EISENSTEIN AT 100

EISENSTEIN AT 100
A Reconsideration

Edited by Al LaValley and Barry P. Scherr

Rutgers University Press
New Brunswick, New Jersey, and London

Library of Congress Cataloging-in-Publication Data

Eisenstein at 100 : a reconsideration / edited by Al LaValley and Barry P. Scherr.

   p. cm.

Includes bibliographical references and index.

ISBN 0-8135-2970-0 (cloth: alk. paper) — ISBN 0-8135-2971-9 (pbk.: alk. paper)

   1. Eisenstein, Sergei, 1898–1948—Criticism and interpretation.
I. Title: Eisenstein at one hundred. II. LaValley, Albert J. III. Scherr, Barry P.

PN1998.3.E34 E325 2001

791.43′0233′092—dc21   00-045898

British Cataloging-in-Publication data for this book is available from the British Library.

Manufactured in the United States of America

CONTENTS

Part Three
**RECONTEXTUALIZING THE LATE FILMS:
HISTORY, FILM, AND POLITICS**

ACKNOWLEDGMENTS

This volume is based on papers that were presented at a conference hosted by Dartmouth College in November 1998. We are grateful to the Dickey Center and to the Dean of Faculty Office at Dartmouth College, which provided financial support for the conference. Bill Pence, Director of Film at Dartmouth's Hopkins Center, arranged a complete retrospective of Eisenstein's films in conjunction with that conference, and also commissioned the Alloy Orchestra to write a new score for *Strike,* which was performed for one of the first times at that conference. His assistant, Sydney Stowe, offered valuable assistance in locating some of the stills for this volume, while David Bordwell and Kristin Thompson provided many of the other illustrations. Susan Bibeau provided design help with the poster and brochure for the conference. We are grateful to several people at Rutgers University Press for their valuable guidance in preparing the manuscript: Leslie Mitchner, Marilyn Campbell, and our copy editor, Anne Sanow. Several of our colleagues at Dartmouth helped with our work on the volume; in particular, we would like to acknowledge the assistance of Jim Brown of the Film and Television Studies Department, Lev Loseff and Richard Sheldon of the Russian Department, as well as Bruce Duncan and Gerd Gemünden of the German Studies Department. June Solsaa, from the Dean of the Faculty Office, provided valuable and speedy administrative assistance.

We thank Northwestern University Press for permission to use the article by Peter Kenez, a slightly different version of which appears in *Enemies of the People: The Destruction of Soviet Film, Theater, and Literary Arts in the 1930s* (Northwestern University Press, Studies in Russian Literature and Theory, 2001). We would also like to acknowledge the Museum of Modern Art as the original source for several of the stills.

A NOTE ON TRANSLITERATION

When Russian names are cited within the text, we have used a popularized form of transliteration, while for the footnotes, as well as for titles and Russian words within the text, we have employed, for the convenience of scholars, the Library of Congress System without diacritics. Hence Yuri, Pyotr, and Shklovsky in the text, but Iurii, Petr, and Shklovskii in notes. Commonly accepted spellings for well-known figures (Prokofiev) or titles (*Alexander Nevsky*) have been retained.

EISENSTEIN AT 100

INTRODUCTION
Rethinking Eisenstein

Al LaValley and Barry P. Scherr

The year 1998 marked the centennial of Eisenstein's birth, and was coincidentally also the fiftieth anniversary of his death. This milestone year was also nearly a decade away from the collapse of the Soviet Union. It was an ideal time to reconsider Eisenstein, and at a conference held in the fall the contributors to this volume began a radical reassessment of his life and work.

Even before the fall of the Soviet Union, glasnost and perestroika had resulted in a new openness within Russian society. Specifically in reference to Eisenstein, access to previously closed portions of his archive led to new discoveries about him and his films. The atmosphere of glasnost also allowed an exploration of the way in which his films are infused with sexuality, politics, and religion — areas which had previously been largely avoided by Soviet commentators. Western scholars had also left these topics largely unexamined. Suddenly the films, which had always been celebrated as formally innovative and groundbreaking but which had been seen as largely straightforward in terms of their thematic content, were viewed as more complex and problematic. A wide range of interpretations took into account issues of historical revision, the interweaving of autobiographical material, and Eisenstein's later elaboration of his own theories. Along with these developments in Russia, new trends in critical theory among Western film scholars also challenged conventional attitudes toward Eisenstein, redefining his role in the history of film. In particular, during the past decade scholars have attempted to embed Eisenstein in a more intricate and richer historical and cultural context. In doing so they have also paid increased attention to the importance of his last films as well as to the later theoretical and autobiographical writings which so informed their content and style.

This collection reflects these recent developments at the same time that it advances a new picture of Eisenstein. It also represents an important coming together and collaboration of film theorists, who have written defining books about Eisenstein, and Slavic scholars, who have worked directly on archival material connected with the Soviet director. Both groups join in the use of new methodologies and knowledge about Eisenstein, refocusing on the way the films are situated in relation to their Soviet context and the director's biography and theoretical writings. This in turn helps explain the concentration on the later works, especially a more nuanced reading of *Ivan the Terrible,* the film where the relationship of the artist to the state becomes most complex.

Eisenstein's problems with Soviet officialdom arose both because of changes within official art policy and because of the evolution in his own thinking and art. By the 1930s his relationship with the political authorities and the dominant film style of socialist realism had become uncomfortable. Eisenstein's methods were less congenial to socialist realism, which put constraints both on the subject matter and the style of the artistic work, than they were to Constructivism, the reigning manner of the 1920s, which was closely allied to revolutionary themes at the same time that it allowed considerable freedom of artistic expression. Eisenstein's theories of montage had also evolved so that his theoretical pronouncements—as so many of the writers here note—became more complex and all-embracing, concerned with the links between film and culture and with the problem of how to achieve an artistic organic whole. The multidimensional films of his last period sometimes seem to move beyond the power of his own explanations and into the realm of the metaphysical.

In an effort to cope with these later films, and in some cases to reopen issues related to earlier ones as well, the articles in this book explore such issues as gender and autobiographical elements in Eisenstein's work and how specific political and social pressures shaped individual films—often forcing major changes in the original conception. Also examined are the ways in which his later ideas about montage relate to socialist realist aesthetics and how alternative creative forces, especially Eisenstein's highly original ideas about mise-en-scène, served to structure both the early and especially the later films. Eisenstein's late style, which has not received the critical attention of that devoted to the early films, in fact turns out to be as important as his earlier methods; this new methodology, rooted in his notion of overtonal montage, was much more concerned with a wider range of emotional effects and buried meanings and less so with the dialectical clash of images stressed in his earlier work. Some contributors examine the nature of Eisenstein's reception by the larger film community and public both in Russia and abroad. The popular image of Eisenstein may still be that of the "inventor" of montage, the director of *The Battleship Potemkin,* and an enthusiastic supporter of the Bolshevik revolution in its early years. However, the figure that emerges from this volume is more complicated and equally important for his influence on subsequent generations: that of an artist in an often uneasy relationship with a totalitarian state, a theorist whose ideas were constantly evolving, and a filmmaker whose works responded to a murky combination of sociopolitical and autobiographical impulses.

The earlier image of Eisenstein nonetheless lies behind many of the articles in this book, and it is important to say a word about it. Eisenstein emerged almost suddenly as a director of worldwide prominence—an important innovator in film method, whose films were an integral part of the revolutionary impulse in the heady years of the new Soviet state. His first major film, *Strike*, was made when he was just twenty-six years old, and a short while later, in 1925, he completed *The Battleship Potemkin*, which in 1958 a panel of film historians from twenty-six countries selected as the best film of all time. To this day his work on *Potemkin* has come to represent who he is as a director: a master of Constructivist montage, of powerful imagery and film rhythms, and of revolutionary political cinema. He then directed *October* (known in the West as *Ten Days That Shook the World*) in honor of the tenth anniversary of the Bolshevik revolution, a delicate topic that for the first time brought him into some conflict with Soviet censors despite the work's pro-Bolshevik stance.

By the end of the 1920s there are clear hints of the divergence between Eisenstein's creative tendencies and the political situation. Increasingly, his work came to diverge from the official party line, marking him with disfavor by the authorities. *The Old and the New* came out in 1929, with less acclaim and after more conflicts with the authorities; between then and 1938, when *Alexander Nevsky* was released, he was not able to complete a single film. In the interval Eisenstein remained highly creative and active, but a combination of internal searching, governmental opposition, and simple bad luck kept him from finishing any of the numerous projects that he began. Another Eisenstein begins to emerge during this time, as he seeks to articulate his artistic vision within changed circumstances. He begins the period with a trip to Western Europe and then to North America, which resulted in several aborted projects while he was in Hollywood, as well as a privately sponsored film in Mexico (*Qué viva México!*) that remained incomplete but nevertheless allowed him an important period of self-development and self-exploration. Upon his return to the Soviet Union Eisenstein continued his prolific writing and emerged as a master teacher to numerous important filmmakers and film historians, testing his developing theories in the classroom more than in the studio. His one major project at this time, *Bezhin Meadow*, had to be reshot to bring it closer to Communist Party doctrine, and yet was never approved for distribution; the film was eventually destroyed. By shaping his late films, *Alexander Nevsky* and *Ivan the Terrible*, around heroic historical figures, he was able to accommodate the demands of socialist realism in terms of subject matter, while at the same time actualizing in film his newer theories of sound and image, and his explorations into their psychological impact on the spectator. Although Part I of his final film *Ivan the Terrible*, while controversial, was nonetheless admired by Stalin and received a state prize, Part II (1946) was condemned by the authorities and not released until 1958. For the decade after his death in 1948 from a heart attack his reputation in Russia remained under a cloud, and relatively little was written about the person now acknowledged to be the most influential Russian director of all time.

Despite his controversial status in the Soviet Union, by the 1930s Eisenstein's innovations in film method had secured him a firm place in the pantheon of great directors among Western filmmakers and scholars. Many of his theoretical essays were quickly translated into major European languages and together with his early films were responsible for his being celebrated; nearly all film histories in Europe and the United States came to acknowledge his central significance. The influence of the early Eisenstein on Western filmmakers has been immense: on documentary films and on the avant garde, on the presence of social themes in classical European film, on Neo-Realism and the New Wave, and more recently on politically radical filmmaking. In Russia and Eastern Europe, however, the later films have had an equally great impact, and these works are now seen as all-important for understanding Eisenstein's general theorizing about the relationship of image to experience, as well as for his growing interest in larger cultural issues, such as power. This volume concentrates on this later and, for the West, lesser known Eisenstein, at the same time that it discusses as well the earlier films in the context of this broader, richer, and more complex Eisenstein.

We have divided the articles into three parts, each of which examines Eisenstein in terms of these new approaches and contexts. The first part, "Eisenstein's Theory and Practice: New Perspectives" contains two kinds of papers. The two opening articles show how Eisenstein's original theories and practice were expanded to become a total theory of art shaping the later films; these are followed by studies examining sexuality, religion, and allegorical mythmaking, vitally important topics that have previously received little attention. Part Two, "Eisenstein and Cultural Interactions: An Anxious Influence," examines Eisenstein's cultural impact both in the United States and England, and it traces the impact of Eisenstein on film culture and film style, (with particular emphasis on Tarkovsky) in Russia and Eastern Europe during the quarter century after his death. Throughout this section we see Eisenstein's troubled status as a cultural figure, both during his lifetime and in his subsequent legacy. The final part, "Recontextualizing the Late Films: History, Film, and Politics," investigates the troubled history of the films' production, in which Eisenstein's imagination found itself partly in conflict with Stalinist politics during their creative shaping, and offers new ways to read his final and most complex film, *Ivan the Terrible*.

The first two essays of Part One explore overarching continuities in Eisenstein at the same time that they account for changes in his theory and practice. David Bordwell, focusing on specific stylistic techniques, examines the apparent change from an early cinema dominated by montage to Eisenstein's late manner of long takes and deep focus photography. He finds continuities between the two periods, in part through a consistent interest in mise-en-scène but also through developments in the notion of montage, exemplified particularly by the technique of axial cutting in the late films. Oksana Bulgakowa examines three theoretical constructs created by Eisenstein at different periods as part of his efforts to explain and unify his work. In each of them Eisenstein maintains an interest in montage, but constantly broadens the notion of that device until it comes to embrace not just his films but a wide range of cultural phenomena.

The other three contributors to this section shed light on the issues of gender, religion, and allegorical mythmaking—topics that during Soviet times received very little attention and that are now coming to take a more central position in studies of Eisenstein. Al LaValley shows that while Eisenstein throughout his career did privilege male figures, thereby leaving little room for strong female characters, he nonetheless did create a strong (albeit in some senses androgynized) female figure in *The Old and the New*. The paper then goes on to treat Eisenstein's more explicit treatment of gay themes, from *Qué viva México!* to *Ivan the Terrible*. Rosamund Bartlett notes similarities between Eisenstein and the contemporary religious thinker Pavel Florensky, suggesting that Russian Orthodoxy, the religion in which Eisenstein was raised, may have been a source for some of Eisenstein's notions of organic unity. Beyond that, Eisenstein's ostensibly negative portrayal of religious figures and motifs turns out to mask a deep impulse toward religion and mysticism that permeates the films. In many cases Eisenstein's own inclinations as a mythmaker came into conflict with the state's efforts to control the interpretation of history. In the earlier films, despite certain changes forced by the exigencies of the moment, Eisenstein's vision is much closer to that of the state. Thus Håkan Lövgren explores key images in *October* in order to extend the notion of history into allegory and Soviet myth, emphasizing the continuity between Eisenstein's practice during the 1920s with his larger theoretical concerns about allegory and myth during the 1930s and 1940s.

Part Two contains papers that deal with Eisenstein's impact within his intellectual milieu, and with his reputation and influence in several countries and especially in Russia, where it has been most troubled. The first article, by James Goodwin, sheds new light on the significance of Eisenstein's stay in America. He describes Eisenstein's fascination with the new technology and how he hoped to employ it for a serious treatment of Dreiser's *An American Tragedy,* as well as his subsequent disappointment with Hollywood's agenda for the scenario. Eisenstein's disillusionment was furthered by Red-baiting and anti-Semitism in attacks from popular journalism. Jewish Hollywood producers, intent on assimilation, especially feared the linkage of Bolshevism with Jewishness. Although Eisenstein was raised within the Russian Orthodox church he was part Jewish, and that heritage first emerged as an important factor with these attacks in America; his experiences in Hollywood in some ways foreshadowed certain difficulties he was to have later in the Soviet Union. Ian Christie discusses Eisenstein's visit to England, the specific impact of *Potemkin,* and Eisenstein's subsequent influence on British documentary filmmaking and more generally on British thinking about film. He goes on to discuss a second influence, that of *Alexander Nevsky* on Laurence Olivier's *Henry V* and the entire Shakespearean film revival that followed the Olivier film. Focusing on Eisenstein and his compatriots back in Russia, Nikita Lary and Omry Ronen describe Eisenstein's complicated reception, particularly as exemplified through his relationship with the prominent Formalist critic and screenwriter Viktor Shklovsky. Lary examines the long but difficult relationship between the two, while Ronen points out that Shklovsky, perhaps to protect all concerned, failed to point out obvious references to Eisenstein and some of his associates in a contemporary novel. Lary focuses on Shklovsky's mixed reactions to both an early and a late film, specifically *October* and *Ivan the Terrible.* Ronen's main concern is the novel that Shklovsky reviews, demonstrating that children's literature, even under the harshest conditions of Stalinism, could express subversive content. Josephine Woll traces Eisenstein's reputation back in Russia during the decade after his death, noting how he goes from being a virtual nonperson before the period of the Thaw that followed Stalin's death to recovering, albeit in fits and starts, some of his earlier renown. Strikingly, the Thaw affected film more gradually and less radically than it did literature.

The remaining three papers in this section all discuss Eisenstein's influence on subsequent generations of filmmakers. Despite Tarkovsky's well-known public rejection of Eisenstein's theories, Vida Johnson shows that Eisenstein's filmmaking techniques—framing, mise-en-scène, composition—had a profound influence on Andrei Tarkovsky's *Andrei Rublev,* as did the historical epic quality of *Ivan the Terrible.* Andrew Barratt focuses on the issue of Eisenstein as mythmaker, showing how Tarkovsky transformed Eisenstein's myth of the historical hero into a myth of the artist, while Alexander Askoldov, in his film *Commissar,* denies the myth, presenting a bleak view of historical forces. Herbert Eagle shows how Eisenstein, even from his earliest films, develops sets of imagery that take on semantic meanings of their own. He notes that the films often express meanings that Eisenstein either did not or could not express directly, and which are frequently subversive. He then goes on to note the manner in which leading film directors of Eastern Europe as well as Russia use similar techniques as a subversive tool to express ideas that go beyond their works' ostensible narratives, making of Eisenstein a rebellious precursor.

The first three articles in Part Three are based on close readings of variant scripts and related documents, and detail the changes that Eisenstein made in his films due to political considerations. Peter Kenez shows in his analysis of *Bezhin Meadow* how under pressure from film authorities, Eisenstein altered the interpretation of the incident on which the film was based from a classical father–son conflict to a narrower and more politicized tale of informing and revolutionary martyrdom. Nonetheless, the changes proved insufficient to satisfy the political demands, and the work was never released. Barry P. Scherr notes that in making *Alexander Nevsky* Eisenstein was forced to simplify his conception of the hero and of history by omitting what was to be an extensive epilogue to the main action; only in his next work, *Ivan the Terrible,* was he to offer a multi-sided portrayal of a historical figure.

As Joan Neuberger points out, even in *Ivan,* Part I, Eisenstein was forced to eliminate some of the negative material that would have made the tsar a still more complex figure. Alexander Zholkovsky's close analysis of the dialogue in the childhood sequence of *Ivan,* Part II deals with one of the scenes Eisenstein was forced to omit from Part I. Interestingly, Neuberger and Zholkovsky disagree about the extent to which Eisenstein actually dissents from the demands for conformity. On the one hand, Neuberger contends that if, in his earlier work, Eisenstein was more clearly an enthusiastic supporter of the new regime, by the time of *Ivan* his vision had diverged from the dominant socialist realist traditions and Stalinist policies, and the demanded changes were a distortion of his art. Zholkovsky, in contrast, like many Russian intellectuals who matured under the Soviet regime, sees Eisenstein as conforming more closely to the aims of the state, and thus interprets the film as rehabilitating Ivan as a model leader; Neuberger believes that the film critiques Ivan's tyranny. Interestingly, both validate their readings of *Ivan* by grounding them in the famous childhood scene, in which Ivan's mother is murdered, an act for which both scholars see him seeking revenge. Their contrasting views on that revenge represent the main divergent attitudes toward Eisenstein, particularly in his later period, among contemporary commentators.

The remaining two articles in this section, by Yuri Tsivian and Anne Nesbet, offer ways of getting beyond the opposition implied by the readings of Neuberger and Zholkovsky. They offer a "vertical" way of looking at the film — that is, they suggest that it is structured not solely by its linear narrative but also by sets of images and motifs with multiple and buried meanings. These writers tap further into Eisenstein's later theoretical and autobiographical writings, and show their profound importance for the creative process that resulted in the completed work. Thus *Ivan* emerges as a more fluid film in which the significance of the main figure shifts its meaning in various contexts. Specifically, Tsivian looks at the buried meanings of the film's title imagery and how the work is structured around the principles of ambivalence and internal contradiction, while Nesbet meditates on Eisenstein's own deathbed meditations, aligning dominant scenes with key passages in his autobiographical writings. Nesbet also raises the crucial issue of sexuality, both for Eisenstein and the films, noting that, like Freud, Eisenstein sees the dialectic of sexual identity resolved in bisexuality.

While the articles in this section exhibit divergent attitudes toward Eisenstein's political stance, they all agree on several crucial points: the increasing methodological complexity and metaphorical density of his filmmaking; the close link between the large-scale later theorizing and the films, a juncture of theory and practice; the growing autobiographical thrust behind Eisenstein's work, be it the father–son conflict in *Bezhin Meadow* or Eisenstein's quasi-identification with historical leaders in his last films; and finally the dark atmosphere that comes to dominate his work. What remains in question is the extent to which this darkness points to a critique of the system itself.

The contributors to this book offer a fuller and more intricate understanding of Eisenstein than that which we have had until now—yet they represent only a beginning. An important start has been made in analyzing Eisenstein both from the viewpoint of contemporary cultural studies and from a post-Soviet historical perspective, as well as from reflections on his own expanded theory and the later films. As with other figures who were closely associated with the Soviet state, Eisenstein's reputation has been undergoing fresh scrutiny. There are those, like Solzhenitsyn in his famous passages in *One Day in the Life of Ivan Denisovich,* who to this day see Eisenstein as essentially an apologist of the Stalinist regime, a view reflected to some extent by both Kenez and Zholkovsky in this collection. Meanwhile, others, such as Naum Kleiman, the director of the Eisenstein archives in Moscow, have taken pains to assert that Eisenstein's relationship with the state was far more troubled and marked by dissidence than many would assert. However, the divergent views of Eisenstein seem at times to hinder the creation of a multi-sided interpretation. As a result it still remains difficult for critics to embrace all the dimensions of the films, which can at the same time seem both to support and subvert images of tyranny. The autobiographical motifs that appear in the films also pose further problems and have yet to receive sustained attention; more needs to be done to elucidate both the homosexual and religious motifs that seem to permeate his work. And as the only film figure who has striven to develop a complex, "scientific" theory of film in all its dimensions, Eisenstein deserves much more exploration.

Still, more than a hundred years after his birth, a richer and more profound image has emerged of Eisenstein the man, the director, and the film theorist. The contributors to this volume have uncovered central metaphors that allow a new view of the late films and theory in particular, and have also delved into aspects of the films, such as issues of gender and religion, that have previously not received the attention they deserve. They have also situated Eisenstein in his political and cultural context, exploring the ways in which contemporary pressures shaped the films and showing that a reading of the films is itself a complex task, requiring familiarity with the biographical, historical, and political background. Several of the contributors have unearthed new materials in the archives and have used them in fresh and creative ways. Eisenstein, a canonized figure since the release of *Potemkin,* was understandably the central figure in Russian cinema for his contemporaries in the Soviet Union and abroad; in this volume we see also that his centrality only grows due to the influence of the multi-layered epic films and his own rich theorizing toward the end of his career. While embodying the tensions between the creative imagination and politics that affected many artists who began as supporters of the new revolutionary era, he also found artistic solutions that allowed him to produce innovative works up to the end of his career. What emerges in the final analysis is that the Eisenstein of the 1930s and 1940s is every bit as important, and in some ways even more complex, than that of the silent filmmaker who first came to fame during the 1920s.

Part One

EISENSTEIN'S THEORY AND PRACTICE

New Perspectives

EISENSTEIN, SOCIALIST REALISM, AND THE CHARMS OF *MIZANSTSENA*

David Bordwell

Few filmmakers have been so insistently identified with particular techniques; Eisenstein is known as the prime theorist and practitioner of "Soviet Montage." Yet we still haven't charted the full range of his stylistic strategies. This supreme technician, who devoted volumes to explaining the purposes behind his artistic choices, remains imperfectly understood. I suppose that this is partly because of what literature Anglophone readers have had available; perhaps if some transcripts of his classes at the All-Union State Institute of Film (henceforth referred to by the Russian acronym VGIK, for Vsesoiuznyi gosudarstvennyi institut kinematografii) had been translated in the 1940s, we would have understood sooner that "montage" was only one tool in a well-stocked kit. We would have known that he was as interested in staging and framing as in cutting; and that he developed a sophisticated account of staging in depth well before André Bazin launched his famous defense of *profondeur du champ* in Orson Welles and William Wyler.[1] Perhaps too we are still only partly aware of the range of Eisenstein's aesthetic because contemporary discussions of his films tend to be broadly interpretive—more interested in the what than the how, more intent on his gender politics or his *politics* politics than on matters of craft, which are often harder to spot and demand intensive analysis. The Old Man would be the last to deny the importance of those phallic symbols which inevitably attract commentary; but he was at least as interested in the filigree of shot design and cutting—topics which after many decades remain relatively unexplored.

There is yet another block to understanding Eisenstein's style: our imperfect knowledge of the work of his contemporaries, particularly in the sound era. As a stylistic phenomenon socialist realist cinema is routinely dismissed, even though it constituted a powerful and enduring body of norms for a very important national cinema. How do Eisenstein's films relate, stylistically, to the socialist realist canon? We know too little about this canon to come to any definitive conclusions, but I think that we can make headway by looking at some distinctive qualities of his late films in relation to the reigning norms.

So through-composed is Eisenstein's work that we could start at almost any point, but let me launch my inquiry by recalling a curious detail from the first part of *Ivan the Terrible*. Ivan is standing in the opening of his tent during the

1–3. *Ivan the Terrible.*

siege of Kazan, but suddenly, in the space of two more shots, he is now standing outside it, glaring majestically at the camera (Figs. 1–3). He is never shown moving toward us; the shots thrust him forward like a chess piece. The startling effect depends upon cutting that enlarges the view at the same time as the figure pops forward. I want to ask simply: Where could such a strange moment come from? This question, opening out from an anomalous moment, carries us quickly into forces at work across the history of socialist realist filmmaking.

E. H. Gombrich has usefully proposed that one motor of stylistic change in art history is the process of schema and revision. For the sake of new expressive purposes, an artist can rework a reigning stylistic convention. Gombrich suggests, for instance, that a change in the function of art during the Renaissance led to the development of conventions for rendering an event as a unique action at a specific moment, as if seen by a witness.[2]

It seems to me that the stylistic history of film can also be treated as a process of norm-following and norm-revision. However innovative we may find the montage filmmakers of the 1920s, most of them followed schemas developed in Hollywood and Europe. From U.S. practice Lev Kuleshov and Vsevolod Pudovkin took the technique of "constructive editing," whereby detail shots are combined to create an impression of a whole. At the same time, these directors pursued more radical implications of the technique. For example, they argued that the director should avoid overall establishing shots, which were in fact distracting and uneconomical; a more forceful presentation would be laconic, using detail shots to coax the spectator into mentally constructing the action. Similarly, Eisenstein's 1920s films draw on editing schemas of classical Hollywood cinema: crosscutting, analytical editing, the eyeline-match, and so forth. Yet he goes on to revise devices in ways that exploit possibilities minimized by American filmmakers. Thus the match on action, normally overlapped only a little in the Hollywood continuity system, becomes the prolonged overlapping we associate with Eisenstein's silent style. Eisenstein "refunctionalizes" the received devices in order to fulfill a new task: the creation of a perceptually, emotionally, and cognitively engaging "agitprop" cinema.

The picture gets a little more complicated, however, if we take up the Russian formalists' suggestion that no revision of a reigning norm arrives out of the blue. To Gombrich's "Making precedes matching" I would add: "Revising invites reviving." That is, transformations of reigning norms often draw upon earlier devices, often minor or subordinated ones.

If we want to understand Ivan's popping out of his tent we can start by considering one example of this revision: what we would now call the axial cut (sometimes a "concertina" cut). This is a cut in or back straight along the

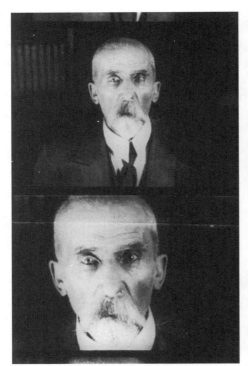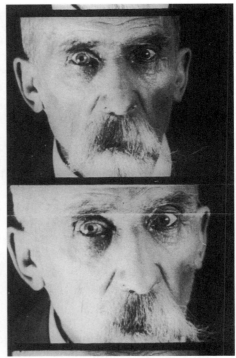

4. *Arsenal:* At a moment of high tension, one cut directly inward . . .
5.   . . . is followed by two more, in a paradigm case of axial editing.

lens axis. The axial cut became a minor stylistic convention of Soviet montage cinema, as witness Grigori Kozintsev and Leonid Trauberg's *Devil's Wheel* (1926) and Alexander Dovzhenko's *Arsenal* (1929; Figs. 4–5). The device was prominent enough to be discussed in S. Timoshenko's 1926 book on editing, which labels axial cut-ins "concentration cuts" and the axial cut-backs "expansion cuts."[3]

It is likely that Eisenstein helped popularize the axial cut; we can find examples in *Potemkin* (Figs. 6–9) and *October*. Indeed, this construction seems to have preoccupied him, as we can see from an illustrative image in his 1929 essay "Beyond the Shot" (Fig. 10).[4] While this is meant to illustrate how the Japanese artist uses the frame to "carve" a composition out of reality, it also presents a diagrammatic equivalent of axial cutting. Two points deserve attention. First the *scales* of the frames vary, yielding "larger" or "smaller" views of the object. More important, the *angle of viewing* does not change: all the framings are, necessarily, located on the same axis perpendicular to the object. If we made a movie sequence out of the framings Eisenstein indicates, the cherry blossom would constantly jump toward and away from us, shift rightward and leftward, but always with respect to a unitary axis linking picture and perceiver. This is what happens in the *Potemkin* shots illustrated (Figs. 6–9). By the time Eisenstein launched his VGIK courses in the 1930s, the idea becomes a major tactic for handling action; each cluster of shots constituting a "montage-unit" is unified by axial cuts.[5] More significantly, we can find in this rather small-scale device one source of broader strategies of mise-en-scène in his late films.

Soviet montage filmmakers normalized a second device during the 1920s: wide-angle depth composition. Exaggerated foregrounds and steep perspectives can be found in several montage classics (Fig. 11). Again, it is likely that Eisenstein led filmmakers toward this option. One can find occasional shots of this sort in nearly every silent Eisenstein film, but with *The Old and the New* he develops this technique very extensively, with many grotesque foregrounds (Fig. 12). We have his word for the fascination such images held for him, and again a flowering branch triggers his explanation. As he recalls his

6–9. *The Battleship Potemkin.*

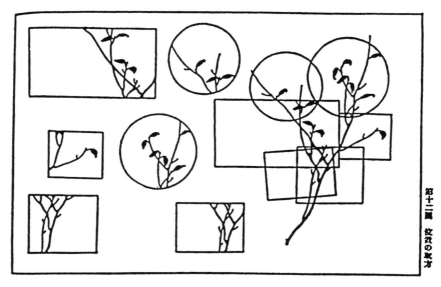

10. Eisenstein's example of alternative framings of a cherry blossom, taken from a 1910 drawing manual for Japanese grade-school children.

"first childhood impression," a white lilac branch seen through the window, he remarks: "The branch was a typical Japanese foreground. . . . And so I was aware of the beauties of foreground composition before I saw Hokusai or was entranced by Edgar Degas."[6] In his 1930s projects the same concern is evident: both *Qué viva México!* (Fig. 13) and *Bezhin Meadow* display strikingly exaggerated depth within the frame. According to Eisenstein, these images fulfill many expressive functions: they integrate various scenic elements into a tense unity, they add a monumental effect, and the 28 mm lens yields a grotesque distortion, a "Gogolesque hyperbolization" that shakes the viewer out of his accustomed relation with things.[7]

Deep-space and deep-focus techniques in his earlier films put static elements into relatively independent juxtaposition. At the limit, objects and heads float as if in an aquarium, suspended in a space that conceals the ground plane that connects them. In the later 1930s, however, Eisenstein begins to realize that shot depth can articulate the space as a concrete arena for dramatic action—what he called, borrowing from the French term for staging, *mizanstsena*. And this imperative is very likely bound up both with the arrival of synchronized sound filming and the dictates of socialist realism.

For most filmmakers, adopting the policy of socialist realism encouraged a stiff, somewhat academic version of international continuity cinema. Analytical editing, already dominant in popular cinema of the 1920s, became the

11. *Mountains of Gold* (directed by Sergei Yutkevich, 1931).

12. *The Old and the New.*

13. *Qué viva México!*

14–15. *Mashenka* (directed by Yuli Raizman, 1942).

norm for all films. But like their Hollywood compatriots, some filmmakers also organized their scenes in moderate depth.[8] In most cases, the foreground planes tend not to be as aggressively close as we find in the 1920s montage work. Moreover, the deep-space shot is typically used for its more common function of establishing the space of the action. Consider, for example, a brief scene in *Mashenka* (1942). As Alyosha lies in bed, his uncle asks him if he'll marry Mashenka (Fig. 14). As he assures the uncle that he doesn't love Mashenka, there is a cut in to her listening, marking her reaction for us (Fig. 15).

The deep-space composition has served as an establishing shot, laying out the space for us before editing highlights the important information.

Yet in other socialist realist films, particularly those of 1938 and after, we confront a bolder, more exaggerated use of depth. Bodies fill the foreground, often from the waist up; a face may hang very close to the camera (Fig. 16); characters are arrayed in steep diagonals plunging into the distance. Images like these remarkably anticipate the design strategies critics have long identified with Orson Welles's *Citizen Kane* (1941) and William Wyler's *The Little Foxes* (1941). In Soviet cinema the deep-focus look quickly became a significant option, perhaps the dominant one for prestige films of the 1940s (Figs. 17–18). Depth staging and wide-angle shooting remained central to the "official" style well after Stalin's death, being pushed to vivid lengths in such works as *The Cranes Are Flying* (1957) and *The Ballad of a Soldier* (1958).

I am far from offering a fine-grained causal account of why depth staging of this sort emerged so saliently in the USSR during the late 1930s. Certainly technical preconditions had to be present—good wide-angle lenses, fairly sensitive film stocks, and powerful lighting equipment (perhaps even arc lamps, which in the US came back into use for black-and-white filming in order to sustain deep-focus). And doubtless the prestige of theatre encouraged directors to present events in ways which would allow their actors to sustain performances within the shot. There is also, once more, the vigorous influence of Eisenstein. His VGIK courses emphasized depth as a cinematic resource, perhaps most notably in his 1933 *Crime and Punishment* étude (Fig. 19), and many directors of the late 1930s and 1940s would have known these courses.

Once launched, the new depth norm could have been sustained partly by the drive to exhibit technical virtuosity that we find in any tradition. Artists enjoy exhibiting their skill and competing with their confrères. Apart from virtuosic display, though, this sort of staging and shooting enlarges and amplifies. In keeping with that hyperbolic "gigantomania" seen elsewhere in high Stalinist culture, these films monumentalize their subjects. Naturally enough, a historical epic can be expected to display grandiose locales, as in *Kutuzov* (1944; Fig. 20) or *The Battle of Stalingrad* (1950; dir. Vladimir Petrov). But spectacular depth is even found in intimate scenes. Thanks to set design and the exaggerating effects of the wide-angle lens, the modest farm parlor of the family in *The Vow* (Fig. 18) seems as big as their barn. The party meeting room of *A Great Citizen* is more than ample, presenting rich zigzag depth; and the apartment of the Trotskyite plotters, though sparsely furnished, might have made audiences members wonder how enemies of the people could gain such spacious quarters (Fig. 16). Even the cell in which the partisan girl is imprisoned in *Zoya* (1944), is conceived on a grandiose scale and filmed in a

16. *A Great Citizen,* Part 2 (directed by Friedrich
Ermler, 1939).

17. *Admiral Nakhimov* (directed by Vsevolod
Pudovkin, 1946): In a steep low angle, a stretcher is
brought in to a physician.

18. *The Vow* (directed by Mikhail Chiaureli, 1946).

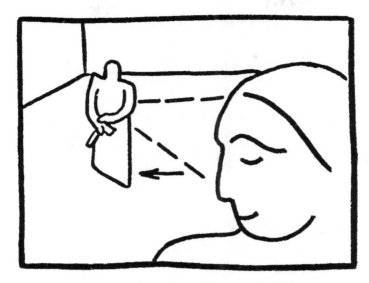

19. Eisenstein's sketch for a phase of the murder of the pawn-broker in his étude for *Crime and Punishment*.

style which can only be called "Wellesian," as if to magnify the significance of her sacrifice (Fig. 21).

During the late 1930s, then, socialist realist directors not only gave up many tactics of montage editing; they also surrended the caricatural deformations of the wide-angle image. Instead, that image was often recast in order to heighten and intensify the heroic side of the stories told. Much as Welles presented Kane as an American colossus, Soviet directors aggrandized their regime's mythology by means of a monumental style. Montage editing had been well suited to suggest mass movements sweeping across cities and continents. The new depth style could present more intimate scenes and focus on individual characters while also inflating them and their enterprises. In gigantic sets, looming figures enact dramas of epochal significance; deep space becomes an arena of momentous treachery and sacrifice, genius and betrayal, military strategy and struggles for the soul of the people.

All these fluctuations in academic socialist realist technique add up to a significant norm against which we may pinpoint Eisenstein's innovations. As socialist realism came to dominate 1930s Soviet filmmaking, Eisenstein's public pronouncements acknowledged the emerging policy. In key essays of 1934 he accepted Maksim Gorky's delineation of socialist realism and firmly put aside intellectual, "de-anecdotalized" cinema. Of course, we can take these claims as defensive gestures, attempts to stabilize his position in precarious

20. A vast set portrays military headquarters in *Kutuzov* (directed by Vladimir Petrov, 1944).

21. *Zoya* (directed by Lev Arnshtam, 1944): A low angle dramatizes the imprisonment of the partisan girl.

circumstances. Still, Eisenstein's late films offer considerable evidence that he sought to imbue the emerging socialist realist norms with genuine aesthetic vitality. And one way he did this was to reshape his style around such devices as the axial cut and staging in depth.

While we cannot say exactly how *Bezhin Meadow*'s scenes were staged, surviving materials suggest that it was a transitional work, utilizing the exaggerated compositions of the late 1920s but anchoring them in a more concrete scenic space. By the time of *Alexander Nevsky*, exaggerated depth within the shot came to be replaced by a progression into and out of depth by means of the axial cut. Indeed, what was a minor device in the hands of many directors was promoted to a major role in structuring several of Eisenstein's scenes.

In an early scene of *Alexander Nevsky*, axial cutting recarves the space in the manner of the Japanese cherry-branch exercise. From an extreme long-shot of Alexander's compound at the sea, Eisenstein cuts to a long-shot view of the old man, and then to a still closer view (Figs. 22–24). After a view of the men trawling the sea, we might expect to move in on a dramatic action; but Eisenstein then cuts back to another, very distant framing, followed by another one that adds new elements and drops others we have already seen (Figs. 25–26). There is a sense that Eisenstein could go on forever in this vein, cutting in and out, reshuffling compositional elements, reshaping shot design.

Most of *Nevsky*'s scenes are dominated by static figure arrangement of this sort. Elsewhere I have traced how the episode showing the Teutonic Knights' domination of Pskov opens with a long shot of a group of knights, then cuts back to place them in their surroundings, then cuts still farther back to convey the devastation of Pskov. Eisenstein then cuts in on the same line, reconfiguring the scenographic elements. The sequence goes on for some time in this way, always establishing a set of elements and then rearranging them, eliminating some and introducing others, putting some in the background while promoting others.[9] The passage constitutes what Eisenstein called a "montage unit," that cluster of shots sharing a predominant spatial orientation.[10] Eisenstein sometimes reworks his compositions more radically, using editing to delete figures or add them to the tableau. He cuts in on Olga, making her suitors vanish (Figs. 27–28). And he will cut back from the Germans' tent in such a way as to make the ominous priests in the foreground pop up startlingly (Figs. 29–30).

So one source of the Tsar's odd movement out of his tent in our first example is Eisenstein's increased reliance on the axial cut, even in defiance of spatial verisimilitude. *Ivan the Terrible* displays the same technique in other scenes, notably the one in which various powerful people wait outside Ivan's bedchamber while he is ill. Starting with a shot of the Christ icon, there comes a series of shots moving more or less steadily backward from the rear wall, reframing the immobile elements in the scene (Figs. 31–33). Nevertheless, what comes to the fore in *Ivan* is a greater use of figure movement in depth.

To put it another way, Eisenstein often replaces lateral staging with action that proceeds toward or away from the camera. Simple instances of this tactic can be found in the deep-space work of other Soviet directors of the period,

22–26. *Alexander Nevsky.*

but in Eisenstein, the spatial dynamic bursts the bonds of the single shot. Axial editing combines with depth staging to create a constantly unfolding foreground, opening up new vistas of space for the characters to hurl themselves into. Eisenstein states the plan explicitly:

> The "set design proper" for my shots never in itself exhausts the real "place of action."

27–30. *Alexander Nevsky.*

> Most often this set design proper seems to be a "spot in the background,"
> which appears through a system of foregrounds placed like "wings"
> attached endlessly in front of it, driving this set design proper further
> and further into the distance.
> In my work set designs are inevitably accompanied by the unlimited
> surface of the floor *in front* of it, allowing a bringing forward of
> unlimited separate foreground details. . . .
> The last point in this method is the close-up of the actor carried beyond
> all thinkable limits.[11]

The "wings" flanking a proscenium stage-space are rotated ninety degrees to
provide playing areas in the distance, in the foreground, and even "behind
the camera"; the action can thereby develop energetically along the lens axis,
achieving maximal intensity as it approaches the viewer.

In my book on Eisenstein's cinema I have discussed the unfolding foreground strategy in some detail, particularly in its more aggressive forms. The
actors' charging of the camera, their ability to burst the frame and force the
camera further back, reaches a kind of culmination late in Part II when Efrosinia and Pimen plan Ivan's assassination. The confrontation in Efrosinia's

31–33. *Ivan the Terrible.*

apartment is played out as a series of thrusts to the foreground, even when the axis of action (as it might be conceived in Hollywood) changes. The scene reaches its climax when Efrosinia runs to the camera and announces to the viewer: "It is God's will!"[12]

This culminating moment can be seen as a kind of paroxysmic reworking of the stylistic premises of one sequence in Part I. As Ivan lies ill, various factions gather around his chamber to plot how they may benefit from his death. Moving across different locales, the entire episode articulates the drama as a series of framings that move back farther and farther to a kind of "foreground climax"—somewhat more optimistic and exuberant than that of the assassination plot in Part II. The sickbed scene opens, as we've seen, with a string of "expansion" cuts back from the icon, showing a cluster of courtiers and boyars awaiting news of Ivan's health (Figs. 31–33). Efrosinia enters with Vladimir and comes to Kurbsky in the foreground; against all plausibility, they stand side by side and twist their bodies for our benefit (Fig. 34). Straightforward axial cuts lay out their dialogue, yielding framings very different from the angled shot/reverse-shot of Hollywood and orthodox Soviet practice (Fig. 35). The next bit of action in Ivan's chamber is introduced by a string of axial cuts to him on his sickbed. When we return to Efrosinia and Kurbsky, he is declaring his loyalty to Ivan and she is offering him reign over Moscow; at the same time, from the foreground Malyuta is spying on them.

So far the scene has been played out principally in static arrays captured in "concentration" or "expansion" cuts in the *Nevsky* manner. But now things become more volatile, presenting a series of diagonal movements—some slow, others swift. From the foreground, Efrosinia leads Vladimir and the other boyars into the chamber, blotting out the space with their dark shapes. Such front-to-back movements, so atypical of the film, serve as a kind of ballast to the predominantly back-to-foreground design of the scene. In a counter-thrust Ivan rises from his sickbed and staggers forward to beg the boyars to kiss the cross for his son Dmitri. He crawls painfully to them, and they turn coldly away—a gesture accentuated by a hulking foreground and a reverse tracking shot, a very rare device for the film (Fig. 36). Ivan retreats to the bed, cursing them, and collapses grandly. It looks as if death has come. As the boyars quarrel over the kingdom, Kurbsky enters from the rear and prowls forward to the bed to study Ivan's face. After the emblematic shot showing Kurbsky torn between Efrosinia and Anastasia, Efrosinia leads Vladimir out ("Hail to the boyar Tsar!") from the bed to the foreground through the cluster of onlookers, an inversion of their entry into the sickchamber. Kurbsky leaves along the same diagonal, and the boyars follow him.

A new phase of the scene takes place in the long corridor outside, and here the diagonal thrusts turn into zigzags. Kurbsky comes toward us (Fig. 37), and a string of axial cut-ins juxtaposes him with the icon, stressing the all-seeing

34–35. *Ivan the Terrible.*

eye. Anastasia enters in zigzag fashion from the rear, and as he tries to seduce her, more axially organized inserts follow their interchange. When she pushes him away to leave, she turns to go, as if to retrace her path into the scene. But he rushes back to grab her (Fig. 38) and drag her forward (Fig. 39). He detains her in a series of close views that highlights the icon's eye. This reminder of the all-powerful Tsar (identified throughout with the eye of God) underscores the pivot of the scene, Anastasia's line: "You should not bury someone before he's dead."[13] She glides back into the recesses of the corridor and vanishes.

This stretch has consisted of symmetrical thrusts to and from the camera,

36. *Ivan the Terrible.*

broken by short, sharp interchanges in medium close-up; but what follows creates an unbroken flow of action forward, revealing ever-new "foreground wings." Realizing that Ivan lives, Kurbsky rushes forward (Figs. 40–41), pauses by the icon for brief contemplation (and more juxtapositions with the omniscient eye), before hurling himself forward again (Figs. 42–43). He strides into the chapel, the shot revealing a new space in the foreground, the stand holding the Bible. Kurbsky hastens to it (Fig. 44) and kisses the cross, pledging loyalty to Ivan's son Dmitri. Pimen and Efrosinia are aghast, and they turn behind them to see Ivan, now recovered, shakily entering on the arms of Malyuta and Anastasia. A new editing unit presents his progress to the front of the chapel to meet Kurbsky, being blessed on the way by Pimen (Fig. 45). Then, with Kurbsky's loyalty apparently assured, Ivan tells him that he will lead the army to Livonia and the sea. Given the constant diagonal pitch of the staging, it is appropriate that when Ivan orders Kurbsky to lead the army to Livonia, this region is suggested to lie in the left foreground, diagonally just off-camera (Fig. 46): yet another foreground space to explore! One step more and we are with our initial example of the Tsar at his tent, a passage which simply dispenses with figure movement and lets the cutting propel Ivan out toward the viewer.

Eisenstein's fusing of axial cutting and deep space into a pervasive principle of staging springs out in even sharper relief if we consider what his most famous rival was up to during the same years. Pudovkin's films after *Deserter* (*Dezertir,* 1933) have been unjustly neglected, for they bristle with many striking visual ideas. In his productions of the late 1930s and the 1940s he

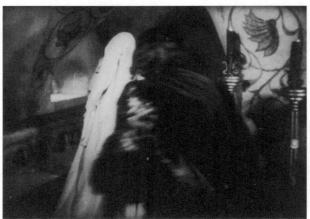

37–39. *Ivan the Terrible.*

40–46. *Ivan the Terrible.*

followed the trend toward a stolid deep-focus look (Fig. 17). He did not explore to-camera movement with the single-minded brio that Eisenstein displayed, but at some moments we find him working his own variations on foreground-background interplay while keeping camera orientation constant across the cut. The result is a peculiar editing tactic.[14]

In these passages, Pudovkin sets up a shot with a center of interest in the middle ground, but he then blocks our view of it by having something else pass straight across the foreground. As the foreground element slides by, Pudovkin cuts. Sometimes he simply makes a jump cut, keeping the middleground element still visible but making the foreground character vanish abruptly. Alternatively, he may cut smoothly from the foreground movement to *another* foreground element passing through the same screen area, then revealing either the same middle-ground object or a different one. In all cases, camera distance remains constant.[15]

For example, during a welcoming parade in *Victory* (*Pobeda,* 1938, co-directed with Mikhail Doller), a man's face passes in the foreground (Fig. 47). As he starts to leave the shot, revealing the man standing behind (Fig. 48), Pudovkin cuts smoothly to another shot of a foreground shoulder in almost exactly the same place, moving in the same direction (Fig. 49). This figure moves aside to reveal a cheering woman (Fig. 50). This pulsating, shearing effect reappears during the jolting battle sequence of *Admiral Nakhimov* (1946); here infantrymen fall in the foreground again and again, and jump cuts strive to keep our view fastened on a soldier in the middle distance.

Apart from showing that editing experiments did not wholly cease with the arrival of socialist realism, Pudovkin's jump cuts and deceptive matches on foreground movement reveal an effort to develop his own ideas of axial matching and depth composition. It is as if he is trying, like Eisenstein, to reabsorb these devices into a viable sound film style. Intriguing as the results are, however, they remain fairly simple, one-off effects. Pudovkin treats depth as a static biplanar array, and he uses cutting to mask or reveal action in a peekaboo fashion. The devices are strictly local, working up visual excitement in narrative contexts that call for kinetic energy (public celebration, intense combat). The devices do not fundamentally recast ways of staging and shooting sustained scenes.

By contrast, Eisenstein's late work "refunctionalizes" aggressive depth and axial cutting by making them the premises of an entire scenography. The dynamic interplay of exaggerated foreground and background elements found in the late 1920s and early 1930s work gets transformed into a constant movement to and from us and by cuts which unfold ever-new playing areas "behind the camera." The action takes place not in Pudovkin's parallel planes but in vectors thrusting out from the recesses of the shot. It is as if the lens axis, the basis of the "concentration" and "expansion" cuts, has assumed the role of a gravitational field around which the entire action will hover.

47–50. *Victory.*

Why did Eisenstein recast these particular schemas in these particular ways? There are probably several factors at work, but we might usefully recall some tasks he defined for himself during the 1930s and 1940s. Much of the force of the axial cut and the unfolding foreground derives from the montage-unit method articulated in his teaching, and Eisenstein saw this method as reshaping theatrical space according to new cinematic purposes. He compares the unity of shots in the montage unit to the unity of scenes within a drama's act.[16] The method thus solves the problem of integrating theatre and cinema in the sound era.

These stylistic choices also correspond to Eisenstein's later emphasis upon a tightly knit process of formal development within the work. Starting from a detail and cutting back provides a way of controlling the information to which the audience has access; the shots introduce new elements in relation to ones already seen and thus unfold motifs and thematic materials. By contrast, cutting into the scene or bringing the actor forward can intensify the action, building toward a dramatic and emotional climax. The strategy thus answers to Eisenstein's desire to create an organic form governed by a careful retardation of narrative elements and a gradual revelation of the work's theme.

The new scenography also works toward the absorption of the spectator. Eisenstein's 1946–48 essay on three-dimensional film implies that such absorption constitutes a stage in cinema's historical mission. He asserts that throughout the history of the theatre, producers have sought to reconnect the audience with the performance. Efforts were made to bring the spectators into the theatrical space (as in the Renaissance custom of letting some viewers sit on stage) or to fling a bridge from the stage into the audience (as in the Japanese *hanamichi*). Eisenstein insists that the modern cinema transcends these rather artificial solutions and moves closer to forging a unity between the consumer and the spectacle.[17]

The montage-unit method forms an important part of this scheme. The spatial devices we have considered either pull the viewer into the represented space or thrust the action out to the viewer. Eisenstein remarks that pushing figures into foreground close-up is an "'ecstatic' method of construction . . . based on the telescope."[18] By breaking the barrier between spectator and spectacle, these scenographic tactics help the filmmaker create a rich, organically unified work that can provoke ecstasy.

From this standpoint, the abrupt, isolated moment of Ivan popping out of his tent can serve as an emblem for many qualities which continue to fascinate us about Eisenstein—his drive to violate realism for the sake of dynamic effect; his search for a pictorial impetus directed straight at the spectator; his effort to forge a formal principle encompassing overarching dramatic development and moment-by-moment stylistic texture; and his willingness to revive techniques which others had compromised or abandoned but which in his hands carry a fresh, splendid force.

Notes

1. See André Bazin, "The Evolution of the Language of Cinema," in *What Is Cinema?*, ed. and trans. Hugh Gray (Berkeley: University of California Press, 1967), 23–40.

2. See E. H. Gombrich, *Art and Illusion: A Study in the Psychology of Pictorial Representation* (Princeton: Princeton University Press, 1961), 146–173.

3. Semen Timoshenko, *Iskusstvo kino: Montazh fil'ma* [Art of the Cinema: Film Montage] (Leningrad: Academia, 1926), 46–49.

4. Sergei Eisenstein, "Beyond the Shot," in *Selected Works, 1: Writings, 1922–34*, ed. and trans. Richard Taylor (London: British Film Institute, 1988), 147.

5. See my discussion in *The Cinema of Eisenstein* (Cambridge: Harvard University Press, 1993), 146–150.

6. Sergei Eisenstein, *Selected Works, 4: Beyond the Stars: The Memoirs of Sergei Eisenstein*, ed. Richard Taylor, trans. William Powell (London: British Film Institute, 1995), 462.

7. Sergei Eisenstein, *Nonindifferent Nature: Film and the Structure of Things,* trans. Herbert Marshall (Cambridge: Cambridge University Press, 1987), 48.

8. I try to situate Soviet directors' use of depth within international sound film traditions in *On the History of Film Style* (Cambridge: Harvard University Press, 1997), 217–221.

9. For further examples from this sequence, see *The Cinema of Eisenstein,* 217–220.

10. Vladimir Nizhny, *Lessons with Eisenstein,* trans. and ed. Ivor Montagu and Jay Leyda (New York: Hill and Wang, 1962), 77.

11. Eisenstein, *Nonindiffierent Nature,* 152.

12. See *The Cinema of Eisenstein,* 245–247.

13. For a discusssion of the visual motifs pervading this sequence, see Kristin Thompson, *Eisenstein's "Ivan the Terrrible": A Neoformalist Analysis* (Princeton: Princeton University Press, 1981), esp. chapter four.

14. The device is foreshadowed in a moment of *Deserter* (1933).

15. Since camera distance does not change, this device is thus not the same as that now-common editing device of cutting in to closer views of a figure, using a passing foreground element, such as a car or a person, to mask the cut.

16. Nizhny, *Lessons with Eisenstein,* 77.

17. Sergei Eisenstein, "Du cinéma en relief," *Le Mouvement de l'art,* ed. François Albera and Naum Kleiman (Paris: Cerf, 1986), 109–156.

18. Eisenstein, *Nonindifferent Nature,* 152.

THE EVOLVING EISENSTEIN
Three Theoretical Constructs of Sergei Eisenstein

Oksana Bulgakowa

Eisenstein's theory of film and art developed intermittantly and found its fixed point in ways most uncommon for scientific papers: through drawing or set design, film projects, theater production, and as a course in film directing. He also explored his theories in essay collections and books, in which sharp analytic passages were offset by belletristic memoirs or collages of quotations. The script of "The Glass House" (1926–1930), like the project of filming "Capital" (1927–1928), are drafts of a new film theory as much as they are screenplays. This nonacademic form of theory reveals a very substantial point: Eisenstein's analytic manner (which emerged from psychology and psychoanalysis, anthropology and etymology, linguistics, mathematics and geometry, literature, theater, art and music theory) and his artistic practice had been united all his life. Theory, which projected the work of art, the artist, and the spectator into a net of complex relations, directly continued his experimental practice, and practice itself was a form of elaborating theory. Both also stand in a rich and intricate relationship with the scientific and artistic developments of his time.

Eisenstein aligned his theoretical systems to offer a multifaceted model that could describe and analyze the heterogeneous phenomena of all the arts. I wish to explore here three partially realized theoretical projects that Eisenstein developed in three unfinished books. In all three projects Eisenstein looked for an absolute (and utopian) theoretical system, which was understood in very different ways:

- as an artistic device—as montage—which he explored in "The Spherical Book" (1929) but left unfinished;
- as global correspondences between the senses and their materialization in art (e.g., the effect of sound and color, sound and line, or the synaesthetic effect of audio-visual counterpoint), examined in the second unfinished book "Montage" (1937–1940);
- as a universal "method" of art (i.e., a universally analytical model applicable to a broad array of material), in the book "Method," 1939–1947.

In all three cases Eisenstein used new and unusual analytical methods. In the "Spherical Book" he introduced a model partway between linguistics and psychology. In the second book, "Montage," he tried to formalize unconsciously perceived compositional structures in order to capture the effect of color, sound, and picture in their counterpoint. Finally, in "Method" he suggested a simple bipolar model for the description of structures in the work of art. Eisenstein envisaged that his method could be used universally for the analysis of nearly all art practices and forms: Dostoevsky and Disney, Rublev and Ilya Repin, Utamaro and Shakespeare, circus and music.

Eisenstein's projects examine the basic material and the possibilities of film—the illusion of movement, the specific qualities of the film image, the relationship between the seen and the unseen—yet at the same time they are applicable to broader fields: the analysis of historical processes through film, the basic structures of consciousness, and the dynamics of personality.

The focal points of these different theoretical constructs and their analytical approaches emerged from scientific discourse and various other sources (constructivism, Hegelian aesthetics, Ernst Cassirer's new ontology, psychoanalysis, etc.). But on the way to a universal theoretical solution these theoretical projects experienced a kind of shift. Eisenstein's initial investigations were broken off and displaced by still new theoretical beginnings.

THE FIRST MODEL: "THE SPHERICAL BOOK" (1929)

At the end of the 1920s Eisenstein conceived his first book. The internal necessity to write it lay first of all in a desire for demarcation from his rivals. In 1926–1929 formalist critics and the film directors Vsevolod Pudovkin, Semyon Timoshenko, and Lev Kuleshov had published their own books on film theory.[1] But Eisenstein aimed for much more in his; he aspired to expand the common forms of writing theory as a manifesto, an article, or even a book. His project was also not conceived as a technical classification of montage devices, like Timoshenko's book; nor as a traditional account of filmmaking, like Kuleshov's *My Experience in Film Art;* nor as a comprehensive guide on how to write film scripts and make films, like Pudovkin's work. He noted in his diary on August 5, 1929:

It is very hard to write a book. Because each book is two-dimensional. I wanted this book to be characterized by a feature that does not fit at all into the two-dimensionality of the printing process. This demand has two sides. First it supposes that this collection of essays is not to be regarded successively. In any case, I wished that one could perceive them all at the same time, simultaneously, because they ultimately represent a set of clusters, which are arranged around a general, determining point of view and aligned to different areas. On the other hand, I want to create a spatial form, that makes it possible to step from each contribution directly to another and to materialize their relationship . . . Such a synchronic manner of circulation and mutual penetration of the essays could be carried out only in the form . . . of a sphere. But unfortunately books are not written as spheres . . . I can only hope that they will be read in accordance with the notion of a sphere—and with the hope that we will learn to write books like rotating balls. Now we have only books like soap-bubbles. Particularly about art.[2]

At this time he composed many plans for the possible anthology: a collection of writings he had already published (like "The Montage of Attractions," "Beyond the Shot," "Perspectives," and "The Fourth Dimension in Film"); as well as unpublished material (like "The Montage of Film Attractions" or "The Dramaturgy of Film Form"); and texts he had conceived but not written ("John and Schopenhauer," "Le Paire," and "Khlebnikov" among others). The focus of the book would be on montage.

Eisenstein probably did not give up the idea of finishing the book until 1932. We can still discover some traces of this project in his letters. On August 23, 1929, four days after his arrival in Berlin, Eisenstein wrote to Kenneth MacPherson, the editor of the English film review *Close Up,* in which Eisenstein had published some texts like the "Statement" on sound in film and "The New Language of Cinematography": "I have a manuscript of a book written by me about film theory. We could discuss it."[3] He also wrote from Mexico (probably in 1931) to MacPherson when he sent him the English translation of "The Dramaturgy of Film Form." "I hope you will like Film Form—I think it one of the most serious and basic in what I think about cinema—and it might be presented as a page of my still (and I am afraid forever!) 'forthcoming' book!"[4]

Only a few sections of the proposed book, however, were written and eventually published as separate articles. What, then, was lost? Montage, which Eisenstein mentions characteristically as a "method," is analyzed in this published cluster of essays in the frame of different systems: music ("The Fourth Dimension in Film"), Japanese theater art ("An Unexpected Juncture") and Japanese ideographs ("Beyond the Shot"), linguistics ("Perspectives"), reflexology ("The Montage of Attractions" and "The Montage of Film Attractions"), and dialectic ("The Dramaturgy of Film Form"). As a consequence of the linear process of publishing and reading these texts, however, we can no longer perceive the constant change in points of view and frames of discussion and analysis that seemed to be so important to Eisenstein at the end of the 1920s—that is, the most essential characteristic of the project that sets it off against the background of most theory formation then and even today.

It is symptomatic that three sophisticated scholars—François Albera, Annette Michelson, and David Bordwell—in their analyses of *one* essay in the proposed "Spherical Book" come to opposite conclusions regarding Eisenstein's development in this period. Albera dedicates an entire book to the essay "The Dramaturgy of Film Form," using this text to argue for his vision of Eisenstein as a constructivist and finding in the theory of the photogram a basis for his interpretation of Eisenstein's montage.[5] "The Dramaturgy of Film Form," commissioned for the catalogue of the FiFo (Film und Foto) exhibition of European constructivists in 1929, terminated the cycle of essays (in the linear sense). Eisenstein, a radical avant-garde artist, having analyzed the basic phenomenon of the medium (the emergence of the illusion of movement), could reject the common illusionist mimetic representation of movement in film and come to an understanding of true filmic movement. He could deal instead with the possibilities of the medium for freezing movement, for playing with immobility and intervals, and for shifting between shots and creating a nonexisting movement through the montage of photograms. This praxis was continued in the experiments of the later avant-garde: Charles Dekeukeleire, Paul Sharits, Werner Nekes, and Hollis Frampton.

Albera's analysis and conclusion are correct, but his is not the only way to understand Eisenstein's theory. At the same time that he wrote "The Dramaturgy of Film Form," Eisenstein wrote "The Fourth Dimension in Film." Michelson's brilliant essay on this text develops the idea of a transformation of the constructivist Eisenstein, after he is affected by the concept of synaesthesia, as elaborated by the Russian symbolists and Alexander Scriabin.[6] Eisenstein was reading Leonid Sabaneev's book about Scriabin and Joyce's *Ulysses*. Michelson concludes that we could observe in Eisenstein's concept a revival, a stimulation of romantic and metaphysical strains, the union of Hegel and Madame Blavatsky. Bordwell suggests another interpretation in his 1974 essay, "Eisenstein's Epistemological Shift," which is dedicated to the same period and to the same texts.[7] Bordwell notes a change in the development of Eisenstein, from reflexology and materialism to psychology and dialectics.

These analyses of "The Dramaturgy of Film Form" seem mutually exclusive. But the radical constructivist in fact stands close to the metaphysical symbolist and the dialectic psychologist. Furthermore, parallel to his project of the "Spherical Book" Eisenstein conceived of writing a psychoanalytical book about himself and his art, to be called "My Art in Life." These three brilliant and informative investigations of Eisenstein's theoretical work must themselves be read in a dynamic relationship with each other, very much as a spherical ball, in order to attain their implicit multidimensionality.

We can also find in the "Spherical Book" other different and contradictory concepts meant to exist simultaneously, such as montage understood as a construction of attractions and as a construction constituted over the dominant. Whereas the montage of attractions is justified through an appeal to the reflexological stimulus, the construction over the dominant can only be understood in the frame of Gestalt psychology.

Eisenstein approached even the term "attraction" from different points of view and stressed the following:

- the visual moment (in analogy to elements of photo-collages by Alexander Rodchenko or George Grosz);
- the direct shock-effect that comes with such phenomena as the representation of violence, the stimulation of fear, surprise, and so forth;
- physiological changes that can be achieved in the muscles of the spectators through the new school of acting, based on Eisenstein's concept of expressive movement;
- emotional ambiguity (the spectator must be forced relentlessly into a state where the emotions shift constantly; Eisenstein called this kind of stimulus "compound attraction" and refers to lyric and grotesque moments in the films of Charlie Chaplin and to pathos and sadism in religious ecstasy).

Moreover, the psychoanalytical concepts of satisfaction (real in life, fictive in art), of violence (film and theater are forms of exercising violence toward the spectators) and energy support the larger explanation of the attraction, which expands and explodes the framework of the constructivist or reflexological program.

Montage is also interpreted within many frameworks: (1) in reference to reflexology (the montage of attractions tends to create a chain of conditioned reflexes; the film-engineer develops a combination of stimuli, a classical conditioning, by assembling arbitrary shocks in order to train social reflexes like class hate and class solidarity); (2) in reference to the dialectic (montage as a unity of oppositions, in "The Dramaturgy of Film Form"); (3) to the linguistic (montage as a chain of oppositions, in "Beyond the Shot" and "Perspectives") and (4) to a psychological model, in "The Fourth Dimension in Film," where montage is understood as a dynamic structure, a process of dynamic integration. In "The Dramaturgy of Film Form" Eisenstein argues that the production of the kinetic illusion through photograms and intervals increases the intensity of meaning just as rhythmic shifts do in verse. The new qualities of this construction are defined in "The Dramaturgy of Film Form" in relation to conflict and in "The Fourth Dimension" in relation to the dominant that makes the shots correlative. The word "dominant" in Eisenstein's use blends the definition provided by Yuri Tynyanov, Sabaneev's interpretation of Scriabin's music, and William James' psychological term.[8] The interpretation of montage as a chain of conditioned reflexes is replaced by the vision of a dynamic hierarchical system with a changing dominant, but in the "Spherical Book" both models exist at the same time.

The polarity of the positions Eisenstein suggests creates a tension between the sections, due to the principle of simultaneity. But it is the only project in which such polarity is actually implied as a constructive principle. Perhaps it is only logical that the book could not be finished.

THE SECOND MODEL: "MONTAGE" (1937–1940)

"Montage" is the opposite of "The Spherical Book." During their encounter in Paris on November 30, 1929, Joyce showed Eisenstein the scheme of *Ulysses* (1922), which he also gave to his own first interpreter Stuart Gilbert.[9] This outline is a universal map of correspondences. Each of the book's episodes has a place in the real geography of Dublin; at the same time, it is a map of a universal city and the outline of a human life, whose symbolism—birth, encounters, farewell—transforms the individual experience into the general. The majority of the episodes correspond to an organ of the human body, and taken as a whole symbolize the entire body; each episode has a color and a semantic leitmotif that corresponds both to a concrete art and a concrete science. In this way the novel is a gigantic symbol—not a single book, but an encyclopedia of universal knowledge.

Eisenstein was excited by an art of such totality. He wrote his second book about montage as a book of universal correspondences, and he looked for these in different areas. The correspondences between the arts—word and picture, line and music, and color and music—are finally only partial solutions. Eisenstein dreamed as well about even larger agreements, between art, the human being (in his book, concretely, the human body) and the cosmos in its metaphysical totality.

This was a new understanding of totality and a new concept of the book. "Montage" is no longer a sphere, but a reservoir of universal knowledge. Eisenstein's writing changed to accommodate this new view. In the 1920s his phrases were like theses or aphorisms, discontinuous, filled with breaks and unfinished sentences that were often composed only of nouns or verbs. By contrast, in the 1930s his text is a continuous flux, which can flow and grow ever further, to 800 or 1,000 pages, and include empirical studies, quotations, and analyses, all leading to still new correspondences.

The terms with which he worked changed as well. In the 1920s Eisenstein invented nearly all his terms himself (for example *"Film-Ausschnitt"* instead of "shot," derived from the German *Schnitt,* to cut). In the 1930s he changed his basic vocabulary and used the accepted terms of the period, like image (*obraz*), pathos, and ecstasies—terms, however, which he often equipped with his own semantics, differing from the accepted meanings of his day. Discontinuity, fragmentation, and stimulus disappear, as do all traces of constructivism and of the modern. In its place is a holistic system in which such qualities as synaesthesia, wholeness, organic unity, and ecstasy play central roles. The determination of montage also becomes something new.

Eisenstein proves that montage is the basic principle for creating the image (*obraz*), which in turn constitutes the work of art. This concept of the image resolves the opposition between the visible and the invisible, which had its basis in the opposition of representation (picture) versus image. Now there is the concept of an organic unity of both, which can be seen in the example of the synaesthetic effect of audio–visual counterpoint. All this completely displaced his concept of montage from the 1920s. The difficulty of understanding this new book occurred because Eisenstein took excerpts out of nearly all his essays from the 1920s about montage, included them in his new text and reinterpreted them within the framework of his new theory of correspondences. Rather than conflict, jumps, and contrasts, Eisenstein uses unity, synthesis, ecstasy, organicity, and image to clarify the phenomenon of montage. Montage is also understood as expressing the internal laws of all artistic thinking. With this in his mind, Eisenstein intended the book "Montage" as a cultural study, in which he could examine all art forms (architecture and painting, literature and music, theater, circus, music hall and film). This is his "Laokoon" after Lessing, but his goal is not the elaboration of the distinction between poetry and painting, architecture and film, but the discovery of larger correspondences between all the arts. The basis of these corresponding relationships lies in the *obraz*/image that each work of art aspires to produce and which each perceiver absorbs in the act of perception. The image is therefore a product of montage that establishes the basis for relations of correspondences.

In each art the creation of the image is carried out by different means. Eisenstein examines the commensurability of picture and melody, of color and music beyond their semantics (as, for instance, in "Vertical Montage," where he analyzes the commensurability between the visual and acoustic levels in their counterpoint).

The number of different stimuli increases tremendously with the technical development of film. Color and stereoscopic effect, touch, smell, and taste can be activated; the senses can enter into communication with each other. Film can develop into a synthesis of all arts and senses, transcending Richard Wagner's conception of the *Gesamtkunstwerk*.

Eisenstein's task consists in delineating these unconsciously perceived moments, in translating units of perception into the level of cognition, and even in finding a mathematical expression for them. In the context of the book, montage becomes increasingly a metaphor for a universal law. The single term "montage" no longer seems adequate for describing the various techniques for creating the image (*obraz*) in all the different arts. Literature involves a relationship between word and concept; painting between depiction and semantic conceptualization. The universal law, which earlier Eisenstein simply labeled "dialectics," requires now a reinterpretation, a modification for art. The dialectic is now decoded as the feeling that arises through the perception of the image. The path from the level of representation to that of the image involves a semantic conceptualization which includes the sensual perception that Eisenstein defined as ecstasy.

In Marxist aesthetics the concept of the image involves the unity between the representation of reality and its scientific analysis, which the work of art clarifies through the representation of the special as the general, of the concrete fate of fictitious individuals as the objective tendency of history. The representation in art evokes reality and at the same time a general construct of a priori knowledge, with which the reader/spectator carries out the task of synthesis, perception, and interpretation.

Eisenstein, however, bases his thought not on this understanding of history, but on the concepts of "organicity" (derived from "nature") and of unity which derives from correspondences between the human body and the cosmos. Nature is structured by a unity of a higher order than the regularities of historical development. This unity is understood as an organic system in a metaphysical way. This unity cannot be intellectually understood, but only sensually and ecstatically experienced (that is why the concept of montage is not presented as a scientific but as an aesthetic system). Eisenstein sought universal correspondences between body and cosmos, with art mediating between the two. He described these correspondences in the essay "On the Structure of Things" (1939), which concluded this period and introduced a still new field of research, serving as the bridge to the book on "nonindifferent nature."[10]

In "On the Structure of Things" Eisenstein analyzed the "magic effect" of the Golden Section, perceived as something absolutely "harmonious" and "organic." He explored this notion with examples of fine art, by comparing their geometrical and mathematical expression to the proportion fixed by the formula for the Golden Section. He transferred this proportional relationship onto another level and recognized in it a general formula: the mathematical and the geometrical expression of the Golden Section has the same mathematical proportion as the proportion of the growth of plants, human bones, and animal horns. Those artists who built their works intuitively oriented to the Golden Section reproduced the regularity of nature in an artificially created form. The artist does not create these regularities, nor are these regularities recognized in a rational way, but they are intuited in the unconscious act of inspiration. The artist is a medium of nature, and the work mediates between the human and organic worlds. This is possible because all these phenomena have larger isomorphic structures. The work of art stands between nature and humans as a model, which is isomorphic in relation to both. This is the culmination of the complete set of correspondences: body—art—cosmos.

Eisenstein's anthropological interpretation differs strongly from the anthropological models of art discussed in the 1930s and derived from the concepts of Georgi Plekhanov or Valeryan Pereverzev. Plekhanov understood art as a playful reproduction of the work process, while Pereverzev interpreted art (literature) as a model of actual situations, whose social significance was to prepare and educate people for resolving similar conflicts in real life. For Eisenstein it is not play, but a critical ritual which helps shift spectators into an ecstatic condition and prepares them to experience physically the dialectic of nature. Eisenstein's anthropological perspective is something of an illusion. He did not clarify the basic human needs (play, mimesis, etc.) as anthropologists would, but tried to explain their projections onto the work of art.

This new concept of art undoubtedly parallels Eisenstein's shift from cultural paradigms derived from 1920s constructivism to the universal thinking of the 1930s, while Soviet aesthetics at the same time turns to Hegel's metaphysics. Art for Eisenstein is still a medium of the dialectic. But the notion of the dialectic in 1939 lies in the abolition of the contrasts between the general and the special, the mental and the sensual, concept and representation, subjective and objective. This model of art aspires to dissolve completely all dichotomies and this is what Eisenstein describes as dialectic.

Despite the framework of the old-fashioned holistic system and the metaphysical conception of the book, Eisenstein elaborated numerous very modern devices in his concrete analyses of works of art. For instance, he applied to fine art of the former century the cinematic perspective of the twentieth century, and he could therefore interpret the compositions of Honoré Daumier or Valentin Serov as an embodiment of the polyfocal perspective that replaced the monofocal one of the Renaissance.

THE THIRD MODEL: THE METHOD (1932–1947)

The term "method," which replaced the previous theoretical focus on "image" (1937) or "montage" (1929), seems to come from the discursive system of the period. This term, which defines the relationship of the artist on the one hand to reality, and on the other to the transformation of reality in the work of art, was used in the 1930s to elaborate the main characteristics of socialist realism. However, the semantics and function of this category in Eisenstein's manuscript differ strongly from this interpretation.

In this book Eisenstein understands the structure of a work of art as a form isomorphic to the structure of multilayered consciousness. On the basis of this assumption he advances the idea of isomorphic structures that offer broader possibilities of application than the organic correspondences between the human body, art, and nature, and also allow him to situate the analysis *within* the frame of this assumption (which was not always possible in "Montage"). He reduces the entire theoretical system to a universal model of analysis, with whose assistance all phenomena can be described, structured, and understood. Even more: what is analyzed is actually human consciousness, of which the work of art is only its trace and imprint.

"Method" describes the special quality of human consciousness, its ability to perceive and to reproduce reality (in behavior, language, and works of art) in a bidirectional way and to react in the same bidirectional way that implies the unity of the logical and the prelogical, the conscious and the unconscious or, in Eisenstein's terms, the rational and the sensual mental activities.

Eisenstein studied the forms of early sensual thinking (mythological in the terms of Nikolai Marr, symbolic in the terms of C. G. Jung, unconscious in the notions of Freud or prelogical in those of Lucien Lévy-Bruhl) through James Frazer's *The Golden Bough* (1907–1912), Lévy-Bruhl's *La mentalité primitive* (1922, Russian edition 1930), Marcel Granet's *La pensée chinoise* (1934), Wilhelm Wundt's *Elemente der Völkerpsychologie Grundlinien einer psychologischen Entwicklungsgeschichte der Menschheit* (1912), and Heinz Werner's *Einführung in die Entwicklungspsychologie* (1926). The norms of early thinking (the nondifferentiation between the "inner world" and "outer world," "micro" and "macro," the specific kind of overcoming of contradictions, the elaboration of the *pars pro toto* principle and the "I"-concept, which does not know a separation from subject and object, etc.) become palpable in pictures and symbols and their recasting in myths, fairy tales, early cultures, and works of art.

The study of the unconscious by Freud and his pupils, as well as studies of symbolic forms by Jung, of prelogical mental structures by Lévy-Bruhl, and of the language of children and of inner speech by Lev Vygotsky, and of the emergence and development of language by Marr, of mythological thinking by Wundt, Granet, and Frazer were all based upon extensive empirical and experimental material. Eisenstein carried their search further by seeking dynamic cross connections between psychology, ethnology, etymology, anthropology, aesthetics, and art, and he discovered traces of early prelogical thinking not just in everyday behavior (in the remnants of rites, superstitions, and uncontrolled reactions) but also in the process of creating and perceiving works of art. Eisenstein came to the conclusion that artistic devices are the formalized regularities of sensual thinking, like *pars pro toto* realized as close-up or metonymy in film. Psychologists, ethnographers, and etymologists provided the descriptions to enable recognition of the structural patterns of this thinking. Eisenstein went on to discover how they were used in the practice of art and how artists can use them operationally.

One can relate Eisenstein's concept to the ideas of Freud and Marx, because their aims reveal a structural analogy. Freud looks for some basic substance in order to unveil the human psyche and to discover in its structure something simple and universal. Marx did the same thing with the economic structure of society. In a similar way, Eisenstein is also looking for a basic substance, that will or can unveil the secrets in the structure of art.

The work of art provokes in the recipient—in the moment of ecstasy—a shift to prelogical, sensual thinking that penetrates consciousness, like Freud's unconscious. However, Eisenstein understood the effect of a work of art and its aesthetic perception as a dynamic unity of polarizing reactions, aligned both upward to consciousness and downward to the unconscious, the prelogical or sensual thought.

The work of art is an imprint of this double reaction. In an analogy to the psychoanalytical hermeneutic with its double reading of primary and secondary characteristics, Eisenstein proposed to transform or convert a dialectical law about the unity of contradictions into a binary opposition. With this he could describe and classify cave painting and cubism, Japanese graphics of the seventeenth century and American films, ornament and musical counterpoint, acting schools and construction of plot in classical Spanish plays. His simple but universal analytical model presages a total semiotization of the world, where all phenomena are seen as an endless chain of the invariant. The circle inscribing an artist, the artistic work, and perception is closed—not by the conditioning method as in the first book, nor by the isomorphism between the human body and the universe as in the second book, but by the structure of consciousness itself.

The twentieth century is characterized by a pluralism of theories; each theory treats an aspect without aspiring to cover the whole. Eisenstein followed different theoretical discourses, but his aspiring toward a whole remained, even if it was understood differently at different times. In this aspect he remained a personality between the nineteenth and twentieth centuries, striving toward universality and yet very concrete in his analysis.

Three times Eisenstein tried to project a universal model for art or film theory. In "The Spherical Book" he demonstrated the new theoretical mentality of the twentieth century in a very impressive way. In the beginning of the century the idyllic world of holistic systems had broken down. The fundamental transformations in the natural sciences led to the fragmentation into single sciences; the split between the natural and human sciences implied that the humanities had to accept the exactness of the natural sciences and establish analogous methods in order to be recognized as science. The debate during the 1896 First Psychological Congress in Munich over whether aesthetics belonged to psychology or to philosophy illustrates this situation very convincingly. At that time Theodor Lipps argued that only psychology could investigate logic, ethics, and aesthetics because it alone possessed an exact methodology, which was lacking in philosophy.[11]

The ideal of totality is dismissed as utopian, but the results of a single science are instead often adapted as a conception of the world in the older utopian vein, and the two ways of thinking, the old and the new, become mixed. The theories of the 1920s have functional or operational meaning: ontology is banished, and "modest" professional analysis becomes generally accepted as a methodological restriction. However, the variety of different types of discourse still described the work of art in all its aspects. Eisenstein's "Spherical Book" is a product of this time: he steps into the circle of specialists. Like the formalists who can determine what is literary and what is cinematic, he belongs to the 1920s, but he behaves like a figure of the earlier century, looking for totality. But he would like to achieve this totality with all the ability of a specialist. His first model constitutes his most radical effort to find a unity which does not exist and which could only be achieved through constant shifts from one level to another, based on reinterpreting incompatible sections of the book in varying ways.

Eisenstein's model is not only relevant retrospectively as an attempt to overcome discursiveness without giving up fragmentation. He also aspired to an interdisciplinary view, which film actually required and which could not be achieved from existing film theory. The ideas of sociology, semiology, psychology, and communication research could not be unified; scholars used many methods and could not often establish connections between their results. The model which Eisenstein sketched in the "Spherical Book" is to be understood as a request to bring the disintegrated disciplines into a dynamic exchange.

Eisenstein's second theoretical model is very traditional, especially in comparison with the radicalism of the first one. At the end of the 1920s Ernst Cassirer came into his field of vision. Cassirer renewed the negated ontology with his notion of the symbol. Eisenstein found his correspondence to this ontology in the term "image" (*obraz*).

The vision of organic unity, of a holistic system, became more attractive for Eisenstein in the 1930s, and in "Montage" he turned to a traditional ontological philosophy of art. In this view art emerges from the totality, although for Eisenstein this totality is not static but dynamic. Regarded retrospectively, Eisenstein's second theoretical model is interesting as an unorthodox variation of the "old new aesthetics" in the context of discussions on socialist realism in the Soviet Union of the 1930s. This traditional model applied to the new medium of film still offered a surprising result. Eisenstein elaborated in this framework the opposition between the visible and invisible for film and insisted that only the invisible (image) is the essential substance in this visual art. It is no coincidence that Jean-Luc Godard was so impressed by the opposition of picture to image, of visible to invisible in Eisenstein's sense, that he realized it in his self-portrait *JLG/JLG* (1995) as an attempt of the film director to shoot and to edit the true film, which is invisible.

Parallel to this book Eisenstein worked on his third theoretical project and decided on an elementary model, which is universally applicable. This analytical model is shaped by its own reductionism as a provocative answer to the universalizing trend of the 1930s. Both Freud and the dialectic were reinterpreted in terms of binary oppositions, and all phenomena were rendered with an appeal to the same invariant scheme; the total semiotization of the world then offered another kind of universal thinking. This semiotic of Eisenstein is supported by psychology. The union between structure and consciousness implies a similar approach to the cognitive direction in film research in recent times. David Bordwell begins from another theoretical platform, but in his study *Narration in the Fiction Film* he aspires to resolve the basic problem of Eisenstein by studying the reaction of the film viewer in order to find a similar hypothetical unity of unconscious, preconscious and conscious processes.[12] The neoformalist analyses of Kristin Thompson and her exploration of the dynamic interaction between the structures of film and the hypothetical responses of the recipient to it are also affected by Eisenstein's orientation.[13]

In recent times it has not been the theory of Eisenstein that has spurred discussions in his homeland, but rather his person: Was he a homosexual? A Stalinist? An opportunist? A dissident?[14] We must attempt to reconstruct the figure of Eisenstein from a variety of points of view. In a certain sense we must try to follow his "Spherical Book," seeking a unity that can be achieved only through the dynamic change of perspectives.

Notes

1. Boris Eikhenbaum, ed., *Poetika kino* (The Poetics of Film), (Moskva–Leningrad: Academia, 1927); Engl. trans. Herbert Eagle, ed., *Russian Formalist Film Theory* (Ann Arbor: University of Michigan, 1981). Vsevolod Pudovkin, *Kinorezhisser i kinomaterial* (The Film Director and Film Material) (Moskva: Kinopechat', 1926). Semen Timoshenko, *Iskusstvo kino: Montazh fil'ma* (Art of the Cinema: Film Montage) (Leningrad: Academia, 1926). Lev Kuleshov, *Iskusstvo kino (moi opyt)*

(Moskva–Leningrad: Teakino-pechat', 1929); Engl. trans. and ed. Ronald Levaco *Kuleshov on Film: Writings by Lev Kuleshov* (Berkeley: University of California Press, 1973).

2. RGALI (Russkii gosudarstvennyi arkhiv literatury i iskusstva) (Russian State Archive of Literature and Art), *fond* (holding) 1923, *opis'* (list)1, *delo* (folder) 1030, published in Sergej Eisenstein, *Das dynamische Quadrat: Schriften zum Film* (The Dynamic Square: Writings on Film), ed. and trans. Oksana Bulgakowa and Dietmar Hochmuth (Leipzig: Reclam, 1988), 344.

3. "A Statement," *Close Up* 3: 4 (October 1928), 10–13; "The New Language of Cinematography," *Close Up* 4: 5 (May 1929), 10–13. Quotation cited in Marie Seton, *Sergei M. Eisenstein: A Biography* (London: The Bodley Head, 1952), 127.

4. Seton, 218. The letters are written in English.

5. François Albera, *Eisenstein et le contructivisme russe* (Eisenstein and Russian Constructivism) (Lausanne: L'Age d'Homme, 1990).

6. Annette Michelson, "Reading Eisenstein Reading *Ulysses:* Montage and the Claims of Subjectivity," *Art & Text* 34 (Spring, 1989), 64–78.

7. David Bordwell, "Eisenstein's Epistemological Shift," *Screen* 15: 4 (Winter, 1974/75), 32–46.

8. Iurii Tynianov, *Osnovy stikhotvornogo iazyka* (The Fundamentals of Verse Language) (Leningrad: Academia, 1924). On the semantics of the Russian formalist term "dominant," borrowed from Brøder Christiansen (*Philosophie der Kunst,* Hanau 1909, 241–42; Russian trans., 1911), see Åge Hansen-Löve, "Dominante," *Russian Literature* 19 (1986), 15–26. William James, *Psychologie* (Leipzig: Verlag von Quelle & Meyer, 1909), 164.

9. Stuart Gilbert, *James Joyce's* Ulysses: *A Study* (New York: Alfred A Knopf, 1931).

10. "On the Structure of Things," in Sergei Eisenstein, *Nonindifferent Nature: Film and the Structure of Things,* trans. Herbert Marshall (Cambridge: Cambridge University Press, 1987), 3–37.

11. Ernst Cassirer, "Psychologie und Philosophie," in his *System, Technik, Sprache: Aufsätze aus den Jahren 1927–1933* (System, Technology and Language: Essays of 1927–1933), eds. W. Orth and J. M. Krois (Hamburg: F. Meiner 1985), 161.

12. David Bordwell, *Narration in the Fiction Film* (Madison: University of Wisconsin Press, 1985).

13. Kristin Thompson, *Breaking the Glass Armor: Neoformalist Film Analyses* (Princeton: Princeton University Press, 1988).

14. Discussion in *Iskusstvo kino* (Film Art) (1996), 5, 11–21.

MAINTAINING, BLURRING, AND TRANSCENDING GENDER LINES IN EISENSTEIN

Al LaValley

This article was originally going to be called "Why do my female colleagues in the Film Department not want to see *The Battleship Potemkin* again?" One of them, upon learning she was going to teach the introductory film course, had as her first reaction the hope of never having to show *Potemkin* again; the other said she would teach Eisenstein if she had to, but only *Strike* in a near perfect print, which with great difficulty and expense she obtained from Eastman House. Both of their reactions go beyond the duty of screening an established and too-familiar classic film and, I think, speak to their reactions also as women. Put simply, many women feel his films are too male and find little in them which resonates with their experience.

Eisenstein's enduring fame hardly rests on his handling of gender in his films, but in a period when gender issues are so central to our reading and teaching of films it is increasingly difficult to ignore a topic which we associate more closely with the less established field of cultural studies and not those of aesthetics, history of ideas, and art theory—the ones in which Eisenstein and his work are most frequently discussed. Furthermore, an examination of gender roles in Eisenstein offers a chance to shed new light on other core issues in the films: the relationship of sexuality to pathos and ecstasy, the intertwining of violence and power, and the homoerotic overtones of the portrayal of males.

In answering my colleagues, I find it initially easy to counter their objections by pointing to the presence of strong and often heroic women in the films and to awaken them to the heroic central presence of the peasant woman Marfa Lapkina in the little seen *The Old and the New*. I also find myself having to admit that power—and male power in particular—is central to Eisenstein's films and that Marfa Lapkina's prominence is something of an oddity in his work.

There are, of course, many reasons for the strong feeling that his films are very male. First, this is due to the activity the films portray: the revolutionary events of Soviet history, which, even though women were deeply important to them have always been depicted as largely male; and historical kings and strong leaders, often involved in great causes but also in political intrigue and power games to further them. The desire for a plotless cinema in the early films makes them focus on typical male-dominated actions or historical processes—a strike, a mutiny, the revolution itself—necessarily subordinating women.

Secondly, however deep and close his friendships with women were, Eisenstein, as a homosexual (or as he seems to be called more frequently these days, a bisexual) seems to be drawn deeply to portraying male society. As Parker Tyler notes in *Screening the Sexes*, he was attracted to strong male heroes like Nevsky and Ivan because their folk myths were universal and at the same time dealt with "powerful, physically forceful and handsome men." Beyond this, Tyler points out that "Eisenstein had a great personal eye for human beauty, and more especially male beauty."[1] Men are therefore privileged in his films, often in ways that women are in the works of other filmmakers. In many of the films, all male societies are dominant. *Potemkin*, for instance, begins with a kind of semitropical male utopia of men sleeping in hammocks, which is disturbed by repressive authority. The final "act" of the film restores the harmony of an all male world, men now working together empowered by their revolt. Similarly in *Alexander Nevsky* and *Ivan the Terrible*, society is largely male. *Nevsky* relegates women to Shakespearian-like parts with the minor characters; unlike Laurence Olivier's *Henry V*, which it inspired—and which probably also inspired it as a play—there is no concluding romance for Nevsky. The romance instead is relegated to Eisenstein's subordinates who act as aspects of Nevsky. And in *Ivan*, once Anastasia is eliminated in Part I, she is replaced by the all-male *oprichniki*, many of them young and beautiful; Part II culminates with them in an all-male dance with Fyodor playing the woman's role as the queen or princess.

Eisenstein, like most of his contemporaries, even those with very progressive views about women, is also very careful to maintain traditional gender lines. Men for Eisenstein connote physical strength, power, and leadership; women, by contrast, offer softness, maternity, support, and moral strength. Eisenstein regularly uses the crossing and blurring of traditional gender lines to caricature figures he does not like. The manlike woman and the effeminate man who cross gender lines are villains. Yet, ironically and paradoxically, as we shall see, some of his most arresting and admirable figures cross these lines while maintaining their traditional gender qualities, thereby offering a fresh view of gender and a new type of character.

For the moment, keeping our focus on the presence of positive women's roles, we can see that with the possible exception of *October*, Eisenstein creates important moments, and occasionally strong roles, for women in revolutionary events. Deviating from the traditional marginalization of women that still continues without apology in mainstream films of men at sea and involved in a mutiny—*Crimson Tide* (1995) with Denzel Washington facing off against Gene Hackman is a recent typical example—Eisenstein makes a strong point in carrying the effects of the Potemkin mutiny into the citizens of both sexes in Odessa and not just staying on board with the mutineers. Similarly in *Strike,* Eisenstein carries us into the strikers' homes and families and their involvement in the strike itself.

In *Potemkin* and *Strike,* one might reasonably complain that women are chiefly victims, used—often with their dead children—to further revolutionary outrage and a sense of the horrors of pre-revolutionary Russia. While this is true, Eisenstein also makes women heroic and gives them major political moments: the mother in *Strike* who makes her way against the reactionary police to the fire alarm box, the heroic schoolteacher and the mother with her child who fearlessly confront the soldiers on the Odessa steps. *Potemkin* also makes prominent a revolutionary woman who whips the crowd to fervor over Vakulinchuk's body on the quay. Marfa Lapkina is the ultimate and successful embodiment of this heroism, occupying the center of *The Old and the New,* where she takes on an embattled role against backsliding peasants and a dilatory party bureaucracy to bring new technology to the countryside.

Why then hasn't Marfa been celebrated more? Here the fault lies, I think, with Eisenstein scholarship and what traditional film history has most celebrated. *The Old and the New* (still currently available only in poor 16mm prints) has been treated as a lesser work, not a major achievement. Its marginalization is probably due to several factors: unlike the previous films, it popularizes its use of montage in ways that seem less innovative; further, the presence of a single heroine links it too closely to socialist realism; and, probably most importantly, it does not deal with the serious—that is, male-centered—revolutionary events of *Strike, Potemkin,* and *October.* (Even Eisenstein might have demoted it for this latter reason.) I am of the opinion that with our present-day interest in gender roles, the film needs to be re-seen and re-evaluated for its place in the Eisenstein canon. It is unfortunate that it was not rediscovered in the late 1960s when women's issues achieved a new prominence and the didacticism of Brecht in films like *Kuhle Wampe* (1932)—also newly resurrected then—was seen as a new film method and not a heavy-handed erasure of cinema. Seen today, the similar didacticism of *The Old and the New* melds with its folkloric charm in a mix of sophistication and simplicity. It also offers more comic touches and a more open sexuality than any other Eisenstein film. And it certainly offers Eisenstein's most positive depiction of a woman transformed by revolution.

However, even with Marfa Lapkina, whose plainness and lack of traditional feminine glamour is celebrated, Eisenstein is careful not to make her too masculine and to maintain the traditional divisions of gender around her. In her daring actions she is assisted throughout by urban males and on one occasion is rescued by an agronomist who looks like Lenin.[2] He concludes his film with a romance and marriage, a conventional ending for many films, but one that is unique for a main character in Eisenstein. Earlier he takes care to tie Marfa closely to feminine sexual roles that prepare for her final marriage: the marriage of the bull and the cow and Marfa's ecstatic glowing face covered with cream from the cream separator and its highly phallic faucet. One could presumably criticize Eisenstein for needing these traditional roles, but they

51. *The Old and the New:* Spigot of the cream separator.

52. *The Old and the New:* Marfa's ecstasy at the workings of the cream separator.

seem to offer him the narrative support for envisioning Marfa in more masculine areas throughout the film.

These roles may also allow him to envision one of his most daring and
affirmative moments of crossing gender lines. Eisenstein inverts the ending
of Charlie Chaplin's *A Woman of Paris* (1923) at the end of *The Old and the
New.* In Chaplin the urban ex-lover of Marie St. Clair passes her country cart
in a fashionable new car without knowing she is in the cart, traveling in the
opposite direction. "Whatever became of Marie St. Clair?" his friend asks, and
he shrugs as she passes by. The ending is highly ironic. Eisenstein instead
places his urban resident, a man who has come to teach peasants how to drive
a tractor, in the rural cart, while Marfa drives up in the new technology of a
motorcycle, stops beside the cart, and glowingly greets him with a sense of
her newfound power. At first he cannot recognize her; she looks like a man
and is wearing goggles that hide much of her face, as well as a leather hat and
coat. Her smile suddenly tells him (and us) it is Marfa. Eisenstein confirms
this liberation of Marfa from traditional roles as the climax of his "story of
Marfa," placing this final image of her into a quick review of shots we have
already seen of her from other major moments in the film that highlight her
growth. The ending is comic, romantic, politically affirmative, and suggests
a strong positive change in gender roles through revolution and technology.

Is Eisenstein then contradictory, praising Marfa and yet putting down the
woman warriors of *October* whom he caricatures as mannish and more suited
for lovemaking than war? Probably so, but it is important to note that caricature occurs only for the villains—those working for the wrong cause. And
it occurs for both sexes. Sometimes those on the evil side are simply grotesque—the fat capitalists of the early films, whether the bosses of *Strike* or
the kulak couple in *The Old and the New,* or the fierce lace-bedecked women
of *October* who help murder a sailor with their parasols as swords. But more
often caricature involves crossing gender lines in the way people look: the
mannish women soldiers of *October* and the effeminate, tired Provisional
Government leaders. Preening peacocks like Kerensky or even Kurbsky in *Ivan
the Terrible* have a touch of the effeminate which makes them narcissistic and
untrustworthy. These caricatures reach their culmination in *Ivan* when Efrosinia becomes monstrous because she is so manlike, and Vladimir, her son,
becomes absurd and pathetic because he is so weak and womanlike.

While there is something of an equal time rule here—men and women are
both subject to caricature—the caricature of men with feminine traits feels
different from that of women who take on masculine traits. Because the films
value and celebrate power, those who lack that male trait are often condemned as weak and womanly, and more easily dismissed: Kurbsky, Vladimir,
and the Polish court in *Ivan,* Kerensky in *October.* As they become more like
women, they become flighty, not to be trusted, and not real threats. By con-

trast, what seems appalling in Efrosinia is that a woman has violated and distorted her feminine nature so strongly and that as a mother she uses her son in the pursuit of power for herself.[3] Her mannishness, reflected in her costume and appearance and in her hard-driving pursuit of power, makes her horrifying and grotesque, but nonetheless powerful and a worthy antagonist to Ivan. By contrast, Vladimir is hardly a serious threat. His adoption of womanly traits makes him cowardly, fearful, and dependent on his mother. Because he is so like a woman, he is an impotent fool who can be simply gulled and disposed of. In neither case does masculinity per se seem to be critiqued. Masculinity is always power. Womanliness, however, can itself seem tantamount to a negative trait, connoting weakness and lack of power.

There are even more complex and intense crossings of gender lines, what we might call "gender transgression," in *Ivan the Terrible.* Such transgression is at its most negative in Efrosinia and her son Vladimir, but achieves a kind of positive transcendence in Fyodor and his dance. Efrosinia and Vladimir are for Eisenstein apogees of gender inversion; for the most part they are totally negative characters, but even they contain hints of a transcendence caused by their violation of taboos. Efrosinia is for the most part a hideous villain—a woman totally defined by the power drive—modeled, it is often said, on Walt Disney's evil queen in *Snow White* (1937), and without any feminine redeeming qualities. We can hardly tell that she is a woman; her hair is concealed by wimples and cowls, her face is craggy like a man's, and her voice deep and masculine. Yet she is also on occasion a complex villain who finds an odd moment of maternal warmth cradling her son's head in her lap and singing him lullabies. At such moments we are not sure whether the concern for boyar power drives and dominates her, as it seems to in most of the film, or simply her more maternal wish to exalt her son on the throne.

Despite her complexity, Vladimir strikes me as a more interesting figure, probably because he is such a negative example of manhood, a key theme of all the films. Also as a stereotypical homosexual in appearance, he has regularly been regarded as a character Eisenstein has a more direct relationship to and whom he fears. Eisenstein caricatures him but in a richer, more detailed way than he does the mother. He stands out from all the other men in the film by his blond locks, his pale appearance, his pursed lips with their overemphatic lipstick, his trembling and cowering manner—often hiding behind his mother, in a grotesque mixture of man and child—and even by his costume which connotes a more modern theatrical flamboyance. Indeed, he is always ready to go onstage for his coronation—once when Ivan appears to be dying and later when Ivan gulls him. In many ways, he appears as a kind of stereotype of a gay Bolshoi dancer. Does he not look a little like an effeminate version of Nureyev? Parker Tyler notes his contemporaneous look too:

"Vladimir is impersonated by a young man so effeminate of face that he looks like the newest photogenic starlet of Hollywood in 1946."[4]

Marie Seton has read him autobiographically, suggesting in a highly Freudian vein that in killing him, Eisenstein was killing what he regarded as the weak homosexual in himself.[5] This may be too autobiographical an immolation, but she strikes me as essentially correct in seeing his death as an attack on what Eisenstein regarded as the deathliness, impotence and uncreativeness of homosexuality. Eisenstein was well aware of the nineteenth century model of homosexuality as a debilitating disease as well as the etiology suggested in the period's more progressive model in Freud, the suffocating and possessive mother and her emasculated child, too strongly tied to her and so vividly seen in Efrosinia and her son. As Håkan Lövgren and others have pointed out, his reading of Freud's book on Leonardo is central to his conception of both the artist and homosexuality.[6] Eisenstein admired this book because it gave him a way to see his homosexuality as debilitating but capable of being sublimated and transcended through art, made into a kind of aesthetic ecstasy. Vladimir is all that Eisenstein would not want to be. But before leaving Vladimir, let me say a few words in favor of his rehabilitation. Though within the film's narrative he is always a negative example, he nevertheless has many positive traits. He is not entirely a figure to be despised or only an image of Eisenstein's self-hate. Note for instance that Ivan feels he is a real threat, and decides to kill him after he has reached out and grasped a crown on one of the swan food vessels and radiates a kind of bliss contemplating its power. And at the film's end, Ivan seems to want to have it both ways about Vladimir: a clown of no worth who can be easily dismissed, and "no clown but my greatest enemy." In what sense could he be seen as himself an enemy and not just a pawn of Efrosinia and boyar power? Perhaps Ivan sees in him the cheapening of the crown to a toy for self-indulgence, a refusal of the crown's heavy responsibilities. Perhaps even a different ethic of power.

One of the positive traits that flows from Vladimir's difference is that he provides the film with humor. And unlike the humorous and grotesque prince also awaiting his coronation in Josef von Sternberg's *The Scarlet Empress* (1934), upon whom he is partly based, he is nonpolitical, innocent and harmless. While part of the humor involves laughing at him—his exaggerated cowering from the palace intrigue, plots, and violence—he also generates a sense of play and humor on his own. Throughout the film he is the only one not engulfed in the palace treachery. His campy gestures, his freedom from the seriousness of the others, his drunken revelry and his delight in mummery push him into another realm which can act as a critique of the savagery of the main narrative. His gestures are regularly articulating a kind of exaggerated camp that threatens to erupt under the film's high stylization elsewhere—for instance, in the melodramatic frowns and looks of Kurbsky, in

53. *Ivan the Terrible:* Fyodor Basmanov replacing Anastasia in his closeness to Ivan.

Malyuta's theatrical pulling down of his eyelid, Ivan's dramatic use of his eyes and beard, in his often too-swift and extreme changes of gesture, as well as in the theatrical movement of his robes and body. That the film moves to color, dance, and a procession which is mummery suggests the movement to an abstract aesthetic realm of play where Vladimir really could be king of the revels. But this is only suggested. Vladimir is a pawn of his mother's pursuit for power, he is killed and the political narrative restores itself as paramount.

It is Fyodor Basmanov, the young son of Alexei, the first of the *oprichniki* who devote their lives to Ivan, who offers a still more intriguing play across traditional gender lines. A kind of masculine counterpart to Marfa, he preserves his original gender traits while increasingly occupying traditional feminine areas. Alexei Basmanov gives him to Ivan after Anastasia's death as a kind of replacement for her, a companion who offers support and trust. Increasingly the handsome young man is shown in poses similar to those of Anastasia, slightly below Ivan and leaning on him. He is also given single closeups, much like Anastasia, which emphasize the iconicity of his beauty. Eisenstein has even referred to him as an "ersatz Anastasia."[7] However, throughout the earlier part of Part II Ivan also insists on his own orphanhood, his aloneness, and how he has no real replacement for Anastasia. But increasingly Fyodor seems to occupy her role.

At the same time, unlike Anastasia, Fyodor's masculinity allows him to act in the political plot—to be not just Ivan's support and consort, but his eyes, ears, and legs, protecting him and warning him in advance. He does not have

54. *Qué viva México!:* Elaborate ritual of the bullfighter getting dressed.

fits of hysterics nor will he be poisoned by Efrosinia. His most daring transgression of gender roles occurs when at the end of the frenzied dance—Parker Tyler calls it "almost paganish,"—and the central dancer, the only one in female attire, wearing a mask with a queen's crown and breastplates—removes the mask and reveals himself as Fyodor.[8] In a strong sense, Fyodor has become another Anastasia. Earlier too he seemed to hint at his replacement of her when he took Ivan to her bedroom and led him through the actions around her death, making him see that she had been eliminated by poison from the cup Efrosinia left for Ivan to hand her. To be sure, at the dance he reestablishes his male identity and soon warns Ivan of Pyotr's presence and the upcoming assassination attempt. But this moment surprisingly remains obscure and hard to read, compared to the aesthetic frenzy of the ecstatic dance in color which soon takes over again, and the shock of the previously revealed transgendered effect. Vladimir may look like a Bolshoi dancer but is not. Fyodor unexpectedly seems to be one, perhaps the "straight-looking" version of Vladimir, and the return of the repressed in disguised form.

There was strong preparation both for Fyodor's gender transgression and for the roles of music and dance in the earlier *Qué viva México!* where Eisenstein's homoerotic fascination with beautiful males seems strongest and most relaxed. In David Laceaga, the young bullfighter, the film reveals little of the machismo that traditionally surrounds bullfighting, but concentrates instead on the elaborate almost feminine ritual of his dress, his parading into the ring like a dancer, and the extraordinary beauty of his near-deathly dance with the bull. Interestingly, his traditional masculine qualities are never compromised; his courage is only heightened. The dance in Part II and its use of masks is also strikingly prepared for in several dances in the film, especially in the positive triumph over death in the epilogue, where the masks of death are removed to show life itself in smiling children.

Even as the political narrative restores itself in Part II of *Ivan the Terrible* with the killing of Vladimir, there is a carry-over of gay iconicity to the subsequent scene. Throughout all the films the presence of naked male bodies has threatened to disrupt the narratives that contain them and to become iconographic gay male images in their own extradiegetic right. Often these bodies have been in a St. Sebastian–like mold—an iconography with a long gay history, so that by the 1920s it was the dominant male image of homosexuality. In a survey of Sebastian's use in art history, Richard Kaye calls him "the single most successfully deployed image of modern gay identity." [9] Though these bodies are plagued by torture and usually bound or restrained in some way, their visualization uses the instruments of torture only partly to signify a repressive outside power. More importantly, the torture of the male figures allows the sight of the male body and its musculature to be heightened and incorporates a note of sadomasochistic sexuality on its own. The sailor in his hammock whose muscled back is whipped by the sadistic officer in *Potemkin*, the Tartars whose hands are pulled back and tied and their chests exposed on the stakes at Kazan in *Ivan the Terrible*, the heroic peasants of the Maguey

55. *Qué viva México!:* Male bodies beautiful in suffering.

episode in *Qué viva México!* stripped to the waist, restrained and put into the sand to be killed: all are examples of the male body, its beauty somehow heightened by suffering.

Part II of *Ivan* does not disappoint in this category either. As Efrosinia rises and throws herself backward with a wail on discovering her son has been killed, a cut on her movement repeats it as Fyodor plucks the shirt from the beautiful young assassin, Pyotr, and Malyuta restrains him from behind, his naked chest straining under the assault. Significantly, Ivan confronts him and pardons him, saving him from certain death by his associates who planned to kill him as a coverup of their actions. Did his beautiful chest have any part in Ivan's pardon?

Eisenstein seems especially careful not to raise such questions. Article 121 of the Russian penal code made homosexuality a crime in 1935; it would have prevented such questions on his part and made him cautious. Eisenstein follows the lead of other gay filmmakers—some closeted, some not—in idealizing young straight-looking males in nominally straight narratives. This is a common enough paradigm that allowed a kind of doublespeak which held until gay liberation in the 1960s and 1970s. Jean Cocteau with Jean Marais and Eduoard Dermit, Pier Paolo Pasolini with Franco Citti and Ninetto Davoli, and Luchino Visconti with Helmut Berger, and many others come easily to mind, though all are more revelatory of their gay subtexts than Eisenstein and all featured their young lovers in their films. In Eisenstein, however, as with the character Marfa, the support of the traditional acts both as a kind of disguise for gender transgression and a support for opening an exploration of it.

Beyond the traditional division of gender lines, there were still other lines and divisions that Eisenstein felt had to be maintained. Eisenstein was both inhibited and buttressed by a deep-seated belief that the ecstasy of true art had to be separated from the false ecstasy of drugs or eroticism, as well as from religious ecstasy. As David Bordwell points out, these were for him surrogates for ecstasy.[10] Religious ecstasy was closer to what he was aiming for, something more like the saint's loss of self in the Other. This is how he preferred to think of the famous cream separator sequence in *The Old and the New,* not in its more obvious sexual implications or its ties to the theme of fecundity elsewhere in the film. Presumably sexual ecstasy—and more importantly homosexual ecstasy—would also be ruled out in Fyodor's frenzied dance with the *oprichniki.*

But as with gender roles, these distinctions do not always conveniently stay fixed. Religious, aesthetic, and sexual ecstasy all seem to mix in the cream separator episode. And in the frenzied dance of Fyodor and the *oprichniki*—as well as David Laceaga's dance with the bull—and the mummery of the pageants that surround these scenes in both films, religion, aesthetics, and sex blend in a form of play beyond politics. Marfa's ecstasy can more easily be termed revolutionary at the end of *The Old and the New,* but the ecstasy of Fyodor and David Laceaga and that of the viewers who witness it comes from a more distinctly aesthetic realm.

Indeed, in its final dance and "mummery" of deception, Part II of Ivan seems to suggest a more abstracted yet highly energized aesthetic realm permeated by Eisenstein's own struggle with alternate versions of masculinity and homosexuality, each of them invading new areas. That he ultimately must kill the weak homosexuality of Vladimir is unfortunate, but that he then absorbs homosexuality into energy and power in Fyodor's dance is also a real breakthrough and akin to letting Marfa gain power from the revolution to don goggles, ride a motorcycle, and master technology. But here power comes from dance, music, color, and a female costume on a male—hardly the sources of power the movie has been advocating to this point. Still, when the political plot returns, we realize there has been little room for the contemplation of other qualities outside of power that seem to be vaguely signaled but unexplored in the Fyodor–Ivan relationship: introspection, quietness, warmth, the traditional female virtues. The queen's mask of the dance is glimpsed lying on the floor, but we don't see what the relationship without the mask will be. These other qualities of life are only too often a sign of weakness. The proposed Part III was to end with Ivan attaining his victory of an expanded and unified Russia, but alone. He orders Fyodor to execute his father for betrayal, then finds he must execute his beloved Fyodor as well for another betrayal. This he does but not without shedding a tear. Victory comes with grief and isolation—much the way Eisenstein said he felt in his own last years. Eisenstein was, I think, right about Mexico—he was more liberated there than anywhere else, even if his film work had not approached a consequent artistic liberation in a solidly affirmed new style. The later films press the investigation into style and ecstasy further but inevitably have an air of constraint in them. But despite that, Eisenstein works toward and often achieves a breakthrough, especially in *Ivan,* where even if the traditional gender norms reassert themselves too quickly there are nonetheless moments of an ecstasy which seems liberating, new, and mysterious—and often include the political, but almost always go beyond it. It is these moments beyond gender for which I prize the films. Thus my thoughts on gender return us to an Eisenstein who has traditionally been valued for the experience of pathos and ecstasy he has achieved in his films, but I hope they have also shown how the violation of traditional gender lines especially fuels their urge toward ecstasy and transcendence.

Notes

1. Parker Tyler, *Screening the Sexes: Homosexuality in the Movies* (New York: Holt, Rinehart, and Winston, 1972), 320–321.

2. David Bordwell, *The Cinema of Eisenstein* (Cambridge: Harvard University Press, 1993), 105.

3. Marie Seton, *Sergei M. Eisenstein: A Biography* (New York: Grove Press, 1960), 436.

4. Tyler, *Screening the Sexes,* 321.

5. Seton, *Eisenstein,* 437.

6. Håkan Lövgren, *Eisenstein's Labyrinth: Aspects of a Cinematic Synthesis of the Arts,* Stockholm Studies in Russian Literature, 31 (Stockholm: Almqvist & Wiksell, 1996), 23.

7. Sergei Eisenstein, *Izbrannye proizvedeniia v shesti tomakh* (Selected Works in Six Volumes) (Moscow: Iskusstvo, 1964–71), 6: 512. Cited in Bordwell, *Cinema of Eisenstein,* 234.

8. Tyler, *Screening the Sexes,* 323.

9. Richard A. Kaye, "Losing His Religion: Saint Sebastian as Contemporary Gay Martyr," in *Outlooks: Lesbian and Gay Sexualities and Visual Cultures,* ed. Peter Horne and Reina Lewis (London: Routledge, 1996), 87.

10. Bordwell, *Cinema of Eisenstein,* 194.

THE CIRCLE AND THE LINE
Eisenstein, Florensky, and Russian Orthodoxy

Rosamund Bartlett

I t has become common to view the trajectory of Eisenstein's career as one going from revolutionary Constructivism to a more conservative organicism. Although the extent to which Eisenstein actually changed course remains open to debate, he certainly seemed outwardly less interested in the collision of opposites and more entranced with the idea of a "synthesis of the arts" in his later years. Various sources of inspiration have been suggested for Eisenstein's cinematic ideal, which he felt was potentially the ultimate *Gesamtkunstwerk* of the twentieth century; proposed sources have included Gothic cathedrals, Hegel's organicist philosophy, Wagner's artistic theories, and socialist realism.[1] I will consider a more unexpected source: Russian Orthodoxy. The point of departure is an article written in 1918 by the theologian Pavel Florensky, in which he likens the Orthodox liturgy to a synthesis of the arts. It is no coincidence that Eisenstein's deepening interest in organic unity coincided chronologically with the development of the doctrine of socialist realism, which has its philosophical basis in the ideas of Hegel. A comparison of Eisenstein's artistic goals with the ideas Florensky expresses in "Khramovoe deistvo kak sintez iskusstv" (The Orthodox Rite as a Synthesis of the Arts) suggests that we should perhaps reconsider our notions about the German provenance of Russian organicist thought. This is not an attempt to argue that Eisenstein the committed Marxist was in fact a closet Christian, but a conjecture that he might unconsciously have remained culturally true to Russian Orthodoxy in his approach to form and structure in art, even if he rejected its theology. Recent studies have revealed the presence of Christian subtexts in Eisenstein's films, but one may also point to his interest in mysticism and ecstasy, and his heavy use of symbolism, which is a cornerstone of Russian Orthodox aesthetics. And it is in the area of aesthetics that we may find common ground between Eisenstein and Florensky.

Their destinies were very different. Florensky's ministry brought him into direct conflict with the Soviet regime, and he perished as a victim of the purges in 1937 in the notorious Solovki labor camp. Eisenstein's fame somewhat protected him from arrest, and despite his work being severely censored, he died at home in Moscow in 1948. At first glance a more unlikely pairing is therefore difficult to imagine, yet there are some intriguing parallels between the aggressive Marxist Eisenstein and the devout Father Florensky. Eisenstein was sixteen years younger than Florensky, who was born in 1882, yet their birthdays are only one day apart (Eisenstein was born on the January 10, and Florensky on January 9). Their fathers were both engineers. Eisenstein's childhood was one of excessive religiosity; Florensky's the absolute opposite. Eisenstein lost faith in God, having gained his highest marks at school in religion, while Florensky acquired it. Both were polymaths. Besides his work as a theologian and priest, Florensky's activities embraced art history, physics, chemistry, philosophy, and philology. As well as being a film and theater director, Eisenstein was an accomplished graphic artist, whose theoretical writings were the fruit of profoundly original research into many different areas including mythology, anthropology, psychology, painting, and literature. Eisenstein and Florensky are the only two Russian figures in the twentieth century who have seriously been compared to Leonardo da Vinci, a figure in whom both had more than a passing interest. Eisenstein modeled himself on Leonardo; Florensky studied him in the context of his work as an art historian. Both Eisenstein and Florensky were serious mathematicians. Eisenstein first concentrated on analytical geometry as a student in Petrograd, while Florensky studied mathematics at Moscow University with Andrei Bely's father, Nikolai Bugaev. Both were interested in the nature of the artistic experience, and wrote a great many wide-ranging theoretical works in an often complicated syntax. Both, finally, were entranced by the idea of artistic synthesis.

In the 1930s, Eisenstein became increasingly obsessed with the idea of wholeness, which came to constitute an ever-elusive goal in his creative work. In his autobiography *Immoral Memories,* written in 1946, he declared: "If I were a detached researcher, I should say of myself: it seems as if this author is obsessed once and for all with a single idea, a single theme, a single subject"— and this "ultimate idea" was the achievement of unity.[2] It is tempting to speculate that Eisenstein's obsession arose partly as a result of the discord in his family life. Like his elder contemporary Andrei Bely, who was also obsessed with synthesis, Eisenstein was a gifted only child of parents who had little in common. Both Bely and Eisenstein felt torn between their scientist fathers and cultured mothers, and Eisenstein's fascination with Freud's study of Leonardo da Vinci (who seems to have had a similar childhood) in this context is well-known. The fact that numerous artists, writers, and musicians of this period (including Alexander Blok, Vyacheshav Ivanov, Vsevolod Meyerhold, Vasili Kandinsky, and Alexander Scriabin) also had an obsession with synthesis of varying kinds suggests the root causes of Eisenstein's quest for synthesis are more complicated. Håkan Lövgren has argued persuasively, for example, that a major source of inspiration was the medieval Gothic cathedral, which, according to Erwin Panofsky, aimed at totality, and "one perfect and final solution."[3] For Eisenstein the Gothic cathedral was indeed "the most historically perfect artistic manifestation of a totalizing world view as well as an unparalleled expression of the ecstatic creative spirit that imbued the artists/architects who built these edifices."[4] In his 1945 monograph *Non-indifferent Nature,* Eisenstein devotes several pages to Nikolai Gogol's hymn to Gothic architecture of 1831, in which the writer expresses its "pathos" by describing in exultant tones how everything in it is unified together. Gogol speaks, for example, of a "forest of vaults rising harmoniously high over your head, windows huge and narrow," of "grandeur as well as beauty, luxury and simplicity, heaviness and lightness."[5]

Wagner was another obvious and more recent source of inspiration for Eisenstein's concept of organic unity, as his production of *Die Walküre* at the Bolshoi Theater in 1940 clearly showed.[6] Eisenstein positioned himself as Wagner's successor, and the cinema as technologically the most advanced form of the synthesis of arts towards which Wagner strove to achieve. But Wagner himself, of course, was inspired by German idealist philosophy, which he absorbed in part through the medium of Romantic literature. And it was this same source, particularly the philosophy of Hegel, which influenced the ideology of socialist realism, in this case through the Russian medium of Vissarion Belinsky. As Victor Terras has observed, "Belinsky's world view remained 'organic.' To the end of his life, he never doubted the unity and interrelatedness of all that is: one universe, one life, one mankind, one historic process." "No matter how hard you try to split up life," Belinsky writes in his "Survey of Russian Literature" in 1847, for example, "it will still remain an integral whole."[7] Eisenstein followed Belinsky and Hegel in believing that artistic content cannot exist independently of its artistic form. His conception of organic unity in a work of art echoed Hegel's belief that all constituent parts should be integrated in such a way that no one part can be altered without affecting the whole. Eisenstein further believed that the organic unity of a work, as well as the sense of organic unity received from the work, arose when the law of the construction of this work corresponded to the law of the structure of organic phenomena of nature, manifested in the ratio of the so-called Golden Section. This for him was the perfect expression of unity between the part and the whole, and he argues that it is to be located in his films in the repetition of motifs at certain visual, formal, or temporal intervals, creating a musical dynamic in the work's emotional landscape. Elements contributing to the work as a whole thus ideally permeate all its individual features. Eisenstein only began developing his theories of organic unity in the late 1930s, but he might have unconsciously absorbed some ideas from his teacher Meyerhold, whose work in the theater was inspired by a similar quest for synthesis. Take his technique of biomechanics, for example, which was an expression for him of the mechanics of organicity and expressivity. For Meyerhold, as Arun Khopkar has commented, gesture was "the result of the whole body working," so that a single muscle moving would produce a response throughout the whole body. Similarly when an ensemble moved, Meyerhold aimed for it to have the unity of a single organism, and result in the sum of its parts.[8] Eisenstein illustrates a similar idea in *Nonindifferent Nature* by asserting—obviously with the benefit of hindsight—that all five parts of his film *The Battleship Potemkin,* as well as the film as a whole, are governed by the same structural law. In each part, according to Eisenstein, revolutionary brotherhood grows from a small incipient cell into a manifestation of greater intensity on a larger scale. The merging of opposites constitutes another and perhaps more questionable dimension of Eisenstein's idea of organic unity. In *Potemkin,* for example, there is a turning point in each of the five parts, according to Eisenstein, when the action

> leaps over from a quieter protest to a more angry and violent clash. And it is also remarkable that the jump at each point—is not simply a sudden jump to another mood, to another rhythm, to another event, but each time it is a transition to a distinct opposite. Not contrastive but opposite, for each time it gives the image of that same theme from the opposite point of view and at the same time unavoidably grows out of it.[9]

This merging of opposites, Eisenstein writes, contributes to the organic unity of the whole, and is what produces the desired quality of pathos. Eisenstein clearly also found a parallel in real life by telling his students that although Konstantin Stanislavsky and Meyerhold opposed each other ideologically and theoretically, they actually sought synthesis rather than compromise.[10]

One source of inspiration for Eisenstein's concept of organic unity that has so far been overlooked is Russian Orthodoxy. Examination of Pavel Florensky's 1918 article however, reveals there are distinct areas of overlap with the views Eisenstein developed in the 1930s. Florensky began developing his ideas of organic unity much earlier than Eisenstein. "The Orthodox Rite as a Synthesis of the Arts" was the first article he wrote after being appointed to the Commission for the preservation of art and antiquities at the Troitse-Sergius *Lavra* (monastery) in Zagorsk, the center of Russian Orthodoxy, in 1918. It was during his work for the Zagorsk Commission that Florensky began to develop his theory of art, which culminated in 1922 in the writing of *Iconostasis,* a work inspired by the conviction that Russian icons of the fourteenth and fifteenth centuries represented a pinnacle which no other artistic works had ever surpassed.

Florensky had been based at the Moscow Theological Academy in Zagorsk since 1904 (first as a student, and from 1908 as a lecturer in philosophy), and was ordained there in 1911. Although his article on the artistic synthesis of the Orthodox rite was written at around the time of the first anniversary of the October Revolution, it was not published until 1922, in the opening issue of the art journal *Makovets*. It is one of Florensky's more popular works, and is now regularly reprinted. "Makovets" was the name of a Moscow-based group of artists formed in 1921 by Vasili Chekrygin, Nikolai Chernyshev, and Lev Zhegin. Members of the group contributed to exhibitions held in 1922, 1924, and 1925, and they produced two issues of the journal in 1922. As John Bowlt has commented, the name of the group (signifying "summit") has both artistic and religious overtones, containing both a response to the ideas of the Suprematist movement led by Malevich and a reference to the hill at Zagorsk, where in the fourteenth century Sergei Radonezhsky founded the famous monastery.[11] Florensky had become involved with the Makovets group after joining the faculty of Moscow's main art school Vkhutemas, where he specialized in the spatial analysis of artistic works. His affiliation with the group came about as a result of a conviction (most notably shared by Kandinsky) that Modernism marked a turning towards the spiritual in art, thus bringing Russian Orthodox aesthetics into a position of contiguity with the European avant-garde.[12] He had a great deal of sympathy with the group's attempts to restore to art a moral and spiritual purpose, and to reconnect with the artistic heritage of centuries past. For Florensky, symbolic art with its images of otherworldly reality was the art of ascent, as opposed to the realism of the Western art of descent, with what he felt was its empty semblance of everyday life. At a time when the abstract ideas of Constructivism were still in the ascendancy, and religion and past culture had been condemned as obsolete, such idealistic sentiments were highly unfashionable, of course, but nevertheless fully in keeping with the utopian traditions of Russian art.

Like many of the Russian Symbolists, the Makovets group was interested in overcoming the "disease" of individualism, and called for the arts once more to be integrated into a harmonious whole, and for artistic images also to be synthetic. Florensky's article on the Orthodox liturgy as a synthesis of the arts is thus closely aligned with the artistic credo of the Makovets group, and also with Russian Symbolist aesthetics (underlined by his use of the word rite or *deistvo*, with its undeniable allusion to Vyacheslav Ivanov's essay "Wagner and the Dionysian Rite," and to Scriabin). As Leonid Geller has noted, the word "synthesis" and related concepts appear often in Florensky's writings between 1918 and the early 1920s.[13] In Florensky's view, the Orthodox liturgy seemed to offer the highest possible synthesis of heterogenous artistic elements:

In a church, everything is fused to everything else, in principle: the church's architecture, for example, which even takes account of such a small visible effect as the ribbons of blueish incense hovering about the frescoes and wrapping themselves round the pillars of the cupola . . .

widening the architectural space of the church almost to infinity, softening the dryness and hardness of its lines, and, as if melting them, bringing them into movement and into life. But we have so far only talked about one small part of the Orthodox rite, and moreover one that is relatively one-dimensional. Let us remember the movement and rhythm of the clergy during the censing, for example, the undulation and rippling of pleats of precious fabrics, the sweet smells, the particularly fiery quality of the atmosphere, ionized by thousands of burning candles, and let us further remember that the synthesis of the Orthodox rite is not limited to the visual arts, but brings into its circle the art of singing and poetry.[14]

As in the performance of a music drama, Florensky maintains that each individual element in the Orthodox liturgy can only be fully understood within the context of the liturgy as a whole, and when linked to every other element: "Here everything is subordinated to one goal, to the supreme effect of the catharsis of this musical drama."[15] In calling the performance of the liturgy a "music drama," with its explicit Wagnerian connotations, and by making an analogy with Scriabin's quest to create a religious, synthetic work of art, Florensky fully acknowledges the extent to which it is an aesthetic as much as a religious experience, in which stylization and symbolism play an important role in raising participants through worship from the world "below" to the world "above" and bringing about spiritual catharsis.[16] For Florensky, as for Belinsky and for Eisenstein, "true art is the unity of content and methods of expression of that content," so that the alteration of any one element destroys its power and impact.[17]

As far as can be ascertained, Florensky never met Eisenstein, nor is there any record of familiarity with each other's work. As a committed Marxist, Eisenstein outwardly turned his back on his Orthodox upbringing, and took pains in his memoirs to stress his atheism.[18] Declaring in *Immoral Memories* a "not too respectful attitude toward the founders of the christian cult," Eisenstein claims he succumbed to the Voltairian "germ of disrespect for the Supreme Being" following what he describes as an "almost hysterical religiosity and the cult of mystical feats" in his childhood.[19] He took confession for the last time in 1916, when he was eighteen, and thereafter used religious symbols to compare Christianity unfavorably with socialism.[20] The church, whether Russian Orthodox (as in *Potemkin*) or Catholic (as in *Alexander Nevsky*) is invariably portrayed in Eisenstein's films as immoral, corrupt, and obscurantist through withering cameos of its representatives that are often deliberately and provocatively blasphemous. In one of the most famous examples of intellectual montage in *October,* he juxtaposes various images of deities from various religions beginning with an ornate baroque Christ and ending with one of a pagan Giliak idol in order to produce feelings of derisive laughter in the spectator. And yet while Eisenstein was producing parodies of religious belief, he was at the same time introducing numerous religious images into his work, leading, as Mikael Enckell has pointed out, to an "underestimation of the significance of the Christian message" in his films.[21] Alexander Nevsky can be seen as a Christ figure, for example, whose moral strength, courage, and simplicity stand in marked contrast to the weakness, arrogance, and brutality of the supposedly Christian Teutonic knights. Enckell draws our attention to the opening of the film, where Nevsky is depicted with fishing nets, surrounded by his entourage in what amounts to a clearly biblical image.[22] In *Ivan the Terrible,* there are strong parallels with Christ's passion, even though the general attitude to the church in the film is a negative one. This contradictory stance is however perhaps typical of a man who inspired contradictory feelings in the people who met him because of the contradictions in his own personality (he was highly rational, but also very superstitious).[23] And it explains, perhaps, why Eisenstein nurtured a deep and enduring fascination with religion and religious forms. He was certainly aware that he was culturally still Russian Orthodox, even if he had rejected the dogma.[24] Whether he repressed it, concealed it, or disavowed it, mysticism, which is an intrinsic part of the Orthodox heritage, remained a powerful current in his work.[25]

Like Florensky, Eisenstein was fully conscious of the aesthetic power of the Orthodox liturgy. In his autobiography he gives a vivid portrait of his spiritual mentor Father Nicholas, who, dressed in a "silvery blue chasuble, and with his arms raised heavenward" would stand during services "in a cloud of incense pierced by the slanting rays of the sun":

> As he performed the sacrament of the Eucharist, the bells, certainly prompted by a mysterious force, pealed from the lofty belfry, and it actually seemed that the heavens had opened and grace was pouring out upon the sinful word. From such moments springs my lifelong weakness for the ornate in religious services: the sunbeams cutting down through the smoke of incense, the standing columns of dust or mist, the luxuriant shocks of priestly hair (from the priest in *Potemkin* to the religious procession in *Ivan the Terrible*), and a passion for sacristies, chasubles, dalmatics, omophorions and epitrachelions. All these I included in my films.[26]

Eisenstein's description of his emotional reaction to the Russian Orthodox liturgy is an eloquent illustration of Florensky's thesis about it being a synthesis of the arts, and indeed very similar to Florensky's description. Florensky speaks at length precisely about light and the importance of the "art of smoke"—the "thin blue veil of incense that melts into the air" which provides an essential "softening and deepening of the aerial perspective" that is not possible in a museum.[27]

Toward the end of his life, Eisenstein explored both in his creative and theoretical work the idea of the circle as a symbol of unity, as he sought ways of transcending diachronic, linear thinking and the dualism that he felt had always been inherent in his films. Håkan Lövgren discusses, for example, the huge ring in the *Walküre* production which hung in front of the stage at the Bolshoi Theater in 1940, in the shape of the alchemical symbol Uroborus, the snake which consumes its own tail, implying unity and return.[28] This is in keeping with the goal of the production, which was to resurrect the supposedly syncretic unity of prehistory, and thus exemplify Mircea Eliade's later distinction between the cyclical time of archaic man and the linear time of modern man.[29] The ideal of organic unity may well have been present as a Slavic ideal even before the advent of Orthodox Christianity. One can find symbolic circular shapes in native Russian culture that are both physically manifest (such as the round dance of the *khorovod*) and implied (the peasant *obshchina,* or commune). It is also no coincidence that Tolstoy deliberately imbues his quintessential Russian characters Pierre Bezukhov and Platon Karataev with round qualities or links them with round shapes in *War and Peace.* The circle was also a figure frequently used in early Russian icon painting as a symbol of higher truths.[30] In the Orthodox world the circle has long represented immortality, while the three lines making up a triangle symbolize the Trinity of God, man, and the universe.[31] One of Eisenstein's last unpublished theoretical works is called "The Circle," and includes discussions of circular shapes in Christian art and as symbols of the womb.[32] The tension between the "circle" and the "line" in Eisenstein's work can be understood, therefore, to be between female and male, and between movement and stasis, as well as between regression and progression.[33] In the context of our discussion of the influence of Russian Orthodoxy on Eisenstein, it is interesting to note Arun Khopkar's description of the last part of *Ivan the Terrible,* in which Eisenstein uses an image of passage from the womb and rejection by the mother when Vladimir goes to meet his death through a rounded passage. As Khopkar comments:

> The experience of birth is crucial for Eisenstein's concept of mise-en-scène because it marks the meeting of so many opposites; passivity and activity; darkness and light, concave and convex . . . it creates a unity of past experience with a vision of the ideal future, and could thus be related

to the iconostasis of Russian Orthodoxy, where past, present and future meet, life and death touch each other, heaven and hell meet.[34]

Eisenstein's use of symbolic images in his films might from a purely technical point of view be compared to the function of icons in the Orthodox liturgy, which are similarly highly stylized. Like Florensky, Eisenstein was also absorbed by the whole process of art, from conception to reception, and his ideas on the relationship of the part to the whole in art are worth juxtaposing with Florensky's description of the function of the icon within the Russian Orthodox church liturgy. Acting as a symbol of the church, which is in itself a symbol of the world, Florensky shows how the icon's material, surface, and design are all directed towards the aim of bringing about the religious ecstasy of spiritual catharsis:

> And many features of the icon, which irritate the satiated modern outlook such as the exaggerated nature of certain proportions, the way lines are underscored, the abundance of gold and precious stones, mounts and haloes . . . all prove in the correct environment to be necessary, absolutely integral, and the only means to express the spiritual content of the icon, rather than appearing as a curious piece of exotica— that is to say, what results is the unity of style and content, and a genuine work of art. [35]

Eisenstein was also deeply interested in the process of catharsis. If he was interested in arousing the emotions of the viewer by means of montage and the collision of opposites at the beginning of his career, he later became more and more fixated with the idea of ecstasy as the cathartic ideal of the aesthetic experience, and, as Jaques Aumont has observed, he understood it in its original, religious sense, as "union with a transcendental object." [36] Eisenstein had visited French Gothic cathedrals in 1930, and discusses religious ecstasy at length in *Nonindifferent Nature.*[37] Although he is careful to note that ecstasy is not restricted to religious experience, it is tempting to think that his own quest for ecstasy was actually inspired by his experience of the Orthodox liturgy as a young boy.

Eisenstein's ambivalent relationship with the Russian Orthodox church clearly warrants further careful inquiry. In some ways the manifestation of Russian Orthodox themes in his work, as well as the coincidence in aesthetic style, is reminiscent of similar facets of Tolstoy's creative oeuvre. While similarly rejecting the theology of the Russian Orthodox Church (which also rejected him, finally), Tolstoy inherited and continued to deploy its aesthetic language.[38] That Tolstoy's "emblematic" realism should indeed be understood

56. "The Flight into Egypt" (pencil sketch from Eisenstein's Mexican period).

in terms of the icon-painting tradition has received unexpected confirmation in Ksana Blank's comparison of Tolstoy's fiction with Kazimir Malevich's Suprematist paintings, whose common ground is a method of representation that unquestionably originated with the early Russian icon.[39] Perhaps it is time to subject Eisenstein's artistic methods to similar scrutiny.

Notes

1. See David Bordwell, "Cinema as Synthesis: Film Theory 1930–1948," *The Cinema of Eisenstein* (Cambridge: Harvard University Press, 1993), 163–198.

2. Sergei Eisenstein, *Immoral Memories: An Autobiography* (Boston: Houghton Mifflin, 1983), 259.

3. Erwin Panofsky, *Gothic Architecture and Scholasticism* (Latrobe, PA: Arch-

abbey Press, 1951), quoted in Håkan Lövgren, *Eisenstein's Labyrinth: Aspects of a Cinematic Synthesis of the Arts,* Stockholm Studies in Russian Literature, 31 (Stockholm: Almqvist & Wiksell, 1996), 62.

4. Lövgren, *Eisenstein's Labyrinth,* 62.

5. Nikolai Gogol, "On the Architecture of Our Time," quoted in Sergei Eisenstein, *Nonindifferent Nature: Film and the Structure of Things,* trans. Herbert Marshall (Cambridge: Cambridge University Press, 1987), 161.

6. See Rosamund Bartlett, *Wagner and Russia* (Cambridge: Cambridge University Press, 1995), 271–281.

7. Victor Terras, *Belinskij and Russian Literary Criticism* (Madison: University of Wisconsin Press, 1974), 77.

8. Arun Khopkar, "Aspects of the art of the 'mise-en-scène'," *Eisenstein Rediscovered,* ed. Ian Christie and Richard Taylor (London: Routledge, 1993), 157.

9. Eisenstein, *Nonindifferent Nature,* 14.

10. Khopkar, "Aspects of the art of the 'mise-en-scène'," 157.

11. John Bowlt, "Pavel Florensky and the Makovets Group," *P. A. Florenskii i kul'tura ego vremeni: (Florenskii and the Culture of His Time) Atti del Convegno Internazionale, Università degli Studi di Bergamo, 10–14 gennaio 1988,* ed. Michael Hagemeister and Nina Kauchtschischwili (Marburg: Blaue Hömer, 1995), 132.

12. See Viktor Bychkov, *The Aesthetic Face of Being: Art in the Theology of Pavel Florensky* (Crestwood, NY: St. Vladimir's Seminary Press, 1993), 20.

13. Leonid Geller, "K diskussii o sinteze v iskusstve: Esteticheskie izyskaniia P. Florenskogo i ikh mesto v kul'turnom kontekste epokhi" (Toward a Discussion of a Synthesis in the Arts: Florenskii's Aesthetic Investigations and their Place in the Era's Cultural Context), *P. A. Florenskii i kul'tura ego vremeni,* 353.

14. Pavel Florenskii, *Izbrannye trudy po iskusstvu* (Selected Works on Art) (Moscow: Izobrazitel'noe iskusstvo, 1996), 210.

15. Florenskii, *Izbrannye trudy,* 210.

16. On the liturgy, Florenskii, *Izbrannye trudy,* 213.

17. Florenskii, *Izbrannye trudy,* 205–206.

18. While Eisenstein's mother was Russian Orthodox, his father came from a Jewish family that had assimilated at least one generation earlier.

19. Eisenstein, *Immoral Memories,* 201.

20. On last confession, Sergei Eisenstein, *Selected Works,* 4: *Beyond the Stars: The Memoirs of Sergei Eisenstein,* ed. Richard Taylor, trans. William Powell (London: British Film Institute, 1995), 73.

21. Mikael Enckell, "A Study in Scarlet," *Eisenstein Revisited,* ed. Lars Kleberg and Håkan Lövgren (Stockholm: Almqvist & Wiksell, 1987), 123.

22. Enckell, "A Study in Scarlet," 123.

23. Herbert Marshall, preface to *Immoral Memories,* viii–ix.

24. See Eisenstein, *Immoral Memories,* 202.

25. Jaques Aumont, *Montage Eisenstein,* trans. Lee Hildreth, Constance Penley and Andrew Ross (Bloomington: Indiana University Press, 1987), 3.

26. Eisenstein, *Immoral Memories,* 201–202.

27. Florenskii, *Izbrannye trudy,* 209.

28. Lövgren, *Eisenstein's Labyrinth*, 95.

29. Mircea Eliade, *The Myth of the Eternal Return* (Princeton: Princeton University Press, 1971), discussed in Lövgren, *Eisenstein's Labyrinth*, 83–84.

30. Mikhail Alpatov, *Early Russian Icon Painting*, trans. N. Johnstone (Moscow: Iskusstvo, 1978), 13.

31. Edoardo Gross, "Eisenstein as Theoretician," *Eisenstein Rediscovered*, 169.

32. Lövgren, *Eisenstein's Labyrinth*, 103.

33. Eisenstein was struck by a Sinclair Motor Oil advertisement of 1947 depicting a line (a supine male figure) cross-sectioned by a circle (a female figure suspended in the air). See Anne Nesbet, *"Ivan the Terrible* and 'The Junction of Beginning and End,'" in this volume. In *Strike* circular shapes symbolize motion (the turning wheels and cogs of the factory) but also stasis (the factory is owned by the capitalist "enemy" which wishes to preserve the status quo). In *Potemkin,* there is a clearer division between the parallel lines of the Odessa steps, the army's rifles, etc., which symbolize repression and the circular shapes symbolic of revolution. See Herbert Eagle, "Visual Patterning, Vertical Montage, and Ideological Protest: Eisenstein's Stylistic Legacy to East European Filmmakers," in this volume.

34. Khopkar, "Aspects of the art of the 'mise-en-scène'," 162.

35. Florenskii, *Izbrannye trudy,* 208–209.

36. Aumont, *Montage Eisenstein,* 59.

37. Eisenstein, *Nonindifferent Nature,* 172–181.

38. Richard Gustafson, *Leo Tolstoy: Resident and Stranger* (Princeton: Princeton University Press), 1986.

39. Ksana Blank, "Lev Tolstoy's Suprematist Icon-Painting," *Elementa* 2 (1995), 67–80.

EISENSTEIN'S *OCTOBER*
On the Cinematic Allegorization of History

Håkan Lövgren

Allegories are the natural mirrors of ideology.

—Angus Fletcher, *Allegory,* 368

October (1927–1928) is Sergei Eisenstein's celebration of the tenth anniversary of the 1917 October Revolution, based on the American journalist John Reed's account, *Ten Days that Shook the World* (1919). Conceptually it is his most sophisticated silent film as it attempted to realize the notion of intellectual montage, essentially an allegorical method intended to forcefully and conclusively impart Marxist and revolutionary political ideas. Despite Eisenstein's insistence on the actually rather limited instances of intellectual montage in the film, *October* is marked by a culture that seeks what Angus Fletcher has called the highest level of allegory: "a symbolism that conveys the action of the mind." [1] *October*'s thesis–antithesis form, the political conflict between the Kerensky government and its sympathizers on the one hand and the Bolsheviks on the other, dominates the realization of the film from the mass scenes down to the behavior of the individual personages, portrayed via Eisenstein's peculiar method of typecasting, *typage.*

A major theme in the artistic embodiment of this class conflict is the dynamic interaction of human beings with statues—most often in a specific architectural setting—and with figurines, a kind of metamorphosis of living and dead matter. The supersession of an obsolete political system by a new and vital one is allegorically reflected in this peculiar relationship between animate beings and their inanimate, though sometimes animated, sculptural representations.

To Eisenstein the development of art in general and cinematography in particular was itself "allegorical"—that is, it represented a parallel process to the overriding historical one inevitably leading to communism via socialist development. Eisenstein's self-perceived task was to give artistic form to this historical process leading to the classless Soviet society, a form that again answered to an analogous "lawfulness" in the evolution and development of art, the pinnacle of which Eisenstein naturally considered Soviet cinematography to be. In this scheme of things Eisenstein had perceived the mass film as the "new progressive phase of the theater in the streets."[2] The most celebrated example of monumental theater in the streets had been Nikolai Yevreinov's 1920 anniversary open-air mass spectacle, *The Storming of the Winter Palace;* the structuring of this mass spectacle could well have influenced the planning of *October.* In an interview for the newspaper *Life of Art* (September 30–31, 1920), Yevreinov said:

> The action will take place not only on the stages, but also on a bridge between them and on the ground, across which the Provisional Government will run attempting to escape from the pursuing proletariat, and in the air where aeroplanes will soar and bells and factory sirens will sound.
>
> Apart from ten thousand performers—actors and persons mobilized from the drama groups of the Red Army and Navy units—inanimate characters will also take part in the production. Even the Winter Palace itself will be involved as a gigantic actor, as a vast character in the play which will manifest its own mimicry and inner emotions. The director must make the stones speak, so that the spectator feels what is going on inside, behind those cold red walls. We have found an original solution to this problem, using a cinematographic technique: each one of the fifty windows of the first floor will in turn show a moment of the development of the battle inside.[3]

We can only speculate on the impact of these dramatic solutions on the emergence and development of cinematic montage, but in *October* Eisenstein certainly allowed the stones and other "inanimate characters" of the Winter Palace and its surroundings to come alive in a manner Yevreinov never managed. After the end of War Communism (1917–1920), however, mass spectacles in Yevreinov's format became rarer and were followed by a more rational and pragmatic approach to theater which moved back onto smaller stages.

In 1927 there was a renewed emphasis on the transformation of man and mass culture. At a Leningrad agitprop meeting in May the theater was again accorded a greater role in the increasingly more instrumental and agitational view of culture. Mass spectacles were again considered workable and one of the first to be performed was the anniversary *Ten Years,* under the leadership of a handful of veterans from the 1920s production which included Sergei Radlov, Adrian Piotrovsky, and Nikolai Petrov as directors and scenarists. This time, however, the spectacle was set on the other side of the Neva River, opposite the Winter Palace, and the spatial scale and distribution, rather than the number of participants, set the tone of the performance. "The audience alone stretched over one and a half kilometers," Katerina Clark writes.

Similarly remarkable was the sense of stage. *The Storming of the Winter Palace* had been largely set on two specially constructed stages on the Palace Square, with a bridge structure joining them. *Ten Years* was given its "stages," too, but they were not specially constructed ones. The set designer, Valentina Khodasevich, identified as the "proscenium" a large stretch of the Neva River between two bridges, while she called the "main stage" the Peter and Paul Fortress, with the Mint nominated as the "rear stage" and the Kronkversky Canal functioning as "wings." The auditorium, she claimed, was "the entire population of Leningrad."[4]

The space of action had thus expanded considerably and the theater of mass spectacles laid claims to a major part of the city. The stage and backdrop were no longer specially constructed but "expropriated" from Leningrad's existing architectural and urban space. This space would also be heavily banked upon by Eisenstein in his own version of the Revolution. But most of the action in *October* would of course center around the area of the Winter Palace and Palace Square, where architecture, architectural details, statues, and figurines were consciously converted into allegorical participants in the battle for revolutionary power, the "last and decisive battle," as one of the film's intertitles declares.

"By their very mass," Hillel Schwartz writes, "colossi assert that someone has *taken place;* by their presence, they maintain the indelibility of power." To these colossi Schwartz counterposes miniatures, which

> subtle with the play-ful-ness of character, extend us toward second chances, times ahead and remediable. Egyptian dolls, Roman puppets, jointed manikins in the studios of Renaissance artists were less mass than energy, always *trading places,* being changed or exchanged. The scale of the miniature encourages impromptu affections, banter, fantasy. [. . .] The colossus is entirely dependent upon an external story; the miniature is that figure through which we collude with personable doubles.[5]

Schwartz's observations are interesting in relation to Eisenstein's use of statues and miniatures in his film. There appears to be a similar stratification of "colossi" versus "miniatures," an opposition of the world of "heavy action," of manly deeds in the realms of giant statues, columns, and immovable sphinxes to the intimate, "effeminate" and obsolete sphere of tsarist power and reformist politics—*replaceable* entities—in which the manipulation of figurines, gadgets, and trinkets of imperial internal palace space signals impotence.

57. Eisenstein and his crew filming *October*.

In the symphonically orchestrated structure of *October* the *Anschlag* is of great importance. The opening series of medium and close-up shots in the film, where the "pawns" go directly for the "king," show the torso and imperial implements in the hands of the tsar, the statue of the seated Alexander III.[6] Angry crowds of the February Revolution surge up the steps leading to the statue, a ladder is raised against the potentate and agile peasants and workers climb the torso, limbs, and head of the statue to attach heavy ropes around it. The multitudinous ropes around the tsar, who looks like a fettered Gulliver, are stretched and tightened as if the crowd were ready to pull it down. There is a cut to a shot of a forest of raised scythes, obviously symbolizing the peasantry, followed by shots of similarly raised rifle butts to indicate "peace-loving" soldiers. Then we see the statue mysteriously starting to disintegrate without a trace of ropes or people around it. It falls apart piece by piece, revealing the banal scaffold propping it up. Bourgeois individuals rejoice, a censer is swinging and an orthodox priest performs Mass in the shots that follow. What we witness in this sequence is thus essentially a violent attack on the statue of Alexander III and its subsequent, curious self-destruction.[7] The form of this self-destruction in turn prepares for the metaphoric reversal of the process later in the film, the specifically "cinematic" reconstruction of Alexander III's statue as a symbol of political reaction.

"Consider how we are still drawn to images of crowds attacking gigantic statues of dead dictators," Kenneth Gross writes, "statues that gain a striking, if sometimes forlorn sort of animation even in the process of being hacked, toppled, hung, burned, defaced; one feels here as if the violence done to such statues becomes an aspect of their peculiar life."[8] His point is that the violent attack on the statue, the attempt to demystify the idol's "magic hold" on its subjects, results in a re-mythification or re-mystification of that very power as well as of the attacker's motives:

> Since the iconoclastic stance depends on its own reductive, projective parody of idolatry, and on a radical mystification of the power that undoes that idolatry, the text's disenchantments remain unsettlingly ambiguous. One result of this ambiguity is that the "enemy" will tend to be pictured as a peculiar composite of idol and demon, as a thing at once dead and uncannily alive.[9]

In terms of Gross's discussion, by dismantling the statue and then reassembling it, Eisenstein seems paradoxically to import more power and life into the statue than it ever had when left in peace: Eisenstein awakens the dormant demon in the sculpture, so to speak. However, Eisenstein's de- and reconstructions of Alexander III's statue in *October* are not just a clever political metaphor. The treatment of the statue, the fact that it comes alive while falling apart, as it were, bears on the perception of all subsequent interactions between or juxtapositions of sculpture / figurine / miniature and woman / man / living being.

Let us look at the shots immediately following the machine-gun attack on the demonstrators, the masterly edited sequence beginning with the text *spasaia znamia,* "to the rescue of the banner," and roughly ending with the First Machine Gun Regiment being herded off. This sequence was barely hinted at in the original script, but the artistic consideration and energy given to it by Eisenstein would seem to underline its importance in the film. The young Bolshevik standard-bearer is trying to find a route of escape from the pursuing police along the Neva embankment. A long series of medium and close-up shots follows. The young man halts, looking around, framed between a sphinx-like pharaoh bust in granite and a large urn, presumably in the same material, all belonging to the embellishments of the river waterfront. There is a cut to the demonstrators dispersing under fire from the machine gun and then a cut back to the young man with the banner. Next we see an image of the Bolshevik and a rounded object with a surface resembling the pattern of the urn, a parasol; a transition, as it turns out, from granite to cloth to the human beings behind it. The significance of this short series of cuts could be that the impassive stone face of despotic power (the granite pharaoh, a king in our political chess game) suddenly comes alive, acquires a living representative in the flirting cadet who begins the attack on the standard-bearer that will rally other bourgeois individuals and result in the martyrdom of the young man. He dies like a St. Sebastian, stabbed by enraged bourgeois women

whose lacy underwear and exuberant attire make them seem unlikely warriors. The martyr sequence is intercut with the drawbridge scene in which a
woman demonstrator and a white horse perish, the horse and the young man
as well as banners and issues of *Pravda* being symbolically claimed by the
water of the River Neva. At the end of the sequence Eisenstein shows a view
of the open bridge with a sculpture indifferently gazing over the scene. There
are also two different close-ups of the same immovable granite pharaoh that
occurred at the beginning of the entire *reaktsiia pobedila* sequence. In other
words, the whole sequence is "framed," or opened and closed by historical
sculptural entities seemingly identifying members of the "Kerensky bourgeoisie and military" with the despotic tsarist power that was overthrown in
the February uprising.[10]

If this sequence represents interaction with colossi—immovable statues
which have *taken place* and assumed a permanent (political) location—the
sequence with a gloomy Kerensky in Tsar Alexander III's study, where the
head of government is being juxtaposed with images of a plaster miniature
of Napoleon and an army of toy soldiers, answers to Schwartz's idea of figurines or miniatures trading places both with one another and with humans
and thus entering into relationships. When Schwartz speaks about the miniature as "that figure through which we collude with personable doubles," he
seems to allude to a certain intimacy. In the film the close-ups of Kerensky
playing with a four-part bottle and a cap in the shape of a crown, of toy soldiers, of a series of devotional figurines in the "In the Name of God and Country" sequence, and of the many objects in the imperial bedchamber, all have
an aura of intimacy that generates curiosity, perhaps even a certain empathy,
through their sensuous immediacy. The effect is one of ambiguity and, to the
extent that it is consistent and pervasive, it must be considered counterpro-
ductive in Eisenstein's effort to debunk these objects and images and everyone
associated with them.

The issue I would like to touch upon here is to what extent Eisenstein's understanding of myth, allegory and the psychoanalytic image of the labyrinth
can be applied to *October* and intellectual montage, although his discussion
of these concepts occurs mostly in the 1930s and 1940s—that is, several years
after the film was conceived and produced. In terms of historical description *October* is, not unexpectedly, a strange mixture of fact and fiction. The
opening scene or sequence has already been mentioned; the rendition of the
storming of the Winter Palace is largely mythical since historically the attack
was totally unorganized and the military cadets in the Palace had already
given up by the time the Red Guards and sailors were penetrating it.[11] But did
Eisenstein strive for a mythical or allegorical form? Was there a self-conscious
mythologizing process in his work? In "Perspectives" (1929), the essay that

tried to sum up the idea of the intellectual film, Eisenstein spoke of the moment when even the driest facts of a lecture on mathematics are enthusiastically absorbed by the audience due to the personality or personal method of the lecturer. "A dry integral is recalled in the feverish brightness of the eyes. In the mnemonic of *collectively* experienced *perception.* . . . What is the difference," he later asks, "between a perfected method of oratory and a perfected method of acquiring knowledge? The new art must set a limit to the dualism of the spheres of 'emotion' and 'reason.' . . . Only *intellectual* cinema will be able to put an end to the conflict between the 'language of logic' and the 'language of images.'"[12] There is only one obstacle in this process, what he calls "living man," who is primarily associated with the culture of Moscow Art Theater performances—that is, naturalism in acting and thinking. Appropriately quoting a speech by Molotov in reference to "inappropriate progress" in agriculture, Eisenstein continues:

> Filling the screen with "living man" would mean precisely the same "inappropriate progress" towards the industrialisation of our cinema culture.
>
> Cinema can—and consequently must—convey on the screen in tangible sensual form the pure, dialectical essence of our ideological debates. Without recourse to intermediaries like plot, story or living man.[13]

This ambition very much resembles the already mentioned "symbolism that conveys the action of the mind," the highest level of allegory.[14] Eisenstein's intention in *October* was to present a historical process, the events leading up to and the storming of the Winter Palace in 1917, in accordance with the laws of Marx's historical and dialectical materialism. Eisenstein did not simply give his own interpretation of the revolutionary upsurge but also strove to convey in visual terms (with a minimum of printed text frames) the abstract categories and principles determining it. The result is realistic, ritualistically repeated and abstracted behavior on the part of the actors and participants who tend to become walking concepts, *figurae* or, in Eisenstein's terminology, *typage* figures. The intellectual montage which is to generate the highest level of abstraction consists typically of combining diegetic and nondiegetic images to form a trope, which serves to justify both the treatment of specific historical characters (ironic caricature) and the historical process as a whole. "Plot, story or living man" is obviously of slight importance in this scheme.

In the most abstract forms of intellectual montage the difficulty seems to lie in control, in limiting and directing the associations between serial images of objects to their intended effect without destroying the entire process. The more grotesque the juxtaposed images appear—for instance, in being diegetically incompatible—the more effort is needed for the analogy-making process because "the grotesque is embodied in an act of transition, of metonymy becoming metaphor, of the margin swapping places with the center. It is embodied in a transformation of duality into unity, of the meaningless into the meaningful."[15] If we consider the sequence of "idols" or religious figurines in the film, we understand from the images following one another, from the nondiegetic nature of some of them and the fact that they do not all belong to the same spatial continuum, that there is a problem of meaning to be solved, a task for a decoder. But what guarantees that the conclusion made by a Leningrad spectator will not be "Aha, these are exotic objects from Peter the Great's *Kunstkammer,* and Kerensky and his cohorts will soon be joining their lot"—a not totally inappropriate deduction, instead of the intended general denunciation of religion to which the "In the Name of God" sequence aspires? From a purist point of view, the intellectual montage in *October* sometimes puts the cart before the horse by using text frames to "assist" in the guiding process, thereby *presenting* the concept rather than *generating* it. Do just the elements of intellectual montage and other nondiegetic and symbolic processes in the film identify it as allegorical? Angus Fletcher considers certain "exotic" and grotesque elements necessary in some romantic subgenres of the allegorical.

Eisenstein's own comments on allegory are interesting since they also involve the notions of myth and mythology. In a speech at the All Union Film Workers' Conference in 1935, Eisenstein pointed to the fact that certain theories and perspectives that were once considered scientific lose their status as science in the course of time, only to be relegated to the sphere of art and imagery where they are permissible:

> Take mythology. We know that at any one stage mythology is, properly speaking, a complex of science of phenomena set out in a language that is mainly figurative and poetic. All those figures from mythology that we regard as no more than allegory, were at one stage an imagistic summary of our knowledge of the world. Then science moved away from figurative narratives and towards concepts, even though the arsenal of earlier, personified, mythological and symbolic beings continued as a series of stage images, of literary metaphors, lyrical allegories and so on. They cannot endure forever in this role, however, and end up in the archives.[16]

Here Eisenstein's evolutionism is setting the terms by allowing art to pick through the rubble on the scrap heap of science. This of course was written during the Stalinist times of cautious and careful treading in the 1930s, and not during the heroic 1920s when *October* was made. There is no real distinction made between the categories of mythology, allegory, and symbolism; they all deal in figurative and poetic language which is doomed either to extinction or to the archives. However, in his autobiographical work *Beyond the Stars,* which was written during the *post scriptum* period after his heart attack in 1946, there is a text called "Dead Souls" which contains a more complex and interesting discussion from our perspective. The paradigmatic genre here is the detective story, with Edgar Allan Poe's "The Murders in the Rue Morgue" as possible forerunner. Eisenstein points to Poe's ubiquitous horror situations of murders or people caught in sealed rooms. He refers to Marie Bonaparte's and Otto Rank's psychoanalytical explanations of memories from our pre-natal existence and the universal trauma stemming from being liberated from the womb and released into the light of day. Following Rank, he associates this *Geburtstrauma* with the myth of the Minotaur and the labyrinth as an archetypal image of this primary complex.

> In the more contemporary derivatives of that legend [Russian *mif*] . . . it is less the situation of the criminal extricating himself from an "impossible" situation into the outside world, than in the way in which the detective draws the truth out into the open: that is, the situation effectively operates on two levels.
>
> In a direct sense and metaphorically—transposed from situation into principle.
>
> At this point we can see that the latter—the transposing of a situation into a principle—can freely exist parallel to the primary, "original" situation. . . .
>
> And so the detective story, as a variety of genre fiction—in any of its forms—is historically allied to the Minotaur legend and by extension to those primary complexes which that legend serves to express through imagery.[17]

Although this is a post–*October* discussion, Eisenstein's familiarity with Otto Rank's works goes back to the 1920s, while issues of myth and allegory had been prevalent in Russian culture since the Neo-romantics and Wagnerians appeared around the turn of the century. But could *October* be seen as a myth in the Minotaur sense, as a narrative that is allegorically self-revelatory, con-taining its own decoder's key, its own Ariadne's thread? Eisenstein insists, however, that the Minotaur myth is not an allegory:

> Allegory *consists* [*sic*] of an abstracted representation intentionally and arbitrarily assuming the form [*odevaetsia*] of a particular image. The figurative form of the expression is then like a myth—the one accessible means of "making it familiar" [*osvoenie*] and a comprehensible expression for consciousness. Only later does it attain the level at which it is able to put abstract notions into formulated concepts.[18]

58. Citizens toppling statue of Alexander III in *October.*

59. Toppling the statue of Felix Dzerzhinsky (founder of the Soviet secret police), Moscow, August 1991.

Does Eisenstein then in some sense subscribe to the Romantic and Neo-romantic distinction between allegory and symbol—which the Russian Symbolists (Vyacheslav Ivanov, for instance) certainly adhered to—that differentiated between an artificial or contrived and a natural and organic use of a symbolic language mode? If we have understood him correctly, there is an appropriate and an inappropriate use of the mythological type of language, a language of images. In ancient times myth served the legitimate purpose of conveying abstract notions and ideas, just as the use of mural paintings or stained glass images in cathedrals helped to convey the lessons of the Bible to illiterate audiences. But to the modern literate mind the systematic use of a mythic language would be an anachronism, a false disguise ("assuming the form of" in the quote is *odevaetsia,* "to dress," in the Russian original). The appropriation of this kind of language would be admissible and defendable under one condition: that the audience primarily consisted of illiterate individuals who had to be inoculated against the ideological and physical threat of an educationally superior enemy. Enter intellectual montage, the principal mode used in the construction of Eisenstein's *October,* a form of expression through images: "*edinstvenno dostupnoe sredstvo 'osvoeniia' i vyrazheniia dlia soznaniia, kotoroe eshche ne dostiglo stadii abstragirovaniia predstavlenii v for-mulirovannye poniatiia*" (the one accessible means of "making it familiar" and of expression for a consciousness that has yet to attain the level at which it is able to put abstract notions into formulated concepts).[19] *October* then, we may assume, was a lesson for the primitive communist mind as to how to understand and effectively reach a political and military organization that could defeat a formally superior enemy. The film as a whole and every other subplot and incident in it serve to teach this lesson which had already in its own way been formulated by Yevreinov's decidedly allegorical mass spectacle of the *Storming of the Winter Palace* in Petrograd, 1920. With *October* Eisenstein may have wanted to demonstrate by what formal cinematic means this task could be achieved, and thus perhaps prove the evolutionary superiority of film over theater. As a whole, however, and as a monument to the Revolution, *October* seems to confirm the suspicion voiced by Kenneth Gross that tearing down the monumental manifestations of despots and thus demystifying their hold on the public mind often amounts to a re-mystification and re-mythification of the political powers to come. The process that began with the ten days that shook the world in 1917, symbolically indicated at the end of the film in images of swirling clocks from some of the world's capital cities, culminated in the dismantling of many statues depicting leading Bolshevik revolutionaries and the final collapse of the Soviet Union in 1991, thus bringing another cycle of Russian history to a close.

Notes

1. In 1935 Eisenstein wrote: "In fact, in practice there are only a few individual parts of *October* which contain practical suggestions for the *possibilities* of an intellectual construction in cinema, which then manifested themselves as *a certain range of theoretical possibilities.*" Sergei Eisenstein, *Selected Works, 3, Writings, 1934–1947,* ed. Richard Taylor, trans. William Powell (London: British Film Institute, 1996), 19. Angus Fletcher, *Allegory, The Theory of a Symbolic Mode* (Ithaca: Cornell University Press, 1964), 278.

2. Sergei Eisenstein, *Vnutrennii monolog* (Inner Monologue), unpublished text, c. 1940.

3. Vladimir Tolstoy, Irina Bibikova, and Catherine Cooke, eds. *Street Art of the Revolution: Festivals and Celebrations In Russia, 1918–33* (London: Thames and Hudson, 1990), 137–138.

4. Katerina Clark, *Petersburg: Crucible of Cultural Revolution* (Cambridge: Harvard University Press, 1995), 244.

5. Hillel Schwartz, *The Culture of the Copy: Striking Likenesses, Unreasonable Facsimiles* (New York: Zone Books, 1996), 90.

6. These shots of the statue may seem to foreshadow the shots of the crowning scene in Eisenstein's *Ivan the Terrible*—this time, however, depicting a tsar very much alive and active.

7. This statue was situated not in Petrograd but outside the Cathedral of Christ the Savior in Moscow, thus giving the impression that revolutionary action in Moscow preceded the events leading up to the overthrow of the Kerensky government in Petrograd. The opening sequence of shots could be seen in part as an internal dialogue, a reply to scenes in his previous films. Consider the working-class and popular defeats and setbacks in *Strike* and *The Battleship Potemkin.* In both films crowds are massacred; in *Potemkin* the Odessa inhabitants sympathetic to the strikers on board the battleship are fired at and forced down the now-famous steps by soldiers who in one shot are clearly seen against the background of a statue at the top of the steps. (The statue portrays Richelieu, the proconsul of Odessa.) In *October* the crowds are triumphantly surging up the stairs to depose the "idol" Alexander III, which could be seen as a victorious rebuttal of the gloomy fate of the people on the steps in Odessa. Cf. Clark, *Petersburg,* 263.

8. Kenneth Gross, *The Dream of the Moving Statue* (Ithaca: Cornell University Press, 1992), xiii.

9. Gross, *Dream,* 50.

10. Marie-Claude Ropars-Wuilleumier has pointed to the "reactionary" function of statues in the film. Cf. Yuri Tsivian, "Eisenstein and Russian Symbolist Culture," *Eisenstein Rediscovered,* ed. Ian Christie and Richard Taylor (London: Routledge, 1993), 81.

11. Cf. Christopher Read, *From Tsar to the Soviets: The Russian People and Their Revolution, 1917–21* (London: UCL Press, 1996), 174.

12. Sergei Eisenstein, *Selected Works,* 1: *Writings, 1922–34,* ed. and trans. Richard Taylor (London: British Film Institute, 1988), 157–158.

13. Eisenstein, *Selected Works,* 1, 159.

14. Cf. note 2.

15. Geoffrey Galt Harpham, *On the Grotesque: Strategies of Contradiction in Art and Literature* (Princeton: Princeton University Press, 1982), 47.

16. Eisenstein, *Selected Works,* 3, 26.

17. Sergei Eisenstein, *Selected Works,* 4: *Beyond the Stars: The Memoirs of Sergei Eisenstein,* ed. Richard Taylor, trans. William Powell (London: British Film Institute, 1995), 128–129.

18. Eisenstein, *Selected Works,* 4, 129.

19. Sergei Eisenstein, "Wie sag' ich's meinem Kinde?!" in his *Memuary* (Memoirs), 2 vols. (Moscow: Muzei kino, 1997), 1, 99.

Part Two

EISENSTEIN AND CULTURAL INTERACTIONS
An Anxious Influence

EISENSTEIN
Lessons with Hollywood

James Goodwin

Whater Eisenstein reflected upon his time in Hollywood two years after leaving, his ideological perspective was framed at a geopolitical distance by the Great Depression and the events of financial ruin and economic dislocation in the United States. At close hand, it was framed by the promises of Stalin's revolution from above in the form of the Five Year Plan for the Soviet economy. At the point when Eisenstein wrote down his first reflections on Hollywood in 1932, Stalin and the Communist Party had proclaimed the First Plan a success one year ahead of schedule, the Second Plan was anticipated, and the new Soviet economic imperative was to overfulfill previous goals, as announced in the watchword "Overtake and Surpass," a phrase which Eisenstein himself repeats. Beyond the formulaic rhetoric on political economy contained in his article "The Cinema in America," however, Eisenstein also reveals sincere admiration for a heroic age in the movie business in the capitalist West.[1]

During the second half of 1930 Eisenstein, Grigori Alexandrov, and Eduard Tisse stayed in Hollywood to learn the new sound technology and advanced studio methods. In his commentary, however, Eisenstein is not inclined to periodize American movie production into silent and sound eras with 1927 marking a pivotal division. Rather, Eisenstein looks upon the year 1930 as the close of a golden age led by "the old romantic pioneers of the movie industry," each one of them an "adventurer, dreamer, sportsman, [and] poet of profit."[2] Among these pioneers Eisenstein reserves pride of place for Jesse Lasky, the head of production for Paramount with whom he had negotiated his Hollywood contract. Nineteen thirty was the final year of glory at Paramount for Lasky, who would fall prey to a boardroom coup within the next twelve months. But in that twilight year the Hollywood entertainment industry as a whole enjoyed the greatest ticket sales, gross revenues, and profits on record and the major studios began to think theirs was a "Depression-proof" industry.[3] In the end it transpired that the effects on the movie business were delayed by only a few more months. When the illusion of commercial invincibility was broken, some studio corporations, Paramount included, undertook extensive financial and managerial restructuring.

While in Hollywood in 1930, Eisenstein observed the effects of the emergence of a new managerial echelon comprised of "creatures of Wall Street without initiative, . . . dry bureaucrats" driven by the "clatter of adding machines."[4] These executives possessed little imagination, not to speak of any pioneering spirit or genuine vision. Despite their soulless pursuit of profit, to Eisenstein's mind the new studio managers lacked the ability even to maintain a sensible balance sheet and as a result the movie business unraveled into a "debauchery of unaccounted volume, large staffs, and useless expenditures."[5] Indeed, while the figures were not available to Eisenstein, we now know that the annual write-offs at Paramount for abandoned or reassigned scripts and projects increased nearly eightfold from 1927 to 1930. Losses in 1930 reached $390,000, including the $30,000 spent in compensation to the Eisenstein group.[6] The economic lesson Eisenstein draws from his professional experience in America—at least the one cast in terms that flatter Soviet claims about the superiority of a planned economy—is that the potential of the "world's most perfect technical apparatus" for movie-making remains unfulfilled due to a chaotic expenditure of talent, opportunity, and capital.[7] Eisenstein's summation in the "Cinema in America" article adopts Stalinist discourse to characterize new studio managers in Hollywood as the wreckers of their own industry.

So much for the official Soviet lesson of Eisenstein's Hollywood experience. The directly personal truths of the experience provide more original and interesting lessons, but Eisenstein largely reserved the consideration of these truths for his memoirs and they remained unpublished in his lifetime since he accounted them as unorthodox and immoral in the contemporary Soviet scheme of things. At the time of work on *An American Tragedy,* Eisenstein observed first-hand the power struggle within studio management over old and new business ways. Mindful of divisions within Paramount Pictures, in the cover letter dated October 5, 1930, accompanying the completed script, Eisenstein invited advice separately from "The East Coast Magnates" headed by Jesse Lasky and "The West Coast Magnates," whose chief executive was Benjamin P. Schulberg. Reviewing the matter in the episode of autobiography entitled "The Road to Buenos Aires," which appears to have been composed in 1946, Eisenstein explains that the project's fate and his own future in Hollywood were tied to the doomed romantic era represented by Lasky and his fellow "'risk-takers [and] seekers after novelty and excitement," as against bloodless financial calculators like Schulberg "who gambled only on certainties . . . and, more often than not, were all for repeating winning formulae."[8]

With adjustments for differences in the economic and bureaucratic situations, Eisenstein could say much the same for his career within his own country during most of the 1930s, given his relationship to the reorganized Soviet film industry under Boris Shumyatsky. Shumyatsky's aim was to centralize and regularize studio management, and to exercise control over production from the earliest script stages, all with the intention to steer Soviet cinema away from avant-garde experimentation and toward popular entertainment.[9] Where his own blocked career was concerned, Eisenstein could not help but find symbolism in the visit to Hollywood and other film capitals in the West by an official commission headed by Shumyatsky during 1935. Upon its return, the delegation published a report that declared the need to create an entirely new *kinogorod,* an idea that became popularly known as "the Soviet Hollywood."

Given the seemingly foreordained outcome of Eisenstein's efforts in Hollywood, it is worthwhile considering what Paramount and the Soviet director had expected from their contract in the first place. To understand Paramount's motivations, one should look first to the company's origins and the early movie business experience of Adolph Zukor, who had concocted the much-imitated idea "Famous Players in Famous Plays" and adapted the phrase as the name for his first production company in 1912. Zukor was a pioneer in the development of a feature-length form for motion pictures, in bringing to the screen great stage figures of the day, and in adapting notable material from drama and literature. One blatant, swift imitator of Zukor and his marketing strategies was Jesse Lasky, who formed his own Feature Play Company in 1913. Famous-Players Lasky became the title to the corporation and Paramount the distribution circuit name and trademark in advertising and publicity after the Zukor and Lasky companies merged in 1916.

Thus was born Paramount's widely self-promoted reputation for the presentation of cultured feature films. In point of fact, the company was particularly zealous in its acquisition of prominent talent from Europe, including the directors Rouben Mamoulian, Josef von Sternberg, and Ernst Lubitsch and the actors Olga Baclanova (who was trained at the Moscow Art Theater), Pola Negri, Emil Jannings, Maurice Chevalier, and Marlene Dietrich. In an investigation into Jewish identity and the power of Hollywood illusions, Neal Gabler singles out Paramount under Zukor and Lasky in this period for its conspicuous efforts to create an aura of sophistication, intelligence, and high culture.[10]

Irrespective of the talents involved and the studio's reputation for refined taste, the truth of the matter is that in sheer volume the Paramount releases for 1929 and 1930 are dominated by romantic comedies, madcap farces, musicals, exotic melodramas, adventure tales, and crime stories.[11] It was in terms of crime story and melodrama that studio supervisors responded to Eisenstein's conception of *An American Tragedy,* while the Soviet director pursued the material as an inarguably tragic story whose implications reached into the foundation of American values. Apart from their mutual esteem, here

Eisenstein was fundamentally at odds with Lasky, who had grumbled over *A Farewell to Arms* with its "tragic unhappy ending" when Paramount acquired rights to the Hemingway novel a year earlier.[12]

And what had been Eisenstein's professional expectations for the Hollywood venture? In the matter of new technology the famous "Statement on Sound," issued in July 1928 and cosigned by Vsevolod Pudovkin and Grigori Alexandrov, acknowledges openly that as a consequence of Soviet industrial underdevelopment "practical implementation of sound cinema is not feasible in the near future."[13] It was not until June 1931—as compared to the October 1927 American debut of *The Jazz Singer*—that the first Soviet dramatic feature film with sound was exhibited. In March 1930, when Abram Room's documentary episodes about the First Five Year Plan (*A Plan for Great Works*) had been exhibited, only two theaters in the entire Soviet Union were equipped to play back the audio track.[14] The growth rate in development of an infrastructure for sound film production and exhibition in the Soviet Union can only be described as retarded when compared to the rapid capitalization and conversion that took place in the United States. In the whole of 1931, less than 10 percent of Soviet releases were sound films. The ratio of sound to silent releases remained less than 50 percent until 1935, when the annual total was 65 percent of the films in exhibition.[15]

The 1928 statement viewed as harmless Hollywood's initial commercial exploitation of the new technology to stimulate the simple curiosity of audiences. In this rudimentary capacity, the innovation was a possible "attraction" in Eisenstein's early sense of that term. Such a popular application, however, leaves unexplored the artistic potential that for Eisenstein is to be found in an "*orchestral counterpoint* of visual and sound images."[16] We may be inclined to overlook some fundamental implications of this musical analogy in the attention given to Eisenstein's preoccupations in the period with compositional conflict among montage elements and with dialectical film form.[17] Indeed, the proposition for counterpoint is immediately preceded by a stipulation that "*The first experiments in sound must aim at a sharp discord with the visual images.*"[18] But orchestral counterpoint is not by any means equivalent to discord or dissonance. For the Western classical tradition, in a rudimentary sense, counterpoint refers to properties of combination and simultaneity that contribute density and complexity to musical texture. To specify an orchestral convention of counterpoint is to stress qualities of harmonic integration and resolution, at least by the standards of classical orchestral music prior to the twentieth century. Counterpoint, by interweaving equally important melodies, creates a unique mass in harmonic structure. In this orchestral tradition, then, counterpoint and harmony are inseparably related.

Eisenstein returned to issues of sound cinema a month later in 1928 in his

commentary "An Unexpected Juncture," written in response to the performances in Moscow by a Kabuki group. For him, the Japanese dramatic tradition proved to be an art of unexpected equivalencies, including one with
a sound cinema founded upon counterpoint. Through interplay, sound and
visual components in the Kabuki ensemble multiply, rather than merely add,
their individual capacities to stimulate audience response. Eisenstein accounts for the process as a matter of substitutions and transferences among
visual and acoustic elements. The central example Eisenstein reconstructs is
an enactment of hara-kiri, rendered through a conjunction of the movement
by the actor's hand controlling a knife with the sound of sobbing delivered
off-stage. The kind of counterpoint here is not differential but combinatory.
In Eisenstein's words, the superimposition of distinct visual and audio effects "doubles up" the power of each component, thus "squaring" the final
impact.[19]

By the time of Eisenstein's trip to America, Hollywood sound production
was not a total cultural wasteland of all-talking and all-singing entertain-
ments. Asked his opinion of American talkies upon his arrival in New York,
Eisenstein said that of those he had viewed he considered Lewis Milestone's
All Quiet on the Western Front (1930) the best. He ranked *Hallelujah* as next best
with the qualification "not as a talkie really, but as a picture."[20] King Vidor's
Hallelujah, a 1929 MGM release, contains some elementary efforts at expressive innovation in audio-visual composition, though these were limited by
the recording methods available on location. With an aim of enriching characterization, a few scenes in this Southern black musical drama overlap individual speech and vocal chorus. And in order to heighten tension, a chase
sequence features off-screen sound in the form of exaggerated, nearly non-
naturalistic effects, due perhaps as much to inadequate pitch fidelity in the
technology as to artistic intention.

At Paramount in 1929, Rouben Mamoulian directed the sound feature *Applause,* which studio executives were likely to have screened for the Eisenstein
group. In this backstage drama about the life of an aging burlesque star, intimate scenes in the dressing room are inflected by passages overheard from
the show numbers performed out front. In one memorable shot the words of
a scheming cad are presented on-screen as delivered from the mouth of his
fantastic shadow cast upon a wall, a compositional arrangement that will be
important to Eisenstein in *Ivan the Terrible.* For other scenes in *Applause,* am-
bient city noises color the dramatic moment, as when the joy of a marriage
proposal is joined with the high-pitched sound of an airplane flying by. In the
film's editing, abrupt changes in the soundtrack on occasion mark transitions
to a new setting.

In 1928 and 1929 Walt Disney launched the *Mickey Mouse* and *Silly Sym-*

phony series. Prior to departure from France to the United States, Eisenstein acclaimed the Disney animation shorts for pointing a way to the future of sound cinema by originating counterparts in "the acoustic domain" for each "optical fact."[21] In explaining this innovation he draws an unexpected analogy between audio-visual composition in the Mickey Mouse series and the traditions of Kabuki theater, invoking the example of the staged act of hara-kiri. With both cases, he maintains, visual perception is intensified by sounds that correspond to the emotional and sentimental reaction that the scene induces. And both are instructive examples of audio-visual counterpoint wherein the sensory components are integrated through "an association or a pure equivalence."[22]

In terms of the spoken word in sound film, Eisenstein thought at the time that its fundamental form for montage cinema was monologue instead of dialogue. Within his conception the monologue, in both the dramatic and interior modes, is overdetermined by social discourses and is structured like polyphony, a musical form closely related to counterpoint. The influences here of James Joyce's *Ulysses* are well documented, but the aspirations of his Hollywood efforts with the monologue were consciously set much lower. Though he had been reading Stuart Gilbert's study of *Ulysses* at the time, in the end he ranked the challenge of the *American Tragedy* project as "making an Emile Zola from a Theodore Dreiser."[23]

For Eisenstein, as one who had been fascinated from afar by glimpses through literature and movies, the Wall Street collapse of October 1929 had opened a gaping crack "in the very armor of the idealized giant [of] American technical civilization, [which represented] exact science and rationalization, from water closets to the higher activities of the nervous centers." Seemingly for the first time in the century, the hypnotic trance of "advertised Americanism" was broken.[24] When Eisenstein gained his own perspective from within the entertainment industry less than one year later, he gauged the narrow moralism of mass culture in the United States as a sign of broader political anxieties over the relative strength of American values. To make this point, Eisenstein's commentary on "The Cinema in America" quotes at length portions of the Production Code formulated by the Association of Motion Pictures Producers and Distributors of America and adopted as enforceable industry regulations in March 1930. The studios had formed a trade organization with its own "Purity Code" in 1922 for the purpose of self-regulation and to avert censorship legislation. In the 1920s under the early stewardship of Will Hays, however, the office was relatively permissive in its application of rules on movie content.

The first section cited in Eisenstein's article demonstrates that the Code's stated intention to maintain movies "as entertainment without any explicit purpose of teaching or propaganda" is in fact an insincere and empty promise since the next clause proceeds to amend that generalization: "the motion picture within its own field of entertainment may be directly responsible for spiritual or moral progress, for higher types of social life, and for much correct thinking." [25] To Eisenstein's mind, "political suppression can be read between the lines" throughout the Code in spite of its claim to be a mandate limited to moral self-regulation on the part of the movie industry. [26] The Code's political scope is made most obvious in one stipulation among the many rules on sexual content: "*Miscegenation* (sex relationship between the white and black races) is forbidden." [27] Eisenstein observed broad permissiveness within certain areas of the Code, particularly those involving criminality and the depiction of murder. In these areas a higher mandate prevails, the profit motive of the entertainment business, formulated by Eisenstein as "Vulgarity— means money, and sensationalism—means money. And money—means everything." [28] Eisenstein cites two crime films of 1932, Charles Brabin's *Beast of the City* and Howard Hawks' *Scarface,* for evidence that it is possible for a score of dead bodies to pass through a loophole in the Code for the greater good of commerce. [29]

Eisenstein discovered that one subject did remain effectively taboo: "The paragraph of the code covering racial problems reigns supreme." [30] As a story of modern black life in the American South, the MGM release *Hallelujah* might seem to be an exception. But, as made clear by the detailed plot synopsis Eisenstein provides in "The Cinema in America," this film's intentions were benign even if largely misguided and stereotypical in their characterizations of black American life. As a story not about relations between the races but rather largely about life among blacks in the South, with particular emphasis on blood passions, superstition, spirituality, and violence, the film remained securely within the parameters of dominant cultural perspectives. Eisenstein remarks that "not without cunning [the script was] passed by the Code" by virtue of its condescending portrayal of the impulsive lives of "a lower race." [31] Nevertheless, given the fact that Vidor was able to complete the film and in light of its exceptional subject matter, the movie business invoked commercial interests rather than morality to limit the availability of this feature to American audiences. Based on information gathered in personal conversation with Vidor, Eisenstein explains that MGM applied the preemptive argument that "Negro films don't pay," restricted national distribution of *Hallelujah,* and thus made the presumption of failure at the box office a foregone conclusion. [32]

In the period just prior to signing a contract with Paramount, while still in Paris in 1930, Eisenstein became interested in the history of slave rebellions in the Caribbean region, particularly in the successful uprising and early years of self-rule in Haiti. [33] By Eisenstein's account, when he broached the idea of a film not only on the subject of race relations but on that of black revolution

60. Alexandrov, Montagu, and Eisenstein.

as well, the studio's rejection was couched in the standard commercial pretext that "Negro films don't pay" rather than in American political truth.[34] Ivor Montagu disputes any claim that the Eisenstein group had proposed the subject to Paramount.[35] But, for the Paris period in question, Montagu had already left for the United States and he no longer had direct knowledge of Eisenstein's activities in Europe. Montagu does remember that during the group's work with Paramount Eisenstein purchased the book *Black Majesty* by John Vandercook on the subject.

Two years later, back in the Soviet Union and on the defensive for his experimentation with montage form, Eisenstein contrives a rather incongruous analogy to an American context of racism. In reference to Party appointees placed in studios to supervise ideological matters, Eisenstein denounces them as a "Ku-Klux-Klan" intimidating Soviet filmmakers to a degree that has "almost eradicated creativity and creative searches in the field of form."[36] This inflammatory analogy is an expression of the passion with which Eisenstein periodically resisted political censorship in his own country and with which he regarded circumstances in America's black communities, which he had sought out in his travels.

Eisenstein's most enduring political memory of his time in Hollywood was the campaign mounted against his very presence on American soil by Major Frank Pease, a rabid self-promoting patriot. Pease's crusade was as much anti-Semitic as anti-communist in its ideology and rhetoric, as he brandished slurs like "Mesopotamian mongrels" and "Jewish Bolshevik." In this respect, Eisenstein's brief Hollywood period is more consequential and world-historical than a mere chronicle of his professional experiences would indicate. Some aspects of the Pease campaign are documented in Marie Seton's biography, so it will be most useful here to add new information and enlarge the political context.[37]

Pease first gained attention in Hollywood during contract disputes between the major studios and the Actors Equity Association in the summer of 1929. Anti-union in his views, Pease formed the Character Actors Association, the first of many organizations with impressive names that in truth were one-man operations. His next cause, launched under the auspices of the newly coined "Hollywood Technical Directors Institute," called for a national ban on further exhibition of Milestone's *All Quiet on the Western Front* until censorship forced major changes to it. Soon after its release in April 1930, Pease branded this Universal Pictures feature as "the most brazen propaganda film ever made in America." His appeal, sent by telegram to President Hoover, cabinet heads in the departments of justice, the military, treasury, and commerce, and to the governors of all forty-eight states, continues: "Moscow itself could not have produced a more subversive film," one that "will go far to raise a race of yellow-streak slackers and disloyalists."[38]

Eisenstein arrived in New York in May, unaware of the kind of political mischief possible in America from a peripheral figure like Pease. As already mentioned, when asked by reporters his opinion of American talkies, Eisenstein stated that of those he had viewed he considered *All Quiet on the Western Front* to be by far the most important. In another document, Pease issued a "Technical Release Report" on *All Quiet on the Western Front,* rating it in terms of 34 qualities and 171 subcategories, including the film's moral worth in matters ranging from the Ten Commandments and civilized conventions of sex down to questions of what double entendres it might contain. Pease issued the report to the press to garner publicity meant to expose the negligent, if not treasonous, practices of the Association of Motion Picture Producers and Distributors and its Production Code.[39]

In short order, Pease added the issue of Eisenstein's Paramount contract to his campaign and made public a directive he cabled to Jesse Lasky on the 17th of June. Its preamble states: "If your Jewish clergy and scholars haven't enough courage to tell you, and you yourself haven't enough brains to know better or enough loyalty toward this land, which has given you more than you ever had in history, to prevent your importing a cut-throat red dog like Eisenstein, then let me inform you."[40] His language makes plain a contempt for all Jews, no matter how Americanized they had become, but the moguls maintained public silence over Pease's vicious anti-Semitism. One journalist of the day found this passivity characteristic of Hollywood's assimilated Jewish elite. When Eisenstein's contract was terminated, Richard Watts, Jr., suggested in an editorial for *The Film Mercury* that the following political rationale was at work: "Eisenstein was [a] threat to the popularity of Paramount and the Jews. . . . [Pease] achieves publicity and patriotic acclaim for the expulsion of the Red. . . . Patriotism seems to be the last refuge of the cinema industry."[41]

In this view, Pease and Paramount ultimately served one another's purposes and the imperatives of assimilation and American acceptance entailed a degree of Jewish self-rejection. Neal Gabler and Michael Rogin, in separate studies of the Hollywood studio system, both conclude that the Jewish moguls of the 1920s and 1930s were effectively engaged in a process of cultural parricide.[42] Prejudices that linked Jews and political radicalism were particularly troublesome and in demonstrating their patriotism studio chiefs found themselves aligned on several occasions with reactionary, anti-Semitic forces.

In Los Angeles on October 8 and 9 of 1930, a congressional committee headed by Representative Hamilton Fish of New York held hearings on the influences of Communist propaganda and subversion in American society. An official from the Hays Office offered to compel Eisenstein to appear before them, but the committee adjourned ahead of schedule. Testimony from a host of friendly witnesses was arranged through the Better America Federation, headquartered in Los Angeles. Each of their sworn statements maintained that in American politics "most of the Communists are Russian Jews."[43] In the final committee report the linkage between family origins and radical politics focussed on "various types of American communists—Jewish, Hungarian, German, Finnish, Greek, Scotch, and Negro."[44] The mix of religious, national, and racial identities in this list reveals a wide range of nativist anxieties. In another area of inquiry, the Fish Committee justified harsh police tactics in the suppression of leftist activities largely on the basis of testimony from a Los Angeles police captain. On this matter, the Fish report furthermore objected that "there has been too much denunciation of the police for alleged brutality by 'pinks' and metropolitan papers."[45] In a similar vein, the studio Production Code, adopted formally in March 1930, classifies among "Repellant Subjects" to be "treated within the careful limits of good taste" any presentation onscreen of "*Third Degree* methods" by police authorities.[46]

From Mexico a few months after his exit from Hollywood, Eisenstein contemplated a fitting revenge on Major Frank Pease and his fellow "Blue Shits," a derisive allusion to the American reactionary organizations of the time known by their uniform dress colors. With the example from *An American Tragedy* of the political purposes served by a jury trial fresh in his mind, Eisenstein raised the possibility of a civil defamation suit, with Clarence Darrow as his attorney, that would at least "paralyze the scoundrel" Pease through prolonged and costly legal action.[47] As the Mexico project ran over schedule and the relationship with its sponsor Upton Sinclair deteriorated, Eisenstein was once again confronted with anti-Semitic scorn. The source now was the project's production manager, Hunter Kimbrough, and his slur was repeated unchallenged in correspondence Eisenstein received in October 1931 from the Soviet film official at the Amkino office in New York.[48]

More than a decade later, while writing his memoirs, Eisenstein returned to the Pease episode on at least three occasions, and for compelling reasons. Eisenstein remained informed on American political events surrounding Pease, which included Congressional investigations during the late 1930s into reactionary organizations like his for possible fifth-column activities.[49] Though not finally proven in the American investigations, Eisenstein imagined Pease as engaged in assembling "underground Fascist detachments—in the shadow of the Statue of Liberty."[50] A similar political scenario had been part of Eisenstein's rhetoric in his 1941 statement "Cinema against Fascism," which points to "the vile activities of Hitler's lackeys amongst the Germans living in America."[51]

The chapter of autobiography Eisenstein entitled "My Encounter with Mexico" provides an expansive consideration of the prominence given to violent death within that country's traditional and colonial cultures. Within this discussion the Soviet director admits to some grain of truth in Pease's fulminations over "this red dog and sadist" Eisenstein. In a candid hypothesis, Eisenstein suggests that Pease is the vicious nemesis he deserved and that some measure of self-betrayal was unconsciously involved. In like fashion, Eisenstein treats the encounter with Mexico as a narcissistic projection of his own complexes, formed long before his actual visit to America, and the complex in question here is a psychological identification between persecutor and victim. A counterpart to this individual complex that Eisenstein discovers within Mexican culture more generally is the habit of *vacilada,* from the Spanish verb "to vacillate" and also, in the idiom of Mexico "to have fun."[52] Furthermore, Eisenstein proposes that on the level of history the counterpart to his identification complex is the cycle of modern nationalism wherein radicals on the right or the left rise to become repressive authoritarians who celebrate their power through sustained terror against political enemies.

As events of the 1930s progressed, Eisenstein fully recognized the extent to which he was enmeshed in similar political dynamics. In 1940 through his production of Wagner's *Die Walküre* at the Bolshoi Theater he participated in the celebration of a part of German high culture most revered by the Nazis. The opera's premiere was met with the condemnation "Deliberate Jewish tricks" from an officer of the German embassy in Moscow, however, regardless of the cultural respect extended from the Soviets with this gala event.[53] Eisenstein's connection to Jewish roots ran along his father's side of the family, which appears to have largely assimilated into the dominant Christian culture at least one generation before Sergei's birth. Among Eisenstein's childhood memories, nonetheless, is one of being costumed as a rabbi in some make-believe game of his own invention.[54] In this particular game transvestism and police authority were two other chief components of the fantasy, thus compounding the possibilities for bipolar projection, identification, and condemnation.

In the Soviet Union during the mid-1920s, Stalin deployed anti-Semitism for the Party struggle with Trotsky and the left opposition, which he condemned for Jewish intellectualism and cosmopolitanism.[55] The state-ordered changes to *October* thus served the purposes of an ethnic purge as well as a political one. One cardinal history lesson re-experienced by Eisenstein in Hollywood fast became a global lesson of the 1930s—namely, that no matter how distant or faint the ancestry and no matter how complete the assimilation, reactionary forces were determined to target Jews as a conspiratorial menace. For successful assimilated Jews from the relatively comfortable distance of the United States, however, the temptations of passivity and acquiescence were strong.

After the Nazi invasion of June 1941, Soviet policy shifted to allow some recognition of Jews as a distinct segment of the population, including permission for a Moscow rally and radio broadcast organized by members of the Soviet Jewish intelligentsia. Held on August 24, 1941, the event issued an appeal to "Fellow Jews the World Over" based on cultural solidarity with "the history of our long-suffering people." The roster of speakers that day included prominent Soviet figures, with Eisenstein among them, whose Jewish or partly Jewish origins had not been public knowledge.[56] Association with this cause and with the Jewish Anti-Fascist Committee of the Soviet Union—which was endorsed at least publicly by the state in the years 1942–1948—proved, however, to be extremely dangerous under the precarious circumstances of Stalin's terror. Two original organizers of a Soviet Jewish anti-Fascist movement were arrested in December 1941, and by February 1943 both men had died in prison. The keynote speaker at the August 1941 rally was the actor Solomon Mikhoels, the head of the State Yiddish Theater in Moscow who would serve as chairman of the Jewish Anti-Fascist Committee for the duration of its existence. In January 1948, one month before Eisenstein's death, and under circumstances reported in the press at the time in vague terms of either an accident or a common crime, Mikhoels was assassinated by the secret police.

As late as July 1946 Eisenstein again brought the American fascist Pease to mind when he returned to intimate psychological themes in an installment of autobiography dedicated to the Marquis de Sade. Among a chain of associations concerning masochism, which Eisenstein traces back to childhood and the relationship to his father, he reiterates the tell-tale insult "this 'sadist' and 'red dog' Eisenstein," whose original context was equally anti-Semitic, as we have seen.[57] Fascinated by the epithet, Eisenstein moves quickly in the chapter to the topic of his childhood desire to fulfill aggressive impulses through games of his invention, games that entailed unjust persecution of the innocent.

Immediately upon his arrival in the United States in May 1930, Eisenstein had been obligated to attend Paramount's annual convention for exhibitors, which was held in Atlantic City.[58] Once there, Eisenstein visited the movie theater located on the city's busy oceanfront promenade where *The Battleship Potemkin* had received an American premiere in December 1926. The manager, who had presided over the film's 1926 run in that theater, related to Eisenstein an odd encounter with an elderly Jewish man who left in tears at the end of one show. While the manager thought at first that he or his family may have been among the victims of Cossack troops in Russia, the Jewish man revealed that in 1905 he had been a volunteer in the Tsar's army serving in the Odessa garrison and that he was among the soldiers who fired upon innocent citizens. In the course of subsequent events in 1905, faced by the spread of pogroms in Russia, the Jewish man deserted the military, fled the country, and soon emigrated to America, where for over two decades he managed to repress specific memories of his army past. Prompted by Eisenstein's film in 1926, the man recognized himself for the first time for having acted the part of a "Jewish Cossack" in the Odessa uprising of 1905.

From this intimation of tragic self-discovery by an Old World Jew, within a month Eisenstein would travel to Hollywood and encounter the often equivocal and absurd expressions of an American identity among very wealthy Jews in the movie business. Ivor Montagu, who was working at Paramount Pictures in advance of the Soviet group, had already witnessed many outlandish examples. Among them was his first glimpse of the Warner brothers "when several large men, like so many sea-monsters, emerged from the surf at Malibu Beach with their names picked out in Hebrew characters in the peeling skin of their sunburnt chests."[59] As amply documented in memoirs about the period by movie people, a paradoxical variant of anti-Semitism—the contempt directed by some secularized American Jews toward Old World Jewry—gave a serious inflection to this Hollywood ethnic comedy.

With sympathy and admiration, Eisenstein refers to the East European heritage and Jewish immigrant identity of many in the first generation of Hollywood bosses and he traces their American business origins back to a "cosmic chaos of speculation" in humble trade goods such as "old clothes."[60] F. Scott Fitzgerald's Hollywood novel *The Last Tycoon* portrays aspects of the cultural predicaments of American Jews in terms relevant to the present discussion. Set in the 1930s, the book establishes from the outset an Old World/New World conflict in having the failed studio mogul Manny Schwartz, described as a "middle-aged Jew," stare with "shameless economic lechery" at his triumphant rival Monroe Stahr, the suavely Americanized Jewish movie tycoon.[61] Schwartz "had come a long way from some ghetto" to phenomenal wealth only in the end to be utterly defeated by the power of a fully assimilated Jewish elite embodied in Monroe Stahr.[62] At a later point, in considering the number of horse fanciers among studio executives, Stahr "guessed that the Jews had taken over the worship of horses as a symbol—for years it had been the Cossacks mounted and the Jews on foot. Now the Jews had the horses, and it gave them a sense of extraordinary well-being and power."[63] This passage is an uncannily apt variation on the Jewish Cossack theme Eisenstein had encountered in Atlantic City.

In closing, it is valuable to note that one of the few tangible results of Eisenstein's time in Hollywood—the completed script for *An American Tragedy*—contained a profound history lesson for Siegfried Kracauer. After publication of his *Theory of Film: The Redemption of Physical Reality* in 1960, Kracauer devoted his energies to a general inquiry into questions of historiography. The study that Kracauer prepared under the title *History: The Last Things Before the Last* invokes as a fundamental methodological model the montage lists Eisenstein composed to render the interior monologue of Clyde Griffiths, his American screen story's protagonist. For Kracauer the script treatment is exceptional in rendering a crucial moment in an individual's life when the utter multiplicity of historical being becomes manifest. Of particular significance for the historian is the excess of audiovisual material, well beyond story requirements, in the montage lists. Kracauer finds in them "a great deal of possibly relevant elements, . . . impressions of the actual environment with projections of motives and splinters of thought."[64] In portraying a condition of overdetermined causation, Eisenstein's montage design conveys to Kracauer the general truth that there is "an infinity of factors" and thus a level of indeterminacy within human events.[65] This condition, in accord with Kracauer's fundamental thesis, offers no last or final cause in historical explanation and it thus provides a humanist alternative to materialist determinism. Kracauer draws insight from the Eisenstein montage example into the "irreducible share of freedom" within human events and thus into the provisional nature of any historical explanation.[66] Such history lessons seem far too intellectual and existential for the purposes of Hollywood, particularly in that era, but they may well be relevant to an understanding of the reserves in spirit and mind required by Eisenstein during the nightmare European and Soviet history became in the 1930s and 1940s.

Notes

I am grateful to the Council on Research of the Academic Senate at UCLA for funds in support of my work on this essay, to Professors Al LaValley and Barry Scherr of Dartmouth College for their invitation to the "Eisenstein at 100" conference, and to conference participants for their ideas on these issues. Thanks also to Michael Baskett and David Halloran for library work and help with some research questions.

1. Sergei Eisenstein, "The Cinema in America: Some Impressions of Hollywood," trans. S. D. Kogan, *International Literature,* no. 3 (July 1933), 97–105. According to the annotated bibliography in Sergei Eisenstein, *Film Essays,* ed. Jay Leyda (New York: Praeger, 1970) the article was published originally under a title that translates "Overtake and Surpass" in *Proletarskoe kino,* no. 15–16 (1932), 20–32.

2. Eisenstein, "Cinema in America," 102.

3. This information and the cited phrase are drawn from Thomas Schatz, *The Genius of the System: Hollywood Filmmaking in the Studio Era* (New York: Holt, 1996), 69–70.

4. Eisenstein, "Cinema in America," 102.

5. Ibid., 104.

6. Schatz, *Genius of the System,* 78.

7. Eisenstein, "Cinema in America," 105.

8. Sergei Eisenstein, *Selected Works,* 4: *Beyond the Stars: The Memoirs of Sergei Eisenstein,* ed. Richard Taylor, trans. William Powell (London: British Film Institute, 1995), 288.

9. Richard Taylor, "A 'Cinema for the Millions': Soviet Socialist Realism and the Problem of Film Comedy," *Journal of Contemporary History* 18 (July 1983), 439–461; and Taylor, "Boris Shumyatsky and the Soviet Cinema in the 1930s," *Historical Journal of Film, Radio and Television* 6: 1 (1986), 43–64. In revised version, the second article is contained in Richard Taylor and Ian Christie, eds., *Inside the Film Factory: New Approaches to Russian and Soviet Cinema* (New York: Routledge, 1991).

10. Neal Gabler, *An Empire of Their Own: How the Jews Invented Hollywood* (New York: Crown, 1988), 202–205.

11. This conclusion is based upon the production lists and synopses provided in John Douglas Eames, *The Paramount Story* (New York: Crown, 1985), 60–75.

12. The statement is made in a memo from Lasky to David O. Selznick dated October 22, 1929 and cited in David Thomson, *Showman: The Life of David O. Selznick* (New York: Knopf, 1992), 98.

13. Sergei Eisenstein, *Selected Works,* 1: *Writings, 1922–34,* ed. and trans. Richard Taylor (London: British Film Institute, 1988), 113.

14. Jay Leyda, *Kino: A History of the Russian and Soviet Film* (New York: Collier, 1973), 280. More recent research by Richard Taylor puts the figure at only *one* as late as May 1931; see "Boris Shumyatsky," 48.

15. The sources for this information are Leyda, *Kino,* 277–288; and the table "Film Production, 1918–41" included in Richard Taylor and Ian Christie, eds., *The Film Factory: Russian and Soviet Cinema in Documents* (Cambridge, Mass.: Harvard University Press, 1988), 424. Valuable discussion of aesthetic considerations in early Soviet sound cinema is provided in Kristin Thompson, "Early Sound Counterpoint," *Yale French Studies,* no. 60 (1980), 115–140; and Ian Christie, "Soviet Cinema: Making Sense of Sound," *Screen* 23: 2 (July–August, 1982), 34–49. In

revised version, the Christie article is contained in Taylor and Christie, *Inside the Film Factory.*

16. Eisenstein, *Writings, 1922–34,* 114.

17. In earlier work, I was so inclined; see James Goodwin, *Eisenstein, Cinema, and History* (Urbana: University of Illinois Press, 1993), 121–122, 175. Jacques Aumont discusses the "Statement on Sound" in terms of conflict between image and sound track and dates Eisenstein's concern for harmonic synthesis to the late 1930s in *Montage Eisenstein,* trans. Lee Hildreth, Constance Penley, and Andrew Ross (Bloomington: Indiana University Press, 1987), 68, 184–185. David Bordwell, in *The Cinema of Eisenstein* (Cambridge, Mass.: Harvard University Press, 1993), 185, points out that Eisenstein's early understanding of counterpoint was incomplete at best and that this led him to emphasize image/sound conflict.

18. Eisenstein, *Writings, 1922–34,* 114.

19. Ibid., 119.

20. Harry Tugend, "Action Beats Dialog: Eisenstein," *Exhibitors Herald-World,* May 24, 1930, 22.

21. Eisenstein, *Writings, 1922–34,* 200.

22. Ibid., 201.

23. Eisenstein, in a letter to Léon Moussinac dated September 12, 1930, published in Moussinac, *Sergei Eisenstein,* trans. D. Sandy Petrey (New York: Crown, 1970), 52. Annette Michelson does consider the *American Tragedy* script to be a response by Eisenstein to "the Joycean challenge"; see her essay "Reading Eisenstein Reading *Capital,*" Part 1 in *October,* no. 2 (Summer 1976), 27–38, and Part 2 in *October,* no. 3 (Spring 1977), 82–89. Artistic relationships between the two figures are the subject of my essay "Eisenstein, Ecstasy, Joyce, and Hebraism" *Critical Inquiry* 26, no. 3 (Spring 2000), 529–557.

24. Eisenstein, "Cinema in America," 97.

25. Since the article's retranslation of the Production Code into Russian and back into English is inexact and incomplete, I have quoted here from the original text, as appended to Raymond Moley, *The Hays Office* (New York: Bobbs-Merrill, 1945). In the two sources, the passage can be found on the following pages: *Hays Office,* 241; "Cinema in America," 98.

26. Eisenstein, "Cinema in America," 98.

27. *Hays Office,* 242; retranslated as "Race mixture (sex relations between blacks and white people) are [sic] prohibited" in "Cinema in America," 99.

28. Eisenstein, "Cinema in America," 100.

29. "Cinema in America" (100) names the two films *Beast Over the City* and *Shame of a Nation. Scarface* is referred to here by the subtitle the film was obliged to adopt, along with several other changes, after a two-year struggle between producer Howard Hughes and the Production Code board, a fact that Eisenstein does not comment upon.

30. Eisenstein, "Cinema in America," 101.

31. Ibid., 101.

32. The account in Donald Crafton, *The Talkies: American Cinema's Transition to Sound, 1926–1931* (New York: Scribner's, 1997), 405–406, attributes the limited

distribution of *Hallelujah* to the refusal by exhibitors, many of them from the South, to book the film. See also Eisenstein, "Cinema in America," 101.

33. Jay Leyda and Zina Voynow, *Eisenstein at Work* (New York: Pantheon, 1982), 74.

34. Eisenstein, "Cinema in America," 100.

35. Ivor Montagu, *With Eisenstein in Hollywood* (New York: International, 1969), 345–346.

36. Eisenstein, *Writings, 1922–34,* 239.

37. See Marie Seton, *Sergei M. Eisenstein* (New York: A. A. Wyn, 1952), 167–176.

38. The quotations are taken from "Little Headway Made in Attack on *All Quiet* As Pacifist Film," *Exhibitors Herald-World,* June 28, 1930, 11; and "Zero for *All Quiet,*" *The Nation,* July 2, 1930, 7.

39. Conflict between Pease and the Production Code Office is mentioned in "Wild To-Do over Russe Director Is Ignored," *Variety,* August 13, 1930, 4.

40. The telegram is reported in "Little Headway Made," 11.

41. Richard Watts, Jr., "The Passing of Eisenstein," *Film Mercury,* November 14, 1930, 8.

42. Gabler, *An Empire of Their Own,* 1–5, 429; Michael Rogin, *Blackface, White Noise: Jewish Immigrants in the Hollywood Melting Pot* (Berkeley: University of California Press, 1996), 84–87.

43. "School Plots of Reds Told," *Los Angeles Times,* October 9, 1930, sec. 1, 1–2.

44. Special Committee on Communist Activities in the United States, House of Representatives, 71st Congress, *Investigation of Communist Propaganda* (Washington, D.C.: Government Printing Office, 1931), 1.

45. *Investigation of Communist Propaganda,* 62.

46. *Hays Office,* 243.

47. In letters to Upton Sinclair from April and June 1930, published in Harry M. Geduld and Ronald Gottesman, eds., *Sergei Eisenstein and Upton Sinclair: The Making and Unmaking of Qué viva México!* (Bloomington: Indiana University Press, 1970), 70–71, 92.

48. See *Sergei Eisenstein and Upton Sinclair,* 167, 172–173, 202.

49. Pease is discussed in the report by the Committee on Un-American Activities, House of Representatives, 76th Congress, *Investigation of Un-American Propaganda Activities in the United States* (Washington, D.C.: Government Printing Office, 1939), vol. 5: 3696, 3699. For a contemporary account of American reactionary movements, see Harold Lavine, *Fifth Column in America* (New York: Doubleday, 1940), which mentions Pease (196).

50. Eisenstein, *Beyond the Stars,* 420.

51. Sergei Eisenstein, *Selected Works, 3, Writings, 1934–1947,* ed. Richard Taylor, trans. William Powell (London: British Film Institute, 1996), 183.

52. Eisenstein, *Beyond the Stars,* 420–421.

53. Leyda and Voynow, *Eisenstein at Work,* 114n.

54. Eisenstein, *Beyond the Stars,* 117. Anne Nesbet's article in this volume also discusses that memory.

55. See Robert C. Tucker, *Stalin in Power: The Revolution from Above, 1928–1941* (New York: Norton, 1990), 41.

56. My principal sources for information on the Soviet Jewish anti-Fascist movement are: Yehoshua A. Gilboa, *The Black Years of Soviet Jewry, 1939–1953,* trans. Yosef Shachter and Dov Ben-Abba (Boston: Little, Brown, 1971), 42–86; Shimon Redlich, *Propaganda and Nationalism in Wartime Russia: The Jewish Antifascist Committee in the USSR, 1941–1948* (Boulder, Colo: East European Quarterly, 1982); and Redlich, *War, Holocaust, and Stalinism: A Documented History of the Jewish Anti-Fascist Committee in the USSR* (Luxembourg: Harwood Academic Publishers, 1995), which publishes the full "Appeal" (174–177), where the phrase I have quoted appears. A *Pravda* report dated August 25, 1941 (translated in Redlich, *War, Holocaust and Stalinism,* 183) lists Eisenstein among speakers at "a rally of representatives of the Jewish people." In a filmed speech delivered in English some time soon after (published in Seton, *Eisenstein,* 429), Eisenstein makes an international appeal against Fascism "as a Russian representative of the Soviet intelligentsia."

57. Eisenstein, *Beyond the Stars,* 548.

58. Eisenstein recounts these events in *Beyond the Stars,* 160–164.

59. Montagu, *With Eisenstein in Hollywood,* 123.

60. Eisenstein, "Cinema in America," 102.

61. F. Scott Fitzgerald, *The Last Tycoon,* 1941 (New York: Scribner's, 1969), 6.

62. Ibid., 13.

63. Ibid., 74.

64. Siegfried Kracauer, *History: The Last Things Before the Last,* ed. Paul Oskar Kristeller (Princeton, N.J.: Markus Wiener, 1969), 29.

65. Ibid., 29.

66. Ibid., 43.

CENSORSHIP, CULTURE, AND CODPIECES
Eisenstein's Influence in Britain during the 1930s and 1940s

Ian Christie

The reader cries out within himself with excitement . . . for the task of inner collaboration as co-author amounts to "unifying" the disconnected series of the author.

—Sergei Eisenstein

Conventionally, Eisenstein had few disciples; many would argue none, apart from his faithful archivists and translators scattered around the world. Yet his influence was pervasive and protean. This is an attempt to trace how such influence shaped the emergence of a film culture in Britain during the inter-war years, where it was arguably decisive. Of course, Eisenstein's influence on the British documentary movement was long considered axiomatic, but to limit his impact to this episode begs many questions, and almost all its assumptions can and have been questioned by revisionist historians. I argue that this is not so much *wrong* as it is a considerable underestimation of Eisenstein's total impact on British film culture, which stretches from filmmakers and critics as early as 1927 up to the rediscoveries of the 1980s.

Act One inevitably revolves around censorship, reflecting Britain's long-standing mistrust of the potentially subversive influence of film. But it is also a complex narrative of reaction and counterreaction to a largely symbolic *Battleship Potemkin,* absent or at least little-seen during the eight or nine years of its greatest notoriety. In fact, the success of *Potemkin* in Germany in 1926 coincided almost exactly with the General Strike in Britain in May of that year, which probably exacerbated an already hostile official attitude towards this latest example of "revolutionary propaganda."[1] Even an avowedly anti-Soviet film was cut to nearly half its original length in late 1925, due to its inclusion of what the British Board of Film Censors would have considered ipso facto inflammatory material.[2] Unsurprisingly, therefore, *Potemkin* was formally refused certification on 30 September 1926, a decision reported in Parliament by the Home Secretary.

Meanwhile, the new journal *Close Up,* edited by English emigrés in Switzerland, referred knowingly to *Potemkin* in its first issue in July 1927: "Then we began to hear from Russia. We had got very sick of Russian novels and

Russian plays, and in spite of a recrudesence of Russian influence in art and decoration, there was prejudice. But *Potemkin* and *Aelita* put an end to that."[3] By the following year, 1928, Soviet cinema had become central to the defense of silent cinema as a distinctive art, now threatened by the talkies, and *Close Up* published the "Statement" on sound signed by Eisenstein, Vsevolod Pudovkin, and Grigori Alexandrov.[4] But it was still British censorship that continued to draw most comment on *Potemkin.* Ivor Montagu, a film editor and later producer with both Alfred Hitchcock and Eisenstein, was the moving spirit behind the Film Society, and he published a pamphlet in 1929 entitled *The Political Censorship of Films* which attacked the draconian powers vested in local authorities and the British Board of Film Censors under the licensing Act of 1909. George Bernard Shaw wrote in similar terms, bracketing *Potemkin* with a British film about Edith Cavell, *Dawn* (Herbert Wilcox, 1928), also banned at this time, pointing to the absurdity that "the screen may wallow in every extremity of vulgarity and villainy, provided it whitewashes authority," with the result that "one of the best films ever produced as a work of pictorial art" is suppressed as "simply a move in class warfare."[5]

Close Up continued to protest against the ban, organizing a petition against film censorship and reporting on continued clandestine maneuvers. It even commissioned an article by the psychoanalyst Hanns Sachs, in which he compared British film censorship with witch trials, diagnosing a "social repetition of [the] individual process of repression" in order to maintain "a fiction—the queer idea that things are not what they are as long as you don't say so."[6]

In spite of the BBFC's ban, the Film Society secured tacit permission to show Soviet and other uncertificated films during the late 1920s, largely due to its elite membership, which included many leading intellectual and cultural figures, and a level of subscription that effectively put it beyond working-class means. Several key Soviet avant-garde works were shown before the Society finally succeeded in presenting *Potemkin* on November 10, 1929—complete with Edmund Meisel conducting his own musical score which had contributed greatly to the film's impact in Germany—and with Eisenstein in attendance. With an apt symbolism, this long-awaited event also included John Grierson's own manifesto for a new program of popular education and information films, *Drifters,* thus securing a form of apostolic succession for the future documentary movement. In fact, *Potemkin* had already played its strategic role behind the scenes, when a private screening organized by Grierson and attended by members of Parliament and other figures of influence so impressed this audience that support was raised for a government-sponsored film unit—no doubt encouraged by the very hysteria that still surrounded *Potemkin* in public.[7] The irony that Eisenstein had already made two subsequent films, and hoped to add sound to the latter of these in Britain, seems to have been ignored. Eisenstein also gave several lectures late in 1929 as part of the Film Society's commitment to foster film culture. No notes are known to exist, but Montagu indicated that they dealt more with literature and art than cinema, encouraging the audience, which included many future filmmakers, "to see much with new eyes."[8]

The following five years saw a prolonged influence of *Potemkin* in Britain which was probably unique. This took two forms: a continuing struggle to screen it beyond the tolerated confines of the Film Society, and a modest degree of emulation among politically motivated filmmakers. *October* and *The Old and the New* were also shown, the latter widely after receiving its BBFC certificate, but neither seems to have had any similar degree of impact. From 1930 a number of Workers' Film Societies developed in London and other major cities, modeled on the original Society; these were supplemented by a smaller network of Kino groups (named pointedly after the Russian word for "cinema"), and by other politically inspired organizations such as the Workers' Film and Photo League and the Independent Labour Party Masses Stage and Film Guild.[9]

The loophole in cinema legislation exploited by Kino was that "substandard" film—meaning 16mm rather than the standard 35mm—appeared to be exempt from licensing control, as did noninflammable film stock. In December 1934 a test case was brought by the police after a screening of *Potemkin* by a miners' lodge and Kino in the town of Jarrow (soon to become famous for the Jarrow Crusade, when 200 unemployed men marched to London to draw attention to the scale of unemployment). The prosecution failed, and in the following year *Kino News* carried details of how to avoid the risk of prosecution by forming a film society and renting 16mm films.[10] The formation of such politically inspired groups would contribute significantly to the growth of a film society network comparable to the ciné-club movement in France.

Whether workers' film societies should be showing Eisenstein's films, or indeed making such a fetish of Soviet cinema, became a major issue for debate during the early 1930s in the sectarian world of British left politics. A group known as the Plebs League proposed a radical strategy of working-class self-education, opposing the more traditional Workers Educational Association. One of its leading spokesmen, Huntly Carter, had written the earliest accounts of the "new spirit" in Soviet theatre and cinema, but became increasingly critical of Eisenstein's veneration. Responding to a counterattack by the Communist Ralph Bond, Carter wrote in 1931:

> I should take *The General Line* [the original title of *The Old and the New*] as unsuited for consumption by British Labour. It is inconceivably old-fashioned. It is a mess of primitive magic and ritual, of religion (in the sense of god-making), of superstition, of faith in and fear of tribal gods

and faith in and fear of the new god of machinery. . . . Is British Labour so unintelligent that it requires this mixture of primitive ignorance and idolatory to stir it to economic action?[11]

Carter himself had been accused by Bond of using "mystic and spiritual phraseology" in his book on Soviet cinema when he called for "the English people [to] build a splendid new Theatre-Cinema temple to initiate all into a new philosophy and a new religion," instead of exposing how capitalist cinema "is used as an ideological force to dope the workers."[12] But Carter's essential argument is that *Potemkin,* along with *Mother,* Pudovkin's *The End of St. Petersburg,* and *The Old and the New,* all belong to the pre–Five Year Plan phase of Soviet development, while Viktor Turin's *Turksib* offers a "glimpse" of "a new Soviet edifice" under construction (November 1930). In this, Carter joined Grierson, who had little time for *The Old and the New,* preferring *Turksib* as a model for the new documentary he was launching.[13]

Turning to the direct influence of Eisenstein on nascent radical filmmaking, Basil Wright suggested in his 1974 memoir that "the only people who went to town on the 1928 Statement on sound and its counterpoint idea were the British documentary filmmakers of the early 30s under the influence of Grierson and Cavalcanti."[14] This was largely because, he explained, they had almost as much difficulty as their Soviet counterparts in obtaining sound equipment: "As late as 1933, I was still shooting without access to sound. Not that this means we were not interested. Certainly when I went on a filmmaking tour to the West Indies in 1933 I had in mind various possibilities for soundtracks to be added to what I was shooting, and was of course acutely aware of the Russian Manifesto."[15] Indeed, Wright's *Song of Ceylon* (1934) does show the influence of thinking about asynchronous sound, with its use of radio and telegraph sounds and a seventeenth-century visitor's account to counterpoint contemporary images. Also within the documentary movement, Len Lye's Post Office film *N or NW* (1937) uses a sophisticated sound–image counterpoint, which probably owes something to the Group Theatre experimentalism that marks Lye's other work, but equally could be compared with Eisenstein and Alexandrov's Paris fantasia *Romance Sentimentale* (1929). And before he joined the General Post Office Unit, Norman McLaren's polemical anti-arms trade *Hell Unlimited* (1936) used a sophisticated range of references, among which he admitted to *Potemkin.*[16] Other amateur films of this period made by Kino and the Workers' Film and Photo League included montage passages, but these suggest the stylistic influence of Pudovkin rather than Eisenstein.

Even as Eisenstein's silent films continued to be shown defiantly at film societies, while their relevance to contemporary politics or aesthetics was increasingly questioned, a second phase of Eisenstein's influence had begun through the agency of Dallas Bower. Despite remaining a virtually unknown figure, Bower could claim to have been one of the most progressive figures behind the scenes in British broadcasting and cinema.[17] Having trained as a radio engineer in the early 1920s, he became a pioneer film sound recordist, working on both Hitchcock's *Blackmail* and its rival "first British talkie," *Under the Greenwood Tree* (1929). In 1936, he published a remarkable survey and prospectus, *Plan for Cinema,* which looked forward from the early stage of talking cinema to a "frameless" medium using stereoscopy and color, which Bower termed "solid cinema." In this, he anticipated by a decade Eisenstein's 1946 essay on "stereoscopic cinema." The book also employed a critical technique that would become familiar after Eisenstein's first collection of essays appeared in 1942, imbricating cinema with the literary, musical, and visual arts to reveal both its ancestry and its common means of signification. Bower's contribution to the study of "pre-cinema" was to claim Thomas Hardy's verse epic *The Dynasts* (1903) as a "work of art bursting its boundaries, groping for a medium not yet come." [18]

Bower's starting point, however, was mockery of the typical contemporary intellectual who railed against American and British cinema only to "fall flat on his face in ecstatic abandon at the feet of the twin-gods, Eisenstein and Pudovkin." [19] His argument, similar to Grierson's and Carter's, was that the Soviet classics were products of their time and there was now a need to move beyond celebrating "revolution" into construction. Bower's own move from theory into practice followed directly from his anticipation that cinema and television would inevitably fuse into one art of the future, synthesizing ballet, music-drama, and poetic drama along with other popular forms of entertainment.[20] When the British Broadcasting Corporation (BBC) launched its pilot television service in 1936, Bower joined as a producer and during the following three years was responsible for a series of pioneering drama and opera productions, including Shakespeare and Wagner. It was during 1939 that Bower saw Eisenstein's *Alexander Nevsky* and was so impressed by its technique that he arranged to buy a copy for use in training novice television camera operators.[21]

The BBC television service was closed at the outbreak of war in September 1939, and Bower joined the Royal Corps of Signals before being drafted into the Ministry of Information and returning to the BBC as a radio producer. It was in this capacity, after Germany's invasion of the Soviet Union in June 1941, that he conceived the idea of re-creating *Alexander Nevsky* as a poetic drama for radio, with the original Prokofiev music. He persuaded the poet Louis MacNeice to write the play and Adrian Boult to conduct the music, and secured a star-filled cast headed by Robert Donat. Coordinating such large forces—some two hundred performers, including the full BBC Symphony Orchestra and Chorus—for a live transmission was a major undertaking, especially in wartime.[22] What transpired was even more dramatic than could have been anticipated: the day before the broadcast, Japan attacked Pearl Harbor, bringing the United States into the war. *Nevsky* was preceded by announcements from Roosevelt, Churchill, and the Soviet ambassador, and was later rebroadcast several times during the war—thus launching the new genre of radio verse drama, to which Bower and MacNeice also contributed *Columbus,* with original music by William Walton.

For Bower, however, the inspiration of *Nevsky* had not yet run its course. Immediately before the war's outbreak, he had been planning a television production of Shakespeare's *Henry V,* which was aborted. According to an obituary of Bower:

> In the spring of 1944, the film department [of the Ministry of Information] was searching for a subject which would brace Britain for the fearful risks and possible setbacks of a seaborne invasion of fortress Europe. Bower had seen Olivier deliver the "Once more into the breach" speech from *Henry V,* dug out his old television script and proposed a film of it.[23]

In fact, Bower had produced a radio program in 1942, *Into Battle,* which included Laurence Olivier performing speeches from the play, and he appears to have been in frustrating negotiations with the producer Filippo Del Guidice during that autumn.[24] After such directors as William Wyler and Carol Reed had declined the film, Olivier took on its direction, as well as starring in it, with Bower credited only as associate producer.

The full details of Bower's involvement with his most celebrated of British wartime productions may never be known, but Ivor Montagu explained in a letter to Eisenstein that Bower was the "medium" by which the influence of *Nevsky* was transmitted to *Henry V,* and that it was only his "enthusiasm for the subject that eventually secured [its] production." He described Bower as "an eccentric who worked on documentaries and for the BBC . . . a passionate devotee of *Nevsky* which he produced for the BBC." From this eloquent letter, we can see Olivier's and Bower's film through Montagu's eyes, as he wished to portray it to Eisenstein. Hailing it as "a very great film achievement" and noting that "there is no doubt that your own work has very much influenced this film," Montagu introduces it as an "unadapted" film of the play, observing that "the formalists that we once were would therefore maybe have objected to it." But Montagu believes that this "transference" is effectively an improvement on any theatrical presentation of the play.

The film's major innovation, compared with all previous Shakespeare adaptations, was its careful re-creation of the Globe Theatre as the primary setting, which then expands in two main ways: through a stylized re-creation of

61. *Alexander Nevsky.* Museum of Modern Art/Film Stills Archive.

62. *Henry V* (1945; dir. by Laurence Olivier).

the late medieval world as represented in contemporary painters and illustrators, and through realistic battle scenes. Montagu observes that "Breughel has undoubtedly been used as [a] model in colouring and perspective, for composition in the interiors." He also praises the film's decorative use of Technicolor in the sequences modeled on the Duc de Berry's *Book of Hours:* "for the first time (outside Disney) colour is used, as we always said it should be, not naturalistically but arbitrarily." Montagu describes the Battle of Agincourt as "an entirely gutless imitation" of the Battle on the Ice in *Nevsky,* perhaps because he is reacting against the praise heaped on this bravura sequence by those who "have never seen *Nevsky* or [have] slept through it." But he goes on to praise its lack of realism as helping to preserve "the play convention of the film" and maintains that "there is no more reason why its spectacular qualities should not be *after* Eisenstein than why its pictorial ones should not be after divers mediaeval ancestors." [25]

Montagu praises "the high standard of research, the delight in costumes, textures, period technical appliances, period faces," characterising this as "historical realism, not mechanically reproduced but creatively selected." Considering *Henry* in the light of *Nevsky* also prompts Montagu to recall "how much the dialogue of the courtship of Olga in *Nevsky* owes to Shakespeare's dialogue in the scene of Henry's courtship of Katherine." "Plagiarism is only a 'revanche',," he concludes. With the knowledge of *Ivan the Terrible* which Montagu did not have, we can reflect further on the profound Shakespeareanism of Eisenstein. [26] Olivier's film was to prove highly influential. Apart from launching his own career as a film director, which would lead to *Hamlet* (1948) and *Richard III* (1955), its considerable commercial success on both sides of the Atlantic helped to establish Shakespearean films as a viable post-war genre—soon to include Orson Welles's *Macbeth* (1948) and *Othello* (1951), Akira Kurosawa's Samurai version of *Macbeth, Throne of Blood* (1957), and, in Russia, Sergei Yutkevich's *Othello* (1956) and Grigori Kozintsev's *Hamlet* (1964). All these, in some measure, could be said to descend from Bower's appropriation of *Nevsky.* [27]

While Bower was translating Eisenstein's example into an English idiom, another important passage from theory into practice was also underway in post-war Britain. Thorold Dickinson had been another Film Society activist and attended Eisenstein's London lectures in 1929 before becoming a filmmaker in the 1930s, although one more drawn to fiction than the Griersonians. He was also politically active: as a founder-member (with Ivor Montagu) of the film technicians' union, the Association of Cine Technicians, he visited the Soviet Union as part of an ACT delegation in 1935, producing a report on his return. In 1948, Dickinson coauthored a book on Soviet cinema in a new series on national cinemas. [28] Here he had no hesitation in devoting more space to Eisenstein than any other Russian director of the silent period, noting that *Potemkin, October,* and *The Old and the New* "are among the few significant silent films of all time."[29] Dickinson's account of Eisenstein favors the first and third of these over *October,* regretting its uneven composition and intellectualism, especially compared with the "deeply satisfying" *The Old and the New.*

Eisenstein's sound films were covered in the second part of the book by Catherine De La Roche, who had worked for various Russian agencies during the war and was clearly a reliable pro-Soviet. Eisenstein's reverses between 1929 and 1937 are conveniently elided, and *Bezhin Meadow* is not mentioned. *Nevsky* is described as a "direct development of the epic style of his silent films," with "optimism [as] the leitmotiv of the production."[30] *Ivan the Terrible,* Part I is praised for its political emphasis on the importance of unifying the Russian state, and also for its own "unity of form and content," which recalls the final, rather ironic paragraphs of Dickinson's essay, dealing with the coming of sound and the use of "formalism" as a condemnation of Eisenstein and others.[31] Perhaps this tone is explained by Dickinson's own excursion into elaborately stylized historical narrative on a Russian theme at almost exactly the time of writing. His film *The Queen of Spades* (1948) invests Pushkin's tale with an imaginative horror not equalled since Yakov Protazanov's version in 1916, helped by outstandingly atmospheric sets from the painter Oliver Messel and starring Edith Evans and Anton Walbrook (en route from his role as a Diaghilev-inspired impressario in Michael Powell and Emeric Pressburger's *The Red Shoes* to the master of ceremonies in Max Ophuls' *La Ronde*). Dickinson could not have known of Eisenstein's own thwarted Pushkin project, *The Lives of a Poet,* but he would certainly have known *Ivan the Terrible,* Part 1 and been aware of the banning of Part 2, on which De La Roche dutifully quotes the Stalinist verdict.[32] Like *Henry V, The Queen of Spades* may well deserve to be counted as another beneficiary of Eisenstein's unfashionable historical dramaturgy.

An important postscript to this account of the 1930s and 1940s is the remarkable conjunction in 1957–1958 of two belated Eisenstein "premieres"—the release of his first film *Strike* and *Ivan the Terrible,* Part 2—both made possible by the Khrushchev "Thaw." Perhaps surprisingly, it was the thirty-year-old silent film that met with a more enthusiastic response than the long-awaited final testament. For while *Ivan,* Part 2 was greeted with reverence by some, and compared with Shakespeare in a climate of Shakespearean adaptation that Eisenstein had indeed helped inspire, it also seemed out of sync with the era that was about to experience Angry Young Men, the Kitchen Sink, and the New Wave. Its full appreciation would not come for another twenty-five years; and yet it clearly held a fascination for the generation that had been formed, at a distance, by Eisenstein. I discovered while interviewing Lindsay Anderson on the subject of Eisenstein that John Ford had asked to see *Ivan,* Part 2 while in London making *Gideon's Day* (probably in 1957), and that Anderson had arranged a private screening at the National Film Theatre. Unfortunately he was unable (or unwilling) to report Ford's response, except to say that he found it "operatic."[33] *Strike,* meanwhile, came into non-theatrical distribution around 1960 (in a version with intertitles well translated by Montagu), and gradually established itself during the next decade as the emblem of a more "revolutionary" face of Eisenstein, supporting a revived image of him as a Constructivist, which would bear fruit in Peter Wollen's major reassessment and in Lutz Becker's film made to accompany the London "Art in Revolution" exhibition of 1971.[34]

What can be learned from this brief chronicle of Eisenstein's impact on British film culture? Most importantly, it is no exaggeration to say that Eisenstein was crucial to the very *idea* of film culture in Britain during the formative period of 1927–1935. His influence would continue to be felt in the growth of criticism and theory: notably, for instance, in the compilation *Film and Reality* made by Alberto Cavalcanti in 1942, which effectively canonized Eisenstein as a Grierson-style "realist," and in Ernest Lindgren's introduction to film appreciation, *The Art of the Film,* which first appeared in 1948.[35] And the legacy of alternative distribution and exhibition, originally established to circumvent censorship in the 1930s, continued to shape these sectors until the advent of video. Unsurprisingly, there was a reaction against this canonized, ossified Eisenstein which would topple him, until a further "new" Eisenstein was reinvented in Derek Jarman's polemical, gay appropriation film *Imagining October* in 1984—a dialectical irony that the sexually ambivalent Eisenstein who relished embarrassing the warders of the Tower of London about their armor's missing codpieces would surely have appreciated.[36]

Notes

Epigraph quoted by N. M. Lary, "Eisenstein and Shakespeare" in *Eisenstein Rediscovered,* ed. Ian Christie and Richard Taylor (London: Routledge, 1993), 150.

1. A phrase used in the 1921 Report of the British Board of Film Censors; quoted in James C. Robertson, *The Hidden Cinema: British Film Censorship in Action, 1918–1975* (London: Routledge, 1989), 28.

2. Ibid., 29.

3. Kenneth Macpherson, "As Is," *Close Up,* vol. 1, no. 1, July 1927; reproduced in James Donald et al., eds., *Close Up 1927–1933: Cinema and Modernism* (Princeton: Princeton University Press, 1998), 37.

4. *Close Up,* 3: 4 (October 1928), 10–13.

5. George Bernard Shaw, "Views on the Censorship," *British Film Journal,* April–May 1928; reproduced in Bernard F. Dukore, ed., *Bernard Shaw on Cinema* (Carbondale: Southern Illinois Press, 1997), 54–55.

6. Hanns Sachs, "Modern Witch-Trials," *Close Up,* vol. 4: 5 (May 1929); reproduced in Donald et al., *Close Up 1927–1933,* 299–301.

7. The exact circumstances of this screening have not been confirmed. Grierson referred to it obliquely in his obituary essay on Eisenstein in 1948, and it presumably formed part of his intensive activity in 1927–1928 in relation to the Empire Marketing Board. He had invoked *Potemkin* in a Memorandum written in 1927, entitled "English Cinema Production and the Naturalistic Tradition," and organized screenings at the Imperial Institute during the winter of 1927–1928. For details of Grierson's role at this time, see Ian Aitken, *Film and Reform: John Grierson and the Documentary Film Movement* (London: Routledge, 1990), 97–109.

8. Ivor Montagu, *With Eisenstein in Hollywood* (Berlin, GDR: Seven Seas, 1968), 36.

9. *Traditions of Independence: British Cinema in the 1930s,* ed. Don Macpherson and Paul Willemen (London: British Film Institute, 1980), 126–164.

10. Articles by Ralph Bond and Ivor Montagu from *Kino News,* Winter 1935, quoted in *Traditions,* 112–117.

11. Huntly Carter, "Labour and the Cinema (II)," *The Plebs,* October 1931; quoted in *Traditions,* 143.

12. Ralph Bond, "Labour and the Cinema: A Reply to Huntly Carter," *The Plebs,* August 1931; quoted in *Traditions,* 141.

13. "There is, I believe, only Turin and *Turksib* which for all its patches of really bad articulation is the single job which takes us into the future." Grierson, quoted in Aitken, *Film and Reform,* 87.

14. Basil Wright, *The Long View* (London: Secker and Warburg, 1974), 71.

15. Ibid., 114. The films Wright made in the West Indies were *Windmill in Jamaica* and *Cargo from Jamaica* (both 1934).

16. David Curtis, ed., *Norman McLaren* (Edinburgh: Scottish Arts Council, 1977), 10.

17. Dallas Bower, b. 1907, died while this paper was in press, in October 1999.

18. Dallas Bower, *Plan for Cinema* (London: J.M. Dent, 1936), 70.

19. Ibid., 7.

20. Ibid., 140ff.

21. Information from an interview by the author with Bower in 1996.

22. A file of production documents exists in the BBC Archives at Caversham and, unusually for this period, there is a recording of the transmission. I am grateful to Simon Elmes for locating these during our work together on *The Eisenstein Enigma,* BBC Radio 3, April 1, 1994.

23. Peter Purser, [Dallas Bower obituary], *The Guardian* (London), October 20, 1999, p. 22.

24. See Sue Harper, *Picturing the Past: The Rise and Fall of the British Costume Film* (London: British Film Institute, 1994), 86; James Chapman, *The British at War: Cinema, State and Propaganda 1939–1945* (London: I. B. Tauris, 1998), 244; Charles Drazin, *The Finest Years: British Cinema of the 1940s* (London: Andre Deutsch, 1998), 21. None of these accounts notes the influence of *Nevsky.*

25. Excerpts from letter dated February 25, 1945, from the Eisenstein Papers, courtesy of Naum Kleiman.

26. See Lary in Christie and Taylor, *Eisenstein Rediscovered,* 140–150.

27. Bower's post-war career produced a number of innovative television productions and one film, *Alice in Wonderland* (1951), which combined live action sequences, directed by Bower in Oxford, with puppetry by Lou Bunin. Unfortunately the color process used (Anscochrome) became obsolete and the film was only restored in 1997. None of Bower's other ambitious projects were realized before his death in October 1999.

28. Thorold Dickinson and Catherine De La Roche, *Soviet Cinema* (London: Falcon Press, 1948). Published as part of a series, "National Cinemas," edited by Roger Manvell of the British Film Academy.

29. Ibid., 23.

30. Ibid., 56.

31. Dickinson writes that "film craftsmen in Russia as elsewhere had anchored the microphone to the film camera and were in full pursuit of the presentation of characterisation which had largely been denied them by the nature of silent film"; then describes "socialist realism" as "a simple naturalism." Dickinson and Roche, *Soviet Cinema,* 37–38. The book was evidently published before Eisenstein's death in the same year.

32. See Håkan Lövgren, "Eisenstein's Pushkin Project," in Christie and Taylor, *Eisenstein Rediscovered,* 126–139.

33. Anderson was outspokenly hostile toward Eisenstein and his influence. See Christie and Taylor, *Eisenstein Rediscovered,* 1.

34. "Eisenstein's Aesthetics" is the first part of Peter Wollen's highly influential book *Signs and Meaning in the Cinema,* first published in 1969 (London: Secker and Warburg). Lutz Becker's collage-documentary *Art in Revolution* was commissioned by the Arts Council to accompany the Hayward Gallery's pioneering multimedia exhibition.

35. For brief details of Cavalcanti's once influential compilation, see British Film Institute Distribution catalogue, 90; Lindgren's book, with its heavy emphasis on Eisenstein, remained the only accessible English introduction to film history and criticism until the 1960s (London: George Allen and Unwin, 1948).

36. *Imagining October* is a 35-minute film, long kept semisecret but now widely considered one of Jarman's best, shot partly in Russia and in the Eisenstein Museum during a visit by Jarman organized by the author. For details, see *Afterimage* (UK) no. 12, (Autumn 1985), 40ff. For the codpiece anecdote, see *Selected Works,* 4: *Beyond the Stars; The Memoirs of Sergei Eisenstein,* ed. Richard Taylor, trans. William Powell (London: British Film Institute, 1995), 314–315.

VIKTOR SHKLOVSKY
The Good and Awkward Friend

Nikita Lary

Viktor Shklovsky was Sergei Eisenstein's loyal friend. He celebrated Eisenstein's work in private and in public, and championed him in better times and worse. Eisenstein's senior by five years, Shklovsky did not always or finally grasp the range or direction of his friend's strivings. He liked to instruct, and made no exception for Eisenstein, who he felt could benefit from his advice. During Eisenstein's lifetime and afterwards, he put forward provocative insights into Eisenstein's artistic struggles and achievements. Shklovsky had a knack for locating problems, and a disturbing talent for providing solutions or prescriptions that Eisenstein found unhelpful. Shklovsky's relationship with him is a history of partial understandings, occasional help, and much advocacy. On both sides there was irritation and even exasperation; there was also indebtedness. Shklovsky's relationship with Eisenstein was, moreover, a difficult attempt to keep open a space for dialogue, criticism, and difference in times of growing ideological conformity and political pressure, when both men were exposed to attack.

THE PERSONAL FRIENDSHIP

During the 1920s the two men met with some regularity; later, the intimate discussions between them recurred only intermittently. Shklovsky's letters to Eisenstein reflect the pain of separation.[1] Thus, on July 4, 1930, when Eisenstein was in Hollywood, Shklovsky writes: "Your postcard gave me great joy, since I continually remember you and am always glad when I hear or read of your successes. . . . Soon it will be a year since our pleasant conversations have ceased." On January 22, 1946: "I am very sad I do not see you." A letter dated April 24 the same year was an attempt to find words that would reach Eisenstein after his heart attack, at a time of uncertainty over the fate of *Ivan the Terrible*:

> My dear friend, I am now writing a history of film, that is, I am writing an analysis of its future. I need a conversation with you about your manuscripts.
>
> Remember that I am the only man in the Soviet Union who knows

63. Viktor Shklovsky.

that everything in books is montage. One must write a book as it has been conceived and not attempt to smooth it out. You have been held up not because your book will not come out but because it is developing. You need to write it in the way it is born, and then write a third or fourth volume. Call me if you need a secretary. I won't reduce the book for the sake of order, but I will get it to hold together. . . .

I love you faithfully and tenderly. My heart hurts middlingly.

It is used to hurting.

We can live without happiness and people will envy us.

We see a lot and what we see we ourselves have made.

I love you a lot, Sergei Mikhailovich.

In this letter Shklovsky was offering to collect and salvage Eisenstein's writings on montage and direction. Shklovsky had long valued the theorist more than the artist in Eisenstein, holding that his struggle to understand what he had created was his second, and more important achievement: "That which came to him as easy inspiration, that which was created by the times working through him, that which was done as easily as a child's drawing—he later worked out, consciously and with difficulty."[2]

For the theoretical work, Shklovsky had been able to give Eisenstein much needed support at one critical juncture; the story comes to us from Naum Kleiman. It was New Year's Day, 1933. Eisenstein was in no mood to celebrate: he had returned to Moscow following the abrupt termination of the *Qué viva México!* project; the script "MMM" had been refused; he had no contracts at a time when others were working. Coming home from a party and passing through the artists' compound in which they both lived, Shklovsky noticed lights on in Eisenstein's apartment, knocked at his door and chided him for staying home. Then Shklovsky added: "Remember you are the Khlebnikov of Russian film. Do not neglect your task." Velimir Khlebnikov's Futurist experiments in poetry had come out of his investigations of the roots of words and meaning. Shklovsky's admonition drove Eisenstein to resume his investigation into the principles of direction (*Rezhissura*), which formed the basis for his lectures at VGIK—Vsesoiuznyi gosudarstvennyi institut kinematografii (All-Union State Institute of Film)—and are a major part of his theoretical legacy.

ARTISTIC AND CRITICAL RELATIONS

Shklovsky's early, intimate discussions with Eisenstein continued in more public forums—in newspapers, at conferences, and in artistic committees in studios. Generally, Shklovsky spoke as an equal, and sometimes as a mentor. Uppermost in Shklovsky's artistic discussions with Eisenstein and critical discussions of his work were commonsensical criteria, connected with his preference for prosaic rather than poetic conventions, and with his views on the place and nature of historical truth. This point could be illustrated in relation to any one of Eisenstein's films; here I will focus on two films, *October* and the uncompleted trilogy, *Ivan the Terrible.*

October (1928)

October crystallized Shklovsky's difficulties with the direction of Eisenstein's filmmaking. He was sympathetic to a degree with Eisenstein's self-conscious film language in parts of *October.* However, while sometimes stirred by the montage effects, he was generally resistant to the way the montage acted directly on the feelings even in this, the least "pathetic" of Eisenstein's films. While he was interested in the director's struggles to forge images and symbols out of the materials of reality, he was resistant to his explorations of subjective experience and dream logic. In all this Shklovsky's willingness to assert contrary insights is sometimes a tribute to his openness, while an assertive, dogmatic tone, reinforced by his own filmmaking expertise, sharpens the contradictions between them.

Opposing commonsense observations recur throughout Shklovsky's early discussions of *October*. For instance, he asserted that *October* was a commissioned piece; its theme was an assigned one, which Eisenstein was supposed to illustrate. But art could not be confined to mere illustration, and thus *October* used history as a pretext for artistic explorations.[3] The film had become "a catalog of inventions arranged in some unknown order—perhaps chronological, perhaps alphabetical."[4] Conversely, Shklovsky claimed that all the artistic detail—the statues and dishes—had swamped the Revolution. The film had essentially lacked a script; Shklovsky charged that Eisenstein had sought to supply one *after* the shooting. For Shklovsky, in his preferred role as a writer in film, the script—and with it the *siuzhet* (narrative plot)—was primary. The film was made out of "an accumulation of bits and . . . close-up shots. The piece was overloaded." It was a "prettification of the Revolution." Eisenstein had gone off "alongside the theme" and had wanted to shoot "everything."[5] There was a divergence of artistic means and significance. "Eisenstein created the 'Soviet baroque' style of film. It seemed that the October Revolution was made by statues"; much of *October* resembled "a meeting of statues in a porcelain shop."[6] And, in another way of formulating the complaint, he said: "Beyond the objects one could not see the 'insignificant' event of the October Revolution."[7]

Common sense of course has its claims; in places we readily forget that *October* is in fact about the October Revolution, while elsewhere we may have a sense that the events of the Revolution are being forced into unconvincing or stereotypical models (the French Revolution, for instance). For Eisenstein personally, Shklovsky's aphoristic quips must have been at once obtuse and stinging:

> Your rebellion of the dishes in *October*—that amazing battle against things in the Palace.
> It was hard to fight against those things, against those elephants.
> You conquered Kerensky, you raised the drawbridge, and yet you failed to take the Winter Palace.[8]

Ivan the Terrible (1944, 1946)

Eisenstein's last work in film baffled Shklovsky. In a draft article in 1946, writing about Parts One and Two of the film (probably before the final official denunciation of Part Two), he says bluntly, "I do not like the script of *Ivan the Terrible*. I wrote about it in detail in long assessments but failed to persuade Sergei Mikhailovich."[9]

His assessments were complicated by several factors. First, Shklovsky had an artist's pride of possession; he too had staked out a claim to the subject of

Ivan the Terrible in Yuri Tarich's 1926 film *The Wings of a Serf,* for which he wrote the script. He had, moreover, a realistic view of the treatment appropriate to this subject. Shklovsky's populist view of history was, he felt, exemplarily realized in *Alexander Nevsky* (which he regarded as Eisenstein's best film). Nevertheless, Shklovsky was often an astute critic, and in the draft article his insights into the two Ivan films struggle against his prejudgments:

> In the script there is a lot that is personal in the old sense of this word. Personal, accidental.
>
> . . . The fabric of the *siuzhet,* made out of conspiracies and cups of poison, is not new, but in Part One there is a conflict. There are the people, who come to the Tsar because he, too, is opposed to the boyars, yet he seems inauthentic, almost like something out of the film *Queen Christina,* in which the Swedish queen speaks in the same way with a man of the same kind, a blacksmith. Nonetheless, the film lives because of the pictorial qualities of its shots and its understanding of Russian iconography and the change that Ivan the Terrible brought about in it.
>
> Even though they do not sing the old chants in the film and they crown a younger Ivan the Terrrible, and come to him with a song that is perhaps from the nineteenth century, and the swans have wreathes around their necks—still there are good things in the film. Nonetheless, a big part of it could have been jettisoned.[10]

And:

> If motion does not always succeed in the shots, those points at which motion congeals and is resolved are done with an accurate, new calculation.
>
> Yet history turns out to be only a pretext for the rhythm of motion. Eisenstein's film has a dual heart and dual artistic meaning, and therefore the film is artistically flawed.[11]

Despite the eccentrically perceptive insights, Shklovsky at this point in time could not allow that Eisenstein had found (or was working towards) a poetic rhetoric of film suited to the exploration of tyranny and terror.

Eisenstein had to contend with the "claptrap of Shklovockery" in a direct way (and not just because of the fact of *Wings of the Serf*) during discussions of the script prior to the shooting of the film. At one point in 1940, he was driven to scribble four pages of notes, entitled "A Snarl at Shklovsky."[12] According to Naum Kleiman, who discussed the circumstances of this "Snarl" with Viktor Shklovsky several years later, it was written in response to some objections to the script that Shklovsky raised at a meeting of the Artistic

Council on August 10, 1940. Some of the notes show that Eisenstein was already dealing with the same objections that Shklovsky was later to make in his draft article of 1946, six years later; Eisenstein writes:

> We are creating anew
> 　　　　a legend
> 　　script
> He is used to ∧ superficiality of the "Minin" type
> He understands nothing from the "Ivan and the people" line [13]

The "Minin" reference here is to the film *Minin and Pozharsky* (1939), directed by Pudovkin, for which Shklovsky wrote the script, dealing with a Russian uprising against Polish occupiers in the seventeenth century and stressing the material conditions determining action.

Some of the notes in the "Snarl" show that there was still another quarrel, this one with Shklovsky's claim that Eisenstein's literary sources included Alexandre Dumas' serial novels *The Three Musketeers* and *Twenty Years Later.*

> Why such contempt for musketeers?
> artillerists and defenders of the King (at any rate in Dumas)
> against the Cardinal, etc.
> Why is the death of Porthos parodic? [14]

Shklovsky illuminated this quarrel when many years later he specifically returned to the subject of the script and reviewed his objections to it.[15] The death of Ivan's henchman Malyuta was, Shklovsky said, modeled on that of Porthos. In the completed film, Malyuta is seen as the Tsar's doglike follower and spy who takes the responsibility for ordering needed assassinations, although he is also an *oprichnik.* (His death would have come in the original Part Two of the film, but was eventually reserved for the never-completed Part Three.) Shklovsky specifically said that Malyuta died the death of a titan, but also the death of a serial-novel hero, and that his death looked like another standard "attraction" (the display of extraordinary strength by both Malyuta and Porthos when, for a few moments following an explosion, each prevented a stone wall from collapsing on him). If Shklovsky said anything like this to Eisenstein in 1940, the extent of the latter's irritation is easy to understand, as is his question "Why is the death of Porthos parodic?"

Shklovsky was imposing a simple scheme on the story: he wanted to show the common interest of the Tsar, the *oprichniki,* and the people in breaking the power of the boyars. However, Eisenstein was not afraid of dramatic complexity—we see this in the death of the boyars' figurehead, Vladimir, who is finally a tragic scapegoat. Nor was Eisenstein going to be afraid of complexity in depicting the death of Malyuta, the *oprichnik* and spy, even if his death did have associations with that of Porthos in Dumas's potboiler.

There was still another reason for Eisenstein's defensiveness regarding Dumas' "artillerists." An early version of the script that was discussed at the August 1940 meeting of the Artistic Council included two comic artillerists, Foma and Erema, who botched an explosives charge at the siege of Kazan. Shklovsky did not like these free-floating artillerists and wanted Eisenstein to integrate them more tightly in the plot, showing them as representatives of the people and giving them a role as Chaldeans in the Fiery Furnace scene in Part Two of the film. In his "Snarl" Eisenstein defended his artillerists and indignantly rejected Shklovsky's prescription. In this instance, however, he later tacitly accepted that Shklovsky had a point: these comic figures did not fit into the tragic conception that was emerging, but rather than turn them into spokesmen of the people, his solution was to eliminate them altogether from the script. At least part of his irritation at Shklovsky was due to his sense that Shklovsky was pointing to a problem in the scheme of the film.

AFTER EISENSTEIN'S DEATH

Shklovsky was always Eisenstein's awkward friend, generally loyal and generous, but not always clear-sighted. After Eisenstein's death, Shklovsky continued to champion him.

In the 1960s Shklovsky praised Eisenstein for taking Ivan's achievements as a politician and artist into account in the aesthetics of the film, but still criticized him for not carrying them into the plot. Shklovsky spoke as though he knew in advance what the basic story of Ivan the Terrible had to be, insisting on the populist treatment of the relations of the Tsar and the people. Although initially he had avoided questions impinging on the Terror, now—at the time of the Thaw—he spoke of its importance:

> Ivan the Terrible was hailed in popular song. . . . The people had been looking for their Tsar. Therefore, they welcomed Ivan the Terrible.
>
> One other aspect of Ivan the Terrible is Terror. This was a very critical question at the time the picture was made.[16]

In his 1973 book on Eisenstein, which was first serialized in the journal *Iskusstvo kino* in 1971, Shklovsky was reading history very differently than in 1946 and he was also a more open reader of Eisenstein's film. He did not view the *oprichniki* simply as a progressive force opposed to the boyars. He now spoke of the importance of the experiments with color in Part Two of the film and no longer dismissed the feast of the *oprichniki* as lurid melodrama. Characteristically, the book contains flashes of new insight and rephrasings of old insights. It first appeared at a time when a veil of official disapproval still surrounded the director's work and his legacy had to be defended. It was another, almost final tribute by Shklovsky to the filmmaker who was for him one of the leading representatives of his revolutionary generation.

Notes

1. The first two of these letters are part of a small collection in the Eisenstein archive at RGALI (Russkii gosudarstvennyi arkhiv literatury i iskusstva) [Russian State Archive of Literature and Art], *fond* (holding; hereafter f.) 1923, *opis'* (list; hereafter op.) 1, *delo* (folder; hereafter d.) 2246, while the third is in the Shklovsky archive (f. 562 op. 1, d. 473).

2. "Pesni Abaia" (Songs of Abai, c. 1943–1946), RGALI, f. 562d. 171, *listy* (sheets; hereafter ll, singular l) 12–18, l. 12.

3. "O zakonakh stroeniia fil'm Eizenshteina" (The Laws of Composition in Eisenstein's Films) (part 2), *Sovetskii ekran,* 1929, No. 7, 5. Also in Shklovskii, *Podenshchina* (Day Work) (Leningrad: Izadatel'stvo pisatelei v Leningrade, 1930), 109.

4. *Sovetskii ekran,* 1929, no. 7, 6 (also in *Podenshchina,* 109).

5. "Veshch' Eizenshteina" (Eisenstein's Piece), 1927–28 (in a collection of various people's comments on the script). RGALI, f. 1923 op. 1, d. 273, ll. 1–9, l. 2.

6. "O spetsifike khudozhestvennykh sredstv kino" (On the Specific Nature of Film's Artistic Means), Lecture, Experimental Workshop, Jan. 17, 1929, RGALI f. 562, d. 218, 17 ll., l. 7.

7. "O spetsifike," l. 5.

8. "Konets barokko," *Literaturnaia gazeta,* 1932, No. 32, July 17. Collected in and quoted from the (new) *Gamburgskii schet,* ed. A. Iu. Galushkin and A. P. Chudakov (Moscow: Sovetskii pisatel', 1990), 448–449, 449.

9. "Neudacha sil'nykh (o kinofil'me *Admiral Nakhimov* V. I. Pudovkina i *Ivan Groznyi* S. M. Eizenshteina" (Failure of the Strong: On Pudovkin's Film *Admiral Nakhimov* and on Eisenstein's *Ivan the Terrible*). Draft article, 1946, RGALI, f. 562, d. 173, 12 ll., l. 5.

10. RGALI, d. 173, ll. 5–6.

11. RGALI, d. 173, l. 9.

12. "Ogryz na Shklvskogo" (A Snarl at Shklovsky, 1940). RGALI, f. 1923, op. 1, d. 1350, 4 ll.

13. RGALI, f. 1923, op. 1, d. 1350, l. 3.

14. RGALI, f. 1923, op. 1, d. 1350, l. 1.

15. Viktor Shklovskii, *Eizenshtein* (Moscow: Iskusstvo, 1973), 269.

16. Shklovskii, *Zhili-byli* (Once Upon a Time) (Moscow: Sovetskii pisatel', 1966), 507.

ONCE IN A LIFETIME
Eisenstein and His Associates as Literary Prototypes in a Novel by Lev Kassil

Omry Ronen

S ergei Eisenstein appears, or serves as a prototype of a semifictional character in various literary works, reflecting a broad range of attitudes, from Katherine Ann Porter's short story "Hacienda" to Vladimir Lugovskoy's long poem "Midcentury" (*Seredina veka*).

One such book, well-known to any reader of Soviet children's literature, has been overlooked by film historians and by the biographers of Eisenstein. It is the first part of the novel *Velikoe protivostoianie* (The Great Opposition) by Lev Kassil, serialized in the Moscow journal *Pioner* in 1940 and released as a book in April 1941.[1]

A few words about this historically important Soviet author of juvenile literature. His literary debut was made in Vladimir Mayakovsky's *New Left Front* (*Novyi LEF*) magazine with a fragment of "factual prose" that was to consist of actual entries in a provincial *Gymnasium* conduct book on the eve of the revolution, and other written records and recollections relevant to the downfall of the old school system. Eventually, after the demise of the *Left Front,* Kassil published the entire *Conduct Book, or a Tale of the Wreck of the Old School* in installments in *Pioner,* and in 1930 it appeared in book form, to be followed in 1933 by its sequel, *Shvambrania.* The twin tale combined a documentary nonfictional account of school life during rather fantastic times with a schoolboy's unrestrained daydream, which, at a closer look, would turn out to be a bricolage of everyday items, foreign-sounding commercial trade names or newspaper entries, and reminiscences of children's books, all fitted in "a golden frame" of a child's imagination. By 1940 Kassil had become immensely popular as a writer for children and adolescents, as well as a sports reporter, an author of several film scenarios, and a radio journalist. His books, along with the books of his friend Arkadi Gaidar, were instrumental in shaping both official and unofficial adolescent culture in the USSR, from soccer and interplanetary travel fads to the rather dangerous fashion for secret societies and esoteric games. Unfortunately for his posthumous literary reputation—he died in 1970—all the recent editions of Kassil's books are based on the cruelly disfigured versions which he himself prepared after the anti-cosmopolitan campaign in order to stay in print and to ensure the appearance in 1960, of his selected writings in five volumes.[2] (This act of personal compromise and literary self-immolation is in sharp contrast with the absolutely honest and consistently courageous political behavior of Kassil attested by such memorialists as Kornei Chukovsky.)

Several books by Kassil appeared in English, and the blurb for the English-language version of *The Great Opposition* is worthy of note: "After starring as a heroic serf girl in a movie about Napoleon's invasion of Russia, a typical Moscow girl must readjust to ordinary life."[3] Here too Kassil retains his invariant plot collision: the everyday life of a schoolgirl and, as an extraordinary, magically heroic digression from it, the production of a movie about 1812. A serious critical analysis of *The Great Opposition* was published by a very competent reviewer, who certainly knew much of what there was to know about literature and cinema: Viktor Shklovsky. It appeared unobtrusively, as part of an essay "O trudovom vospitanii" (Education Based on Work) in *Detskaia literatura* 2 (1941) and reprinted in Shklovsky's collected articles on children's literature.[4] The review was a masterpiece of evasiveness. Shklovsky deliberately refused to notice the real-life people and situations which lurked in the historical and biographical subtext of Kassil's book. Indeed, by following what Shklovsky has omitted from his scrutiny, we should be able to identify what is truly relevant to our topic: Eisenstein as a prototype of an idealized literary portrait, and the moral message of the metamorphosis that the prototype undergoes in the hands of a children's writer.

"Kassil is telling a rather touching story," wrote Shklovsky. "There lives a girl Serafima, she has freckles. Her family is poor, the wall paper is faded, even the ceiling is yellowed from the sun, in short, she lives in a bad house, with a bad superintendant. To complete the misery, her father is almost blind. And then a miracle takes place: she is invited to be filmed in a movie."[5] Here Shklovsky omits a vital motif: the father, a war veteran, and the freckled daughter are deeply and tenderly attached to each other (as parents and children invariably are in the books of Kassil, who worshipped his own father).

"The girl acts in a picture made by a great director, who has no shortcomings, except heart disease." Now Shklovsky takes the author to task for selecting the girl for this particular part in the street because she resembles an old engraving showing Ustya Biryukova, a partisan girl of 1812, who had similar sad eyes without eyebrows, a snub nose, and a dimpled chin (but no freckles). "We sometimes do all kinds of silly things at film studios. But no one has ever done such a silly thing as looking for a girl because of her similarity to a portrait."[6] What Shklovsky deliberately overlooked—because Kassil, naturally, did not use Eisenstein's trademark term typage—was how Maksim Strauch had been sent out to look for faces and figures to suit the typage of the *Potemkin* crew in the streets of Odessa, or how Eisenstein himself looked at hundreds of children until he found the unique physiognomy of Vitya Kartashev (whose curious skin blotches due to lack of pigmentation seem to be the girl Sima's freckles in the negative) for the typage that he associated with Stepok, the sacrificial child of *Bezhin Meadow*. Shklovsky interrupted his summary of the book's plot after he dismissed the scenario of the film about Napoleon and the peasants fighting against him as "second-hand." Here he made a digression on the documentary sources of *War and Peace* and went off on a tangent, never mentioning what happened later to the girl and the director.

Yet, before this cut, Shklovsky dropped a remark that would, ironically, turn out to be true, albeit in a sense quite different from what Shklovsky had intended: "Lev Kassil has an astrological attitude toward life, and he understands it himself." Shklovsky was referring to the allegorical meaning of the book's title: Alexander Rasshchepey the film director was an amateur astronomer, and the "opposition" in question, between Mars and Earth, which he had been looking forward to, would come July 23, 1939, after his death, but the figurative meaning of it was the necessity of being morally prepared for every "great opposition," every decisive turning point in one's personal destiny. Shklovsky interpreted this as opportunistic: predicting and catching a "once in a lifetime" chance. Actually, Kassil proved to be an astrologer in a quite different sense: in retrospect, he seems to have predicted the destiny of Eisenstein.

What personal features of Rasshchepey, admittedly a so-called "heroid" (Marietta Chudakova's term), a ligature of several prototypes, make him resemble Eisenstein, rather than any other director? His passionate intellectual interests and polymath knowledge; his appearance (stocky, with an amusing face, and thinning, halo-like hair); the Native American curios in his apartment. The tragic background of his wife, a former actress who had to abandon her profession, somewhat resembles that of Pera Atasheva. The associates of Rasshchepey, the lanky assistant director (*rezhisser-laborant*) Ardanov, nicknamed "Labardan" (*Ardanov / laborant* ≈ *Tisse / assistent*), and the cameraman Pavlusha appear to be a combination of Dmitri Vasiliev, Eisenstein's assistant director in *Alexander Nevsky,* and the great cameraman Eduard Tisse, with a partial crossing-over of functions. As for the great director himself, another of his prototypes, besides Eisenstein, was, as is noted in the commentaries to Volume II of Kassil's selected writings (1965), the celebrated actor of the Vakhtangov Theatre, Boris Shchukin (who, similar to Rasshchepey in the book, acted the part of Lenin in the movies and died, also like Rasshchepey, holding an open book in his hands, in 1939). The third prototype was the journalist and Kassil's co-author in the early thirties, Aleksei Garri (repressed in 1938, he survived the camps and returned after Stalin's death). The fates of Shchukin and of Garri, as well as the predicament of *Bezhin Meadow,* appear to determine the destiny of Kassil's protagonist in his novel. After the success of his film about 1812, envious enemies of Rasshchepey drew him into political trouble, using Sima Krupitsyna, the girl actress, as their tool. To save Rasshchepey, she wrote a letter to Stalin, and even though Rasshchepey himself prevents it from being delivered to the Kremlin, justice triumphs, the slanderer is fired, Rasshchepey is vindicated and makes another film, entitled *Melkii sluzhashchii* (*A Petty Official*), in which one can perceive, with some effort, what little we know about "MMM." The film is released only after Rasshchepey's death from a heart attack.

What of the films described in *The Great Opposition?* The title of the film is *Muzhik serdityi* (*An Angry Moujik,* a reference both to Napoleon, who was so nicknamed by Russian peasants, and to the angered people, who fought him as partisans). These people, not Ustya, are, as Rasshchepey rather angrily points out to her, the main character of the film. Kassil seems obliquely to contrast here the ideological attitude of *Alexander Nevsky,* in which an auto-cratic prince has replaced the people as the central subject of history, with the attitudes of *The Battleship Potemkin, October,* and, apparently, *Bezhin Meadow,* which is reflected in Kassil's summary of *An Angry Moujik* less obviously, but more poignantly, than *Alexander Nevsky*'s patriotic theme is.

The principal motifs that link Rasshchepey's film and Eisenstein's lost masterpiece involve the peasant-child "activist" and the predicament of peas-antry, with the entire "Pavlik-Morozov" and "peasantry's-salvation-through-sacrifice" myth turned inside out. The child Ustya survives and fights the invaders, though her friend Stepan (a namesake of Eisenstein's Stepok), who has hoped that Napoleon would emancipate the serfs, is shot by the French as a suspected incendiary during the scene of the Moscow fire, which parallels the burning of the farm in *Bezhin Meadow.* The ending of *An Angry Moujik* contains a powerfully ironic rejoinder to the message of Eisenstein's passion play: after the defeat of Napoleon, Ustya returns home from Denis Davydov's partisan detachment. She is a serf actress again, and again her master slaps her face. The final sequence shows her lying face down on the grass. Above her, on the dark sky, a caption slowly fades in. It is a quotation from Alexander the First's victory manifesto: "The peasants, our faithful people, may they re-ceive their reward from God."

The antagonist of Rasshchepey in the book is a certain Prichalin, who is a combination of two main prototypes, Ivan Pyrev and Grigori Alexandrov. Physically he resembles neither of the two tall, athletic former disciples of Eisenstein: Kassil has been very cautious, making Prichalin look like a fat, slimy frog. Serafima's summary of his film, however, bears an unmistakable likeness to the kind of fare that the two made popular in the late thirties:

"I had to play the part of a little collective farm girl who has grown a carrot of miraculous size and made her *kolkhoz* famous, and at the same time won the first place playing the piano at an amateur talent contest [Aleksandrov's

Jolly Fellows and *Volga-Volga*]. The greatest scientists of the country and journalists come to take a look at my extraordinary carrot [in Aleksandrov's *Svetlyi put'* (*A Luminous Path*)—for which Stalin himself offered the title—a new weaving technique, introduced by a young girl worker, is inspected and admired by famous specialists]. The chairman of the collective farm falls in love with a young journalist [*mutatis mutandis;* Pyrev's *The Rich Bride* and *Tractor Drivers*]. At that time, two saboteurs arrive, posing as guests. They plan villainously to kill the chairman; I overhear them and at the very last moment save the chairman. The saboteurs are arrested [Pyrev's *Party Card* and, alas, Eisenstein's own *Bezhin Meadow*]. I play the march from *Aida* at an amateur concert, the chairman embraces his bride, and that is the end of the picture."[7]

The title of the film, *Muzyka, tush!* (*Music, Play a Flourish!*), and some details of the plot hint also at Alexander Ivanovsky and Herbert Rappaport's *A Musical Story,* the star of which, the popular idol Lemeshev, is ironically mentioned in Kassil's book as "the famous Soshnikov" (*lemekh* meaning "ploughshare," and *sokha,* "wooden plough").

None of the directors and scenario authors lampooned in Kassil's book seemed to recognize their films in this set of cliches. Indeed, it is hard to imagine that a figure as powerful as Grigori Alexandrov, who had just been appointed the art director of Mosfilm, would have condescended to notice a book for high school children.

Yet apparently he did, because he eventually responded to it, not without a certain flair, in his first postwar picture, which Jay Leyda would later helplessly but aptly describe as "a strange comedy": the curiously metacinematic film *Vesna* (*Spring*), which was awarded with a special prize for the most original plot in Venice in 1947.

In a sense, the film used Kassil's children's book to answer the remarks of Shklovsky and, obliquely and more generally, the old, suppressed, and almost dead—but not forgotten—challenge of Eisenstein's intellectual cinema. In the beginning of the picture, an assistant director is chasing women in the streets of Moscow. Actually, he is looking for for someone to play the part of a famous woman scholar from "the Solar Institute" (the idea was supposed to have been suggested by the physicist Kapitsa, although Rasshchepey's great scholarly interest was astronomy). A photograph of the woman is used to find its double, an operetta singer and dancer, as if to belie Shklovsky's criticism of Kassil. The doubles briefly exchange roles: the astrophysicist takes a screen test, and the singer takes her part in the institute. The point is supposed to be that intellectuality and "funny tales" are not mutually exclusive (here Nikolai Gogol's words about the world that would fall asleep unless it was told such tales are quoted). It turns out that a scientist, previously nicknamed a "dry shark," *sushenaia akula,* can sing and dance and even fall in love, while an actress can become involved in intellectual matters. Happy end.

In several episodes the director (played by Nikolai Cherkasov, Eisenstein's Alexander Nevsky and Ivan the Terrible, whom Alexandrov had taken over from his politically demolished and dying former teacher), shows the new actress his studio. Kassil's situations here are openly borrowed—as, for example, when two Gogols appear together, arguing with each other, just as in *The Great Opposition* the girl encountered seven Napoleons at once.

In brief sequences, Alexandrov caricatures images out of *October* (a ritual mask from the "gods" sequence), makes an Alexander Nevsky-like medieval Russian hero swing his sword over the heads of *Swan Lake* ballerinas, and has a Kolychev-like boyar out of *Ivan the Terrible* catch the shawl cast aside by Lyubov Orlova during her song and dance routine.

Spring produced a mixed reaction and apparently was not an official success. Indeed, it still reflected the mood of the last war years and the brief post-war thaw, prior to the Central Committee decrees of 1946, and would not fit the canon of high Stalinism, which rejected even *The Jolly Fellows* because it glorified jazz. As an early example of auto-metadescriptive cinema, it certainly deserves attention: one can discern quotations from this picture in Fellini.

What then was the significance of *The Great Opposition,* this obscure and forgotten minor episode in the history of the reception of Eisenstein—particularly the reaction to what was known about *Bezhin Meadow*? (We have no evidence that Kassil saw the picture, but he surely read Alexander Rzheshevsky's published scenario.) It has to do, as far as one can judge, with a vital but little-studied mechanism which sometimes develops in modern totalitarian or other cultures dominated by ideology.

Flaubert suggested in 1852 that while old literature had to put the sweet coating of art over a bitter moral message, to please modern French taste one must hide a grain of poetry in the tasteless powder of common morality and common ideas. Such was the price art—especially cinema—had to pay in totalitarian democracies. To survive as art, art would produce powerful moral toxins. However, even in absolutist totalitarian societies, culture also generated antidotes to these toxins. During the era of socialist realism such a resistance—an opposition to the perverse and inhuman message conveyed by some of the most advanced art, or to the sugary kitsch that pretended to be art—was, for several reasons, found mainly in the books for children. *The Great Opposition,* certainly not a great work of art, is important as a representative specimen of such antitoxic literature.

Notes

1. Lev Kassil', *Velikoe protivostoianie* (The Great Opposition) (Moscow: Izdatel'stvo Detskoi literatury, 1941).

2. Lev Kassil', *Sobranie sochinenii v piati tomakh* (Collected Works in Five Volumes) (Moscow: Detskaia literatura, 1965–1966).

3. For instance, *The Land of Shvambrania* was published by Viking Press in 1934, and the *The Great Opposition,* entitled *Once in a Lifetime,* by Doubleday in 1970.

4. Viktor Shklovskii, *Staroe i novoe* (The Old and the New) (Moscow: Detskaia literatura 1966), 58–71.

5. Shklovskii, *Staroe i novoe,* 68.

6. Ibid., 68–69.

7. Lev Kassil', *Sobranie sochinenii v piati tomakh* (Collected Works in Five Volumes) 2 (Moscow: Detskaia literatura, 1987), 164.

EISENSTEIN
Barometer of the Thaw

Josephine Woll

When Sergei Eisenstein died in 1948, eighteen months after the Soviet Central Committee directed its venom at cinema, the fraught cultural atmosphere precluded much response.[1] *Iskusstvo kino,* then appearing as a bimonthly journal, published an obituary written by director Mikhail Romm. Romm trod a precariously narrow path in order to pay tribute to a man he had consistently championed. He concentrated on Eisenstein's early work, which had never fallen seriously afoul of party dogma; he described Eisenstein's omnivorous curiosity and knowledge, attributes acknowledged even by Eisenstein's ill-wishers. Calling Eisenstein a "brilliant child" (*genial'nyi rebenok*), a characterization he later applied to one of the physicist heroes of his 1961 film, *Nine Days of a Year,* Romm focused on Eisenstein's personal and political radicalism.[2]

Romm adroitly skirted unpleasant issues, thereby managing to avoid outright lies. He made only one reference to the controversies that had bedeviled Eisenstein and plagued his work: "He sometimes made mistakes." (Eisenstein himself would doubtless have—indeed, had, in public—concurred.) However, Romm continued, "if not all of his pictures were equally accomplished, all were exceptionally significant." In his theoretical work, too, Eisenstein sometimes erred, "but overcame his mistakes with stubborn, heroic work."[3]

Compare this obituary, however cautiously phrased, with the tone and language of an article that appeared a few months later. Its author, Ilya Vaisfeld, was a film "theorist" who had been teaching at VGIK—Vsesoiuznyi gosudarstvennyi institut kinematografii (All-Union State Institute of Film)—since 1946 and who later edited a multivolume book series, *Problems of Film Drama* (*Voprosy kinodramaturgii*). He reviewed a history of Soviet cinema, Nikolai Lebedev's *Ocherk istorii kino SSSR,* in which Lebedev discussed Eisenstein's early work in the context of the aesthetics of the Proletkult, Alexander Bogdanov's revolutionary-era organization to promote "proletarian culture."

By 1948, the Proletkult and Bogdanov were officially anathematized. Hence Vaisfeld indignantly complained that the author ignored the Party's critical role in helping Eisenstein overcome the "pernicious influence" of the Proletkult. The critic objected primarily to Lebedev's distortions of cultural history: Lebedev's errors, rather than Eisenstein's. *Strike* and *The Battleship Potemkin* are realizations of communist ideals, not—as Lebedev mistakenly proclaimed—Proletkultist aesthetic theories; Lebedev's assertion that *Strike* demonstrated the influence of "Bogdanovite–Proletkult collectivist ideology" was, in Vaisfeld's view, "a calumny of historical truth."

According to Vaisfeld, Lebedev discussed Eisenstein's work as if it had no relationship whatever to Party policies on art, nor to political and economic circumstances—as if, in other words, Eisenstein's films were simply the external manifestation of the artist's autonomous ideas.[4] Whereas in fact the Bolshevik Party is "obviously" the "healthy, progressive, life-affirming source" of Eisenstein's aesthetic stance and the reason he attained such creative heights.[5]

Compared with Vaisfeld's formulaic rhetoric, Romm's obituary, however incomplete, seems remarkably forthright, if not actually courageous. The two pieces reflect the distinction that consistently differentiated the responses of filmmakers to Eisenstein from those of critics, a gap that continued long after his death. During the Thaw, and particularly after Khrushchev's "Secret Speech" at the Twentieth Party Congress in 1956, many national ideas and ideals were subjected to scrutiny and revision. But film critics remained skittish about Eisenstein. His personal history, his theoretical writings, the films and the treatment of the films by the cultural establishment during Eisenstein's lifetime crept into critical discourse very gradually, and piecemeal.

Filmmakers of the Thaw, on the other hand, consistently contemplated Eisenstein's ideas and studied his movies. In Mikhail Kalatozov's *The Cranes Are Flying* (1957), for instance, the famous *provody* (seeing-off) scene, when volunteers depart for war, recalls Eisenstein's contrapuntal montage. Its interplay of multiple dynamic elements recalls Eisenstein's concept of "mise-en-cadre," in which both back- and foreground are clearly in focus and play a simultaneous and coordinated role in the drama. Romm himself made effective use of mise-en-cadre in *Nine Days of a Year* (1962), where he also emulated Eisenstein's ability to present events simultaneously on epic, dramatic and lyric planes.

Marlen Khutsiev, whose first feature film *Spring on Zarechnaya Street* (1956, codirected with Feliks Mironer) introduced to the Soviet screen key hallmarks of the early Thaw, learned a good deal from Eisenstein despite their aesthetic and political differences.[6] The May Day Parade in his 1961 *Ilich's Gate,* for instance, creates a polyphony of general and particular action, sound and image, conceptual conclusion and emotional shock that owes much to Eisenstein. So does the poetry reading sequence in the same film, with its synesthesia of hearing movement and seeing sound, its dynamization of documentary events to produce emotional effects, and its dramatic handling of time.

Thus Eisenstein cast a long shadow. Yet between 1948 and 1953 *Iskusstvo kino* neither referred to nor published any of Eisenstein's work. This is not surprising: as Naum Kleiman commented in a 1987 lecture at Britain's National Film Theatre, none of Eisenstein's films after *The Battleship Potemkin* could safely be mentioned while Stalin lived; besides, for decades cultural mandarins had dismissed Eisenstein's theoretical work as the meanderings of a "muddler."[7]

The silence continued until 1955. Filmmakers and film critics alike reacted slowly to the possibility of change in the wake of Stalin's death. For more than a year after he died the minutes of weekly sessions at Mosfilm, the Soviet Union's largest studio, record methodical—indeed plodding—discussions of each week's activities. Anonymous bureaucrats, none of them involved in any creative aspect of filmmaking, counted off the number of meters shot for each film, pleased when the advance plan was overfulfilled, dismayed when the figures were low. No lively exchanges—no substantive debates at all—can be found in the documents of 1953 or indeed 1954. In January 1954, ten months after Stalin's death, *Iskusstvo kino*'s editorial begins with references to Lenin's "genius" and Stalin's "greatness."[8] Eleven months later its December editorial continued to hail Stalin as Lenin's great heir.[9]

Despite contradictory demands and entrenched resistance, the film industry began, tentatively and creakily, to change. Plans were made and slowly implemented to resurrect the republican studios, quiescent during the last years of Stalin's life. The Party advocated an increase in film production, and, in the sixth Five Year Plan (announced in 1955 for the years 1956 through 1960), substantial sums were allocated for the repair and expansion of studio facilities and equipment, the enlargement of existing movie theaters, and the construction of new ones. Filmmakers replaced bureaucrats in key positions. Ivan Pyrev, whose directing career began in the late 1930s, became head of Mosfilm in October, 1954.

Eisenstein reappeared to the cinema public in late 1955, when *Iskusstvo kino* marked twin anniversaries: the thirtieth anniversary of the opening of *Potemkin,* and the fiftieth anniversary of the 1905 revolution. The journal published a group of pieces about the making of the film and its reception. In no way anticipating the bombshell Khrushchev was to explode only two months later at the Twentieth Party Congress, the articles ploughed overworked soil. Semyon Freylikh, who had taught at VGIK since the year of Eisenstein's death and who often wrote about film for *Iskusstvo kino,* repeated Party-sanctified clichés about the film, labeling it a "poem of the revolution" and "the expression of an era," and praising Eisenstein's foregrounding of "the people."[10] He identified several faulty critical approaches to *Potemkin,* such as an exaggerated emphasis on its indisputable stylistic innovation. Too much attention to composition, rhythm, and montage obscures the true source of this art, he wrote: "life itself."[11]

Freylikh squeezed *Potemkin* into a socialist realist straitjacket, insisting on the importance of the individual. "In the interests of an accurate assessment of *Potemkin*'s artistic and ideological content," he wrote, the notion of typage, of characters as symbols or signs, must be dismissed as superficial. On the contrary: the Bolshevik Vakulinchuk, the officer Gilyarovsky, the doctor and captain and other characters are "images of living people." [12]

When he turned to Eisenstein's cinematic theories, Freylikh attempted to balance Eisenstein's "errors" with his contributions to Soviet cinema. He opted for a curious compromise. According to Freylikh, Eisenstein consistently strove for the "generalized detail," as much in his 1937 debacle, *Bezhin Meadow*, as in the overwhelmingly successful *Potemkin*. In the earlier film, however, the director understood those details "properly," hence the film's triumph; in *Bezhin Meadow* he did not, hence its failure. (Freylikh omits all reference to objective circumstances.) [13] "The result was a hypertrophied generalization, psychological abstraction, the biblical theme of sacrificial offering. As Eisenstein later understood, his error . . . was one of world-view, a superficial apprehension of the profound meaning of the class struggle during the collectivization years." [14]

The celebration of *Potemkin* continued in 1956 with an article by Sergei Yutkevich. Yutkevich, a cautious man though one deeply committed to cinema, had assailed Eisenstein at the Cinema Conference in January 1935. [15] In January 1956, Yutkevich felt obliged to correct foreign critics who persisted in distorting the importance of *Potemkin* by emphasizing its artistic innovations to the exclusion of its political and social significance. Although Yutkevich was arguing a valid point, he chose to use the highly confrontational language characteristic of Soviet Cold War rhetoric, relying on phrases like "class struggle," "primitive" morphological analysis and "the procrustean bed of prefabricated bourgeois concepts." [16] He chided Paul Rotha, who had cited *Potemkin* and *The Cabinet of Dr. Caligari* as outstanding examples of original filmmaking. How, Yutkevich wondered, could *Caligari*—the epitome of decadence and testimony to the moribund society that produced it—be compared to *Potemkin*, its diametric opposite in every way? [17]

Although socialist realism as a doctrine postdated *Potemkin* by nearly a decade, Yutkevich swaddled Eisenstein's film in its sheets. Just as Soviet literary theorists bent the great fiction of the nineteenth century into precursors of Soviet ideology, Yutkevich considered *Potemkin* a triumph of socialist realism *avant le lettre*, toward which Eisenstein—and other artists responsive to "party, people and nation"—were moving inexorably.

In Yutkevich's tautology, *Potemkin* is a socialist realist work because socialist realist art is the greatest art. A critic can therefore legitimately apply the norms of socialist realism to it, which first of all means querying *Potemkin*'s accuracy in portraying revolutionary reality. From that point of view, Eisenstein made only two historical errors. Yutkevich fully justifies the first, the film's specious conclusion. Indeed, the rapturous ending exemplified socialist realism inasmuch as it resisted simple "naturalistic canons"—that is, factual truth—in favor of the "essential" truth of events, the ultimate victory of 1917. He was more critical of Eisenstein's neglect of the Party: "Had the film portrayed with greater amplitude the leading role of the Communist Party and its individual representatives . . . it would indubitably have connected more clearly and tellingly (*znachitel'no shire, iarche i interesnee*) the sailors' spontaneous uprising with the organized workers' movement."[18]

One month later, in February 1956, Khrushchev delivered his Secret Speech, with its startling indictment of the Cult of Personality. The artistic world, including cinema, responded quickly. By late 1956 *Iskusstvo kino* referred to Eisenstein far less guardedly. In November, for instance, Leonid Kozlov contributed an essay about the syncretic nature of film to an ongoing series about cinema art. Kozlov repeatedly cited Eisenstein's views on montage, on cinematic space, on the time–space entity that viewers perceive as a second space and that is created by the sequence of shots linked by montage. Kozlov grappled with Eisenstein's aesthetic concepts in an unapologetic and straightforward fashion, without historical captioning and with no obligatory references to ideological rectitude or, conversely, to ideological errors.[19]

A month later *Iskusstvo kino* ran a review of two relatively new books, collections of essays by Eisenstein and Vsevolod Pudovkin respectively. The reviewer, Semyon Ginzburg, candidly acknowledged that although cinephiles in other countries had been able to read these articles in translations, Soviet readers had not had access to them. As a result, the young generation of filmmakers knew very little about the "artistic quest" of these two great directors, knowledge essential to a proper understanding of the films of the 1930s. "For many years our critics, if they recalled these masters, did so in order to condemn their errors," Ginzburg noted. He mentioned two dissertations, written in 1941, that "slandered" the best film work of the 1920s; VGIK did not accept them, but they were successfully defended at other institutions.[20]

Cinema "dogmatists," who used the *Bezhin Meadow* affair as a club with which to beat Eisenstein, had artificially separated his creative work from his theoretical writings, and refused even to include the latter in the canonic texts of Soviet film theory. Anathematizing Eisenstein as a leader of the "antirealistic" tradition, they had ignored everything except his mistakes and missteps. "Now our cinematic theory, together with all forms of artistic interpretation, is freeing itself of those dogmatic and mummifying wrappings," Ginzburg wrote.[21]

Rostislav Yurenev was the editor of the Eisenstein collection under review. Yurenev belonged to an influential and powerful clique of cinema specialists. After graduating from VGIK in 1936, he began a publishing and teaching career that lasted for more than four decades. The director Grigori Kozintsev, who recorded his mordant observations of the film world in a diary he kept for many years, despised what he considered to be Yurenev's expropriation and manipulation of the director and his legacy. In a November 1957 entry, Kozintsev described Yurenev as being "like the Lilliputian who remembered Gulliver as being not all that tall, no taller really than I am." In a final acid comment, Kozintsev wrote: "Some people work on something. Others work over somebody. Yurenev works over Eisenstein."[22]

In his introduction to the 1956 edition, Yurenev tried to present Eisenstein as activist citizen, as the first film artist to understand *partiinost* (Party spirit) and as an artistic progenitor of socialist realism. He selected essays that exemplified Eisenstein's search for aesthetic means of conveying ideological messages. Ginzburg openly criticized Yurenev's bias: he faulted Yurenev for detailing Eisenstein's theoretical mistakes of the 1920s, while ignoring the achievements of those same years. Eisenstein was groping for answers to problems; those answers may now be obvious "to any student," but at that time, given the relatively primitive level of Marxist–Leninist aesthetics, they were unclear. Yurenev's description, Ginzburg objected, would give less informed readers the false impression that Eisenstein wrote meaningful theoretical work only in the late 1930s.[23]

While remaining within the parameters of socialist realism, Ginzburg offered an eloquent and more nuanced defense of Eisenstein. The artist made mistakes because he took risks and continually experimented, bequeathing a powerful legacy to subsequent generations. "His artistic ideas and creative principles are visible in literally every single film made nowadays by thoughtful directors of a realistic orientation (*realisticheski mysliashchie*)."[24]

Ginzburg's review, written some time before its publication in the December 1956 issue of *Iskusstvo kino,* was one of the last reasonably objective assessments of Eisenstein for another two years. By the end of the year, domestic political warfare in the wake of the Hungarian revolt threatened the hopes engendered by the Twentieth Party Congress. The media disseminated few details of the intramural tussles between Khrushchev and his chief rivals, Malenkov, Kaganovich, and Molotov, which ended in June 1957 when Khrushchev secured the virtually unanimous support of the Central Committee. Still, ripples reached the arts.

Khrushchev spelled out the new rules when he met with writers and artists in March and again in May of 1957. Ominously, he compared the Soviet literary "opposition" with the Petőfi circle, those Hungarian writers who had played a major role in the events leading up to the revolt. The warning was patent, particularly since all major arts publications reprinted in part or in full Khrushchev's speeches to writers and artists, and editors everywhere recapitulated the main points: artistic obedience to the Party line, conformity to socialist realist patterns, state promotion of ideological orthodoxy.

Anxiety mounted as infractions engendered consequences. The State Institute for Cinematography imposed disciplinary measures, including expulsion, on students who had been too outspoken in their judgments and who had published a *samizdat* (underground) journal.[25] Khrushchev denounced Vladimir Dudintsev, author of the influential Thaw novel *Not by Bread Alone,* for "slandering" Soviet society. He censured the editors of the literary almanac *Literaturnaia Moskva,* Margarita Aliger and Venyamin Kaverin, who had been less than submissive in admitting their ideological errors. He authorized the creation of a Union of Writers of the Russian Federated Republic as a conservative counterweight to the liberal and outspoken Moscow writers' organization. A planned volume of Marina Tsvetaeva's poetry with an introduction by Ilya Ehrenburg was postponed indefinitely.[26]

The Kremlin urged or coerced leading figures in the arts into retreating from the candor many of them had warmly embraced after the Twentieth Party Congress. At meetings held in the spring of 1957, for instance, senior members of the Writers' Union pressured their colleagues to recant and apologize. Stalin had died only a few years earlier, and the entrenched fear that lingered after twenty-five years of Stalinism outweighed the nascent and fragile trust Khrushchev kindled. Most complied.

Liberals and conservatives dueled on the pages of periodicals, among them *Iskusstvo kino.* In the first months of 1957 editorials continued to condemn the detrimental consequences of the "spirit of administrative timidity and deference toward the opinions of officials from the Ministry of Culture or the Writers' Union." Sergei Yutkevich mildly proposed "not condemning films but discussing them" (*ne osuzhdat', a obsuzhdat'*). He also recommended discovering "what our friends and enemies abroad are doing—without a two-year delay."[27] Elsewhere he noted that "the fear of critical comments anticipated from somewhere 'above' . . . is a tradition that should stop immediately."[28]

Increasingly, however, such pleas for boldness, innovation, and the elimination of bureaucratism and red tape coexisted with intensified Cold War rhetoric and confrontational responses to foreign criticism. Because of the politically driven chill, for much of 1957 and indeed most of 1958 as well, lackluster articles, pedestrian memoirs, archival documents, and verbatim citations from or paraphrases of Party directives dominated all major arts periodicals. The upcoming fortieth anniversary of the Bolshevik Revolution contributed to the pressure.

As a result, Eisenstein receded into the shadows. *Iskusstvo kino* published very little by or about him in 1957: a piece on *Qué viva México!* by Eisenstein's colleagues on the project, Grigori Alexandrov and Eduard Tisse, concerning the prospects for completing the project; and the manuscript of *México*'s libretto, written by Eisenstein after returning from Mexico, along with some comments and drawings. In 1958, *Iskusstvo kino*'s editors recalled the twin anniversaries of Eisenstein's birth and death, respectively sixty and ten years earlier, in a muted fashion. They gave the job to Kozintsev, Eisenstein's close friend.

Like Mikhail Romm ten years earlier, Kozintsev managed to avoid lying by electing to write about Eisenstein's eclectic taste and omnivorous curiosity, and by couching his praise of Eisenstein in officially palatable language. In spurning the "cinema of stars," he wrote, Eisenstein sometimes lost sight of individual humanity and threw the baby out with the bath water. But, he was quick to add, if one doesn't drain dirty water, the baby gets mangy and scabby. Eisenstein drained the "dirty water" from cinema; after him, much seemed false and trivial.[29]

For Kozintsev, Eisenstein's greatest achievement was the restoration of "scale" to dramatic art on screen, a quality theater had forfeited centuries before. Eisenstein informed his films with an Aristotelian sense of fear and awe, creating art that disturbed as well as entertained. His films attested to cinema's capacity to depict the combat for justice, not simply rivalries for love — national tragedy, rather than banal passions.

Kozintsev shaped his remarks shortly after releasing his own film about the "combat for justice," *Don Quixote,* in which Nikolai Cherkasov's Quixote confronts rulers who are as arbitrary as they are incomprehensibly cruel. Like Eisenstein, Kozintsev tried to exploit the medium to present Quixote's quest for justice on a large scale. His version of Cervantes' novel is a bleak assertion of the human need for faith, however illusory, in those who do not in the least merit it — rulers and populace alike.[30]

The change of atmosphere empowered by the Thaw, however enfeebled in the late 1950s, is patent in Kozintsev's discussion of Eisenstein's cinematic style. Without feeling obliged to justify his approach, Kozintsev engaged in an essentially formalist analysis (without using the word) of Eisenstein's visuality — the way images permeated his consciousness as dynamic lines, in colors, costumes, make-up, masks, compositional graphics, and the like. Kozintsev considered Eisenstein's overwhelmingly visual imagination the preeminent characteristic of his work.

Apart from Kozintsev's tribute, and some reportage on the screening of Jay Leyda's *Qué viva México!* footage in Paris at the First International Congress of Film Historians, *Iskusstvo kino* neglected Eisenstein until its last issue of 1958. Such silence may have seemed safely noncommittal in the disorienting cacophony of "thaw" and "freeze" signals that characterized the Soviet political and cultural world throughout 1958 and 1959. In May 1958, for instance, the Central Committee revoked one of the bleakest symbols of Zhdanovism, the 1948 denunciation of "formalism" in music. *Iskusstvo kino* reprinted the resolution on the first page of its July 1958 issue. A few months later, however, the "Pasternak affair," initiated with mild mutterings when *Doctor Zhivago* was published abroad in November 1957, blew up into a hurricane when the

Nobel Committee awarded Pasternak the Prize for Literature on October 25, 1958. Venomous censure of Pasternak in major press organs such as *Literaturnaia gazeta* and *Pravda* forced him to renounce the prize and plead with Khrushchev not to force him into emigration.

The film world felt the chill when Ivan Pyrev was replaced at Mosfilm by Leonid Antonov, an undistinguished director and an old Party hack who had held the post from 1946 to 1949, abysmal years for Soviet filmmaking. Khrushchev's pronouncements on "catching up with" and "overtaking" the United States referred primarily to agriculture and industry, but Ministry of Culture bureaucrats and doctrinaire film critics were quick to see their relevance to the arts as well. One scriptwriter reminded his colleagues that they were workers in no essential way different from stokers or miners. If the Seven Year Plan called for one thousand films, then scenarists should produce triple that number of scripts to ensure meeting the quota. Balzac, he thought, had the right idea: the French colossus went to bed at 6 P.M. in order to wake at midnight and work.[31]

That perhaps explains the official response to the release of *Ivan the Terrible* Part 2 on September 1, 1958. *Iskusstvo kino* did devote three articles of its December issue to the film, but omitted all reference to the circumstances of its production and offered no explanation whatever for its belated opening. One article dealt with Eisenstein's concept of Russian history, the second discussed the film's visual style, the third treated Prokofiev's collaboration with Eisenstein and the film's musical score.

The historian, Alexander Danilov, sought an uneasy balance in his article, "With the Eyes of an Artist." On the one hand, he wrote, Eisenstein avoided the blunder of merely "illustrating" history: *illustrativnost'*, and films guilty of it, were favorite targets of critics during the early years of the Thaw. On the other hand, Danilov continued, Eisenstein did commit errors in his portrayals of the *oprichnina* and of Ivan himself. Danilov cites one example of why the film is unsuitable as a high school history textbook: *Ivan* minimizes the violence perpetrated by the *oprichnina* against the working people, who had nothing to do with boyar conspiracies or with traitors abetting the designs of foreign states.

To be sure, Eisenstein was hardly intending to create a textbook. Acknowledging *Ivan*'s status as a work of imagination, Danilov commended Eisenstein for avoiding two traps, two false if opposing images of Ivan—one of Ivan as "father and benefactor" of his people, the other of Ivan as a psychologically unbalanced despot who exterminated tens of thousands of people on a whim, and who impoverished and damaged the population of an enormous empire by his tyranny. No Soviet artist could in good conscience depict Ivan—arch-representative of the exploiting class—with unalloyed praise. Nevertheless, Ivan and his entourage had a positive impact on Russia's history: they fought against dangerously reactionary traditions that fostered an alliance between enemies of governmental unity within and outside of the country. For Danilov, Eisenstein's Ivan, a talented and strong-willed man who manages to resolve complex political problems and whose cruelty matches in both kind and degree the norms of his epoch, approximates the truth.[32]

Natalya Sokolova, in "The Painting of a Film," categorized *Ivan* as a "romantic tragedy" that remained within the bounds of socialist realism. She compared Eisenstein's artistic strategy in representing historical figures and events not to the realistic depictions of artists like Ilya Repin, but to paintings by Viktor Vasnetsov: an art based on legends, folklore, and frescoes, not fact. She regarded Eisenstein's Ivan as a passionate, purposeful, active, and intelligent propagandist for the idea of statism, which explains both the power of the film and its one-sidedness, a characteristic of romantic tragedy. Since everyday detail and rounded characterization would have softened and obscured the fundamental features of what Eisenstein wanted to portray, he eliminated them.[33]

Sokolova confined her analysis of Eisenstein's visual style mainly to generalities, although in discussing the dramatic potential of "mute" images, she astutely observed that Eisenstein transforms the figures in the frescoes into eloquent witnesses to and even participants in the battle occurring before their eyes. While ignoring Eisenstein's fascination with Japanese art and drama, she noted his artistry in using make-up to emphasize certain lines, forms of the skull, and so on.[34]

Given the disquieting climate of 1959 and 1960, the release of *Ivan* had relatively little resonance in the world of film criticism, although filmmakers paid close attention. Even Andrei Tarkovsky, who consistently polemicized with Eisenstein and who disliked what he considered Eisenstein's "despotic" attitude toward his audience and his "cold intellectualizing" of the image, admired *Ivan*.[35] As scholars recognize, *Andrei Rublev* (1966) betrays an Eisensteinian influence. "In the raid on Vladimir, as in the bell-casting, [Tarkovsky] combines the intimate with the expansive, a sense of exact detail and individual activity with a comprehensive overview that seems to take as its model the 'Odessa Steps' sequence of *Potemkin* or the attack on Kazan in *Ivan the Terrible* Part 1."[36]

Over the next few years Eisenstein's writing appeared sporadically in the pages of *Iskusstvo kino.* In March 1959, editor Ludmila Pogozheva prefaced a group of Eisenstein's sketches for *Boris Godunov* with historical background on his planned biofilm of Pushkin. A year later she published the first chapter of what was to have been Eisenstein's book on John Ford, in which he discusses Ford's *Young Mr. Lincoln* (1939) as the film he would have most liked to make because of its "harmonious integration of discrete elements."[37]

By 1960, *Iskusstvo kino* no longer felt the need to excuse, explain, or rationalize its publications of Eisenstein's work, whether theoretical or creative. Neither did it feel obligated either to derogate his "erroneous" ideas or to offset and defuse them by bracketing them with compensatory virtues.

Thus Eisenstein rejoined the critical discourse on cinema once again, his wayward genius reincorporated into the zig-zag pattern characteristic of the Thaw years. Thanks in large part to the dedication and labor of Naum Kleiman, Leonid Kozlov, and other critics and scholars, the first volume of Eisenstein's *Selected Works* appeared, finally, in 1964. By the seventieth anniversary of Eisenstein's birth, Yutkevich could refer openly to "pygmies" who had tried to censor and "spoil" Eisenstein's films, and could call for further investigation of his legacy as scholar, teacher, and historian as well as filmmaker. Thirty years later, in his centenary year, the investigation continues.

Notes

1. Eisenstein's case was not unique. When Georgii Vasiliev died in June 1946, the obituaries omitted all mention of his last "wasted" years, when he made no films because the Ministry of Culture kept changing its directives. Jay Leyda, *Kino: A History of the Russian and Soviet Film* (Princeton: Princeton University Press, 1960), 390.

2. Mikhail Romm, "Pamiati Sergeia Mikhailovicha Eizenshteina" (Eisenstein: In Memoriam) *Iskusstvo kino,* 1948, no. 2, 3.

3. Ibid., 4.

4. I. Vaisfeld, "O knige N. Lebedeva *Ocherk istorii kino SSSR*" (On N. Lebedev's Book, *An Outline of the History of Soviet Cinema*) *Iskusstvo kino,* 1948, no. 5, 22.

5. Ibid., 23.

6. See Josephine Woll, *Real Images: Soviet Cinema and the Thaw* (London: I. B. Tauris and New York: St. Martin's, 2000), 45–50.

7. Cited by Ian Christie, "Rediscovering Eisenstein," in *Rediscovering Eisenstein,* ed. Ian Christie and Richard Taylor (London and New York: Routledge, 1993), 14.

8. "Za dal'neishii rost, za razvitie vsekh zhanrov kinoiskusstva!" (For Further Growth, For Further Development of All Genres of Film Art) *Iskusstvo kino,* 1954, no. 1, 3.

9. "I. V. Stalin—velikii prodolzhatel' dela Lenina" (Stalin: The Great Successor to Lenin's Cause) *Iskusstvo kino,* 1954, no. 12.

10. Semen Freilakh, "Velikoe proizvedenie realisticheskogo iskusstva" (A Great Work of Realistic Art), *Iskusstvo kino,* 1955, no. 12, 45.

11. Ibid., 47.

12. Ibid., 49–50.

13. For a description of these circumstances, see Peter Kenez, *Cinema and Soviet Society, 1917–1953* (Cambridge: Cambridge University Press, 1992), 148–153, and his essay in this volume.

14. Freilakh, "Velikoe proizvedenie," 52.

15. Much later, Iutkevich characterized that conference as "an almighty battle

between the generations" and felt no need to apologize for his own role: "As we were good friends of Eisenstein's we started with him," he recalled. *Cahiers du Cinéma* 125 (1961).

16. Sergei Iutkevich, "Mirovoe znachenie *Bronenostsa Potemkina*" (The World-Wide Significance of *Battleship Potemkin*) *Iskusstvo kino,* 1956, no. 1, 50–54 *passim.*

17. Ibid., 50.

18. Ibid., 53.

19. Leonid Kozlov, "O sintetichnosti kinoiskusstva" (On the Syncretic Nature of Film Art) *Iskusstvo kino,* 1956, no. 11.

20. Semen Ginzburg, "O teoreticheskom nasledii S. Eizenshteina i V. Pudovkina" (On the Theoretical Legacy of Eisenstein and Pudovkin), *Iskusstvo kino,* 1956, no. 12, 82. The Pudovkin collection had appeared in 1955, the Eisenstein in 1956.

21. Ibid., 83.

22. Grigorii Kozintsev, "Iz rabochikh tetradei raznykh let" (From Working Notebooks of Various Years) *Iskusstvo kino,* 1992, no. 8, 70–71.

23. Ginzburg, "O teoreticheskom nasledii," 85.

24. Ibid., 86.

25. Irina Shilova, . . . *I moe kino* (. . . And My Cinema) (Moscow: NIIK/Kinovedcheskie zapiski, 1993), 46.

26. Joshua Rubenstein, *Tangled Loyalties: The Life and Times of Ilya Ehrenburg* (New York: Basic Books, 1996), 302.

27. Sergei Iutkevich, "Razgovor o kinokritike, o zhurnale" (A Conversation about Film Critics and about the Journal), *Iskusstvo kino,* 1957, no. 1, 3.

28. Sergei Iutkevich, "Dorogu talantam!: studiia molodykh" (Make Way for the Talented Ones!: A Young People's Workshop), *Iskusstvo kino,* 1957, no. 1, 89.

29. Grigorii Kozintsev, "Sergei Eizenshtein: zametki o cheloveke i khudozhnike" (Eisenstein: Notes on the Man and the Artist), *Iskusstvo kino,* 1958, no. 1, 70.

30. See Andrei Shemiakin, "Dialog s literaturoi, ili opasnye sviazi" (A Dialogue with Literature, or Dangerous Liaisons), *Kinematograf ottepeli* (Moscow: Materik, 1996), 135–143, on Shakespeare and Cervantes on the Soviet screen.

31. Aleksandr Shtein, "Razgovor s druz'iami" (A Conversation with Friends), *Iskusstvo kino,* 1959, no. 3, 7–8.

32. A. Danilov, "Glazami khudozhnika" (Through the Artist's Eyes), *Iskusstvo kino,* 1958, no. 12, 87–90.

33. Natalia Sokolova, "Zhivopis' fil'ma" (The Painting of a Film), *Iskusstvo kino,* 1958, no. 12, 94.

34. Ibid., 95.

35. Andrei Tarkovsky, *Sculpting in Time: Reflections on the Cinema,* trans. Kitty Hunter-Blair (London: Bodley Head, 1986), 183, 118.

36. Vida T. Johnson and Graham Petrie, *The Films of Andrei Tarkovsky: A Visual Fugue* (Bloomington: Indiana University Press, 1994), 93–94.

37. Sergei Eisenstein, "Mister Linkol'n mistera Forda" (Mister Ford's Mister Lincoln), *Iskusstvo kino,* 1960, no. 4, 135.

IN THE NAME OF THE FATHER
The Eisenstein Connection in Films by Tarkovsky and Askoldov

Andrew Barratt

It is curiously appropriate that the centenary of Eisenstein's birth coincides with an era in Russian cultural life which is in its own unique way akin to the age of anxiety which bred the explosion of creative energy that characterized the country in the first thirty years of this century. Eisenstein's own part in that artistic revolution is so well known that it requires no elaboration. Indeed, his status as one of the world's greatest film directors has been for so long a matter of certainty that it has become customary in recent years to damn him with faint praise. The point has been well made by Ian Christie in his introduction to *Rediscovering Eisenstein,* a work which captures perfectly both in its conception and execution the task facing students of Eisenstein in the post-Soviet world.[1] The contributors to that volume have performed a valuable service, adding significantly to the body of our knowledge while identifying the enormous task of scholarly retrieval which still remains to be done.

The present essay plays no part in this larger venture. On the contrary, rather than attempting to rescue Eisenstein from his decidedly ambiguous reputation as a "Soviet" filmmaker, it is concerned with that very image of "Eisenstein" that so much recent work has sought to demystify. It does so by examining how Eisenstein's work has been appropriated and recirculated in two of the most outstanding films of the post-Stalin era: Andrei Tarkovsky's *Andrei Rublev* and Alexander Askoldov's *Commissar.* My approach is signaled by the title "In the Name of the Father," which pays homage both to Freud and to the critic whose classic study of literary influence has converted Freudian ideas into a powerful—albeit highly controversial—analytical model. I refer, of course, to Harold Bloom's *The Anxiety of Influence.*[2] While I shall not be pursuing a rigorously neo-Bloomian reading of these films, it seems to me that Bloom's ideas acquire an interesting resonance in the context of post-Stalinist culture. This is because the years since Stalin's death—up to the present day—have been concerned, quite crucially and explicitly, with the work of coming to terms with a bad paternity, which has been associated either with Stalin himself as the primal father figure or with those many others—*pace* Yevgeni Yevtushenko's "Heirs of Stalin"—who have been deemed guilty by association. These are the very circumstances which have ensured a place for Eisenstein in the post–Stalinist rogues' gallery. As the "father" of Soviet film, a man whose work both contributed to the creation of a foundation myth for the new Russian state (*Strike; The Battleship Potemkin*) and—more notoriously—to Stalin's campaign of self-justification to the Russian people (*Alexander Nevsky; Ivan the Terrible,* Part I), it is quite obvious in retrospect that he could not fail to inspire those acts of filial rebellion which Bloom advanced as the motive force of poetic tradition.

In order to comprehend the intensity of that filial rebellion, we need look no further than the work in which it receives perhaps its most vitriolic expression—Alexander Solzhenitsyn's *One Day in the Life of Ivan Denisovich.* Such is Solzhenitsyn's concern to vilify Eisenstein that he devotes not one, but two, passages to a discussion of the director's work:

"No, my dear fellow," Tsezar was saying in a gentle, casual way. "If one is to be objective one must acknowledge that Eisenstein is a genius. *Ivan the Terrible,* isn't that a work of genius? The dance of the masked *oprichniki!* The scene in the cathedral!"

"Ham," said X 123 angrily, arresting his spoon before his lips. "It's all so arty there's no art left in it. Spice and poppyseed instead of everyday bread and butter! And then, that vile political idea—the justification of personal tyranny. A mockery of the memory of three generations of Russian intelligentsia."

He ate as if his lips were made of wood. The kasha would do him no good.

"But what other interpretation would be allowed?"

"Allowed? Ugh! Then don't call him a genius! Call him an arse-licker, obeying a vile dog's order. Geniuses don't adjust their interpretations to suit the taste of tyrants!"

Tsezar was arguing with the captain:

"For instance, when he hung his pince-nez on the ship's rigging. D'you remember?"

"Hm, yes," the captain said as he smoked.

"Or the perambulator on the steps. Bumping down and down."

"Yes . . . But the scenes on board are somewhat artificial."

"Well, you see, we've been spoiled by modern camera technique."

"And the maggots in the meat, they crawl about like earthworms. Surely they weren't that size?"

"What do you expect of the cinema? You can't show them smaller."

"Well, if they were to bring that meat here to our camp instead of the fish they're feeding us on and dumped it straight into the cauldron we'd be only too . . ."

The prisoners howled.[3]

This is quintessential Solzhenitsyn, an uncompromising polemic all the more remarkable for its incongruity within a narrative which ostensibly records the mental life of an uneducated peasant. And yet, for all their extremism, these two passages are typical of the post–Stalinist critique of Eisenstein. Most striking of all, perhaps, is the straightforward association of the director with Soviet power and the concomitant reduction of his films to the status of mere propaganda. No less interesting, however, is the tendency to conflate vastly different periods of Eisenstein's career—different both in terms of film style and political significance—into a singular vision of the director as the servant of a dictatorial regime. Finally, there is the cunning movement by which the political critique is assimilated into an aesthetic rejection of Eisenstein's modernist film-making practice. In the remainder of this essay I shall suggest that, albeit in a manner far more subtle and interesting than Solzhenitsyn's direct attack, Tarkovsky and Askoldov contribute to the same broad regime of interrogating the legacy of Eisenstein.

THE TOWER AND THE WINDOW: EISENSTEIN AND TARKOVSKY

The subject of Eisenstein and Tarkovsky is not a new one, yet it has not, to my knowledge, been studied in any real depth. The consensus view, supported by the director's own scattered references to his illustrious precursor, is that Tarkovsky conceived of his own practice as a conscious reaction against a great tradition in which Eisenstein occupied a central place.[4] Certainly, Tarkovsky's celebrated notion of filmmaking as "sculpting in time," with its emphasis on sequence and a reliance on the long take, can perhaps be most readily understood as a radical alternative to the Soviet montage movement with which Eisenstein is inevitably associated. And Tarkovsky's desire to create in his films an impression of an almost tactile physical universe stands in contradistinction to the deliberate artificiality and self-conscious theatricality of Eisenstein's work. In what follows, I would like to identify two moments which suggest a specific connection between the two directors, a connection which will extend the general comparison in a particularly productive manner.

The first moment occurs in the prologue to Tarkovsky's *Andrei Rublev*. The scene is a vast rural landscape and the action concerns the efforts of a peasant inventor by the name of Yefim to launch a primitive hot air balloon. Despite the violent attempt by a superstitious mob to prevent the flight, Yefim succeeds in getting the balloon airborne, a flight which begins with his exhilaration as he looks down on the earth below, but quickly ends in disaster as the balloon loses height and crashes close to a river. On a first viewing, this is a stunning yet puzzling introduction to a film which is no less stunning and puzzling in its overall effect. It is puzzling, of course, because the events it portrays stand in no direct relationship to the main body of a film which concerns incidents from the life of the medieval icon painter Andrei Rublev. It is only after some reflection that the function of this introductory sequence begins to make sense as a powerful initial encounter with a filmic world which is both intensely physical and inescapably brutal. It is an elemental world in which the archetypal components—fire, air, earth, and water—combine in what is effectively a cinematic assault upon the senses. It is also a world in which political and ideological dissension is the rule, rather than the exception: witness the representatives of the church who are instrumental in inciting the mob to violence.

As a number of commentators have suggested, the prologue to *Andrei Rublev* serves also as a self-sufficient parable which provides a model for understanding the larger story that follows. In his daring act, Yefim may be seen as a latter-day Icarus. This is, however, not a case of human arrogance justly punished by the gods. For what Yefim achieves is a momentary act of transcendence, a brief vision of his world from a perspective which liberates him from the quotidian and validates the death which follows so quickly in its wake. In the same way, the sheer beauty of Andrei Rublev's art, specifically the magnificent icon of the Trinity which figures so memorably at the close of the film, serves as a compensation for the cruelty and suffering he witnesses and experiences. There is no escape from the brutal forces which rule Russian life, but human creativity proves in the end a force no less powerful—perhaps even more powerful, given the dire conditions by which it is constantly threatened.

But where does Eisenstein figure in all of this? Let us consider one of his most famous sequences, the conclusion of *Ivan the Terrible,* Part I.[5] Reduced to a condition of despair by the combination of personal tragedy and the prospect of national catastrophe, Ivan has retired to a monastery in the company of a small band of loyal followers, including the infamous Malyuta Skuratov. But this is just the prelude to the film's uplifting conclusion: the people of Moscow, in a seemingly endless religious procession, come to the tsar beseeching him to return to the city and rule over them. All of this converts only too readily—and this, let us remember, was the burden of Solzhenitsyn's complaint—into a convenient Stalinist myth, in which the strong ruler draws strength and legitimacy from the loyal Russian people in his battle against his foes, both internal and external. This is a defense of patriarchy which finds direct and archetypically "Russian" religious expression in the choral appeal by the people to Ivan as "Our Father." There is also a recognizably Stalinist subtext here. As he awaits, and then accepts, the obeisance of the common folk of Russia, Ivan is attended by a faithful son, in the person of the younger Basmanov. The relationship is one which transcends natural parentage: indeed, earlier in the film, Basmanov *père* had delivered his son into Ivan's service as a mark of his devotion. Thus, in true socialist realist fashion, ideology supersedes biology and the surrogate father–son bond reinforces the central Stalinist myth of Soviet society as a "great family" with a "good father" at its head.[6]

When viewed together, the sequences from the two films suggest several points for comparison. In each case, a solitary individual occupies a church building in the midst of a vast Russian landscape. Most striking of all is the moment in each film where that individual looks through a window onto a scene dominated by representatives of the ordinary Russian people. The broad similarity of the two scenes serves above all to emphasize the differences between them. The static, pictorial world of *Ivan the Terrible* with its fixed camera positions and slow pace contrasts with the restless energy of *Andrei Rublev*. Tarkovsky's mobile camera follows the action, enabling the viewer to explore the three-dimensionality of space. There is also a subjectivity here which is quite alien to Eisenstein's film. Whereas Eisenstein, in what is perhaps the most famous expressionist moment in *Ivan the Terrible*, has Ivan's head slowly enter the frame which already contains the image of the approaching procession, Tarkovsky has the camera follow the direction of Yefim's anxious gaze onto the angry crowd below. This subjectivity characterizes what follows, when Yefim undertakes his hazardous aerial journey.

These observations lead toward a rather simple reading of the opening of *Andrei Rublev* as a countertext to the ending of *Ivan the Terrible*, Part I. Instead of Eisenstein's ritualistic representation of a Russia defined by the desire of the people to be governed by a powerful individual leader, Tarkovsky offers a compellingly naturalistic vision of that same country as a place where the daring creative individual stands in opposition to the anarchic presence of the mob. Whereas Eisenstein's film ends with the promise of "romance" in the form of a permanent alliance of the ruler and the ruled, Tarkovsky's begins with a celebration of the inevitably transient moment of ecstasy as the rebellious spirit soars above the realm of brute contingency below.

In his comparison of the two films, Marc Le Fanu suggests the deliberate operation of a historiographical consciousness on the part of the younger filmmaker. Tarkovsky, so his argument goes, deliberately chooses for the subject of his film a period of history *earlier* than the unification of the Russian state under Ivan so as to emphasize its greater proximity to a primeval spirit of "Russianness."[7] This is a persuasive notion, not least because it suggests

Tarkovsky's proximity in this, his most "Russian" film, to the spirit of the contemporaneous Village Prose movement and its search for an authentic national identity.[8] Ultimately, however, I would suggest that it is the mythopoeic
dimension of *Andrei Rublev* which is the most important. If, in *Ivan the Terrible*, Eisenstein draws on the traditional paternalistic myth of leader and
people which for so long sustained the Russian monarchy, Tarkovsky sub-
scribes to an alternative conception with its own venerable (albeit shorter),
history. Tarkovsky's representation of Andrei Rublev and his precursor Yefim
as creative individuals doomed to self-sacrifice places his film within a cor-
pus of Soviet works featuring artist-martyrs—Mikhail Bulgakov's *Master and
Margarita* and Boris Pasternak's *Doctor Zhivago* being the most celebrated
examples.[9]

In the end, however, the comparison of Tarkovsky and Eisenstein points
toward a fundamental similarity between the competing myths that their
films promote. For both films turn on the opposition between the *suffering*
individual—in this respect Eisenstein's Ivan is no different than Tarkovsky's
Rublev—and the undifferentiated mass which is the Russian people.[10] More
interesting still, perhaps, is the way in which each director appeals via the
film's imagery to a recognizably Russian religiosity: in each case, it is a church
building which is the site of mythopoeia.

THE GUN CARRIAGE, THE EYEGLASSES, AND THE BRIDGE: EISENSTEIN AND ASKOLDOV

In the preceding discussion I have been careful not to suggest any deliberate intention on Tarkovsky's part to engage in a polemic with Eisenstein. Although one might reasonably suppose that Tarkovsky could not possibly have
embarked upon his historical epic without the example of Eisenstein firmly
implanted in his consciousness, it would be foolish to insist that the opening
sequence of *Andrei Rublev* was deliberately designed as a riposte to the conclusion of *Ivan the Terrible*, Part I. If, as I have argued, this is to be viewed as an
example of cultural dialogue, this is a dialogue which most probably operates
outside the narrow sphere of conscious intention.

My second example, Askoldov's 1967 film *Commissar*, is altogether more
self-reflexive and far more obviously transgressive than *Andrei Rublev*—hence
the twenty-year ban on its release.[11] A film about the Russian Civil War, it
touches quite directly on a crucial theme: the founding of the Soviet Union,
constituting a radical challenge to the canonical version of modern history so
memorably embodied in the socialist realist classic *Chapaev*, the 1934 film by
Georgi and Sergei Vasiliev. In his engagement with that heroic foundation
myth, Askoldov challenges not only conventional Soviet historiography but

also the very iconology of Bolshevism. This is where Eisenstein enters the scene.

Commissar tells the story of Klavdiya Vavilova. The commissar who supplies the film with its title, Vavilova discovers that she has become pregnant. As it is by now far too late for her to have an abortion, she is billeted with a poor Jewish family, the Magaziniks. Thus begins a journey of discovery in which the experience of maternity and the encounter with Jewishness are inextricably linked. In due course, Vavilova bears a son. But history cannot be kept at bay. The town where the Magaziniks live is recaptured by the White forces and the film ends as Vavilova puts on her commissar's uniform again and returns to the fray, leaving her son in the care of the Jewish family which had taken her in.

Such a bald summary can do little justice to Askoldov's remarkable film, yet it provides the narrative context against which we can explore one of its most memorable sequences—the delirium which Vavilova experiences during the birth of her son. A superb example of cinematic surrealism, it comprises three parts, which punctuate the realistic scenes in the film's "present" depicting the progress of Vavilova's labor. The first of these is a desert-like location, which features, first, a figure in a blindfold who staggers through this harsh environment calling out for help. In the main action which follows, Vavilova is seen as part of a team of soldiers who struggle in vain to shift a gun carriage up a sandbank. The episode ends with soldiers and their horses running down to a river where they assuage their thirst. The second part takes place in the same desert location, where Vavilova and her lover Kirill embrace alongside the gun carriage. The third part begins by showing the death of Kirill, who is shot by a machine-gunner as he endeavors to cross a bridge on

64. *Commissar:* Klavdiya Vavilova.

horseback, a scene which blends seamlessly into a long sequence of running horses, ending again with the drinking of water.

In its length and cinematic intensity, Vavilova's delirium creates a powerful effect. It operates on a number of levels. In purely narrative terms, this sequence provides an answer to the question which Vavilova staunchly deflected when it was asked by the crude commanding officer to whom she had to confess to her pregnancy. Now we know that the father of her child was a fellow servant of the Bolshevik cause. (His name, Kirill, is revealed only towards the very end of the film, when Vavilova bestows the same name upon her child before leaving to rejoin the Red Army.) On the representational level, this is subjective cinema pure and simple. As the film cuts between Vavilova's physical experience of childbirth and the images which invade her consciousness, we are constantly made aware of the connection between the somatic and the mental worlds of the heroine. This is done most obviously through the use of diegetic sound, which crosses the boundary between reality and delirium, and the mirroring of actions, specifically the drinking of water by the men and horses in the first delirium sequence, then by Vavilova as she rests between bouts of exertion. In this way, it is a simple matter to convert major parts of the delirium into a metaphor of the birth itself. Thus, the efforts to shift the heavy gun carriage in the first sequence equate with Vavilova's attempts to engage the child for delivery, and the final scene with the riderless horses running free parallels the moment of delivery itself. These parallels point to one further connection between the world of the mind and the world of the body, and it is perhaps the most interesting of all. For it is the death of the father in delirium which appears to trigger the birth of the son in the realm of the film's present.

It is at a third level that Vavilova's delirium becomes of direct importance to our present concern. As she slips into half-consciousness, the heroine is given access to a state where the symbolic takes precedence over the mimetic. Askoldov, of course, makes no effort to disguise this fact; on the contrary, he employs a film language so extravagantly symbolic as to verge on the parodic. In short, it is a quintessentially postmodern moment, even though the term (like Askoldov's film itself) was to wait two decades before it came into circulation in Russia.

When viewed in this way, many of the details from the delirium yield to that sort of archetypal reading which we associate with the traditional style of dream interpretation as practiced by Freud and Jung. The spare, dry world of the Civil War recasts the historical event as an existential battle between human beings and the elements. It is an environment which seems all the more forbidding due to the contrast with the dark, wet, dense—and "Jewish"—world in which Vavilova gives birth to her child. The desert metaphor is amplified by other self-evidently symbolic details: the row of men "harvesting" the desert sands with their scythes like latter-day clones of the grim reaper; the machine gun which severs the heads of wheat from their stalks; the abandoned plough. The subversiveness of this moment can hardly be exaggerated; no longer the site of a historic struggle between Reds and Whites, the Russian Civil war is here defined above all as the place where no food will grow. Askoldov thus reminds us that for many citizens of the new Soviet state, the price of the Bolshevik victory was a disastrous famine. No less subversive is the first sequence with the gun carriage, with its distinct echo of the myth of Sisyphus. As for the scene between Vavilova and Kirill, this is as remarkable for its lack of eroticism as it is for its almost preposterous phallic symbolism, which equates the man's sexual power as progenitor with the barrel of the cannon caressed by the woman. Again, this is a moment which acquires a greater resonance against the context of the frame narrative. A poignant image earlier in the film depicted the Magazinik children as the machinery of war was brought into their town, their naked bodies half-obscured by the military transport to reveal only their legs and genitalia.

Considered in terms of a conventional mythology of the Civil War as a conflict between the forces of good Reds and evil Whites (witness *Chapaev*), Vavilova's delirium is nothing short of an outrage. But this is not all. The archetypal symbolism of this segment is rendered all the more potent by the manner of its articulation. Throughout this sequence Askoldov draws on a repertoire of readily identifiable images from Soviet film and other visual arts. First among the images here are quotations from Eisenstein. The opening sequence which shows the Red Army troops putting their weight behind the wheel of the gun carriage mimics a moment early in the "To Kazan" section of *Ivan the Terrible,* Part I.[12] The death of Kirill in the third delirium sequence is even more striking, as it conflates a number of recognizable Eisensteinian quotations. The slow-motion photography reminds us of those famous slow-motion shots on the Odessa steps in *Potemkin.* The connection is reinforced by the shot which focuses on Kirill's eyeglasses—an unmistakable echo of what is perhaps the most memorable motif in Eisenstein's early classic, in particular the image of the doctor's pince-nez suspended in the rigging. And Kirill's posture as his body hangs over the side of the bridge invokes both the death of Vakulinchuk, the revolutionary hero of *Potemkin*—the famous shot of his body hanging across the ropes—and the equally celebrated moment in *October,* when the horse dangles from the bridge over the Neva.

These allusions to Eisenstein sit alongside other subversive gestures against the iconology of Bolshevism. The figure of the blind man, for example, recalls Aleksei Radakov's famous anti-illiteracy poster of 1920 "The Illiterate Man is Blind." And that same man's haunting cry of "Help!" repeats the title of Dmitri Moor's 1921 poster encouraging Soviet citizens to offer aid to the victims of the famine. (The poster, which depicts an emaciated peasant with his arms raised above his head, also features a broken stem of wheat, which provides a visual point of contact with the delirium sequence in *Commissar*.)[13] Finally, Kirill's leather outfit alludes to the widespread contemporary practice of referring to the Bolsheviks as "leather jackets."[14]

In every case, Askoldov endows these traditional images with a radically different significance. The Civil War becomes a place where blind men are lost in the desert; where men cry out hopelessly for help; where the classic leather jacket of Bolshevism is almost ludicrously inappropriate; where the weaponry of war condemns individuals to fruitless exertion. Thus Vavilova's words— "Don't torment me" and "I will not survive"—while they refer to the business of childbirth, may be understood equally to describe her reaction to the delirium which accompanies it. As a staunch supporter of the Bolshevik order, Vavilova cannot fail to be "tormented" by a such a vision. (One can readily imagine a similar mood among the censors when they viewed these scenes in the late 1960s.)

There is one last aspect of this crucial scene which requires comment. Vavilova ostensibly experiences this delirium during the Civil War period. Yet the realm of the imaginary into which her vision grants access is self-evidently anachronistic, and nowhere more so than in the allusions to the films of Eisenstein, which were, of course, made *after* the historical period ostensibly represented in the film. As a consequence, Vavilova's hallucinatory experience, although it draws upon the experiences of the recent past, nevertheless acquires the status of a revelation.[15] As it turns out, this is only the first of two such moments in the film. The second occurs after what is beyond any doubt the darkest passage in the film, both literally and metaphorically. This is the scene where Vavilova and the Magazinik family take shelter in a basement as the White forces bombard the town. In a sequence which calls to mind another Eisensteinian tour de force—the dance of the masked *oprichniki* in *Ivan the Terrible,* Part II—Vavilova witnesses a dance performed by the Magazinik family, a dance which is transformed first into a frighteningly distorted personal vision, a sort of *danse macabre,* then into a horrifying premonition of the Holocaust.

These Eisensteinian moments in *Commissar* represent, therefore, an iconoclastic anticipation of the Soviet mythopoeic project. For Vavilova, as a committed revolutionary, they serve as an experience which exposes her Bolshevik idealism to a doubt so potentially corrosive that she is moved to leave it behind, just as she abandons the child who is the biological product of her engagement with the Revolution.

Despite her fears to the contrary, Vavilova does survive the twin experience of childbirth and revelatory delirium. She bears a son and for a brief time enjoys the fulfillment of motherhood. However, her destiny lies elsewhere: the arrival of the Whites in the town serves as a call to duty. But, as I have just suggested, Vavilova's return to active service has a significance which extends far beyond the literal. As she hurries up the cobbled street to join her comrades, Vavilova passes from the "real" world of the urban settlement to re-enter the realm of the symbolic. Once again, the transition is marked not only by the cinematography but also by the operation of a final allusion to a classic Soviet film. For this final sequence, Askoldov draws quite unmistakably on the finale of Pudovkin's *Mother* so as to create a disturbing countermyth. Instead of the heroic act of revolutionary self-sacrifice which brings Vsevolod Pudovkin's film to its end, Askoldov situates *his* mother and her comrades in yet another desolate landscape which bodes ill for the direction of human history.

This is to suggest, then, that *Mother* serves as a sort of metatrope which comprehends the entire allusive practice of *Commissar*. To be sure, it is this connection which brings into sharp focus the disjunction which was so powerfully represented in the delirium sequence. A disjunction between the biological realm in which Vavilova gives birth to her child and the symbolic realm where history resides, it also displays a rift between the place of the living mother and that of the dead father. Finally—and it is here that one discerns the most likely reason for the twenty-year ban on the film's release—this is an opposition between the world of the Jews and the world of the Russians. In this most shocking of ideas, Askoldov offers an antidote to the entire tradition of a revolutionary iconology which was predicated on the belief that art could provide an ideal model for emulation. Askoldov, by contrast, offers a version of Russian life afflicted by a fatal gulf between existential reality and the revolutionary mythology by means of which that country's leaders had sought to envision its place in modern history.

Commissar and *Andrei Rublev* were produced within a year of one another, yet they could hardly be more different in their aesthetic realization. And if, as I have suggested, each film can be understood (at least in part) in terms of a dialogue with Eisenstein, we can see that that dialogue operates in equally different ways. In the case of Tarkovsky, the prologue to *Andrei Rublev* might be described as that kind of revision which Bloom terms "Daemonization," which involves "a movement towards a personalized Counter-Sublime, in reaction to the precursor's Sublime."[16] The key word in all this is "revision," for what distinguishes the relationship between Tarkovsky and Eisenstein, I believe, is the younger man's dedication to the same mythopoeic impulse as his illustrious predecessor. This impulse is most fully expressed in one of the film's most memorable sequences: the raising of the bell constructed by Boriska and his helpers. Not only does this scene bring *Andrei Rublev* to a stunning climax, it also functions as a reprise of the belfry scene from the prologue. The main components here are the same—the tower, the landscape, the scurrying figures of the common Russian folk—as are the filmic qualities, especially the dramatic use of camera angles. In this way—and this is a supreme irony—Tarkovsky effectively ends his film by *reenacting* the conclusion of *Ivan the Terrible,* Part I. As in Eisenstein's film, this sequence emphasizes the significance of the tower as a site which enables the unification of the Russian people. No less important is the event which follows, bringing Tarkovsky's film to its narrative closure: the union of Andrei Rublev and Boriska, who appear, like Eisenstein's Ivan and Basmanov *fils,* in the guise of surrogate father and son. Of course, Tarkovsky invests these "Eisensteinian" moments with new significance. The raising of the bell represents what is, at best, only a momentary respite for the Russian people from the horrors of their historical existence; as Andrei puts it, this is a "holiday (*prazdnik*) for the people." Certainly, there is no hint here of glorification of the ruler or his entourage. By the same token, the bonding of "father" and "son" is less an act of homage and obedience than a moment which restores Andrei as a human being and a Russian, thereby allowing him to fulfill his destiny as an artist. The mythopoesis could not be further removed from that of Eisenstein, yet mythopoesis it most certainly is.

Askoldov, by contrast, displays a thoroughgoing iconoclasm which we can now identify as a characteristic gesture of the postmodern spirit in Russia. This is to say that, while *Andrei Rublev* remains one of the supreme achievements of post–Stalinist culture, it is *Commissar* which takes us closer to an understanding of the predicament facing Russian art today.[17] In his radical gesture against Eisenstein and other makers of the Soviet Union's "great tradition," Askoldov offers no alternative. Instead, he leaves his audience to consider the revolutionary impulse of Bolshevism as a force which opened a fatal gulf between utopian dream and the brute experience of history. In the end, this is a most disheartening vision, especially for a contemporary Russian audience which might be looking for a language from which to construct a new sense of national identity.

Notes

1. Ian Christie and Richard Taylor, eds., *Rediscovering Eisenstein* (London and New York: Routledge, 1993).

2. Harold Bloom, *The Anxiety of Influence* (New York: Oxford University Press, 1973).

3. Alexander Solzhenitsyn, *One Day in the Life of Ivan Denisovich,* translated by Ralph Parker (Harmondsworth: Penguin, 1963), 70–71, 98.

4. Tarkovsky's most famous comments on Eisenstein can be found in Andrei Tarkovsky, *Sculpting in Time,* trans. Kitty Hunter-Blair (London: Faber & Faber, 1986), 118–119, 183–184. See also Andrei Tarkovsky, *Time within Time,* trans. Kitty Hunter-Blair (London: Faber & Faber, 1994), 356.

5. Mark Le Fanu, *The Cinema of Andrei Tarkovksy* (London: British Film Institute, 1987), 50, briefly suggests the possibility of a fruitful comparison of *Andrei Rublev* and Eisenstein's *Ivan.*

6. On the "big family" and its significance for Stalinist culture, see Katerina Clark, *The Soviet Novel. History as Ritual* (Chicago: University of Chicago Press, 1981), 114–135.

7. Le Fanu, *The Cinema of Andrei Tarkovksy,* 36.

8. See Kathleen Parthé, *Russian Village Prose* (Princeton: Princeton University Press, 1992).

9. See the classic study by Rufus Mathewson, Jr., *The Positive Hero in Russian Literature,* 2nd ed. (Stanford: Stanford University Press, 1975).

10. This argument could easily be extended to trace the source of this notion to the ideas of the Russian Populists, particularly the notorious concept of the "hero" and the "crowd." See Richard Wortman, *The Crisis of Russian Populism* (Cambridge: Cambridge University Press, 1967).

11. For a brief discussion of Askoldov's film, see: Andrew Horton and Michael Brashinsky, *The Zero Hour: Glasnost and Soviet Cinema in Transition* (Princeton: Princeton University Press, 1992), 35–39.

12. This was something of a favorite motif in Eisenstein's work. There is a similar shot in *October.*

13. These posters are reproduced, respectively, in *Tradition and Revolution in Russian Art: Leningrad in Manchester* (Manchester: Cornerhouse Publications in association with the Olympic Festival, 1990), 125; and J. P. Nettl, *The Soviet Achievement* (London: Thames and Hudson, 1967), 78 (fig. 46).

14. See Mathewson, *Positive Hero.*

15. I can think of no similar example from other films. There is, however, a remarkably close counterpart to this sequence in Mikhail Bulgakov's novel *The White Guard,* in which the central character, Aleksei Turbin, experiences a prophetic dream which weaves past and future in a surrealistic fantasy.

16. Bloom, *Anxiety,* 15.

17. This conclusion should be compared with the argument advanced by Denise Youngblood, who makes the case in a recent article for *Andrei Rublev* as a "profoundly postmodern, or better yet, 'post-utopian' work." See "*Andrei Rublev:* The Medieval Epic as Post-utopian History," in *The Persistence of History: Cinema, Television, and the Modern Event,* ed. Vivian Sobchak (London: Routledge, 1996), 127–143 (specifically 127–128).

EISENSTEIN AND TARKOVSKY
A Montage of Attractions

Vida T. Johnson

For most students of Soviet cinema the films of Sergei Eisenstein and Andrei Tarkovsky represent two polar extremes in the use of cinematic language: Eisenstein's hallmark rapid, intellectual montage, typical of his early films, is often contrasted with the lengthy, uninterrupted shots and slow-moving camera characteristic of Tarkovsky's mature films. Moreover, in his writings and pronouncements Tarkovsky frequently distanced himself from Eisenstein: "Nor can I accept the notion that editing is the main formative element of a film, as the protagonists of 'montage cinema,' following Kuleshov and Eisenstein, maintained in the 20s."[1]

Tarkovsky's best-known critique of Eisenstein's montage is his analysis of the famous battle scene on the ice in *Alexander Nevsky.* This is found not only in Tarkovsky's *Sculpting in Time: Reflections on the Cinema,* but also in his published Russian lectures from the Advanced Courses for Film Directors, which he taught at Vsesoiuznyi gosudarstvennyi institut kinematografii (VGIK) (the All-Union State Institute of Film). Using Eisenstein as a negative example, Tarkovsky taught groups of aspiring directors their future craft. Rather than being a mechanical or rhythmical alternation of shots,

> editing has to do with stretches of time, and the degree of intensity with which these exist, as recorded by the camera. . . . Eisenstein's own work vindicates my thesis. If his intuition let him down, and he failed to put into the edited pieces the time-pressure required by that particular assembly, then the rhythm, which he held to be directly dependent on editing, would show up the weakness of this theoretical premise. Take for example the battle on the ice in *Alexander Nevsky.* Ignoring the need to fill the frames with the appropriate time-pressure, he tries to achieve the inner dynamic of the battle with an edited sequence of short — sometimes excessively short — shots. However, despite the lightning speed with which the frames change, the audience . . . [is] dogged by the feeling that what is happening on the screen is sluggish and unnatural. This is because no time-truth exists in the separate frames. In themselves they are static and insipid.[2]

Tarkovsky's devastating and perhaps unduly harsh—though perceptive—attack on Eisenstein overshadows a much deeper affinity between the two directors: to borrow Eisenstein's term, a kind of "montage of attractions" where contrasting elements of Eisenstein's cinematic style are borrowed and reconfigured by Tarkovsky. Even the above quote, while stating Tarkovsky's dislike for montage, attests that Tarkovsky must have held Eisenstein in high regard indeed to analyze individual sequences with such precision. Eisenstein himself was "rediscovered" only in the late fifties and influenced a whole new generation of young filmmakers including Tarkovsky, who, as a VGIK student, saw the newly released Part II of *Ivan The Terrible* in 1958.

One needs only to look at Tarkovsky's diploma film, *The Steamroller and the Violin* (*Katok I skripka,* 1960), and the opening dream sequence of his first feature, *Ivan's Childhood* (*Ivanovo detstvo,* 1962), to be convinced that Tarkovsky learned his montage lessons rather well from Eisenstein—and also from Dziga Vertov. Although Tarkovsky was soon to abandon these rapid montage sequences, built on contrasting geometric patterns and dynamic diagonals, they stand as a testament to Eisenstein's and the "montage" directors' powerful influence on the young film makers of the Thaw period. In his very next film, *Andrei Rublev* (1966, USSR release 1971) Tarkovsky abandons montage for a cinematic style characterized by a stately, slow-moving camera and lengthy, uninterrupted shots and seamless editing. Whereas Eisenstein's shots last a few seconds, Tarkovsky's often last a minute or more, culminating in his last film, *The Sacrifice,* in a virtuoso single shot of more than nine minutes.[3]

In opposition to montage Tarkovsky develops his concepts of the "the organic unity of the image," "indivisible and elusive," born of "direct observation of life" with the director "sculpting in time" (phrases which appear throughout *Sculpting in Time*). He also abandons "symbols, allegories and other such figures" strongly identified with Eisenstein's films, and turns to the realistic imagery of the natural world, shot seemingly in real time, so typical of the films of Alexander Dovzhenko.[4]

Yet if one reads Eisenstein's later writing in *Nonindifferent Nature,* a collection from the 1940s, one finds that he was no longer preoccupied with montage but with the "organic unity" of works of art and the "natural world" they reflect. Eisenstein identifies two types of organic unity: one which is defined "by the fact that the work is governed by a definite law of structuring," which he calls *"organic unity of a general order,"* and a second type which "occurs when not only the actual *principle of organic unity* is present but also the actual canon of law by which natural phenomena are structured."[5] He continues: "Here we have a case where the work of art—an *artificial* work—is structured according to the same laws by which *nonartificial* phenomena—'organic,' natural phenomena—are structured."[6] Here Tarkovsky and Eisenstein seem to have much in common, including frequent use of the term "organic unity."

In one of his lectures at the Advanced Courses for Film Directors, Tarkovsky praised *Ivan the Terrible* for its *plastichnost' obrazov*—the supple tangibility of the figures in the film. One could argue that in all his works Eisenstein was intensely concerned with the representation of the natural world in film, especially the human body and its movements—palpable, realistic, sensual. Recall the opening shot of *The Battleship Potemkin* where a bare-chested sailor, Vakulinchuk, rouses his fellow sailors against the injustices of the officers. In the attack on Kazan, bare-chested Tartar prisoners are pierced by Russian arrows. Tarkovsky, too, was concerned with capturing in *Andrei Rublev* an almost visceral experience of the real world. The pagan ritual scene in *Rublev* celebrates the sensuous beauty of the landscape and the bare bodies undulating in the grass. The realistic blow-by-blow torture of the sacristan in the pillage of Vladimir by the Tartars makes the brutality of the era also palpably real.

Both directors make the viewer feel the characters as authentic, tangible persons, despite the distancing effect of historical time. Both wanted to create an emotional, as well as physical, reality: Eisenstein called it pathos; Tarkovsky, emotional truth. The striking differences between the two directors in the style of filming and editing—rapid montage vs. long takes and slow-moving camera—obscure affinities which become evident in a careful viewing of sequences from their films. Moreover, in *Ivan the Terrible* Eisenstein himself was moving away from rapid montage, so much so that Andrew Sarris in his *Interviews with Film Directors* could assert that *Ivan* represented "a virtual repudiation of the fundamental montage theory."[7]

Yes, Tarkovsky clearly rejects, both in his writing and in his films, the basic tenets of Eisenstein's montage, and even his predilection for figurative cinematic language (synecdoche, metonymy, metaphor, allegory), but in his own first attempt to make an historical film, he turns to Eisenstein's least montage-driven film, *Ivan the Terrible*. A close textual comparison of *Ivan the Terrible* (especially Part I) and *Andrei Rublev* reveals that Tarkovsky learned a number of lasting lessons from Eisenstein and continued to polemicize with him in his films. Besides the already mentioned similarities in *plastichnost' obrazov*, the use of tangible, sensuous human forms, there are three more areas of potential influence where Eisenstein had something to say to Tarkovsky: cinematic mise-en-scène, sound, and the historical film genre and thematics.

If cinematic mise-en-scène encompasses both the staging of the action (the composition of elements) and the way it is photographed, these are the lessons Tarkovsky could have learned from Eisenstein: how to create dynamism within the shot through use of geometric and graphic patterns (already seen in Tarkovsky's *Ivan's Childhood,* 1962); the importance of framing; the creation of *massovka* (crowd scenes) through very careful staging and the use of deep-focus photography which reveals the complexity of sets and actions on several planes.

Critics like Mark Le Fanu have already noted general similarities between the scene of the attack on Kazan from *Ivan the Terrible,* Part I and the scene of the attack on Vladimir in *Andrei Rublev.*[8] But these similarities, I believe, are more thematic than cinematic. In purely cinematic terms there is a closer parallel between the preparation for the attack on Kazan in *Ivan the Terrible* and the bell-casting scene in *Andrei Rublev.* In the famous cannon scene in *Ivan,* the men drag huge cannons, cutting diagonally across the screen in increasing, larger-than-life close-up (Eisenstein's quote of the famous Repin painting of the Volga Barge Haulers), and later they repeatedly roll the barrels of gunpowder in preparation for battle. The men work in rhythmic precision, filling the screen with their powerful bodies and sheer numbers. The deep-focus photography allows the viewer to be overwhelmed by the grandeur of men and machines. Ivan himself is seen as orchestrating the attack, but it is the men—strong, powerful Russian men—who will carry it out.

Throughout the bell-making scene in *Andrei Rublev* the viewer is impressed by the mass of human bodies and the huge machinery filling the screen in complex geometric patterns, all shot in deep-focus. Just as the peasant-soldiers in *Ivan the Terrible* need coordinated brute power to pull the cannons, the peasants in *Andrei Rublev* push, with rhythmic precision, the huge wheel which in turn lifts the giant bell. It is the collective work and force of the simple peasant that in this case creates a beautiful, giant bell. Here, too, the Grand Prince is an observer, taking credit for the work done by his men. (I will pick up the significance of the role of simple Russians in the historical process below, in the discussion of the historical film genre.)

Despite Tarkovsky's rejection of symbolism, he, like Eisenstein, foregrounds sets and objects to give them if not symbolic, certainly thematic import in the film. The alternation of churches and palaces as major sets in both *Ivan* and *Rublev* focuses on the tension or collusion of the spiritual and secular powers, and their roles in Russian history. In *Nonindifferent Nature* Eisenstein writes extensively about architecture and its symbolic meaning in film. Tarkovsky was a perfectionist about his sets, shooting on location in monasteries and churches. Both directors were fanatical about details, selecting for a close-up the right individual out of the crowd or the telling object. The note in the hands of the dead Vakulinchuk in *Battleship Potemkin* is quoted by Tarkovsky in the small plate nailed to the cross with Christ's name on it in the Russian Golgotha in *Rublev.*

A second area of confluence, if not influence, is in the musical and sound texture of Eisenstein's and Tarkovsky's films, in the realization of a complex relationship between sound and image. The similarities are not found in direct musical or sound quotes, but in methodology and the acute awareness and desire to marry sound and image. Despite the fact that for Tarkovsky *Ivan the Terrible* was "removed from the principle of direct observation," and that it

> consists of a series of hieroglyphs—major, minor and minute . . .
> nonetheless, the film is astonishingly powerful in its musical and
> rhythmic composition. Everything about it, editing, shot transitions,
> synchronization, is developed with subtlety and discipline. That is why
> *Ivan the Terrible* is so compelling; for me, at least at the time, the rhythm
> of the film was positively bewitching. The characterization, the
> harmonious composition of the images, the atmosphere, take *Ivan the
> Terrible* so close to the theatre (the musical theatre) that it almost ceases—
> in my own purely theoretical view—to be a cinematic work. . . . The films
> made by Eisenstein in the 'twenties, above all *Potyomkin* were very
> different; they were full of life and poetry.[9]

The renowned Eisenstein scholar Naum Kleiman confirms that Tarkovsky watched and studied *Ivan* with rapt attention. (In his writing Tarkovsky does not differentiate between Parts I and II of *Ivan the Terrible,* although I suspect this quote most likely refers to Part II.) This very telling quote expresses Tarkovsky's conflicting feelings about Eisenstein's films. At the same time that he is denying *Ivan* its cinematic status (what amazing hubris!), he praises the early films—the ones whose montage he disparages elsewhere. But then, quickly, he points out the elements which he found to admire and which also influenced his own filmmaking: "the characterization"; "the harmonious composition of images" (*plastichnost' obrazov*); the "atmosphere" (sets, costuming, and presumably the historical past); and, most important, the "musical and rhythmic composition." Eisenstein's principle of "vertical montage," where the musical score literally follows the action on the screen, is magnificently realized in Sergei Prokofiev's original scores for both *Alexander Nevsky* and *Ivan the Terrible*. This is some of the most striking and complex film music in all Soviet cinema. For *Rublev* Tarkovsky chose the well-known composer Vyacheslav Ovchinnikov, who gave the film a complex musical texture recreating in an eerie fashion the conflict of pagan and Christian medieval worlds.

When Tarkovsky was considering making a historical film about the medieval monk and icon painter Andrei Rublev, was it possible that *Ivan the Terrible* provided the impetus? Did Tarkovsky look to *Ivan* for the treatment of history, the role of the people and their leaders? In terms of the historical film genre, *Ivan the Terrible* and *Andrei Rublev* will always be linked not only

65. Andrey Rublev.

because they are the most famous Soviet historical films—and arguably the best—but also perhaps because they both challenged the canons of the genre.

Furthermore, *Ivan,* Part II and *Rublev* suffered similar fates under censorship. Both films were banned for several years, harshly attacked by critics, and became (in)famous before they opened to wider audiences, primarily because they subverted the genre of the glorifying historical epic. Neither *Ivan* nor *Rublev* were released in their original director's versions; substantial cuts were required. Both *Ivan* (especially Part II) and *Rublev* have complex narrative structures and problematic protagonists. There are no clear heroes, no linear chronological progressions through battles and trials to final victory. Panoramic establishing shots, standard in historical epics, are often absent. The "enlightened" Ivan of Part I sinks into ecstatic madness in Part II. The uplifting ending and victories of Ivan in Part I are transformed into a carnivalesque parody of religious and monarchic rites in the conclusion of Part II. *Rublev* has a mostly passive hero who wanders through the Russian countryside, witnessing the brutality of the times. Rulers indulge in fratricide, and the beating, maiming and blinding of their subjects. Rublev's beautiful icons, scanned in color at the end of the film, stand as both a silent commentary on and a marvel of the times.

Eisenstein and Tarkovsky deconstruct the genre of the historical epic and complicate our understanding of Russian history. Both were roundly criticized by historians for historical inaccuracies, large and small. Yet both studied historical materials and in their writings wondered how to make history relevant, how to achieve authenticity rather than verisimilitude, how to deal with sets, costumes, makeup, acting, and dialogue, in order both to respect and to bridge the distance of time. And they are not afraid to implicate themselves and their own personal stories in their historical representations. As the historian Joan Neuberger has pointed out, there is another figure to complicate the obvious parallel of Ivan–Stalin: that of Eisenstein's stern, authoritarian father. Tarkovsky had planned to have scenes of his childhood intercut into *Rublev,* scenes which eventually found their way into most of his other films. A film about the tribulations of a creative artist undoubtedly had strong personal meaning for Tarkovsky. Both films clearly belong to the realm of *auteur* cinema in terms of their style, instantly recognizable as an "Eisenstein" or "Tarkovsky" film.

Finally, both directors ask questions about the nature of the Russian state, the role of rulers and the people, and the formation of Russian national consciousness. And here, just as he had challenged Eisenstein's reliance on montage and symbolism, Tarkovsky polemicizes with him on the questions of who or what will save Russia. On the one hand, in the impressive crowd scene discussed at the beginning of this article, the power and the strength of the Russian people, the *narod,* is affirmed in both films. (A nod to socialist realism?) But there the similarity ends. In the Russian Golgotha sequence in *Rublev,* which is visually quite similar to the very ending of *Ivan,* Part I, Tarkovsky answers Eisenstein. In white, snowy, Russian landscapes, processions of Russian peasants pray. In Eisenstein's film, they pray to the ruler Ivan and beg him to return and lead them; in *Rublev* they follow Christ, a Russian peasant, and bow down in prayer as he is crucified. For Tarkovsky it is not the ruler, not the power from above, but the faith and creativity of the Russian people—of Rublev—of the bellmaker and his helpers, that will save Russia. Despite Tarkovsky's protestations and critiques of Eisenstein's films, it is hard to imagine *Andrei Rublev* without *Ivan the Terrible.*

Notes

1. Andrei Tarkovsky, *Sculpting in Time: Reflections on the Cinema,* trans. Kitty Hunter-Blair (London: Bodley Head, 1986), 114.

2. Ibid., 119–120.

3. A shot is defined as one camera action without a cut, or an unedited strip of film.

4. Tarkovsky, *Sculpting,* 66.

5. Sergei Eisenstein, *Nonindifferent Nature: Film and the Structure of Things,* trans. Herbert Marshall (Cambridge: Cambridge University Press, 1987), 10–12.

6. Ibid., 11–12.

7. As quoted by Kristin Thompson in *Eisenstein's "Ivan the Terrible": A Neoformalist Analysis,* (Princeton: Princeton University Press, 1981), 4.

8. *The Cinema of Andrei Tarkovsky* (London: British Film Institute, 1987), 50–51.

9. Tarkovsky, *Sculpting,* 67–68.

VISUAL PATTERNING, VERTICAL MONTAGE, AND IDEOLOGICAL PROTEST

Eisenstein's Stylistic Legacy to East European Filmmakers

Herbert Eagle

For Eisenstein, the task in filmmaking was not simply or primarily to create a *diegesis,* a story world, but rather to create an intellectual and emotional experience. As he put it in the essay *The Montage of Film Attractions* (1924): "A film cannot be a simple presentation or demonstration of events: rather it must be a tendentious selection of, and comparison between, events, free from narrowly plot-related plans and moulding the audience in accordance with its purpose."[1] This early statement turned out to be remarkably accurate in predicting Eisenstein's approach to cinematic art. His films always told stories and had plots in the conventional sense, but he expended most of his effort in drawing meanings directly from correlations of images, and in structuring visual (and later aural) parameters so as to evoke and intensify emotions. Eisenstein's understanding of art was distinctly semiotic; he termed a work of art "a construction which . . . serves to embody the author's relation to the content, at the same time compelling the spectator to relate himself to the content in the same way."[2]

Although Eisenstein's subject matter usually consisted of historical events, it is clear that he did not attempt to represent or replicate them as a whole in a manner faithful to the historical evidence, even where his mise-en-scène imitated film documentaries. He did not reflect worlds, he built them, and very tendentiously indeed. His legacy to East European filmmakers lies in the methods for building a film world with clear semantic dichotomies, thematic implications, and emotional engagements—and not necessarily those derived from the story as such. From Eisenstein they learned that meanings and emotions were to a degree separable from story representation, and that it was possible to evoke and provoke them in ways which ran counter to the logic of the story or its ostensible moral. Such strategies proved to be critical during the era of socialist realism.

Eisenstein's films and his theorizing about them distinguished two distinct registers, which he called the "thematic-logical" and the "image-sensual." The former conveys intellectual meanings, the latter emotions which are sense-based, primitive, and physiological. Eisenstein believed that these two kinds of processes took place in different parts of the brain, and he sought to provoke activity on both fronts simultaneously—to fuse strong emotion with "progressive" meanings.[3] The separability of the two kinds of processes is reflected in his practice and theory, even though he viewed them as mutually reinforcing and wanted to deploy them in tandem. I would like to focus my attention on three strategies in Eisenstein's films, two of them semantic and one affectual.

First, Eisenstein patterns the images in his films *globally.* He foregrounds sets of images based on similarities and differences, sometimes by repeating certain objects or categories of objects, sometimes by repeating patterns of motion, geometrical shapes, lighting patterns, or arrays of colors. He does this in a very systematic way so as to foreground particular semantic oppositions or similarities by association with the respective sets of formal features. Images in Eisenstein's films usually (although by no means always) serve the needs of the diegesis, but their particular nature, their framing, their other stylistic attributes, and their specific placement in the edited sequence are motivated primarily by the film's alignment of classes of signifiers—what I term the film's *paradigmatic* structure. A second strategy is also semantic, but—as opposed to the global patterning, which typically involves rather large numbers of images with similar characteristics—it consists of individual *collisions,* metaphors or similes formed either by visual matches or by an abrupt cut from one context to another (and frequently by both at the same time).

The third strategy is purely affectual. Here, elements of style are deployed in such a way that they produce an icon of an emotion (i.e. a sign where the structure of the signifier resembles the texture of the emotion, in Eisenstein's view). Such affectual signs assault the viewer directly. In other words, we are moved not primarily through associations with the meanings in the story or because we empathize with a character, but because we are provoked by those formal features of the image track or soundtrack (preferably both) which mimic the desired emotional response. Eisenstein went to great lengths in post-analyses of his own films to explain how such devices work. In spite of the fact that Eisenstein's conjectures about creating emotions through such resonance are controversial, his delineation of the "image-sensual" or affectual as a separate track called attention to it as a resource, and his own treatment of the banquet of the *oprichniki* in *Ivan the Terrible,* Part II, illustrated how emotions (in that case, uncontrollable frenzy) inappropriate in terms of the announced theme of the work can be evoked.

Global patterning is everywhere evident in Eisenstein's approach to personages and objects within his films. As his contemporary and friend the Russian Formalist Tynyanov suggested: "The visible world is presented in cinema not as such, but in its semantic correlativity. . . . The visible man and the visible thing constitute an element of cinematic art only when they serve as a semantic sign."[4] In *Strike* (1924), for example, Eisenstein delineates each category of characters stylistically. The capitalist businessmen and the police bureaucrats are presented as hyperbolic caricatures: corpulent, dressed in suits and top hats, or in uniforms, with grimacing faces. The Cossack army, on the other hand, is depicted realistically, albeit with very synchronous choreography, in its relentless assaults on the workers. The *lumpenproletariat* (recruited as spies and provocateurs), as well as the bosses' underlings (a foreman and a clerk), are portrayed as clowns, complete with acrobatic turns and pratfalls. The workers are also portrayed realistically, even naturalistically, but are heroicized through mise-en-scène and framing. In each case, characteristic semantic values are brought out through the style of depiction. The capitalists and their lackeys are not to be taken too seriously, even though they are the villains; the comic depiction reminds us that they are exiting the stage of history, and, particularly in the case of the impish criminals and prostitutes, that they, too, are human beings and unfortunate victims of the system. Implacable, unrelenting violence, is, on the other hand, starkly negative. The workers' suffering, courage, and fortitude are reflected straightforwardly to underscore that these are the positive values in the narrative.

Visual motifs involving objects and gestures play a major role in the paradigmatic organization of Eisenstein's films.[5] Such motifs interweave with one another across an entire film, and frequently collide with one another to create binary oppositions; the formal oppositions become semanticized because of the opposing contexts in which they occur. Not only objects and gestures, but, more abstractly, shapes and geometrical patterns, lighting, and color are all organized so as to give rise to semantic correlations. Returning to *Strike,* we find that an entire series of shots of workers in their factory emphasize not oppressive working conditions (as might be expected in a film about capitalist exploitation), but instead the energetic motion of man and machine—highlighted by the continued presence, in as many as ten consecutive shots, of turning wheels and the pulleys and piston-like rods which connect them. In most of these shots we see parts of workers as well, and the wheels are located in roughly the same position to call attention to their continued presence. This metaphorical association of the workers' energy and power with wheels is established so firmly in the opening sequences that Eisenstein can create visual puns on it later: a wheel being swung on the end of a crane knocks over the foreman, a capitalist lackey; after the strike has spread throughout the factory, a shot shows three standing workers, their image superimposed over that of a spinning wheel. As they slowly fold their arms over their chests, the wheel stops; the workers' strike committee meets in a yard filled with discarded engine wheels, to underscore the result of workers' inaction.

Later, when the firemen stand idly by during a fire set as a provocation,

66. Water motif in *Strike* as it "changes sides."

67. Lattice of circles in *Strike*.

a worker's wife attempts to reach a wheel to turn on the water to the hoses. She is stopped, and instead the firemen turn the wheels of the water-engine against the workers. From this point in the film, the workers' momentum is stemmed and their liquidation begins. As Bordwell has perceptively noted, water, another important motif, also "changes sides," as it were, at this point in the film.[6] Circular shapes, in and of themselves, constitute a related, though more abstract, graphic motif. Whereas in the workers' case circles become associated with their energy, the circular shapes which characterize their enemies suggest stasis and stagnation. The very round bodies of the capitalist bosses and the police captain suggest gluttony and excess. The thieves and prostitutes who are recruited as agents provocateurs live in barrels sunk into the ground, their domain appearing as a lattice of circles. Here, similarity in form calls attention to contrast in meaning.

Other motifs, such as animal imagery, also characterize both the workers and one group among their adversaries, the *lumpenproletariat*—in Bordwell's analysis, "a motif initially associated with one side of the political struggle becomes transferred to the other."[7] But this motif can be viewed as stressing a certain common humanity and victimization among the workers and the *lumpenproletariat*. The capitalists dehumanize both, treating them as animals. First, the faces of the spies are superimposed onto those of animals, later seen in a nearby pet shop. The dwarves who dance on a table in a fancy restaurant as an attraction for the decadent clientele are also like captive animals; as soon as the police detective walks away from the table, they stop their tango and fall upon the food buffet like starved animals. And, in the film's famous finale, the massacre of the workers is intercut with the butchering of a cow in an abbatoir.

Eisenstein's visual patterning extends into the realm of mass choreography and mise-en-scène as well. At the outbreak of the strike, a thin stream of workers runs between files of machinery directly at the camera, which is positioned above the oncoming stream and then begins to track backward with it. As the strike is being spread from one workshop in the factory to another, the moving stream of workers is seen in long shot, running in one direction across the film frame, but then making a sharply angled turn before reaching its edge. Graphically, the pattern resembles a moving wedge of particles in motion. *Strike*'s epigraph, from Lenin, had read in part "organization means unity of action," and indeed the graphic pattern suggests a unified and directed process—the sharply defined current of workers moves in a consistent, precisely angled way; the movement is not chaotic. Eisenstein's treatment of the sailor's rebellion in *The Battleship Potemkin* uses similar visual patterns and choreography, the angled streams of sailors emphasized even more markedly by having them run along gangways at different levels.

Eisenstein employs an expanded and more monumental version of this movement in portraying the way in which the people of Odessa come to the docks to view the body of the martyred sailor Vakulinchuk. An opening matte shot, which isolates a single stairway and then superimposes a shot of it filled with a stream of people, is followed by another in which we see the stream reaching the bottom of the stairway and turning sharply to the right. There follows an entire sequence of shots consisting of angled compositions of the people descending stairways and turning; first two directions of motion are visible in each shot, then three or four. An arc motif is introduced in a shot where the people move along a thin pier which seems to stretch endlessly into the sea, as the panning camera never shows us the end of it. The arc motif and the angled compositions are combined in one of the last shots in the sequence: we see two "streams" of people flowing down the hillside and joining a broad river which is passing under an arched bridge, over which yet another line of people moves. These are breathtaking compositions whose function is affectual as well as semantic, mirroring a desired surge, an amplification and multiplication, of sympathetic feeling in the viewer.

In contrast to the angled compositions which characterize the workers, the repressive forces are marked by parallel line compositions, a suitable choice to express regimentation and control. The first physical assault on workers in *Strike* occurs when the fire brigade stands in a straight file and directs parallel streams of water at the workers. In the scene of the final massacre of the workers in their tenements, bars and railings form parallel arrays at the gateway. The two separate buildings are linked by parallel connecting bridges, emphasized in a slow pan which reveals them one after another. At the end of the massacre they will be shown again in this way, but now with a mounted Cossack, surrounded by dead bodies, on each parallel bridge. In *Potemkin,* this paradigm is developed even more consistently. The mess hall where the sailors are to be forced to eat the rotten borscht has parallel tables which swing from parallel ropes. The sailor who will suddenly smash a plate at the climax of Part I is first seen laying out washed spoons in a parallel line, with parallel vertical lines of a corrugated metal wall behind him, while wearing a jersey of parallel stripes. In Part II, the sailors are ordered to line up in parallel ranks, which are parallel to the ship's railings. When a platoon of marines is called up to carry out the execution, they raise their rifles, creating yet another set of parallel lines. Here occurs the climax of Part II, Vakulinchuk's cry: "Brothers, whom are you shooting at?" Interestingly, the shots which immediately follow this intertitle show the horizontally parallel rifles wavering, and then being shifted from shoulders to ground, now skewed, at acute angles to one another. This is the first signal in the film that tsarist regimentation has been broken. The amorphous group of sailors whom Vakulinchuk has gathered behind the gun turret (here, Eisenstein actually uses the same shot twice, of heads and shoulders bobbing) now turn into the directed lines of sailors who go racing through the ship spreading the mutiny.

The Odessa steps sequence is probably the most horrific display of parallel lines in cinema history. The troops descend the parallel steps in parallel ranks, in steady rhythm, inexorably; the rifles are raised and held in parallel horizontal positions as they fire, simultaneously casting parallel shadows across the parallel stairs. They move in precise cadence, as the amorphous mass of the people of Odessa flee helter-skelter down the steps—Eisenstein at times repeats the very same shots of the fleeing crowd, but the emotional affect seemingly overrides any perception of temporal illogic.

There are other recurring patterns in *Potemkin* as well: the circular motions which accompany both the energetic work and the protest of the sailors (the sailor smashes the plate, ironically inscribed with "Give us this day our daily bread"; he winds up his arm twice, in a sequence actually doubled by Eisenstein's using parts of two separate takes and editing them together); the soft curves of the sailors' hammocks, the tarpaulin which covers the unfortunate sailors about to be executed, the billowing sails of the boats bringing food to the mutineers, the parasols on the steps. This pattern has to do with softness: humanity, compassion, and peaceful relations between people.[8] In his book on Eisenstein, David Bordwell has traced other object and gestural motifs in *Potemkin* (the cross, wringing of hands, agitational motions, hanging images, the single eye motif, eyeglasses, worms, and so on), emphasizing that "Eisenstein's 'orderly aesthetic system' requires a moment-by-moment control over the metaphorical or emotional implications of each motif."[9] In his analysis of *October,* Bordwell shows how the network of motifs brings forward semantic oppositions between the Bolsheviks and their enemies ("Tsarism, Provisional Government, Mensheviks, and Social Revolutionaries")—"heroes" versus "clowns," "purposeful activity" versus "languid inertia," "streamlined functionality" versus "ornate decadence."[10]

In her book *Eisenstein's* Ivan the Terrible: *A Neoformalist Analysis,* Kristin Thompson shows how several dominant gestural and graphic patterns relate to the film's semantics. The idea that unity behind the Tsar is essential to Russia's survival is stressed via these paradigms. Compositions place the Tsar at the center of the frame, often flanked by symmetric elements of architecture or character position. In contrast, the sequences involving the conspirators against the Tsar (and, in terms of the film's semantics, the enemies of Russian unity) are marked by asymetric figure placement. The interlocutors strike rather unlikely poses whenever they are plotting; two characters face in opposite directions, and turn their heads so as never to look directly at one another. Heads are arranged with one in the lower left corner of the frame, another in the upper right—and, in scenes with three conspirators, they are placed on different levels, receding from the camera along a diagonal across the frame. The compositions, given their contexts, come to embody duplicity and disunity.[11] Thompson also explores two other patterns which recur in connection with the Tsar: "the ray motif" and "the power gesture." The first involves a circle (for example, the Tsar's head, the emblem of a sun on his shield, or the face of an icon) with visible rays emanating from it. When the Tsar stands outside his tent overseeing the battle at Kazan, thin clouds form rays around his head. The pattern is echoed in the battle sequence by the spokes of a wheel on an artillery cart, and the symmetrical fuses running from a centrally placed candle. All of these images emphasize unity and power—all rays point to the center, the Tsar—and amplify this meaning whenever they recur. The "power gesture" involves the Tsar most often, as well as his servitors when they are loyal to him; it consists of characters flinging out their arms in imitation of an explosion. Interestingly, the Tsar's enemies, in instances where they believe they have seized the advantage (as in the staging of the play of Nebuchadnezzar in the cathedral, or when Efrosinia believes that the Tsar has been killed) are also given symmetrical compositions or the power gesture.[12]

Beyond the overall organization of images into paradigmatic sets, Eisenstein's films abound in individual metaphors established through cuts and visual rhymes. In *Strike,* a capitalist's hand pressing down on a lemon squeezer is matched in the next shot by a Cossack's rearing horse coming down almost on top of a crowd of workers seated on the ground—a metaphor for oppression, suggesting squeezing the blood out of the workers. Later, when an inkwell is overturned over a map of the city, we cannot help but see that ink as the workers' blood flooding the streets. When the workers are being massacred at the end of the film, Eisenstein cross-cuts these scenes with shots of a cow having its throat slit in an abbatoir; we can quite clearly see the blood pouring out of the cow's neck while its legs still thrash and the butchers press on the body. Eisenstein succeeds in turning more abstract political terms like "oppression" into the very real pressing of life out of living things. He uses a similar metaphor in *October,* where a soldier cowering in a trench is followed immediately by a shot of a gun carriage being lowered from an assembly line, so that it looks like the individual soldier is being literally crushed by the military-industrial machine (of course, in the diegesis, the soldier is ducking exploding artillery shells). Often Eisenstein uses material nondiegetically to create metaphors. Even where the objects exist somewhere in the story world—as is true, for example, of the architectural monuments of Petrograd and the art objects in the Winter Palace in *October*—their abrupt insertion into new contexts and the punning visual matches favor metaphorical interpretations over any search for connections in the story world. When Kerensky is matched to a mechanical peacock we understand that he is narcissistic and also a mere puppet bureaucrat, in spite of his royalistic preening. We are unlikely to wonder where in the Winter Palace this little toy is located. When the Menshevik and Socialist Revolutionary orators are matched with cuts to balalaika and harp players, we are unlikely to wonder whether there is some musical event being staged elsewhere at the same time. In the famous montage of the Gods sequence, where Eisenstein satirizes the notion of fighting "For God and Country" by rapidly following an icon of Christ with a sequence of Asian and African deities, ending with animist wooden idols, we are again unlikely to wonder where these museum exhibits are located as Kornilov attacks the city and the Bolsheviks prepare to defend it. As Bordwell puts it, commenting on these devices in general, "the toys, cutlery, plates, glassware, and other luxury goods are evidently in the palace, but they are filmed in such intense close-ups or framed against such neutral backgrounds that they seem to hover in a purely symbolic space."[13] These examples of what Eisenstein termed intellectual montage (what can be called nondiegetic visual metaphors) are the kind of authorial commentary which East European directors learned to deploy within otherwise acceptable narratives. These units constitute narrations in the nominative as opposed to the predicate narrative of actions—narration through *things*.[14]

The notion of "vertical montage" was central to Eisenstein's writings toward the end of the 1930s, after his collaboration with Prokofiev on *Alexander Nevsky*. However, it is an extension of ideas and terminology already explicitly present in his films and in his theorizing of the 1920s, as reflected in terms like "tonal" and "overtonal" montage. It is the culmination of Eisenstein's search for what he would later term "a compositional structure identical with human behavior in the grip of pathos."[15] Eisenstein came to see such structures as composed of visual and audial "lines" which interacted with one another so that, in the organic fusion of their rhythms and textures, they reproduced the very structure of the desired emotion. He returned to some of the most affectually powerful moments in his films in order to analyze how they managed to produce pathos. The fact that Eisenstein's conjectures remain highly controversial has not prevented such audio-visual structures from being used by later directors. Although Eisenstein's explanations of them as largely physiological responses to physical stimuli appear inadequate, he was without a doubt aware that their effect is also the result of existential, experiential associations as well as of preexisting artistic conventions.

Eisenstein drew attention to those stylistic features that can be modulated, shaped, or formed to produce icons of emotional experience. One of the earliest examples he focuses on is the fog sequence in *Potemkin,* which he cited in the late 1920s as an instance of "tonal montage." The light vibrations in the air (seen as flickering intensities of grey), augmented by overtones such as the ripples in the water and the gentle rocking of the boats, in his view resonated with the emotion of sadness.[16] In his famous post-analysis of the sequence in *Alexander Nevsky* where Nevsky and his peasant army await the onslaught of the Teutonic knights, Eisenstein wrote: "We will try to discover here that 'secret' of those sequential *vertical correspondences* which, step by step, relate the music to the shots *through an identical motion* that lies at the base of the musical as well as the pictorial movement." Eisenstein notes the similarity between the path he claims the eye would take as it scans the shot sequence and the structural path of Prokofiev's melody, concluding: "If we try to read this graph emotionally in conjunction with the thematic matter of the sequence . . . , we can find the 'seismographical' curve of a certain process and rhythm of *uneasy expectation.*"[17] This process and rhythm, Eisenstein goes on to say, is like holding one's breath and then allowing oneself a deep sigh.

Many of the montage effects in Eisenstein's early films, including some of the examples I have already discussed, have an *affectual* component. When Eisenstein places the camera above the charging stream of workers in *Strike* and then begins to dolly backwards, he makes the spectator experience the sensation of running, as well as the exhilaration of movement. The same can be said of the tracking shots which rapidly pull us down the stairs along with the fleeing citizens of Odessa (Eisenstein had to construct a track for the camera alongside the steps so that we physically experience the panic of headlong flight). More abstractly, the rhythm of the advancing soldiers, echoed through the rhythmic units of the steps and the rhythmic cutting, suggests an inexorably approaching doom. One could compare this with the scene in *Ivan the Terrible* where the Tsar advances through the parallel lines of *oprichniki,* only now there is a musical track as well which rhythmically punctuates his steps and a melody which evokes solemnity and awe; the extreme depth of the shot also suggests profundity. Of course, the musical effects do not rely only on resemblances between their structure and the structure of particular emotional displays; there is a history of musical semiotic systems, wherein certain music will signal solemnity, sadness, happiness, reckless abandon, and so on. This is a result of a long and complex process of semanticization within music as an art, and the musical signs, even if iconic in origin, are also symbolic in terms of conventionalized systems.

Eisenstein usually deployed visual patterning, metaphorical cuts and matches, and vertical montage all with a common intellectual and emotional aim. Conflicting patterns within the montage were usually resolved through the emergence of a synthesis forwarding the same progressive theme as the narrative. For example, in the scene in *Ivan the Terrible* following Anastasia's poisoning, Eisenstein uses elements which are contradictory to one another and which he later described in terms of polyphony:

> The line of *death and constraint of will* enters with the immobile face of the dead Anastasia, passes into the constrained, immobile shots of Ivan, develops in the theme of Pimen's reading (*"exhausted* from wailing," "my throat *dried out,*" "my eyes grew weary") . . . The line of affirmation—Malyuta's line—is taken up by the Basmanovs (father and son), the inflammatory nature of the old man's speech passes into the fiery "Two Romes fell, and a Third stands" of the tsar, and ends with the flight of servants in the real fires of the torches.[18]

Eisenstein's full analysis attempts to demonstrate how the complex interplay of moods and drives within the Tsar is rendered by diverse levels of the audio-visual montage: the sharp camera angles, the graphic lines of the mise-en-scène, Ivan's gestures, and the multidimensional soundtrack consisting of a choir singing a sacred psalm while Pimen recites verses from *Lamentations,* Malyuta and the Basmanovs interject alternately despairing and hopeful words, and Ivan moves through guilt and self-pity to defiance. According to Eisenstein, these shifting emotions and moods are echoed by graphic composition, the play of light and shadow, the modulations of voices, and the timbre, melody, and rhythm of the music.

Such contradictory emotional effects in the vertical montage in *Ivan the Terrible,* Part II contributed to the condemnation of the film by Stalin and the Party's Central Committee. Stalinist historiography had assigned to Ivan IV and his *oprichniki* a progressive role in advancing the survival of the Russian state against the threat of internal and external enemies, and it was well-known that Stalin considered himself a modern-day Ivan and his militant and loyal bureaucracy a version of the *oprichnina.* The narrative in *Ivan the Terrible* supports this view; those who suffer violence and death at the hands of the Tsar and the *oprichniki* are consistently shown, beforehand, to have been plotting against him. The Tsar suffers from loneliness and guilt as a result of his actions, but we are given to understand that those actions were necessary and correct in terms of Russia's survival. But the *vertical montage* in a number of places throws our sympathy toward the victims of these purges, and portrays the Tsar and the *oprichniki* as demented and bloodthirsty rather than merely justly stern. For example, in the scene where Efrosinia sings a lullaby to her son Vladimir, the lyrics metaphorically represent her plot to kill the Tsar, but the opening part of the melody combined with her gestures, his pose in her arms, the lighting, and the soft focus, embody a mother's love and hopes for her child, an innocent child—and thus work against the grain of the depiction of Efrosinia as a ruthless villainess.

The dance of the *oprichniki* which precedes the sequence of the murder of Vladimir is the most glaring example of vertical montage which undermines the narrative's ostensible message. The primary components are the choreography, the costuming, the lyrics of the song sung by Fyodor Basmanov, and the use of color. The dance steps are aggressive and frenzied, matched in syncopation with similar movement in the music. Fyodor wears a mask of a woman with gold braids, and the lines of *oprichniki* on either side of him mimic the pattern of village-taunting dances with sexually suggestive meaning. The lyrics celebrate the destruction, looting, and burning of the boyars' estates, with the chorus refrain—"*Zhgi, zhgi, zhgi*" ("*Burn, burn, burn*") matched to the most energetic portion of the dance and the music, and the prevalence of red in the images. In his articles on vertical montage in 1940,

Eisenstein had given a great deal of thought to the use of color to convey meaning and emotion. He believed that there could be instinctive biological responses associated with certain colors, but saw more certain evidence of indexical associations (for example, the association of yellow and red with warmth, in connection with the sun and with fire). He also traced the semiotic development of color meanings in culture, noting the propensity of colors to signify both one thing and its near opposite. Finally, he saw that the systematization of color meanings within a specific work of art could play upon, or contradict, conventional associations. As he put it: "In art it is not the *absolute* relationships that are decisive, but those *arbitrary* relationships within a system of images dictated by the particular work of art."[19]

The most important colors in the banquet sequence are black, red, gold, and blue. Gold figures prominently in the Tsar's vestments (later worn by Vladimir) and in the costumes of one group of *oprichniki*. The primary association here is with the glory of the state. Blue appears only as the background of an icon painted on the ceiling, thus associating it with the Tsar's "heavenly" role, the role of a just god (blue is usually regarded as placid, calm). During the dance sequence, this blue largely disappears and the ceiling, when visible, is red instead. The blue ceiling reappears only in the film's final sequence when, in a symmetrical shot dominated by blue and gold, the Tsar reasserts his role as the unifier of the Russian land and people. Black is the color of the robes of another line of *oprichniki;* it does not necessarily have to signify evil, but earlier in the film Efrosinia had said of the treacherous and calculating Pimen: "White is the cowl, but black is the soul." The increasing prominence of red augments the already violent and rapacious sequence with a dominant meaning of blood. In terms of the film's narrative, the *oprichniki* do not do anything unjust in this sequence, but the vertical montage no doubt had something to do with the condemnatory words of the Central Commitee resolution of September 1946: "Eisenstein in the second part of *Ivan the Terrible* displayed his ignorance of historical facts by portraying the progressive army of the oprichniki as a band of degenerates similar to the American Ku Klux Klan."[20] Whether completely conscious and intended, or a less-than-deliberate manifestation of repressed sorrow and guilt, the vertical montage here conveys an emotional protest against Stalin's purges, and was understood that way by many viewers. This is a meaning that Eisenstein could not have stated or acknowledged explicitly without risking his life.

After the death of Stalin and Khrushchev's condemnation of Stalinist terror, a number of filmmakers in the Soviet Union and Communist Eastern Europe adopted the methods of visual patterning, metaphorical matching and cutting of images, and vertical montage to register views and feelings at odds with those of the reigning Communist Parties, in the context of narratives which could be approved within the state-run industries and by the censorship. These filmmakers, most of them trained after World War II in the state film schools, were, to varying degrees, familiar with Eisenstein's films, particularly his early, ideologically approved work and with his theories. The early stages of the approval process for films focused on the scenarios—that is to say on the narratives, the main line of actions and the dialogue. Thus, it was important for filmmakers to represent these aspects in an appropriate and progressive way from the point of view of Party ideology. However, the material of the image and soundtracks provided a rich potential for suggesting other, dissonant meanings and emotions. Eisenstein's theory and practice provided a blueprint for conveying ideas and feelings other than those presented by the narrative alone. What happened after such films were completed is a complex matter which I do not propose to discuss here, since to a considerable degree it depended on factors other than the formal structure of the films: the intra-Party politics of the period, the sympathy of unit chiefs within the film industry with the somewhat hidden thematics of the films and their willingness or unwillingness to take risks, the tenacity and reputation of the filmmakers, and so on. Some dissonant films were released and shown, but many of them had limited distribution, were officially condemned, or were withdrawn; others were subject to cuts and revisions; some were banned and only released in more liberal periods—or after the fall of Communism. I will examine here a few of the more prominent and well-known examples.

The narrative in Andrzej Wajda's *Ashes and Diamonds* (Poland, 1958) concerns the struggle for political power between Communists and anti-Communists at the end of World War II. It is loosely based on Jerzy Andrzejewski's novel of the same name, and, like that novel, it explicitly portrays the Communists in a positive light. A local Party secretary, Szczuka, and his associate, Podgorski, are working to set up the infrastructure for the postwar government. They are dedicated, hard-working, and willing to sacrifice for their country. Opposing them are two members of a Home Army band now committed to assassinating Communist officials. The local leader of the Home Army operation portrays the need for killing Szczuka in a way that clearly reveals the socialist realist bent of much of the speechifying in the film: "Szczuka . . . is a civil engineer, a graduate, a communist. An excellent organizer. A man who knows where he's going. . . . The skillful removal of such a man should have considerable impact; it would be very effective propaganda for us." Szczuka himself, a solid, grey-haired man in his late fifties, is, on his first appearance, filmed from an extreme low angle in a trench coat that makes him look even more monumental. His reaction to an assassination attempt which results in the murder (by mistake) of two innocent cement workers, Gawlik and Smolarski, is reflected in the following canonical speech for positive heroes: "I'd be a bad Communist if I tried to comfort you as if you

68. Eisenstein and his crew; his cameraman, Tisse, is seated at
the lower right..

were children. The end of the war doesn't mean the end of our fight. . . . And
each one of us may be killed . . . any day. . . . Don't think I'm not grieved,
because I know full well that these bullets were intended for me."

His would-be assassins, Maciek and Andrzej, are portrayed negatively. The
latter usually seems disciplined, but cold and unfeeling. Maciek, on the other
hand, is initially depicted as a casual crazed killer. When the cement workers
are ambushed, Smolarski dies in their jeep, but Gawlik escapes and tries to
seek shelter in a small chapel; Maciek pursues him and machine-guns him
in the back, riddling his body with bullets in an act of gratuitous violence.
Gawlik's shirt bursts into flame around the bullet holes, as the chapel door
suddenly swings open and he falls before a statue of Christ as king. The
Communist Szczuka and the anti-Communist Maciek, the film's main protagonists, seem to be complete opposites. But as Wajda unfolds a tight and sus-
penseful narrative, covering only a night and the next dawn, he patterns the
film visually so as to create semantic parallels between Szczuka and Maciek.
First, there are the pairs of characters, often filmed alongside one another:
Maciek is solid, Andrzej thin; Szczuka is solid, Podgorski thin (even the unfortunate Smolarski and Gawlik share these properties when their bodies are
laid out alongside one another). Maciek and Andrzej, on the one hand, and
Szczuka and Podgorski, on the other, are given scenes which match one another in content, props, and soundtrack. In one scene, Maciek lights shot
glasses of vodka along a bar as he reminisces about his Home Army comrades

who have fallen fighting the Germans; "The Red Poppies of Montecassino," a song about Polish troops who lost their lives fighting as part of the British Army in Italy plays in the background. In another scene, Szczuka lines up the recovered assassin's bullets on his table as *he* reminisces about his Communist comrades who fell in the Spanish Civil War and in the French Resistance; on a victrola in the background, the Spanish Civil War song about the battle at Gandesa plays.

The characters in all three pairs (Szczuka-Podgorski; Maciek-Andrzej; Smolarski-Gawlik) are repeatedly matched to images of Christ and adopt Christ-like poses themselves. The very first shot in the film is of the cross atop the small chapel. When we see Smolarski shot in his jeep, in one half of the frame, a wooden roadside Christ-on-the-cross occupies the other half; Gawlik's arms are outspread as he is shot; he falls before a statue of Christ. Later, Maciek plays an entire scene with the barmaid Krystyna before a large, inverted, partially burned crucifix which looms large in the foreground of the shot, swinging in front of us as water drips from the rays surrounding Christ's head. When Maciek finally does manage to shoot Szczuka, the latter falls into his embrace with outstretched arms. And when Maciek himself is mortally wounded, he hides with his back against a T-shaped pole supporting a laundry line, covered with a white sheet (matching the white sheet which had covered the bodies of Gawlik and Smolarski in the church in an earlier scene). Maciek reaches around the white sheet and presses his hand against his side; a bloody patch appears exactly in the place Christ was speared.

Even denser are the images which refer to a stanza from the Romantic poet Cyprian Norwid, from which the film gets its title. In that stanza, Norwid describes a burning hemp torch, which spews burning flakes as it burns; the poet asks: "Flaming, you know not if the flames bring freedom or death, consuming all that you most cherish; If only ashes will be left and want, chaos and tempest shall engulf. . . . Or will the ashes hold the glory of a starlike diamond, the morning star of everlasting triumph." Flames and smoke recur throughout the film. Gawlik bursts into flame; Maciek and Szczuka run into each other casually in the smoky bar of the Monopol Hotel, where twice Maciek lights Szczuka's cigarette. A banquet where Red Army commanders, local Communists, and the town elite preparing to collaborate with them are celebrating is engulfed by the smoky fog of a fire extinguisher. When Szczuka is being shot, a burst of fireworks erupting into the sky seems to emanate from his shoulder. Amidst the smoke of the bar, the very blonde and beautiful Krystyna shines in her white blouse. When Maciek leaves her, after carrying out his destructive mission, she opens a window and a beam of white light makes her literally disappear from sight. In addition, there are deliberate cuts from one subplot to another which link Krystyna to Christ to Poland, "the Christ of nations." What does this network of image motifs suggest? First it implies that both committed Communists and sincere anti-Communists were martyrs to the dream of a liberated Poland. And secondly it implies that a diamond, an ideal Poland, has not emerged with the postwar Communist regime; the diamond disappears, is swallowed up in the smoke quite literally at the end of the film when Krystyna is pulled into the off-key Polonaise and lugubrious victory march of those who are destined for political power.

The visual patterning in Jiří Menzel's *Closely Watched Trains* (1966) completely transforms a canonical World War II plot wherein Communist partisans blow up a Nazi ammunition train, turning the film into a critique of the stodgy, bureaucratic Communist regime of the 1960s. Menzel relies primarily on bureaucratic trappings and a pervasive network of sexually suggestive shapes. At the beginning of the film, in shots filmed against a sterile white background, the hero Miloš Hrma is crowned by his mother with a railway dispatcher's cap, in a shot sequence where the framing imitates that of Tsar Ivan crowning himself in *Ivan the Terrible*. This crowning, and a slow vertical pan of Miloš's uniform, are accompanied by a pompous sound track. Miloš's cap, his phallus-shaped dispatcher's signal, the soiled uniform of the stationmaster Lansky (who loves his pigeons and craves sex, but tries to discipline himself so as to insure his promotion and his new uniform with gold braid), Lansky's prized Austrian leather couch, and the station's official rubber stamps become major players in the film, whose plot arguably depends more on the adventures of such objects than on the actions of the characters.

Miloš is agonized by his inability to consummate his relationship with his girlfriend Maša; he learns much later that he suffers from *ejaculatio praecox* (premature ejaculation). What strikes the viewer as unusual earlier, however, is that Miloš wears his railway cap to bed with Maša; being capped by his bureaucratic function prevents him from acting in a sexually free manner. He finally succeeds in having sex with the *partizanka,* Viktoria Freie, who brings the bomb to blow up the train—but only after Hubička, his womanizing mentor, takes off Miloš's cap as he pushes him into a room with Viktoria. All of Miloš's bold moments in the film involve the removal of his cap (when he attempts suicide in despair, when he is almost shot by SS men, and finally when he blows up the train and the resulting explosion sends his cap rolling back to his puzzled girlfriend Maša).

Another extended play with objects involves the station's rubber stamps. In the first sequence in which they are foregrounded, the railway official Zedníček uses them to notarize official documents related to the station's responsibility for high surveillance trains (the "closely watched trains" of the film's title—this is the implication of the original Czech in the context of official military jargon). However, then Zedníček uses the rubber stamps as markers for armies as he unfolds a map and describes the brilliant tactical retreats of the German army all over Europe. Zedníček's hypocrisy, the fact that he is

69. *Closely Watched Trains* (1966; dir. Jiří Menzel). Museum of Modern Art/Film Stills Archive.

saying not what is true but what he must say as a loyal collaborator with the Nazi regime, is quite evident. Later, these same rubber stamps play a major role as surrogate phalluses in train dispatcher Hubička's eccentric seduction of the station's telegraphist. Hubička turns out to be a member of the underground; he is the one who gets the message about the bomb and is the one who is supposed to drop it on the train. However, Miloš has to act in his stead because, at the crucial moment, Hubička is detained in the station for an inquest into his use of the rubber stamps, which is found (upon the telegraphist's testimony) to be not forceable rape, but a desecration of the German language. Thus, the rubber stamps which are not successful bureaucratically (the official admonition they stamp fails to protect the "closely watched" ammunitions train) or in military support of the Nazi regime (the armies they represent in Zedníček's speech are in fact in retreat) are successful sexually and in terms of rebellion against the regime (they distract the officials at the inquest while Miloš is dropping the bomb on the train).

The rubber stamps form only a small part of the film's sexually suggestive imagery. Hubička's sexual dalliance leaves a triangular-shaped tear in Lansky's Austrian leather couch, from which horsehair protrudes like a woman's pubic hair. Upon discovering this, Lansky bemoans the desecration of his bureaucratic trophy, but his wistful fingering of the horsehair suggests something else. Later, Miloš makes an identical tear with Viktoria. Viktoria's bomb, which comes in a box, is fingered in this same way by Hubička; Viktoria slaps his hand away. Virtually every bureaucratic or military prop in the film is given sexual meaning through its shape or through the gestures associated with it. Thus Menzel turns an appropriately tendentious narrative subject into a comedy about sex and an endorsement of political rebellion. Sexual release becomes associated with success, not only in matters personal but also in the struggle for Czech national identity and freedom. Bureaucratic "official" behavior is characterized as stifling, boring, cowardly, and ludicrously ineffective. Politically rebellious and personal sexual action are conflated by the film's signifiers. Sexuality stands in for politically dissident action. There is one piece of *realia* in the film which cues the viewer that the target is not the World War II Nazi collaborators; on the wall in one scene is a Nazi propaganda poster which shows a clawed, bloody hand, marked with hammer and sickle, descending over Hradčany Castle, the site of political power in Prague. The caption reads: "If it seizes you, you die." This was the Nazi line during the war, but the direct meaning of the poster in the political context of 1966 would certainly strike the Czech viewer.

Of the East European filmmakers who constructed their films using a dense patterning of visual motifs with a particular penchant for graphic resemblances, Dušan Makavejev did so most explicitly. (He could get away with much more in the Yugoslavia of the 1960s, where the Marxist humanist theoreticians associated with the journal *Praxis* had made the critique of Stalinist authoritarianism legitimate.)[21] The cuts in Makavejev's films of this period function in the manner of nondiegetic metaphors, because the films themselves are composed of several separate *strands,* most of them in completely distinct story worlds. In describing the structure of his films, Makavejev frequently made reference to Eisenstein: "We can no longer speak simply of two pieces of film together giving a third meaning: now we know that two scenes are giving a third meaning, and a number of scenes together are multiplying each sequence times each sequence, so it means we have thousands of meanings in a collage film of the kind I am making."[22]

Beyond cutting from a shot which is part of one strand to a shot which is part of another, Makavejev uses both visual and aural matches in the spirit of Eisenstein's practice. Not only do similar objects appear in shots from different strands, but composition within the frame creates parallels between graphically similar patterns. The same musical motif occurs together with shots from different strands, thus causing the receiver to correlate and associate these shots (Eisenstein does the same thing with the motifs in *Ivan the Terrible,* albeit in the context of a single narrative); verbal texts in similar declamatory styles occur in sequences from the various strands, and so on.

Films as openly dissident as those of Wajda, Menzel, and Makavejev were not made in the Soviet Union, except toward the very end of the Gorbachev era. On the other hand, the affectual potentials of vertical montage were used by directors like Mikhail Kalatozov, Andrei Tarkovsky, and Yuri Ilyenko to channel the viewers' emotional response in ways which went counter to official ideological imperatives. Kalatozov's *Cranes Are Flying* (1957) ilustrates this contrast especially well. While this is a film about World War II whose narrative strongly endorses Soviet patriotism, vertical montage is most evidently effective in conjunction with other themes: personal loss and suffering. The heroine of *Cranes,* Veronika, and her fiance Boris, are carefree young lovers at the outbreak of the war. They are soon to be married; nonetheless, as soon as war has been declared Boris enlists (even though as an engineer, he could have gotten an exemption). After briefly being upset by his son's recklessness, Fyodor Ivanovich, a surgeon, accepts his son's patriotism and makes a very inspiring speech about how those who do not return will be remembered by stars in the heaven. Veronika is very upset, but she soon swallows her sorrow and goes to work in a wartime factory. Her parents are killed in an air raid. Later, she is seduced, actually raped, by Boris's cousin Mark, a spoiled concert pianist who has managed to get an exemption through illegitimate means. Out of shame she marries Mark, who is unfaithful to her. In the meantime, Boris is killed at the front while trying to rescue another soldier. Fyodor Ivanovich's entire family (including Veronika and Mark) is evacuated from Moscow to Western Siberia, where, in a hospital, Fyodor Ivanovich delivers yet another patriotic speech, in which he condemns women who have been unfaithful to their men at the front. Veronika, now a nurse working at his side, runs off and seems about to commit suicide, but doesn't. Instead she saves a young child, also named Boris, from being run over by a jeep and adopts him. At the end of the film, she finally manages to accept her lover Boris's death (she has doubted it since no official word was received). At the train station, her tears turn to a smile as she gives the flowers she brought for Boris to other soldiers and their families.

I have deliberately retold the plot without mention of the film's rather dazzling cinematography, which is not deployed in any of the sequences involving patriotic dialogue (although Fyodor Ivanovich does get centered in the frame in monumental or very low-angled compositions). Instead, dramatic camera movement is reserved for scenes with purely personal meaning. During the opening sequence of a lovers' tryst between Veronika and Boris, he runs breathlessly up three flights of steps to her apartment because he has forgotten to fix the time of their next date. The camera follows him in one continuous shot, craning upwards and spinning rapidly in a circular pan in order to keep him constantly in view, while the soundtrack plays a lively light-hearted melody. Later, when Veronika is riding on a trolley to bid farewell to Boris, the camera fixes on her sitting and then—in a single shot—rushes through the trolley's door with her, loses her as she struggles through a crowd, makes its own way through the crowd to catch up with her again, and finally cranes upward to keep her in view as she makes her way through a formation of tanks. The camera involves us totally in Veronika's emotion, mimicking both her helter-skelter frenzy and her determination.

When Veronika later tries to find Boris at the volunteer's rallying point, the camera adopts her point of view as she moves along a crowd, constantly peering through an iron fence. The efforts of Boris to find Veronika are treated in the same way, from his point of view. The camera becomes a seeking and desiring subject. Finally, Veronika spots Boris marching, and races along the fence trying to catch his attention; faces rush by us on the screen. Veronika never manages to bid her lover farewell. The camera has caught the viewer up, physically, in the frantic effort to prevent separation, and has prolonged it visually and temporally. When Boris is shot at the front, the camera turns upward and spins to create a whirling pattern of trees over which is superimposed first a reprise of Boris's headlong rush up the stairs to Veronika (only now he is dressed in his dirty army uniform), and then, from the top of the stairs (the doorway to Veronika's apartment) a slow-motion panning shot of a wedding party, including Boris and Veronika, making its way eerily down the stairs, looking ghostly because of the slow-motion, the superimposition of the whirling trees, and the gauze of Veronika's veil through which we view all of this. We go in a few seconds from the memory of happy carefree love to a slow sad contemplation of the happiness that will never be.

The sequence of Veronika's apparent suicide is filmed as a racing tracking shot, with a fence's slats flying by up-close in one direction while Veronika moves in the other. Rapid intercutting of shots of her outstretched hands and of an oncoming train make it seem as though she has jumped from the railway overpass. Instead we are given an abrupt sequence of three rapidly edited shots. In each, the same jeep, approaching from different angles, almost hits little Boris. In the first shot, he wanders into its path alone; in the second, Veronika is seen dashing toward him; in the third she grabs him up and clutches him in her arms. But in *all three shots* the jeep has almost reached Boris. They are mutually contradictory in terms of Veronika's location and actions, and impossible to understand as temporally contiguous. But the editing is too fast for most viewers to become consciously aware of this. Kalatozov here employs a favorite device of Eisenstein's — contradiction between an event and its duration. Eisenstein conjectured that both the overlapping of the same event twice (as in the smashing of the plate in *Battleship Potemkin*) and the presentation of a spatially and causally ambiguous series of shots (as in the child overturning in the baby carriage, the saber-slashing Cossack, and the intellectual woman with her eye shot out at the very end of the Odessa Steps sequence) intensified the emotional impact of a shot sequence because of the shock of confusion it subconsciously caused. In the final analysis, all of Kalatozov's cinematographic moves are related to the characters' feelings of love, separation, loss, and grief. They urge and allow the spectators to feel these things. And the devices are never used in conjunction with civic and patriotic thematics alone. The success of the strategy was evident in the strong reaction of Soviet audiences to the film. It was the first film that really invited audiences to re-experience and express their grief.[23]

Wajda, Menzel, Makavejev, and Kalatozov are among the many East European filmmakers who have used visual patterning, metaphorical cutting, and elements of vertical montage as parts of their own unique systems of representation. None could be called derivative from Eisenstein in their approach as a whole, but each creatively applied and extended methods which he pioneered in order to express themes which exceeded or even diverged from the films' officially acceptable narratives.

Notes

1. Sergei Eisenstein, "The Montage of Film Attractions," in *Selected Works,* 1: *Writings, 1922–34,* ed. and trans. Richard Taylor (London: British Film Institute, 1988), 41.

2. V. V. Ivanov's book *Ocherki po istorii semiotiki v SSSR* (Essays on the History of Semiotics in the USSR) (Moscow: Nauka, 1976) is devoted largely to the significance of Eisenstein's theories. Eisenstein's own quote is from his "O stroenii veshchei" (On the Construction of Things), *Iskusstvo kino,* 1939, no. 6. Citation is taken from the English translation by J. Leyda in Eisenstein, *Film Form: Essays in Film Theory* (New York: Harcourt, Brace & World, 1949), 168.

3. For further discussion of this dichotomy, see V. V. Ivanov, *Ocherki,* 113. Eisenstein saw expressive forms as provoking a "regressive" emotionality, in the sense that it could be linked to any meaning, even anti-humanistic meanings.

4. Iurii Tynianov, "Ob osnovakh kino" (On the Fundamentals of Film) in *Poetika kino (The Poetics of Film)*, ed. Boris Eikhenbaum (Moscow-Leningrad: Kinopechat', 1927), 61–62. English translation in H. Eagle, ed. *Russian Formalist Film Theory* (Ann Arbor: Michigan Slavic Publications, 1981), 85.

5. David Bordwell, *The Cinema of Eisenstein* (Cambridge, Mass.: Harvard University Press, 1993); Kristin Thompson, *Eisenstein's Ivan the Terrible: A Neoformalist Analysis* (Princeton: Princeton University Press, 1981).

6. Bordwell, *The Cinema of Eisenstein,* 54–56.

7. Ibid., 54.

8. For a more detailed exposition, see Herbert Eagle, "Visual Patterning and Meaning in Eisenstein's Early Films," in *Russian Literature and American Critics,* ed. K. Brostrom (Ann Arbor: University of Michigan, 1984), 331–346.

9. Bordwell, *The Cinema of Eisenstein,* 66.

10. Ibid., 83.

11. See Thompson, *Eisenstein's Ivan the Terrible,* 113–136.

12. Ibid., 149–152.

13. Bordwell, *The Cinema of Eisenstein,* 85.

14. Ivanov, *Ocherki,* 181.

15. Eisenstein, "O stroenii veshchei"; English translation as "The Structure of the Film" in *Film Form,* 171.

16. See Eisenstein, "Methods of Montage," in *Film Form,* 75–78.

17. Sergei Eisenstein, "Vertikal'nyi montazh" (Vertical Montage), *Iskusstvo kino,* 1940, no. 9. The citations are taken from J. Leyda's translation in Sergei Eisenstein, *The Film Sense* (New York: Harcourt, Brace & World, 1947), 173, 212. The full analysis can be found on pages 173–216.

18. Sergei Eisenstein, *Nonindifferent Nature: Film and the Structure of Things,* trans. Herbert Marshall (Cambridge: Cambridge University Press, 1987), 313. For Eisenstein's full analysis see 309–322.

19. Sergei Eisenstein, "Vertikal'nyi montazh," *Iskusstvo kino* 12 (1940). Citation from the English translation by J. Leyda in *The Film Sense,* 150.

20. See Jay Leyda, *Kino: A History of the Russian and Soviet Film* (New York: Collier Books, 1960), 390–391.

21. See Herbert Eagle, "Yugoslav Marxist Humanism and the Films of Dusan Makavejev," in *Politics, Art and Commitment in the East European Cinema,* ed. David Paul (London: Macmillan, 1983), 131–148.

22. Robert Sitton, James Roy MacBean, Ernest Callenbach, "Fight Power with Spontaneity and Humor: An Interview with Dusan Makavejev," *Film Quarterly* 25: 2 (Winter 1971), 3–9.

23. See Mira Liehm and Antonin Liehm, *The Most Important Art: East European Film After 1945* (Bloomington: Indiana University Press, 1977), 199–200.

Part Three

RECONTEXTUALIZING THE LATE FILMS
History, Film, and Politics

A HISTORY OF *BEZHIN MEADOW*

Peter Kenez

The enormous propaganda apparatus was an indispensable part of the Stalinist state. The propagandists created a fictitious universe of rich, happy, and class-conscious workers and peasants, constantly and courageously fighting dastardly enemies, and there was no one who could demolish this picture. The state controlled information by suppressing hostile voices, and the authorities were extraordinarily careful about what could reach the citizens. Under the circumstances it is not surprising that during the 1930s it became increasingly difficult to make a film. First of all, the proposed script had to pass through a number of institutions, and each of them had veto rights. Since bureaucrats were afraid of appearing too liberal, they were likely to err on the side of caution. Even though scriptwriters knew full well what was expected of them, most of the projects were turned down for one reason or another. For example, in 1933 the largest Soviet film studio, Soiuzfilm, paid advances for 129 scripts, but ultimately only 13 were accepted for production.[1] Even under these circumstances many of the completed films were never publicly exhibited. In 1935 and 1936 alone, 37 films were declared to be unacceptable, about one-third of the total film production of Soviet studios for those two years.[2]

Sergei Eisenstein's *Bezhin Meadow* belongs to the category of films that were made but ultimately found to be unacceptable for Soviet audiences. In this sense there was nothing unusual in Eisenstein's fiasco. However, Eisenstein was not just an ordinary Soviet film director; as the creator of the greatest Soviet revolutionary spectacle *The Battleship Potemkin,* he was internationally the most admired Soviet director. When *Bezhin Meadow* was shelved in 1937, it became a subject of widespread discussion within and even beyond the industry.

The unfinished film was destroyed during a bombing raid in the fall of 1941. In 1964–1965 the film director Sergei Yutkevich and the Eisenstein scholar Naum Kleiman made a 15-minute film consisting entirely of still photos drawn from picture material in Eisenstein's archive, to which they added a soundtrack from the music of Sergei Prokofiev. Although this film shows Eisenstein's pictorial talent, it is impossible on the basis of it alone to form an opinion of the director's artistic achievement. On the other hand, two scenarios and numerous descriptions by those who worked with Eisenstein are available, and these enable us to form a judgment of the political content of the film, if not of its artistic worth.[3]

The events surrounding the making of *Bezhin Meadow* and its subsequent suppression are particularly interesting, for they are revealing of the intellectual and political world of Stalinism in the 1930s. The evolution of the story from the actual event that took place in a remote village in Gerasimovka in the Ural Mountains in 1932 to the almost-finished film in 1937 is an instructive example in mythmaking. Eisenstein's work on this film and his behavior at the time—which must have been a personal crisis for him—tell us much about the director's politics and degree of collaboration with the regime.

When we think of censorship, we tend to think of a courageous artist battling a repressive state. In fact, as this incident shows, the picture is neither as pretty nor as clear-cut as it seems. Eisenstein was both a collaborator with and a victim of the regime that he chose to serve; at times he accepted the fundamental principles of the system, but on other occasions—one assumes admittedly without hard evidence—he must have hated Stalinism. He was an extraordinarily talented Soviet artist. His talent was always evident; he always succeeded in putting his individual stamp on whatever he attempted, and in this respect he was superior to any Soviet film director who worked in the age of Stalin. At the same time he was a Soviet artist, which meant that he never attempted to go against what he believed the regime demanded of him. Without a second thought he removed Trotsky from his almost-finished *October* when Trotsky lost the battle for leadership to Stalin. After all, *October* was never meant to be history; it was created to support a myth. Now the myth slightly changed—and that was all.[4] In the 1920s when the regime desired "revolutionary spectacles," he made *Battleship Potemkin* and *October*. Vsevolod Pudovkin, Alexander Dovzhenko, and many others made similar films at this time. Before and during the Second World War the leadership demanded biographical films of Russian heroes in order to encourage "Soviet patriotism." Directors responded by making films about such historical personages as Peter the Great, Mikhail Kutuzov, Alexander Suvorov, Yemelyan Pugachev, and so on. Eisenstein's contributions were *Alexander Nevsky* and *Ivan the Terrible*.[5] *Bezhin Meadow* was also part of a group of films serving an identifiable political purpose, films which implicitly justify terror. The Soviet citizen was to understand that no one was to be trusted, for the enemy could be your best friend (as in Alexander Dovzhenko's *Aerograd*) or your husband (as in Ivan Pyrev's *Party Card*). In these and in numerous other films, the hero was the denouncer, one who put the state's interest over any other human tie. Indeed, in the Soviet Union in the 1930s denunciations became a widespread disease, poisoning human relations. The great irony of the *Bezhin Meadow* fiasco is that the only film of Eisenstein that the Soviet regime never allowed to be distributed was the one which from an ethical point of view was the most reprehensible. Arguably, the Soviet regime performed an unintended service to the beleaguered director.

Eisenstein had last completed a film, *The Old and the New,* in 1929, after which he was allowed to travel abroad, to spend some time in Western Europe, then traveling to the United States and Mexico to work. Unfortunately, none of his artistic plans worked out and he returned to the Soviet Union in 1932, where he soon realized that the political life of his country had profoundly changed. In the following three years he attempted three different projects but was not allowed to work on any of them. He must have been anxious to return to directing, and it was under these circumstances that in early 1935 Alexander Rzheshevsky approached him with a scenario that was to be the film *Bezhin Meadow.* Rzheshevsky had been an actor in the 1920s and had become an experienced scriptwriter, providing material for the famous directors Vsevolod Pudovkin and Nikolai Shengelaya.[6]

One suspects that one appeal of the scenario was that Eisenstein assumed that this time there would be no difficulty in getting permission to make the film. Rzheshevsky, after all, had written the scenario at the request of the Central Committee of the Komsomol (Young Communist League). Unlike other films made during these dark times on the theme of unmasking hidden enemies, this scenario was based on a real event. This "event" was well-known to every politically conscious Soviet citizen. According to the story, in 1932, in the Ural village of Gerasimovka, a fourteen-year-old Pioneer, Pavlik Morozov, denounced his father, the head of the village Soviet, for providing false documents to kulaks who had been deported to this region. The father was arrested and sentenced to ten years. For his denunciation Pavlik was killed by his relatives.[7]

The Soviet authorities, who carried out collectivization with the greatest brutality, benefited from pretending that it was not they, but the enemies of collectivization who used violence against the innocent. From their point of view it was especially poignant that the victim was a young boy. The murder of an innocent child, of course, is horrifying in any culture, but in Russian tradition it had a special, almost religious meaning. The murder victim in Soviet mythology was always portrayed as younger than a fourteen-year-old, which the real Pavlik was, in order to increase the effect. Eisenstein, for example, chose an eleven-year-old to play the role. Pavlik became a martyr and was celebrated in operas and songs; innumerable paintings and statues came to depict the young hero. He retained his martyr status until the era of Gorbachev.

As a result of the work of the dissident Russian scholar, Yuri Druzhnikov, who traveled to Gerasimovka in the 1980s and interviewed survivors, we know now that the story of Morozov was almost wholly invented to serve political purposes and celebrate informers.[8] To the extent that it is possible to establish the facts of the confusing story after the passage of five decades, it appears that Pavlik had never been a Pioneer, but a rather disturbed young boy unaware of the consequences of his acts. He turned against his father not for political motives, but because the father had abandoned his wife for a younger woman. Pavlik and his brother in fact were murdered, but the circumstances of the murder remain murky and it is not clear that the family had anything to do with this atrocity. The fact that members of the family confessed and several of them were executed is by no means a proof of their guilt.

Of course Eisenstein had no way of knowing the real story that had taken place in a remote Ural village three years earlier. But we can take it for granted that it would not have mattered too much. The director was not averse to myth creation, and like the Soviet authorities he was willing to use the story for the expression of his own ideas, which overlapped with those of the authorities even if they were not exactly the same.

Eisenstein regarded Rzheshevsky's scenario, which he liked very much, as only a starting point. According to the current dogma of the political masters of the film industry, films belonged primarily to the scriptwriter, whose instructions the director was compelled to follow blindly. The all-important ideological message was to be in the script. Furthermore, if the director could make any changes he wanted in the process of making his film, then there was not much point in the careful examination of the script by the authorities. In spite of all the denunciation of the "emotional scenario" (i.e., the director using the scenario as merely a source of inspiration, a starting point), Eisenstein handled Rzheshevsky's work precisely in that spirit. He liked the scenario because it was simple and therefore he could expand and rework it.[9]

As was Eisenstein's custom, he re-fashioned the scenario to suit his own artistic, ideological, and even psychological purposes. The director had little interest in the niceties of Marxism and most likely disapproved of many aspects of Soviet reality which surrounded him. On the other hand, although he had no first-hand knowledge of life of the peasants, it is clear that he shared the Bolsheviks' distaste for the traditional Russian village and wholeheartedly supported its destruction. At least to that extent this was to be an honest film. His film was not so much to celebrate the informer (unlike for example Pyrev's *Party Card*) but to contrast the old and the new. In every way Eisenstein sharpened this contrast. He depicted the new village in glorious bright colors, depicted gleaming tractors and clean, attractive peasant faces, as opposed to those who represented the old, who were always dark, threatening, ugly, and sinister. The parallel between this film and his earlier one, *The Old and the New,* is clear.

But consciously or unconsciously, he also used the film to deal with his own individual preoccupations, such as the father–son conflict. Yon Barna analyzed Eisenstein's relationship with his father in discussing *Ivan the Terrible,* and made the point that this topic preoccupied the artist. In *Bezhin Meadow* this is, obviously, a central issue.[10]

Rzheshevsky prepared himself for the work not by going to Gerasimovka, a remote, extremely poor and backward place, but to Bezhin Meadow, in the region of Oryol, a place that not only had once belonged to the great Russian writer Ivan Turgenev but came to be associated with one of his stories in *A Sportsman's Notebook.* Turgenev's tale of peasant boys in the 1850s and of a death foretold had very little to do with the scenario. Quite unnecessarily and inappropriately, the original scenario began with quotations from Vissarion Belinsky, Alexander Herzen, and Mikhail Saltykov-Shchedrin concerning Turgenev. Eisenstein cut all references to Turgenev except for the original title, *Bezhin Meadow.*

As always, Eisenstein went to extraordinary lengths to prepare for the shooting. He made elaborate drawings for the envisaged scenes. He conducted a remarkably wide search for the ideal boy to play the central role. Out of two thousand children at first six hundred, and later two hundred, were selected to be interviewed by Eisenstein before the right boy was chosen.[11] Unlike his previous films, in which he did not work with actors but chose people who represented types, now, in the age of socialist realism, he gave in and was willing to use some professional actors. Eisenstein, Pudovkin, and Grigori Alexandrov in 1928 published a brief, but important statement about the use of sound. They advocated a nonrealistic, contrapuntal use of sound in which, at least at times, there would be a clash between the moving image and the soundtrack. Now, for the first time, Eisenstein was ready to try out his theory. He also made extraordinary efforts to find the right location for filming. The real Bezhin Meadow would not do, and the idea of going to Gerasimovka did not even emerge. Besides the studios in Moscow, the shooting took place in widely different parts of the country, the Ukraine and the Caucasus.

The film, as everyone connected with it repeatedly emphasized, was inspired by Pavlik Morozov's martyrdom. Indeed, the scenario begins: "Dedicated to the bright memory of Pavlik Morozov, a small hero of our time."[12] However, Rzheshevsky chose to tell a story rather different from Pavlik's. The film, after Eisenstein cut the irrelevant references to Turgenev, started with pictures of flowering orchards and blue sky and among the branches an obelisk which had the name Turgenev on it. The idyllic pictures are followed by a sad procession of Stepok, as Pavlik is called in the film, and an older peasant, accompanying the dead body of Stepok's mother who has been beaten to death by her husband. (Ironically, in the actual ill-fated Morozov family no one survived but the mother, who lived to a ripe old age.) Thereby the father–son conflict is established at the outset. The son's future motivation in betray-

70. *Bezhin Meadow:* The dead Stepok and his father.

ing his father is justified: he has, after all, murdered Stepok's mother. The next scene takes place in the dark interior of the peasant hut. The father complains about his son's allegiance to the Soviet power. Stepok enters, carrying books, and with him comes the light of a bright day. The father utters portentous words, quoting from the Bible: "If the son betrays his father, kill him like a dog!" Only from this reference can the viewer deduce what has happened. Eisenstein delicately chose not to present the actual betrayal of the father by the son. The father is arrested for arson, and Stepok leaves his father's hut with the kolkhoz chairwoman. The other kulak arsonists, surrounded, take refuge in the church and open fire. The church is besieged and the arsonists arrested. Next we see the contrast between the bright, clean-cut, strong, and happy peasants with their extraordinarily long column of tractors on the one hand, and the four dark, ugly, arrested arsonists accompanied by two guards on the other. The peasants' hatred for their enemies is so great they they want to lynch them, but the arrested men are saved by Stepok, who tells a joke. Eisenstein does not share this joke with the audience; we only hear the laughter of the strong and victorious, who have contempt for their miserable enemies.

The peasants decide to turn the church into a club house. They dismantle the church and the scenes provide an occasion for Eisenstein to ridicule the clergy. From the surviving stills it appears that this was the most interesting and powerful segment of the film. To be sure, the scenes are aimed against the Orthodox church, but they also betray a certain ambivalence (perhaps unconscious) on Eisenstein's part toward religion. There are biblical references to Samson, and as the peasants play with the icons, they portray themselves as saints. Several times in the film there appears to be a strange halo around the head of little Stepok; the collective farm peasants are the Samsons and saints of the modern world, Eisenstein seems to be saying. These scenes came to be the most discussed and heavily criticized ones in the film. The critics who later argued that these scenes were unnecessary and that they did not advance the action were correct, but most likely what disturbed them was the mixed ideological message and their sheer exuberance. The arsonists meanwhile manage to overpower and kill their guards. One of them even has time and energy to rape a woman. At night the father finds his son among those who guard the harvest and shoots him. The criminals are arrested once again and Stepok dies in the arms of the leader of the collective farm's political department.

According to Jay Leyda, the film was sixty percent finished when Eisenstein contracted smallpox in the fall of 1935.[13] After spending weeks in a hospital in isolation and then in a sanatorium in the northern Caucasus, the director was ready to return to work, but could not. What happened was not at all unusual in the atmosphere of the 1930s. Boris Shumyatsky, the chief of the Main Film Directorate (GUK), without the permission or even knowledge of the director, showed an unfinished version of the film to leaders of the film industry and later to members of the Politburo.[14] These people viewed the unfinished work and subjected it to heavy criticisms. It was a sad Soviet irony; the director was attacked for not making a picture about a real Soviet village, but instead engaging in mythmaking, raising the level of conflict between father and son to Biblical proportions, a fight between good and evil, light and darkness.[15]

Eisenstein was compelled for all practical purposes to start the work anew. It was to be a different film, with different actors, in which only the basic outline of the story and isolated scenes survived from the original. The roles of the father and of the head of the political department were assigned to different artists. The resolution included yet another irony: the rewriting of the script, in order to make it more politically correct, was entrusted to Isaac Babel, whose last work it was before his destruction as an enemy of the people. The subtlest of Soviet writers was asked to make the work of a far from first-rate author cruder and more explicit. The shooting of the new version began only in August 1936.

It is interesting to compare the two versions because by doing so we can see how Eisenstein hoped to satisfy his critics and make a genuine Soviet film, suitable for the 1930s. Undoubtedly, this was to be a much cruder, one might say much less Eisensteinian film. The most criticized segment of the film was the destruction of the church, and that had to be cut. It was substituted by scenes in which members of the collective farm fight a fire which was the work of the arsonists. At the same time it must be admitted that from the point of view of storytelling the fire scenes are much more relevant than the transformation of the church into a clubhouse.

Some of the nonpolitical elements were removed: there is no mention of the death of Stepok's mother, and consequently Stepok's motivation is exclusively political. Eisenstein was criticized for using myths and Biblical references, rather than showing concrete events. In the new version little is left to the imagination. Now the father has a name, Samokhin. In the previous version his participation in the crime, whatever it was, took place before the first scenes of the film. In Babel's version the boy wakes up and overhears the father and his comrades expressing their loathing for Soviet power, and planning to destroy the harvest: matches will be placed in smoldering sunflowers and thrown into the room where the fuel is kept for the tractors. The awakened boy sneaks out of his father's hut and we see him informing the head of the political department of the planned arson.

The head of the political department has a much greater role. As he should be in a proper socialist realist film, he is a class-conscious positive hero who knows what to do, who is decisive and tender at the same time. He and the chairwoman of the kolkhoz, who at one point breastfeeds Stepok's little sister, are the real parents of the young hero. The leadership of the Party is emphasized. At the end of the film the father shoots his son and tells him: "They took you from me, but I did not give you to them. I did not give my own flesh and blood." It is the political officer who carries the young hero in his arms and more and more Pioneers join as the funeral procession becomes a victory march.

The verbiage is also more didactic. There is nothing of the sly sophistication in Babel's great works. Before he is killed little Stepok goes out to join those who watch the harvest at night in order to protect it from the enemies. This scene is a reference to the Turgenev story where young boys discuss abstract matters at a camp fire. Stepok is surrounded by younger children and he tells them a story about a revolutionary hero who resists the tsarist police and emerges victorious. "And they lead him through a line of soldiers. They beat him with rods. He walks but does not bend. Blood is flowing on his back. Flows like rain. And he walks and keeps silent. And the drum beat rolls." The children are enthralled. Stepok continues: "He walks and keeps silent. And the Tsar asks: Why is this revolutionary silent and does not moan. The general answers the Tsar: Your excellency, revolutionaries do not moan when they are in pain . . ."[16] We are to understand that Stepok is a hero, made of the same material.[17]

On March 17, 1937 Shumyatsky halted production of the film. Two days later he published an article in *Pravda* bitterly criticizing the director.[18] He described the film as a slander against the Soviet countryside, and wrote: "As before, the film's conception is based not on the phenomena of class struggle but on the struggle between the elemental forces of nature between 'Good and Evil.'"

He also wrote: "Now that these deep-rooted errors have been repeated by the director, there can be no doubt that S. Eisenstein was interested in producing *Bezhin Meadow* solely as a pretext for harmful Formalist exercises." Unfairly, but characteristically, he blamed Eisenstein for the scenes depicting the destruction of the church, even though those scenes had been removed.

Shumyatsky's article was followed by a predictable deluge of denunciations of Eisenstein for being "abstract," for being a formalist, for cutting himself off from the people. He was criticized for not showing the leading role of the Party and for depicting collectivization as an elemental process. In a particularly distasteful article, Ilya Vaisfeld maintained that Eisenstein's theory of filmmaking was profoundly hostile to socialism. The director was cut off from reality and deluded by his own mistaken theory concerning "intellectual cinema." According to Vaisfeld, "in the film there is no passionate hatred for the class enemy and there is no genuine love for those who build kolkhozes." It seemed that Eisenstein had depicted the enemies in a positive light, as people who were noble carriers of an incorrect, but nonetheless consistent theory, in the name of which they were willing to accept sacrifice.[19]

Nikolai Otten attacked Eisenstein's approach to the scenario, attributing the failure of *Bezhin Meadow* to the so-called "emotional scenario," which allowed the director to regard the scenario merely as a starting point. In his view montage implied "formalism," the supremacy of the director in the creative work as against the work of the scenarist and actor. The director labored under the illusion that working with an "emotional scenario" freed him from the control of the leadership of the studio. Otten drew the lesson that in the future only fully developed scenarios should be allowed to be staged.[20]

Never publicly shown and seen only by a handful of people, *Bezhin Meadow* became one of the most discussed films of the decade. In the age of show trials, film organizations and studios in Moscow, Leningrad, and Kiev each held meetings for the purpose of discussing the "lessons" of the film. In Moscow the meeting lasted three days, March 19–21, 1937.[21] Shumyatsky himself opened the attack by blaming the director, the film studio in which it was made, and GUK itself. While the director was responsible for the political import, the studio and the higher bodies were guilty of "rotten liberal-ism," allowing Eisenstein to proceed without knowing exactly what he was up to. GUK had asked for a copy of the completed portions of the film but had not insisted when they were not forthcoming. The head of Mosfilm, Boris Babitsky, accepted responsibility and blamed himself for not exercising daily control and therefore not stopping the project earlier. Within a short time Babitsky was arrested.[22] G. Zeldovich of GUK expressed concern that a man of Eisenstein's political unreliability was allowed to work with students at the Film Institute.

Perhaps more interesting than the predictable statements of officials were the opinions expressed by Eisenstein's peers. In their speeches we find a wide spectrum, from courage and decency to villainy. An ex-student of Eisenstein, Pyotr Pavlenko, whose name deserves to be remembered for his courage, de-fended his master at a meeting in the Kiev studio.[23] Eisenstein's former col-league Alexandrov stayed away, earning himself a denunciation in *Kino* for "raising himself above the community." Others managed to speak in such a way as to avoid attacking the man whom they respected. Boris Barnet spoke without saying anything substantial; Grigori Roshal stressed that whatever the circumstances, artists had to trust the leaders. Esfir Shub spoke ambi-guously, suggesting that Eisenstein's absence from the country during the period of the First Five Year Plan rendered him unable to draw the correct political lessons. Calling Eisenstein an urbanist, Alexander Dovzhenko, the reformed arch-formalist, saw the source of formalism in Eisenstein's lack of knowledge of the countryside. Probably "urbanist" was an allusion to Jewish-ness. Ivan Pyrev was as harsh as one would expect from the director of the loathsome *Party Card*. He blamed Eisenstein for not wanting to be a "Soviet person," and wishing to be somewhere else. In his evaluation the formalist Eisenstein had steadily declined after making *The Battleship Potemkin*.[24]

The most bitter attack came from a third-rate director, David Maryan. First he blamed the director for looking down on others, for taking no pleasure in the achievements of others and for being a loner. Then he went on:

> Formalism, formalism and once again formalism. This is a terrible disease with you. Formalism condemns you to loneliness; it is a world view of pessimists, who are in conflict with our era. I should say that I hate formalism with all my being, hate its elements in works of art, even when they are done by such masters as you. I became your opponent when I saw *October*. I saw the Revolution through your eyes. I did not see *Bezhin Meadow,* only excerpts concerning the fire, but that was enough. How could you make a fire the central episode in kolkhoz building? I do not understand what the artist wanted to say by that. We feel that we cannot express in our films even a part of the great thoughts which we want to

express. How do you dare to give a part of your film to show a fire? This is the best testimony of your poverty. You said that the fire represented the struggle of the kolkhoz peasants against anarchy. But don't fascists and capitalists also fight fires? There was no socialist element in it.[25]

Eisenstein's response was extraordinary. First he expressed the inevitable contrition and asked his comrades' help in overcoming his errors. He asked permission to work in the theater, where mistakes could be more easily corrected. Then he went on to make an ambiguous self-criticism, which can also be read as a frontal attack on Stalinist art. He accused himself of believing "that talent and glory gave me the right to have an original vision of the October Revolution. In *The Old and the New* I once again attempted to give my own special, as if it were independent views of the world, instead of carefully studying the statements of the Party and expressing them. I thought I had the right, but it turned out I did not." One can sense bitterness between the lines. He had confided in Rzheshevsky that he would admit being guilty in all instances, whether he was or not.[26] He must have had loathing and hatred for the Stalinist system.

Self-criticism at a small scale gathering was not enough; the director had to make a public statement which appeared in *Sovetskoe iskusstvo* April 17, 1937.[27] After repeating the criticisms made by Shumyatsky, he denounced himself for having been self-absorbed and for not having studied reality. Discussions continued for months. Vsesoiuznyi gosudarstvennyi institut kinematografii (VGIK) (All-Union State Institute of Film) had special meetings scheduled on April 25th and on May 13th. The same themes were repeated ad nauseam and some of the same people gave their denunciations several times. Maryan, for example, spoke again on April 25th. During the May meeting Kuleshov could not avoid making a speech; however, in every criticism he made of his colleague, he included himself. He began: "Comrades, I must speak of the errors of Sergei Mikhailovich in a special way because my own artistic work went on the same incorrect path as the work of Sergei Mikhailovich. I have made special errors, but my artistic work is so full of errors that I cannot speak of the errors of others without remembering my own."[28] He then specified the source of their errors as their having been too preoccupied with the artistic aspects of filmmaking and not knowing Soviet reality.

In conclusion, we may speculate what the real reasons were for the *Bezhin Meadow* fiasco. We should remember that the Stalinist system, like all totalitarian regimes, was highly arbitrary. We may surmise that those films which were not allowed to be shown in the 1930s were not very different from those that actually appeared in the cinemas. Nonetheless, after the state had spent two million rubles on this film, why did it become the only film of Eisenstein which could never appear in the theaters? Most of the criticisms cannot be taken seriously. It is absurd to suggest that the "enemy"—arsonists, rapists, murderers—were depicted with sympathy. It is enough to look at the stills of their faces to understand that these people are monsters. Nor is it a convincing argument that the director depicted collectivization as a destructive process. There were plenty of other films made in this period which showed the dreadful consequences of the work of "wreckers." It is true that Eisenstein operated in the realm of myth, but surely mythmaking was at the heart of socialist realism. Only one of the charges was genuine: Eisenstein was a "formalist," according to the 1930s Soviet understanding of this concept.

Shumyatsky's great and openly expressed dislike of everything that Eisenstein stood for was the decisive reason for stopping production. The boss of the Soviet film industry was a man of primitive tastes, who had neither background nor a particular interest in cinema before his appointment. As long as he headed the industry, Eisenstein was never able to complete a project. In Shumyatsky's view, as he expressed it in his book *Kinematografiia millionov*, the great artists—Lev Kuleshov, Dziga Vertov, and especially Eisenstein—rebelled against bourgeois culture, but in fact they themselves were representatives of that culture. Had these "formalist artists" lived in Italy, they would have become fascists. By describing them as "formalists" Shumyatsky meant nothing more than that they had individual styles, and to that extent never accepted socialist realism.[29]

Eisenstein would have liked to make a genuine socialist realist film, but he was incapable of it; he could not make films which were not in his own, inimitable style. Other great directors, Pudovkin and Dovzhenko, made films at this time that were indistinguishable from those made by less talented people. Eisenstein weathered this storm and soon—but only after Shumyatsky's arrest—started to work on his next project, *Alexander Nevsky*. Eisenstein, the artist, still survived. In this respect he was different from other filmmakers.

Notes

1. "Partiia proveriaet svoi riady" (The Party Examines Its Ranks) *Sovetskoe kino* 10 (1933), 3.

2. *Pravda,* January 9, 1938.

3. R. Iurenev, *Sergei Eizenshtein: Zamysly, Fil'my, Metod* (Eisenstein: Projects, Films, Method), 2: *1930–1948* (Moscow: Iskusstvo, 1988), 100.

4. Grigori Alexandrov writes in his memoirs, *Epokha i kino* (Film and the Era) (Moscow: Politizdat, 1976), 104–105 that Stalin walked into the cutting room of Goskino and announced that "a movie about Trotsky cannot be shown." Eisenstein without a second thought cut out the relevant scenes and re-shot those which were necessary.

5. See my *Cinema and Soviet Society, 1917–1953* (Cambridge: Cambridge University Press, 1992).

6. "O sebe" (About Myself) in A. G. Rzheshevskii, *Zhizn', Kino* (Life, Film) (Moscow: Iskusstvo, 1982), 33–96.

7. It is remarkable that both Jay Leyda in *Kino: A History of Russian and Soviet Film* (Princeton: Princeton University Press, 1983), 329 and Marie Seton in *Sergei M. Eisenstein* (New York: A. A. Wyn, 1952), 353 make the story even "better" than the Soviet myth. In their version the father was a kulak, and the boy was killed because little Pavlik organized the boys to defend the harvest against sabotage. How Leyda, who after all lived in the Soviet Union at the time, came to confuse the official Pavlik Morozov version with Eisenstein's film is an interesting example of the power of mythmaking.

8. Iurii Druzhnikov, *Voznesenie Pavlika Morozova* (The Ascension of Pavlik Morozov) (London: Overseas Publishers, 1988) and a somewhat different English version, *Informer 001: The Myth of Pavlik Morozov* (New Brunswick: Transaction Publishers, 1997).

9. He was not alone in his admiration for the scenario. E. Zil'ber, one of the major critics of the day, also praised Rzheshevskii's work: E. Zil'ber, "K probleme siuzheta" (On the Problem of Plot), *Iskusstvo kino* (1936), no. 3, 15. Zil'ber particularly liked the fact that the major confrontation occurred not between father and son, but between the representatives of two worlds—that is, Rzheshevskii depicted types rather than individuals. Ironically, Eisenstein was attacked in the following year for precisely this characteristic of the film.

10. Yon Barna, *Eisenstein* (London: Secker and Warburg, 1973), 241.

11. On making the film see Leyda, *Kino,* 327–334, who acted as one of the assistants of the director.

12. Rzheshevskii, *Zhizn', kino.* In this collection the entire scenario is reprinted. 215–298. The scenario was first published by Kinofotoizdat in Moscow in 1936.

13. Leyda, *Kino,* 334.

14. E. Levin, " . . . na sud obshchestvennosti . . ." (. . . Into the Court of Public Opinion . . .), *Isskustvo kino* (1988), no. 8, 76–77.

15. Iurenev, *Eizenshtein: Zamysly,* vol. 2, 107.

16. S. M. Eizenshtein *Izbrannye proizvedeniia v shesti tomakh* (Selected Works in Six Volumes) (Moscow: Iskusstvo, 1964–1971), 6, 14.

17. The text of Babel's script is to be found in Eisenstein's *Izbrannye proizvedeniia,* 6, 131–152.

18. *Film Factory: Russian and Soviet Cinema in Documents, 1896–1939,* ed. by Richard Taylor and Ian Christie (Cambridge, MA: Harvard University Press, 1988), 378–381.

19. I. Vaisfel'd, "Teoriia i praktika S. M. Eizenshteina" (Eisenstein's Theory and Practice), *Iskusstvo kino* (1937) no. 5, 25–28.

20. N. Otten, "Snova ob 'emotsional'nom stsenarii'" (Again on an "Emotional Screenplay"), *Iskusstvo kino,* 1937), no. 5, 30–35.

21. *Kino* published two major articles summarizing some of the speeches and giving others verbatim. March 24, 1937, 1–2 and April 11, 1937, 1. Interestingly, Rzheshevskii was not only not invited, but was not allowed to enter the hall. Rzheshevskii, 87.

22. A. Latyshev, "Khotelos' by vsekh poimenno nazvat'" (One Would Like to Call Everyone by Name), *Sovetskii ekran* (1989), no. 1, 23.

23. *Kino,* April 11, 1937, 1. P. A. Pavlenko, aside from this moment of decency, was an unsavory character. According to Nadezhda Mandelshtam, Pavlenko was not only a writer of dreadful conformist novels and scenarios but also an informer, who actually witnessed Osip Mandelshtam's interrogation. The record of human beings at time of extraordinary repression is always complex.

24. N. M. Lary, *Dostoevsky and Soviet Film. Visions of Demonic Realism* (Ithaca: Cornell University Press, 1986). Lary in his chapter on Pyr'ev, 111–129, gives a psychological interpretation of Pyr'ev's hatred of Eisenstein.

25. *Kino,* March 24, 1937, p. 2.

26. Rzheshevskii, *Zhizn', kino,* 87.

27. *Selected Works, 3, Writings, 1934–1947,* ed. Richard Taylor, trans. William Powell (London: British Film Institute, 1996), 100–105. This article, together with other criticisms of the film, appeared in a separate pamphlet in 1937.

28. *Iskusstvo kino* (1988), no. 8, 86–88. Kuleshov and Eisenstein had made an agreement with each other that when one of them was attacked the other would participate in it. After this meeting Kuleshov brought a box of chocolates to Eisenstein, who loved sweets. This story was told to me by Vyacheslav Ivanov, who had heard it from Kuleshov's wife, Khokhlova. Interview with Ivanov on May 14, 1990.

29. *Kinematografiia millionov: opyt analiza* (Cinema for the Millions: An Attempt at Analysis) (Moscow: Kinofotoizdat, 1935), 48–60.

ALEXANDER NEVSKY
Film without a Hero

Barry P. Scherr

Although Andrei Tarkovsky, perhaps the most accomplished Russian director of what may now be termed the "late Soviet" period, was by no means an uncritical admirer of Sergei Eisenstein, the two directors had much in common. One of the more intriguing points of contact concerns a nonexistent echo of an unfilmed sequence. The original screenplay for the work that brought him world renown, *Andrei Rublev,* indicates that Tarkovsky intended to begin the film with a prologue depicting the 1380 Battle of Kulikovo Field, where the Russians inflicted their first major defeat on their Tatar conquerors, a defeat that would, a century later, finally lead to the complete removal of the Mongol Yoke on Russia. The expense of filming this scene caused it to become the first of several cut from the script; even Tarkovsky's "cheaper and artistically more interesting idea" of just showing the corpse-strewn field after the battle was never realized.[1] Thus, *Andrei Rublev* was to have begun precisely where Eisenstein's *Alexander Nevsky* was to have ended: with the Battle of Kulikovo Field, and Dmitri Donskoy, the great-grandson of Alexander Nevsky, leading the Russian troops into victorious battle against the Tatar-Mongolian forces that had dominated the region for a century and a half. But the conclusion to Eisenstein's film, like the prologue of *Andrei Rublev,* was to remain on paper only.[2]

The argument that I shall pursue in this paper is that the absence of the intended final scenes reflects a battle between Eisenstein and others who reviewed the script, and that the inability to include the episode helped make the figure of Alexander Nevsky become both less interesting and ultimately even less central than the director had wanted. Eisenstein seems to have had at least two motivations for his attraction to the topic: on the one hand, he was interested in an epic depiction of Russian heroism, and on the other he found himself fascinated by the figure of Alexander Nevsky. However, for a whole complex of reasons (interference by the authorities, differences between himself and the coauthor of the original screenplay, and very possibly his own lack of readiness to tackle such a topic), he fails to pursue his examination of Nevsky as fully as he might. In retrospect, *Alexander Nevsky* can be seen as a kind of intermediate piece between the earlier films and *Ivan the Terrible,* where he does delve far more deeply into his hero's psychology. The

results for this film are twofold: music and song (but, significantly, not dialogue) take on a heightened importance in the film; second, the work's true
"hero" becomes not Nevsky himself but Russia—the land, the people, and its
spirituality.

As made, *Alexander Nevsky* concludes with the Russians and their leader in
liberated Pskov, shortly after the film's climactic (and longest) scene, the Battle on the Ice. The entire action of the completed work takes place over a
relatively short period; indeed, within the film it seems as though only a matter of days pass from the fall of Pskov to Alexander's being summoned to
assume leadership of the Russian forces in Novgorod, to the climactic battle on
5 April 1242. Historically, though, the events stretched over many months.
Pskov was captured by the Teutonic Knights late in the summer of 1240. The
twenty-year-old Alexander, who had received the sobriquet Nevsky for his
victory over the Swedes at the Neva River earlier that year, left Novgorod in
November for Pereyaslavl after quarreling with the city's leaders; early in
1241, with the threats from the West looming larger, Alexander was recalled
to Novgorod. From the autumn of 1241 onward Alexander led the city's
forces to a series of victories, culminating in the Battle on the Ice the following year.

Even if taking liberties with historical precision to condense the events,
the film deals with a relatively confined period. In the screenplay as Pavlenko
and Eisenstein first published it, however, the victory scene in Pskov was to
be followed by a leap forward in time of some twenty years, when Alexander
is summoned to visit the Golden Horde. The Khan makes Alexander get down
on his knees to show his allegiance, but then ostensibly treats him with respect (while behaving contemptuously toward two Russian princes who have
come over to the Mongols' side). But the Mongols treacherously poison Alexander, who dies on the way home—not in the town where his death actually took place, but at Kulikovo Field, and the film then flashes forward once
again, this time by nearly 120 years, to the time of Dmitri Donskoy and the
Russian victory.

These scenes were among the portions of the proposed film that came in
for the harshest comments by historians. Shortly after the screenplay was first
published in the journal *Znamia* under the title *Rus'* (the old name for Russia), a panel of experts was convened to discuss the historical accuracy of the
script.[3] This must have been a tense occasion; we need only recall that Eisenstein had not completed a film in some nine years and that just a year earlier
production of *Bezhin Meadow* had been halted due to its ideological "errors,"
for which Einstein apologized in an article. That was early in 1937, just as the
purges were about to reach their height; now it was the beginning of 1938,
when countless members of the intelligentsia had been arrested and many

had already perished. Yet the discussion, to the extent that it has been preserved, seems to have focused more on historical than on overtly political
matters. Most of those present praised at least some aspects of the proposed
film, but nearly all had objections as well. Thus one scholar, who was already
carrying out important archeological work in Novgorod, pointed out that the
city was basically an agricultural center and not so much a mercantile one, as
the screenplay indicated. Another complained about the scenes showing the
Teutonic invaders burning and crucifying their captives in Pskov: as Catho-
lics the Teutons would have attempted to convert nonbelievers, rather than
destroy them. That scholar and others were bothered by glimpses of other
foreigners in thirteenth-century Novgorod, which simply would not have
happened at the time. Another described as absurd a scene in which Tverdilo,
the traitorous mayor of Pskov, is seen riding on a troika pulled by three maidens. And numerous complaints were voiced about linguistic anachronisms
in the text. The scenes containing Alexander's visit to the Golden Horde
were critiqued on a number of grounds. Some did not like the relocation of
Alexander's death to Kulikovo Field, but others saw it as a permissible artistic
liberty. More serious were objections that the Khan, who wanted Alexander
Nevsky as an ally, would hardly have poisoned him (though the rumors to
that effect were around long before the screenplay), and that the link between
Alexander's deeds and Dmitri's triumph three generations later was hardly as
direct as the film made it appear.

Some of those experts on the panel tried to be helpful by pointing to specific details that needed correcting, and even the harshest critics provided
useful information. Eisenstein and Pyotr Pavlenko set to work revising the
screenplay, even hiring one of those at the meeting as a consultant on the
project, and by the time the shooting script was prepared they had removed
much of the material that the historians found objectionable.[4] However, not
everything was changed: Eisenstein clung to the scenes showing the violence
committed by the Teutonic invaders against the inhabitants of Pskov, and he
also retained the scenes depicting Alexander's visit to the Golden Horde, followed by his death and the Battle of Kulikovo Field. The script was approved
by the Main Film Directorate (GUK), but with a fourteen-page commentary,
containing numerous suggestions and comments. Among them was a request
to consider dropping these final scenes, which were judged to be poorly developed.[5] Still, Eisenstein continued to make plans to film the conclusion,
until, in March of 1938, the scenes were excised. A few years later Eisenstein
wrote that "A red pencil line was drawn by a hand other than my own after
the scene depicting the defeat of the German hordes. 'The script ends here,'
were the words conveyed to me, 'such a fine prince cannot die!'"[6] When the
scholar Rostislav Yurenev presents his own account of this event, he twice

uses the same phrase that appears in the title marking the start of the Odessa steps scene in *Potemkin:* "And suddenly . . ." [7] Implied here is that the removal of these scenes was ordered at the highest levels; however, given the negative reviews by historians and the generally cool response by the film authorities, the decision could well have been made at the Mosfilm studios.

A detached observer could easily conclude that the person whose hand drew the red line had done Eisenstein a favor, despite his spirited defense of the scene's importance. In a note accompanying the first published version of the screenplay, Eisenstein claimed that the visit to the Golden Horde was vital for showing Russia's struggle against "interventionists." This, he claimed, was the chief theme of the film; while Nevsky embodies that theme, the film was not meant to be just a chronology of his life and deeds. Eisenstein again pointed to a direct line stretching from Alexander's victory on the Neva, to the Battle on the Ice, and concluding with the Battle of Kulikovo Field nearly a century and a half later. [8] Historians, as we have seen, were not convinced. What is more, despite Eisenstein's insistence on a thematic unity between this episode and the rest of the film, it is hard to imagine that audiences would not have instead seen a disjunction. Nearly everything that comes before the visit to the Horde consists of the battle and the events leading directly up to it; the complex epilogue seems to deal with an entirely different topic. On a more mundane level, the film, already longer than average at just over one hundred minutes, would have been extended substantially.

And yet the episode, like the others that were cut from the original screenplay, would have served a purpose in the film, structurally as well as thematically. In satisfying the various objections of the historians and in bowing to the demands of whoever ordered the removal of the final scenes, Eisenstein weakens the series of parallels that impart to the film a sense of harmony and wholeness. For instance, the scene in which Tverdilo rides a troika pulled by three maidens may have been as absurd as the historians claimed, but it would have allowed a moment near the end of the completed film, where Tverdilo himself is seen harnessed in front of a wagon as a prisoner of the victorious Russians, to provide an ironic echo to his earlier moment of triumph. The foreign visitors in Novgorod, who were to have come from both East (Persia, India) and West (Venice) would have shown that Russia meant more to the rest of the world than a convenient territory to be invaded from the East (the Mongols) or the West (the Teutonic Knights). [9]

As for Alexander's visit to the Khan, it would have served to complete the theme introduced by the problematic early scene in which a band of Mongols confront some Russian fishermen and carpenters by the shore of Lake Pleshcheyevo. Alexander is one of the fishermen; as only a historically aware viewer would realize, he has exiled himself from Novgorod after his victory at the Neva due to a dispute with the city's leaders. When a Mongol whips one of the Russians who have been ordered to bow down, the Russians are about to battle back, until Alexander comes over and calms the situation. In the ensuing conversation with the Mongol ambassador who is traveling with the party, Alexander refuses an offer to join with the Golden Horde by referring to a proverb that professes loyalty to one's native land (a theme oft-repeated in the film and another of the parallels so important to the film's structure).[10]

Alexander's leadership, bravery, and patriotism all appear here, but without the planned finale, some troubling questions arise. The sequence concludes with a triumphant song proclaiming that the Russians will never yield their native land, and yet the Mongols are clearly accompanied by a group of Russian prisoners. It is the Mongols, not the Russians, who are triumphant, despite the song.[11] Meanwhile, Alexander insists that the Mongols can wait while the immediate threat of the Germans is confronted. His strategy seems reasonable, but what about those Russian prisoners who are led away, not to be seen again? On the one hand, this opening scene is necessary to show the historical situation and the fact that Russia was threatened from the East as well as the West. However, the film, by raising the issue and then simply dropping it, ends up providing a perhaps unconsciously discordant note to Alexander's triumph.

After the film was completed, Eisenstein offered further reasons for his bitter disappointment at not being able to extend the film as he had wished. The portion of his memoirs that refers to the excision of the final episode contains a remarkable discussion as to how self-abasement can serve as a prelude to attaining one's true position.[12] Eisenstein points out that in his next film Ivan the Terrible has to go through just such a process. He then notes that he himself, like Ivan, also had to submit to self-abasement all too often, but at least sometimes, like Ivan, he was able to rise from that to his highest strivings. The broader psychological implications of these remarks are worth considering; for present purposes, though, the chief point is that in commenting on *Alexander Nevsky* Eisenstein draws a parallel with Ivan's temporary submission.[13] Suffering is seen as a prerequisite to ultimate triumph.

That Eisenstein in fact viewed Alexander Nevsky, along with himself and Ivan the Terrible, as a fellow sufferer, is hardly evident from the completed film, but the point is made explicitly at the end of the preface to the original publication of the screenplay:

> After his death he [Alexander] received the sobriquet "Sufferer for the Russian land"—not "the Conqueror," " the Brave" or "the Glorious," but "the Sufferer." This is characteristic. Nevsky's life was not a series of

military feats. It was lived in service to Russia, and the conqueror of the Swedes and the Germans more than once sacrificed his glory as an undefeated military leader to the Russian national cause.[14]

The last portion of the preface, at least, appears to reflect Eisenstein's thinking, not Pavlenko's. The sequence in which Alexander goes to the Golden Horde at the Khan's bidding was to be viewed both as a subtle strategy on his part, buying time for the Russian forces while they gathered strength over the years, and also as his willingness to suffer humiliation for the greater cause of the Russian people. That is, temporary self-abasement would lead to an ultimate conquest. Elsewhere, Eisenstein states that this episode was to have provided a "Shakespearean reversal" in Nevsky's character—implying, it would seem, a more multisided depiction of the purely heroic figure who appears in the actual film.[15] Thus Eisenstein also saw these scenes as imparting a needed degree of depth and subtlety to the figure of Alexander: with them, he would have become a figure of tragic import who must suppress his personal impulses and desires for the sake of a higher, national goal that would be realized only more than a century after his death.

Taken together, Eisenstein's various remarks about the absence of the visit to the Golden Horde indicate something that bothered him greatly about the film as it was finally made: despite its title, the work does not fully come to grips with the figure of Alexander Nevsky. The project was one of several historical topics that were suggested to Eisenstein in the spring of 1937, while he was resting at a spa in Kislovodsk after the disaster with *Bezhin Meadow*. He was attracted to the idea of working on Nevsky, and was told that Pyotr Pavlenko—a writer who had traveled to and written about Central Asia and the Far East, and for whom this historical topic was thus a natural extension of his interests—was already working on a screenplay.[16] While the title of the first published version was *Rus'*, later Pavlenko was to suggest *Novgorod the Great* and Eisenstein *The Battle on the Ice* as more suitable; only in March of 1938, as filming was about to begin, did Eisenstein insert the title *Alexander Nevsky*. As has often been pointed out, this title, with its focus on a key historical figure, was typical for many films of the 1930s when historical and patriotic films were very much in vogue: *Baltic Deputy, Lenin in October, Peter the First, Minin and Pozharsky, Shchors,* and *Lenin in 1918*.[17]

These films do not so much offer historically accurate portrayals as a Party-line view of the past that could also be applied to the (Stalinist) present. In many ways *Alexander Nevsky* fits into this mode. As Western critics have long noted, the theme of internal subversion (Tverdilo in Pskov) was a favorite of Stalin's, but just as important are, for instance, the scenes in which Nevsky (as a stand-in for Stalin) is shown listening attentively to the voice of the people.

The armorer Ignat (i.e., the ordinary worker) meets death as a result of both his one bit of inferior work as well as his momentary lack of vigilance with the enemy. Similarly, the better-off classes (read: bourgeoisie) are depicted as less reliable and patriotic than the simple peasants, while ultimate wisdom is shown as residing in the supreme leader. All of this combines to make the film the most schematic and accessible by Eisenstein, and also, in the opinion of most Western critics, a largely static work, shackled by its efforts to glorify the Stalinist personality cult.[18]

This criticism is true enough, and yet the record indicates that Eisenstein was all too aware of his failure to provide a psychological portrait of Alexander, and that the removal of the visit to the Golden Horde deprived him of whatever opportunity he had to probe more deeply into his hero. It is perhaps not surprising that he preferred the title *The Battle on the Ice*—since that is what he ultimately filmed—rather than a full study of Alexander. His work was left with a rather unidimensional and isolated figure at its core, with Alexander more typical of the hero in epic songs that served as a source for elements in the screenplay than the kind of psychologically complex figure Eisenstein was to depict in *Ivan*. To the extent that romantic relationships play any role in the work, they are given over to the two Novgorod heroes, Vasili Buslay and Gavrilo Oleksich. These same two figures represent the intelligence (Gavrilo) and the bravery (Vasili) that Alexander combines. Alexander was to have a wife in the original screenplay, and she was to appear, along with their children, at the beginning of the sequence depicting Alexander's visit to the Golden Horde. As the film stands, however, Alexander is shown without a wife and for that matter without a constant confidante—at various times, first one person and then another speaks with him, but he does not appear to have a close relationship with any one individual. In writing about the film, Eisenstein emphasized his efforts to show the brilliance of Alexander, but in fact the strategy that wins the battle is inspired by Ignat, the armorer who is also a representative of the masses. Alexander remains above such mundane matters as ordinary human relationships and is seen primarily making speeches, giving commands to others, or receiving encomia from those around him. The film never provides the kind of mystery or depth in his portrait that could make him a more fascinating person.

It is in fact doubtful whether the final sequence alone could have rescued the film from what is, after all, a superficial and all-too-worshipful treatment of its key figure. The work as a whole would still have lacked the intricate and ambiguous identification with authority that profoundly affects Eisenstein's technique in *Ivan the Terrible*.[19] Instead, one is left with something that resembles a child's hero-worship, in which the great one is held up as the saintly and heroic figure of boyish fantasies.[20] In this regard *Alexander Nevsky* is a transitional work, where Eisenstein (who, during the purges, was himself hardly a figure beyond suspicion) is aware of but not yet ready or able to realize fully the dimensions that will make *Ivan the Terrible* a great film.

This failure to probe more deeply into the personality of Alexander Nevsky results as well from the differing sensibilities behind the original screenplay. Russian contemporaries of Eisenstein simply regarded Pyotr Pavlenko as the writer; indeed when it was first published, in the December 1937 issue of *Znamia,* only Pavlenko was listed as author, with Eisenstein's contribution acknowledged in parentheses.[21] In fact, the very first treatment of the topic, written by Pavlenko alone, already contains much of what went into the final film: the visit of the Horde to Alexander while he is cleaning nets near Pereyaslavl; the defeat of Pskov; the friends Buslay and Gavrilo, along with their rivalry over Olga; the Battle on the Ice; and Olga's request in the final scene for Alexander to choose between her rivals. In putting together this version Pavlenko referred to chronicle accounts of the battle and of Alexander, but also incorporated elements taken from Russian folk sources.[22] Several details in this variant did not make their way into the final film (an opening scene showing the fall of Pskov, a third Novgorodian hero named Sadko, the previously mentioned foreign merchants in Novgorod, the capture of Tverdilo by Pskov maidens), and others are altered. The Battle on the Ice is presented in this early version only in outline form. When Eisenstein joined the project he gathered whatever material he could (including a specially commissioned translation of the one German account of the famous battle) and consulted with numerous experts about details connected with the period. The hundreds of notes and drawings that he prepared during the early stages of his work on the project contain much that relates to the visit to the Golden Horde, attesting to the special importance he attached to that sequence.[23] A second version (which was to undergo many changes before the *Znamia* publication) is already much closer to the film as Eisenstein ultimately envisioned it: several more scenes that eventually went into the completed work are included, others are brought closer to their final realization, and the visit to the Golden Horde now appears.[24]

The evolution from conception to the final film reveals differences between Pavlenko and Eisenstein in their approach to the material.[25] Indeed, when Pavlenko republished the screenplay under his own name after World War II, he went back to the *Znamia* version as (presumably) representing more of his own vision: he again begins in Pskov with the taking of the city, reintroduces foreign merchants and the figure of Sadko in Novgorod, and goes back to the original versions of many other scenes.[26] In keeping with his preference for the film's title, and also reflecting the article entitled "Alexander Nevsky" that he wrote during World War II, emphasizing the importance of Novgorod for thirteenth-century Russia, this treatment sharpens the differences between subjugated Pskov and vibrant Novgorod.[27] In the first sections of the screenplay, other than a few stylistic revisions the major difference with the *Znamia* publication is his omitting references to the three maidens from Pskov who originally pull Tverdilo in a troika and later capture him; oddly, the names of three Pskov maidens (Sofia, Nadezhda, and Lyubov—i.e., Wisdom, Hope, and Love) still appear in his cast of characters. He also retains (or reintroduces) Alexander's visit to the Golden Horde, an addition that seems to have belonged largely to Eisenstein, but leaves out a scene in which Alexander gets on bended knee before the Khan's tent, and with it the "Shakespearean reversal" that was so vital to the director.

Pavlenko's final version indicates, first of all, that in his conception Alexander Nevsky functions only as a symbolic figure of Russian heroism—nothing in his treatment indicates an interest in looking deeply into this figure, who, according to many Western commentators, was perhaps a less positive force than Russian historical myth would imply.[28] The element of self-abasement, so important to Eisenstein, is eliminated by Pavlenko, no doubt because it would have made the figure appear less purely heroic. And if anything Pavlenko sees Novgorod itself as no less a "hero" of the period, introducing both historical and folklore figures connected with its past and, in his article, glossing over the differences between its leaders and Alexander that caused the latter to leave the city. In other words, the basic material that Pavlenko presented to Eisenstein did not leave the director much opportunity to develop a more multifaceted figure. And all of this is not surprising, given Pavlenko's own political views.[29] On his behalf, it can be said that his work reflected some extensive reading in both historical and folk sources, which resulted as well in a play bearing the title of the greatest Russian epic hero, Ilya Muromets.

Pavlenko's introduction of folklore heroes, perhaps unwittingly on his part, helps diminish the role of Alexander. Alexander resembles the legendary figure about whom Pavlenko wrote his play, *Ilya Muromets.*[30] Indeed, his unquestioning bravery and loyalty to a cause for its own sake bring Alexander very much into line with folklore heroes in general and specifically with those of the Russian epic songs, or *byliny,* thereby making him a less realistic and more abstract figure. Whether or not he had Ilya Muromets in mind, Pavlenko did borrow the two most prominent figures who appear specifically in *byliny* that belong to the Novgorod tradition: Vasili Buslay and Sadko. Sadko has only a fleeting role in any of the scenarios and does not appear at all in the film; Vasili of course does appear, as does his mother, also a figure in the *byliny* that were sung about him. Buslay is hardly a conventional figure; in the main story that is told about him he is something of a rebel, who gets into a fight on a bridge over the Volkhov River during which he commits mayhem, until his mother stops him.[31] This episode was to be echoed in the scene contained in the "missing reel" of *Alexander Nevsky,* but with the disappearance of that reel, so too disappeared the clearest folklore influence on the film.[32] What is left is something of Vasily's personality, but virtually nothing of his story.

Eisenstein, unlike Pavlenko, had doubts about using characters from the *byliny,* believing that the exaggerations fundamental to that genre's poetics could not be conveyed on the screen.[33] And in fact, by placing Nikolai Okhlopkov (a sometime actor and prominent theater director) in the role, Eisenstein employed a person already identified in the public mind with another figure named Vasili. Okhlopkov had played the ordinary Russian of that name in the film *Lenin in October* from the previous year and was to do so again the following year in *Lenin in 1918;* to the extent that Eisenstein is typecasting here, he purposefully chooses an actor whose popular image was hardly that of an epic hero. Indeed, with his humorous traits and down-to-earth quality, Eisenstein's Vasili seems more like a good-natured peasant. Thus, if Pavlenko's script uses folk figures that deflect some of the heroic aura from Alexander, Eisenstein's realization of Buslay also affects Alexander negatively: the character played by Okhlopkov, for all his warrior-like manner, nonetheless displays a simple, open nature that makes him a much easier figure than Alexander with whom to empathize: the film's title character becomes all the more remote.

Eisenstein's inability to probe deeply into the film's title figure may also be responsible in part for the role that music, rather than dialogue, plays in this, the first sound film that he completed. As James Goodwin has remarked, "*Alexander Nevsky* is truly a sound film and not a talking picture."[34] Dialogue is minimal, and in many scenes there is no talking at all while the camera offers a panoramic sweep of fields or battle (compare in this regard the opening shots in devastated Pskov). In other instances, the words primarily consist of the songs that serve as background to several moments, most memorably perhaps the mezzo-soprano aria sung during the scene showing the field of dead and wounded soldiers after the battle. Thus it is a film of music and panorama, lacking in the speech that would have allowed for psychological probing.

With this film Eisenstein put together the collaborative team with which he was to work from then on. Vladimir Lugovskoy, a well-known Russian poet, wrote songs for *Alexander Nevsky* and then for *Ivan the Terrible,* while Sergei Prokofiev, of course, composed the music for both films. Prokofiev has been called a composer with a highly visual talent; he had already worked on film and, earlier in his career, had composed operas that could be described as cinematic in their structure.[35] In addition to both his experience and his skill, Prokofiev simply enjoyed a fine working relationship with Eisenstein; the story of their collaboration has been oft-told (not least by Eisenstein himself)

71. Eisenstein with Prokofiev, who composed the scores for
Alexander Nevsky and *Ivan the Terrible.*

and seems to have been an instance where two creative geniuses in different fields had a genuine understanding of and respect for each other.[36]

Many have bemoaned the poor quality of *Alexander Nevsky*'s soundtrack, which was recorded with a small ensemble using equipment that was clearly not up to Western standards of the late 1930s; André Previn has referred to the result as "the greatest film score ever written trapped inside the worst soundtrack ever recorded."[37] Nonetheless, and in contrast to *Ivan the Terrible,* the score has received more attention among critics than the script—perhaps due in part to the well-known cantata that Prokofiev derived from the score.

Eisenstein, in his well-known essay on "Vertical Montage," began the tradition of analyzing the score in great detail. Eisenstein's remarks take up a good portion of this lengthy article and deal with only the twelve shots, accompanied by seventeen measures of music, that comprise the scene of anticipation just prior to the Battle on the Ice.[38] The thrust of Eisenstein's remarks is to claim a correspondence between image and sound, thereby creating a different type of montage than that discussed in his earliest articles, where the term referred to a succession of shots. While some critics have reacted skeptically to Eisenstein's specific claims about the resonances between sound and image in this specific scene, others have commented positively on the music itself, especially that which accompanies the Battle on the Ice.[39] Here critics have discerned a clear use of musical motifs that distinguish the Russian and German forces, with the result that sound and image do indeed reinforce each other in the manner that Eisenstein intended.[40] Indeed, the music—however distorted it may be—provides many of the most striking moments. Much of the sound is nondiegetic: indeed, the powerful effects accompanying the Battle on the Ice will in many ways seem among the least original to today's viewer, since what might be called "battle music" has become almost a cliché in the years since *Alexander Nevsky* was made. More unusual are the songs, such as those that accompany the scene with the Mongol band early in the film or the battlefield at the end; here the sound might be termed "quasi-diegetic"; in that it seems to belong to figures within the film (to the ordinary Russians in the first scene, to Olga in the second), but we do not actually see the figures singing. And then there is the diegetic music: the variety of folk instruments associated with the Russians, the organ played by the ominous cowled figure among the Teutonic Knights, the Knights' own trumpet-like horns. Note in this regard that the foreign visitors to Novgorod were to have been shown playing instruments as well. All of this is no doubt one reason why the film has so often been characterized as "operatic."

And yet it needs to be kept in mind that Lugovskoy's songs and Prokofiev's music are also to be found in *Ivan the Terrible,* for which the term operatic, when applied at all, is done so less pejoratively. The key difference once again concerns the relative absence of dialogue. The Battle on the Ice occupies thirty-five minutes and consists primarily of spectacle and music, interrupted by only a few short exchanges. The scene of the waiting before the battle, so painstakingly analyzed by Eisenstein, is in fact only one of several moments in which a series of shots, accompanied by music but no dialogue, provides an interlude. The first of these depicts the field with the bones of Russian soldiers killed by the Mongols, and appears immediately following the opening credits; another occurs during the scene in which Russians gather to join with Alexander's forces as he returns to Novgorod. At all of these points the focus is not on "character" as such, but on mood, and shots of land and sky, rather than of people, predominate within the image.

As for Alexander Nevsky, his words in the film are few in number and often consist of short speeches, as when he addresses the people in Novgorod before the battle or in Pskov afterwards; his longest dialogue may well be his exchange with the Tatar ambassador at the beginning of the film. When he does speak he often uses brief, elliptical phrases or proverbial constructions. All of this again helps set Alexander apart from others, in keeping with his general depiction. The reliance on speeches and slogan-like proverbs could well have made Eisenstein's contemporaries think of Stalin, and it also makes Alexander's role somewhat "operatic" in that his very words, and often the formal poses that he takes when he utters them, seem no less stylized than the songs that often appear just after his speeches.

And it is precisely in this regard that the poetics of this film seem confused. A heavy reliance on music in early Russian sound films was hardly unusual. Eisenstein's erstwhile colleague Grigori Alexandrov created musical comedies at about this time (*The Jolly Fellows,* also known as *Jazz Comedy; Volga-Volga*), which, whatever their artistic merit, nonetheless could blend music and story no worse than the typical Hollywood musical. In the early 1930s Dziga Vertov directed such documentaries as *Three Songs of Lenin,* in which character as such plays only a small role and the images themselves form a kind of symphonic structure. By the time Eisenstein himself got to *Ivan the Terrible,* he was able to incorporate music while still creating a powerful and complex central character. *Alexander Nevsky,* though, remains very much a transitional film, in which Eisenstein is still tied to building scenes through montage, much as in his silent films where the mass scene and the succession (or clash) of images drives the individual sequence. His essay on "vertical montage" indicates that he viewed sound essentially as music, as an element that can combine smoothly with the image, which contains the "linguistic" message he wants to convey. In all of this there is little room for speech, which almost seems to be an afterthought in both the screenplay and the final film.

And for that matter there is little room for acting as well. As Stanley Kauffmann has pointed out, Eisenstein in general employed "a style of acting that is diametrically opposed to the conventions and scope of the cinema," combining "the large-scale abstraction of romantic acting with the agility and intimacy of the camera." [41] In *Ivan the Terrible* this type of acting produces some unsettling effects, but through it all one can sense the internal struggles of the central figure. In *Alexander Nevsky,* on the other hand, the roles, including that of Alexander, are largely one-dimensional, and there was little need for the fine actors whom Eisenstein recruited to call upon the full-range of their talent. [42] Again, it is possible to sense the influence of Eisenstein's experience in silent film, in which he frequently cast "types" rather than professional actors for certain roles: he was often more concerned with attaining striking effects that he could contrast and mix through montage than in exploring depth of character. Costume turns out to be at least as important as dialogue or the actual acting for characterization of his figures: Alexander, with a tunic that sets him apart from the other Russians fishing in the lake; the cowled organist; or the Teutonic Knights, whose helmets totally hide their faces (and whose "individuality" seems to be determined solely by the strange decorations, such as a set of claws or a hand, on their helmets). [43] The sharply angled camera shots also reduce the need for refined acting; Alexander, for instance, is frequently shot from a low angle and often accompanied by another figure who looks up at him, thereby imparting to him a sense of grandeur.

Still, *Alexander Nevsky* is ultimately a film without a hero. Like so many of his contemporaries, Eisenstein tackled a grand historical theme with a major figure at its center. He then goes on to place the true "heroic" elements elsewhere: by emphasizing the role played by "the people," by highlighting the Russian land as an opponent to the foreign invaders, and by assigning a prominent role to Russian spirituality.

Only the first of these seems to have been motivated by the script and by efforts to please the authorities. In the notes that accompanied the first published version of the screenplay, Eisenstein cites several ways in which he has responded to an earlier critique; he now shows peasants to be taking a more active role in the events, ranging from their appearance in the early confrontation with the Mongol band to their gathering en masse and joining forces with Alexander, to the peasant detachments being given a specific role in the Battle on the Ice.[44] In one of his autobiographical notes Eisenstein also discusses the manner in which Ignat, the armorer, became a major figure in the film.[45] His chief point seems to be to trace how the role of what was initially an insignificant figure grew; however, as mentioned earlier, in making Ignat's off-color folk tale the source for Alexander's strategy in fighting against the Germanic forces, Eisenstein also makes Alexander less of a brilliant strategist and more of a figure who simply is able to translate folk wisdom into action. This is just one of the ways in which Alexander becomes a strangely passive figure. People certainly believe in him and call upon him to rally the Novgorod forces, but within the film he appears to be strangely above much of the action. Key actions by the people are shown as spontaneous: the gathering of the forces that will defeat the Germans, the killing of Tverdilo by the people of Pskov.

More subtly, and more critically, it is the Russian land itself that seems to provide a powerful answer to those who would invade Russia.[46] Most prominent in this regard are several of the scenes without dialogue. The opening sequence begins with shots showing skulls and other remains of the defeated Russians on a battlefield.[47] As the camera pulls back to reveal more of the devastated land, it then takes in the large sky, lingers on a shot showing the

72. Alexander Nevsky: Russian forces set off against the sky.

73. *Alexander Nevsky:* The fall of Pskov is announced against backdrop of church in Novgorod.

vast expanse, and then goes on to the water, with its promise of life. Even more striking in this regard is the scene where the Russians rally to join with Alexander when he sets out to Novgorod. The Russians seem to be springing out of the land itself in the early shots, which are filmed at a very low angle so as to take in the sky as well. Then the marching forces are shown set off against the sky, in one shot with the land itself almost invisible, so that earth and sky seem to have merged and all embody a sense of Russia.[48] Also important are the "weapons" carried by the Russians: farm implements, such as axes and pruning hooks. Axes play a significant role throughout the film (Vasili has one in the first Novgorod scene, and later the Russian forces will be shown wielding them in battle); it is as though this basic tool, like the Russian land itself, takes on an emblematic significance in the struggle against the foreign forces.

And finally, there is the role of Russian spirituality. The surface thrust of the film is clearly anti-religious: the monk Ananias is one of the traitorous Russians, many of the Teutonic Knights have crosses on their uniforms and even the slits in their helmets are in the shape of a cross, and an evil-looking archbishop blesses the Knights. Yet religious symbolism also has a positive import. Eisenstein, deciding that the existing churches in Novgorod bore too many of the ravages of time, relied instead on a set that he had built in which a gleaming white St. Sofia church figures prominently throughout the scenes in the city.[49] When Pavsha, the martyred Pskov defender, is hauled up on ropes against the wall of a church, the figure of an angel or saint on the church wall seems to be looking at him with compassion. Bells, long associated with Russian spirituality (once again, compare Tarkovsky's *Andrei Rublev*), are heard ringing at the beginning of the scenes in Novgorod and call the people to an assembly when the word of Pskov's fall arrives; later, they accompany the victorious Russians in Pskov. In that later scene the fallen Russian heroes bear candles as they are conveyed into the city, in keeping with Russian Orthodox tradition.

What I am suggesting, therefore, is that a subtext accompanies the heroic but also shallow and circumscribed portrayal of Alexander Nevsky: in nearly all of the film's most successful scenes the focus is not on Alexander, but on the Russian masses, on shots of earth and sky, on aspects of Russian spirituality. The psychological drama that attracted Eisenstein was blocked by Pavlenko's original treatment, by the decision to omit the sequence with Alexander's visit to the Golden Horde, by the necessity for a reverential treatment in 1938 toward the figure who would be construed as a stand-in for Stalin himself, by Eisenstein's inability (or unwillingness) at this point to integrate issues of personality and power, and perhaps simply by his failure here to shed fully the poetics of the silent film in which he had done all his completed work until then.[50] But, particularly in the scenes where music and image are allowed to stand on their own, Eisenstein creates a separate homage to the Russian spirit, one that stands apart from and—consciously or not—in the final analysis becomes more interesting and more powerful than the one-dimensional figure who appears as the film's ostensible hero.

Notes

1. See Vida T. Johnson and Graham Petrie, *The Films of Andrei Tarkovsky: A Visual Fugue* (Bloomington: Indiana University Press, 1994), 80; Maya Turovskaya, *Tarkovsky: Cinema as Poetry,* trans. Natasha Ward (London: Faber and Faber, 1989), 47.

2. The original ending appears in the appendix of Eisenstein, *Izbrannye proizvedeniia v shesti tomakh* (Selected Works in Six Volumes) (Moscow: Iskusstvo, 1964–71), 6, 453–455; for an English translation see *Eisenstein: Three Films,* trans. Diana Matias, ed. Jay Leyda (New York: Harper and Row, 1974), 182–186.

3. For the information in this paragraph, I am indebted to Rostislav Iurenev, *Sergei Eizenshtein: Zamysly, Fil'my, Metod* (Eisenstein: Projects, Films, Method), 2: *1930–1948* (Moscow: Iskusstvo, 1988), 144–146.

4. Ibid., 145–146.

5. Ibid., 147.

6. Eisenstein, *Izbrannye,* 1, 500.

7. Iurenev, *Sergei Eizenshtein,* 147.

8. Eisenstein, *Izbrannye,* 6, 546.

9. Part of the historians' objection stemmed from the intention to have the

various visitors carrying musical instruments (e.g., the Venetian was to have a mandolin); while this would have contributed to the musicality that pervades the film, many felt that these secondary figures belonged more in an opera than a purportedly historical film (Iurenev, *Sergei Eizenshtein,* 146).

10. David Quint points to another, somewhat ironic parallel between the missing ending and the completed film: Dmitri's forces were to be shown defeating the Tatars by employing the same wedge-like formation that the Germans had used against the Russians. As Quint remarks, this scene would have had the Russians taking over the Teutonic Knights' role of "Western imperialists," using brute military force to attack and subdue the East. See his *Epic and Empire: Politics and Generic Form from Virgil to Milton* (Princeton: Princeton University Press, 1993), 368.

11. Russell Merritt, "Recharging *Alexander Nevsky:* Tracking the Eisenstein–Prokofiev War Horse," *Film Quarterly,* 48: 2 (1994–1995), 39.

12. Eisenstein, *Izbrannye,* 1, 499–501; cf. the English translation in his *Selected Works,* 4: *Beyond the Stars: The Memoirs of Sergei Eisenstein,* ed. Richard Taylor, trans. William Powell (London: British Film Institute, 1995), 740–742. The memoirs were unpublished in Eisenstein's lifetime; given the frankness of many passages, it is almost certain that he would not have tried to publish them while Stalin was still alive.

13. Leon Balter, in highlighting potential homosexual motifs in *Alexander Nevsky,* notes the role that submission plays in two of the film's negative characters, Tverdilo and Ananias, but, not discussing this ending in the film, Balter sees Alexander Nevsky himself only in terms of a "manly ideal." "*Alexander Nevsky,*" *Film Culture,* no. 70/71(1983), 65–70.

14. Petr Andreevich Pavlenko and Sergei Eisenstein, "Rus'" (Russia), *Znamia,* 7: 12 (1937), 103. The preface links Alexander Nevsky not just to Dmitri Donskoy, but also to Peter the Great—both with an epigraph from Pushkin's poem "Poltava," dealing with Peter's victory over the Swedes, and by pointing out that Peter began building his own fleet at Pereyaslavl (the location of the ship-building in the opening scene of *Alexander Nevsky*) and later moved Alexander Nevsky's remains to the Neva, the site of Alexander's own defeat of the Swedes.

15. Eisenstein on "Shakespearean reversal," *Izbrannye,* 5, 119.

16. Eisenstein, *Izbrannye,* 6, 545.

17. E.g., by Mira Meilakh, *Izobrazitel'naia stilistika pozdnikh fil'mov Eizenshteina* (The Graphic Style of Eisenstein's Late Films) (Leningrad: Iskusstvo, 1971), 43.

18. David Bordwell comments on the film's accessibility in *The Cinema of Eisenstein* (Cambridge, MA: Harvard University Press, 1993), 211. Its stasis is discussed by James Goodwin, *Eisenstein, Cinema, and History* (Urbana: University of Illinois Press, 1993), 177.

19. Alexander Zholkovsky, "Eisenstein's Poetics: Dialogical or Totalitarian?" In *Laboratory of Dreams: The Russian Avant-Garde and Cultural Experiment,* ed. John E. Bowlt and Olga Matich (Stanford: Stanford University Press, 1996), 245–256. An earlier version of this article appeared in *Wiener Slawistischer Almanach—Sonderband* 31 (1992), 481–501.

20. Jacques Aumont, *Montage Eisenstein,* trans. Lee Hildreth, Constance Penley, and Andrew Ross (Bloomington: Indiana University Press, 1987), 18.

21. Pavlenko is discussed by Viktor Shklovskii, *Eizenshtein* (Moscow: Iskusstvo, 1973), 244.

22. Iurenev, *Sergei Eizenshtein,* 136–137.

23. Ibid., 140–141.

24. Ibid., 138–139.

25. The two men did go on to write the screenplay for *The Fergana Canal,* an aborted film which was to have been Eisenstein's next project, and there Eisenstein's interest in the past came into direct conflict with Pavlenko's desire to emphasize contemporary themes. Petr Andreevich Pavlenko, *Sobranie sochinenii v shesti tomakh* (Collected Works in Six Volumes) (Moscow: GIKhL, 1953–55), 4, 375.

26. Pavlenko, *Sobranie,* 4, 189–231. Pavlenko also goes back to the earlier dialogue, with its many turns of phrase that historians found to be linguistic anachronisms. He does not include the preface to the *Znamia* publication; the part of the preface that glorifies Novgorod is in keeping with Pavlenko's views, but Pavlenko almost certainly would not have been happy with the sections that link Alexander to Dmitri Donskoy and to Peter the Great and that talk of Alexander as a "sufferer."

27. Pavlenko discusses Norgorod in *Sobranie,* 6, 108–109.

28. Cf. John Fennell who, among other things, questions the significance of the victories for which Nevsky has been glorified and suggests that his subsequent policies as Grand Prince eliminated Russian resistance to the Golden Horde for many years to come. *The Crisis of Medieval Russia 1200–1304* (London: Longman, 1983), 97–124.

29. Cf. note 23 to the Peter Kenez article in this volume, who points out that Pavlenko, despite a moment of decency toward Eisenstein, was an unpleasant figure who seems to have been an informer for the secret police. Cf. the memoirs of the poet Osip Mandelshtam's widow, Nadezhda Mandelshtam, *Vospominaniia* (Memoirs) (New York: Izdatel'stvo imeni Chekhova, 1970), 89–90. Earlier, Pavlenko had a promising start in literature, and in fact co-authored his first story with the well-known writer Boris Pilnyak. Less attractively, he grew into an uncompromising ideologue and supporter of the regime, culminating in a novel called *Happiness* (*Schast'e,* 1947), as perfect an example as any of the socialist realist novels that blatantly echoed the party line in the post–World War II period.

30. Meilakh, *Izobrazitel'naia stilistika,* 45.

31. Iu. I. Smirnov and V. G. Smolitskii, *Novgorodskie byliny* (Novgorod Byliny) (Moscow: Nauka, 1978) 367–369.

32. Eisenstein says that the reel was not ready for viewing when the film, which was completed well ahead of schedule, was to be reviewed prior to its release (*Izbrannye,* 1, 292). Shklovskii (*Eizenshtein,* 249) adds the tantalizing detail that it was Stalin himself who asked to see the rushes. Eisenstein later requested that the scene be included in the final film and that he be given an opportunity to finish editing the entire work (among other things, he wanted to eliminate two hundred meters from the Battle on the Ice) but the film was released in the form

that the authorities reviewed it. The reel was never restored and remains lost. The name of the film's other main figure from Novgorod, Gavrilo, is taken from the chronicles, not from a folklore source.

33. Iurenev, *Sergei Eizenshtein,* 141.

34. Goodwin, *Eisenstein, Cinema, and History,* 174.

35. Harlow Robinson, "'The Most Contemporary Art': Sergei Prokofiev and Soviet Film," *Studies in Contemporary Communism,* 17: 3–4 (1984), 205 et passim.

36. On their collaboration see, for instance, Eisenstein's essay "PRKFV" (*Izbrannye,* 5, 457–473) as well as comments in "Vertical Montage" (*Izbrannye,* 2, 236 and *Selected Works,* 2: *Towards a Theory of Montage,* ed. Michael Glenny and Richard Taylor, trans. Michael Glenny [London: British Film Institute, 1991], 371).

37. Merritt, "Recharging *Alexander Nevsky,*" 44. In the late 1980's the producer John Goberman arranged for live orchestral performances of a "re-created" film score; for the background to his efforts, see Nancy Shear, "*Alexander Nevsky:* A Masterwork Restored," *Ovation,* 8 (November 1987), 20–22; and her "New Life for a Russian Film Classic," *Symphony Magazine,* (February/March 1988), 8–11. The production was generally well-received in the United States, though John Gillett, reviewing a British presentation, pointed out that the screen and theater performances never quite meshed: "Prokofiev, Cairns and Ashkenazy," *Sight & Sound,* 58: 4 (1989), 200.

38. Eisenstein, *Izbrannye,* 2, 244–266; for an English version, see *Selected Selected Works,* 2: *Towards a Theory of Montage,* 370–399.

39. See Theodor Adorno and Hanns Eisler, *Composing for the Films* (London: The Athone Press, 1994), 157, for a skeptical view of the film's sound and image.

40. See, for instance, Philip D. Roberts, "Prokofiev's Score and Cantata for Eisenstein's *Alexander Nevsky,*" *Semiotica,* 21: 1–2 (1977), 151–166; and John Mowitt, *Text: The Genealogy of an Antidisciplinary Object* (Durham: Duke University Press, 1992). For a dissenting view see D. W. Gallez, "The Prokofiev-Eisenstein Collaboration: *Nevsky* and *Ivan* Revisited," *Cinema Journal,* 17: 2 (1978), 17–20.

41. Stanley Kauffmann, *A World on Film* (New York: Harper & Row, 1966), 21.

42. Iurenev, *Sergei Eizenshtein,* 141.

43. These helmets are said to have inspired George Lucas when creating the figure of Darth Vader for *Star Wars.* George Turner, "*Alexander Nevsky* Comes Back in Style," *American Cinematographer,* 68 (November, 1987), 96.

44. Eisenstein, *Izbrannye,* 6, 545–546.

45. Eisenstein, *Izbrannye,* 1, 176–184; cf. *Selected Works,* 4: *Beyond the Stars,* 751–771.

46. Quint, *Epic and Empire,* 362–363, refers both to the importance of the land and (366) to the prominence of the ax within the film.

47. Note that Eisenstein, who carefully spread bones over a field to create this scene, was not happy with the result: *Izbrannye,* 1, 299–300; cf. *Selected Works,* 4: *Beyond the Stars,* 406–409.

48. As David Brandenberger has pointed out to me, this patriotic use of Russian imagery is generally associated with the period 1941–45; Eisenstein's use of it in this earlier period is highly innovative. See also his article, "'Whosoever comes

to us with the sword shall perish by the sword': Historicizing the Production and Reception of S. M. Eisenstein's *Aleksandr Nevskii,*" forthcoming in *Epic Revisionism: Tsarist History and Literature as Stalinist Propaganda,* ed. by David Brandenberger and Kevin Platt. I am indebted to Brandenberger as well for several other comments on an earlier version of this article.

49. On Eisenstein's interest in cathedrals, Western as well as Russian, see Håkan Lövgren, *Eisenstein's Labyrinth: Aspects of a Cinematic Synthesis of the Arts,* Stockholm Studies in Russian Literature, 31 (Stockholm: Almqvist & Wiksell, 1996), 59–67.

50. After this article was completed, David Brandenberger called my attention to a Russian editorial, which similarly stated that the lack of probing into Nevsky's motives and his inner state is detrimental to the film. "Patrioticheskaia tema v iskusstve" (The Patriotic Theme in Art), *Literaturnaia gazeta,* April 20, 1939, p. 1.

THE POLITICS OF BEWILDERMENT
Eisenstein's *Ivan the Terrible* in 1945

Joan Neuberger

When *Ivan the Terrible,* Part I opened in Los Angeles in 1946, its gala Hollywood audience reacted with stunned outrage. *Ivan the Terrible* had "the usual quota of Soviet propaganda that is so obvious it screams its meaning," the *Variety* reviewer concluded; for the *New York Times'* Bosley Crowther, the film's "conception of Ivan . . . is conspicuously totalitarian." [1] These views dominated the first interpretations of the film in the United States, and they have had extraordinary longevity. Almost fifty years after Crowther first reviewed *Ivan,* musicologist Richard Taruskin denounced the film (and its Prokofiev score) as a "blatant piece of Stalinist triumphalism" which "conveyed as poisonous a message as art has ever been asked to monger . . . that abstract historical purposes justify bloody acts in the here and now." [2] Despite the fact that an alternative view emerged in the 1970s that saw Eisenstein's last film as critical of the Stalinist regime, the original views have had a tenacious hold on popular perceptions and in scholarly circles as well. Textbook histories of film routinely assume that Soviet artists could only produce the most craven art during the Stalin regime.[3] In the only existing book-length study of *Ivan the Terrible,* Kristin Thompson flatly states that Eisenstein had no choice but to adhere to Stalinist orthodoxy in politics.[4] Finally, in what is becoming a new orthodoxy denouncing the Soviet avant-garde's complicity in the coming of Stalinist socialist realism, Alexander Zholkovsky has written that in *Ivan the Terrible,* "Eisenstein's merciless poetic machine was, indeed, part and parcel of a totalitarian complex . . . and a typical, if outstanding, instance of the avant-garde's metamorphosis into Stalinist culture." [5]

In Russia, until very recently, similar interpretations dominated public and scholarly discourse on *Ivan the Terrible.* Alexander Solzhenitsyn set the tone in *One Day in the Life of Ivan Denisovich,* where one of his mouthpiece characters denounced Eisenstein as an "ass-kisser, . . . geniuses don't suit their work to the taste of a tyrant."[6] In the 1980s, Eisenstein's official biographer, Rostislav Yurenev, cited selectively from the director's archive to exaggerate the ways in which Eisenstein seemed to follow the political line expected of him.[7]

But the release of Part II in 1958 and the publication of Eisenstein's six-volume collected works in the 1960s and 1970s led to a new appreciation for the complexity of the film and a reevaluation of its political stance. Part II came to be seen by some as a serious, and perhaps even suicidal, critique of Stalinist despotism and terror. The earliest expression of this view in print can be found in Naum Kleiman's appendix to volume 6 of the collected works.[8] The argument has been developed since by Leonid Kozlov in a series of articles about *Ivan* from the mid-1970s. But Kozlov, like many viewers, saw a critical disparity between *Ivan the Terrible* Parts I and II.[9] As Neya Zorkaya put it in 1965, "Eisenstein produced the official version of *Ivan* in Part I, and the tragic truth of the epoch in Part II." [10] But not all Russian critics were inclined to let Eisenstein off the hook so easily. In many post–Soviet film circles in Russia, Eisenstein is still seen as the exemplary "totalitarian" filmmaker and *Ivan the Terrible* the exemplary "totalitarian" film.[11]

Such one-dimensional political views have flourished because assumptions about Stalinist control over art have obscured the depth of Eisenstein's political analysis in *Ivan*. Recent studies have shown, however, that while cultural control was often harsh and obstructive it was also contested and partial. The state's need for some cultural legitimacy insured that state cultural regulators would themselves be artists with contradictory, variable, and changing notions of the acceptable. On the other hand, artists in all fields pushed the limits of the acceptable, manipulating the conventions of socialist realism and testing its boundaries.[12] The early reception of *Ivan the Terrible* reveals the kinds of difficulties cultural leaders and institutions faced in dealing with such a slippery work of art. These, in turn, reveal something of the internal complexity of Eisenstein's masterpiece and of the director's extraordinary ability to turn the conventions of socialist realism to his own ends.

If *Ivan the Terrible* were indeed the Great Totalitarian Epic or if the party *apparat* controlled the film industry, we would expect to find unambiguous praise for the film in reviews, in prize committees, and in public recognition of the film in the Soviet Union in 1945 when it was released. But we do not. Soviet film critics, industry insiders, professional historians, and ordinary filmgoers responded to *Ivan* Part I with ambivalence, outright criticism, and plain bewilderment. The primary function of socialist realist art as propaganda required clear messages, unambivalent lessons, identifiable heroes, and unambiguous themes. Even when artists found room to modify these conventions, they could not stray too far from the master narrative and the reigning aesthetic.[13] Recorded responses to *Ivan the Terrible,* however, fail to recognize the film as "conspicuously totalitarian" or "Stalinist triumphalism," nor do they resemble anything like the official rhetoric that we expect to hear in this period. More often than not, responses to the film show surprise at the *absence* of official narratives and orthodox politics in Eisenstein's cinematic portrait of the powerful ruler and founder of the centralized state.

It was well known at the time that Stalin had commissioned and approved

Eisenstein's screenplay for *Ivan the Terrible;* indeed the project was widely publicized from start to finish. When the film finally appeared, it was reasonable for viewers to assume that it had run a gauntlet of official viewings—release itself provided the official stamp of approval. If *Ivan* had been perceived at the time as a piece of zealous nationalism or even successful patriotism, one would expect that its release in January 1945 (when victory in World War II was more or less assured) would be accompanied by the kind of warm critical praise that greeted other wartime films, with due references to its Russian heroism, its stalwart leader, and its depiction of the glorious defeat of the perfidious "enemies of the people." Soviet citizens in all walks of life had good reason to say as little as possible in 1945. However, had *Ivan the Terrible* been viewed as a celebration of state power and victory, anyone could have felt safe speaking about it in such terms.[14] The fact that both public and official audiences went out of their way to avoid the safe response, to eschew orthodox Stalinist rhetoric and openly question the film's political postures, suggests that there was space in Stalinist society for people to recognize the film's moral ambiguity and dangerously critical politics. Discussions of *Ivan* Part I reveal a widespread perception that Eisenstein's film broke some important rules: it was seen as incomprehensible, aesthetically eccentric, and politically suspect. But if there was room to acknowledge Eisenstein's political critique and aesthetic challenge, there was no safe space to praise the film, or even discuss it coherently in public.

These highly conflicted responses to *Ivan* Part I indicate some of the parameters of public discourse in Stalinist Russia; they also offer clues to Eisenstein's own conception of the powerful rulers of Ivan's time and of his own. As noted previously, many viewers who read Part II of the film as anti-Stalinist emphasized, by contrast, the orthodoxy and caution of Part I. The assumption of political orthodoxy in Part I seems further to have been sealed by the political fate each part was destined to suffer. That Part I was anointed (or tarnished) with a Stalin Prize, while Part II was banned and its director censured only months later, has reinforced the impression that Eisenstein somehow changed his mind midstream. As a recent cultural critic wrote, "the first part of *Ivan the Terrible* justified and glorified the sixteenth-century leader's reign of terror; it won the highest prize the state could bestow, the Stalin Prize, after its release in 1945. The second part, however, showed Ivan's descent into madness, completed in 1946, it was not released until 1958."[15] But when we return to the original sources, we find that the differential treatment accorded Parts I and II may have had more to do with changing state aims during and after the war, than with the content of the films themselves.[16]

If the cultural propaganda system operated rigidly, official views would be expressed and then reproduced by those whose function it was to disseminate them. Public discourse would be circumscribed by fear and common sense, and dissenting views would be silenced or expressed only in subterranean "Aesopian" forms. Those who conformed to the general line would be rewarded and their achievements publicly framed in terms of the official discourse.[17]

The initial reviews of *Ivan the Terrible,* Part I seem to follow this pattern. We know now, for example, that Vsevolod Vishnevsky was one of two critics asked to prepare a review of *Ivan the Terrible,* Part I for *Pravda,* and that his review (the more positive assessment of the film) was chosen only at the last moment, after a final Kremlin screening.[18] Vishnevsky's review and another one in *Izvestiia,* praised *Ivan* for Eisenstein's presentation of the progressive establishment of central state power, imperial expansion, and the support Ivan enjoyed among the people.[19] Vishnevsky explains that Eisenstein justifies executing boyars as enemies of the people, but he downplays the violence and does not emphasize the political lessons of the film. Following directly the specific points addressed in the opening titles, Vishnevsky relates the ways in which Ivan the Terrible "first united our country . . . out of separate discordant . . . principalities" against the opposition of the greedy boyars, who "spread military glory of our motherland to east and west" and who "took upon himself the crown of Tsar of all Rus." In Vishnevsky's view, Eisenstein offered an "historically accurate" portrait of Ivan as a "progressive leader," who, with the support of the people, struggled against the boyars at home and Germans in the Baltic to unite the country and expand it to its historical territorial borders. However doubtful or reprehensible the justifications for these events, Vishnevsky relates them dispassionately—and more importantly without any effort to make claims for the film's uses as propaganda or its resonance with contemporary politics. He does not neglect to mention Eisenstein's supposed justification for centralized power and for the beheading of the treasonous boyars, but at the same time he makes efforts to emphasize the essential historicity and complexity of Ivan's persona, as well as the aesthetic qualities of Eisenstein's treatment of Ivan, rather than the film's contemporary political relevance or its lessons for moviegoers of the 1940s. Vishnevsky states the official line, as was his task. We know that he genuninely liked the film—but he explicitly resists endorsing Eisenstein's treatment of its political themes, its justification of terror, or its use as propaganda.

The film's limits as propaganda directly surface in ordinary viewers' responses. There are not enough letters in Eisenstein's archive to provide unequivocal evidence of viewer response, but those that exist are exceptionally revealing.[20] Despite the heavy penalties for expressing dissenting views on any subject in the 1930s and 1940s, millions of Soviet citizens nonetheless wrote letters to officials and official publications to complain, to question public policies, and to hector public officials.[21] We would not expect the letters to Eisenstein and to *Pravda* to address the Ivan/Stalin metaphor directly, so its absence is not surprising. On the other hand, no one wrote solely to congratulate the director for *Ivan the Terrible,* as they had done for *Alexander Nevsky.* The letters are passionate, heartfelt, and informed (either aesthetically or historically). They come from all over the country, from Moscow and from small-town Siberia, and from a variety of backgrounds. But the one feature that almost all the letters about *Ivan* share is an astonished bewilderment in the face of the film's unexpected historical narrative.[22] Whether they praise or admonish Eisenstein for departing from socialist realist convention, letter writers emphasize *Ivan's* unfamiliar narrative murkiness. And most of the letters, while paying lip service to the film's "achievement" (a neutral enough word), questioned the meaning and purpose of its portrait of the tsar. One viewer wrote to explain that the film would never "enjoy great success among the majority of the population" because the historical events and their purpose are hard to understand and barely explained. "I loved the screenplay," said one writer, who nevertheless found the movie disappointing.[23] Another self-described "friend of cinema" wrote to congratulate the director on his next step forward in the annals of film art. The writer goes on to say that, "I don't want to speak about the historical-political meaning of the film — it is entirely obvious, in that you refute the *vulgar* understanding of the role of this tsar as the unifier of Rus and clearly prefer his qualities as servant of the people." But then the writer adds that "the only thing, that one might like to see clarified in the next Part II, is the *narod,* the Russian people. How the people felt and acted in that epoch."[24] In other words, this viewer found that Eisenstein depicted Ivan as the people's tsar but failed to make their support for the tsar comprehensible. This is typical of the kind of confusion Eisenstein created with his layered, contradictory, and elastic use of official symbols and rhetoric. A number of correspondents took it upon themselves to correct Eisenstein's historical mistakes in the film. One professor was offended at the erroneous images appearing in the fabricated frescoes decorating the Kremlin and cathedral walls, and at the fact that Eisenstein placed Anastasia's coffin in the Uspensky Sobor, when historically corpses were never allowed there. "The things you make up like Staritsky's death, aren't secondary things, but serious distortions, which mislead our youth, who believe everything they see on the screen."[25]

As if in rebuttal, one extensive and thoughtful letter from a student (who claimed to speak for many others) at the Moscow Institute for Engineers of Communal Construction, shows that there was plenty of robust critical thinking among young people who saw *Ivan* and that they found ways to express it. This student was disappointed by the film and baffled by the *Pravda* review. "The audience expects to see a film of great transformation and reform." But what appeared on the screen was more or less incomprehensible: Ivan was shown "as far too long-suffering, when he should be more energetic." Kurbsky appears to be "nothing more than a man suffering from his

illicit love for the wife of another and dreaming of the tsar's crown," his political relationship with the tsar subsumed by melodrama.

> We could not figure out who the boyarina was leading the opposition . . .
> Events in the film were hardly connected and seemed to develop
> independently of one another . . . The passage of time was revealed only
> by the growth of Ivan's beard . . . And what became of the campaign
> against Livonia after Kurbsky's betrayal? The answer to this is known only
> to Ivan the Terrible and the director of the film, but Ivan is dead and the
> director does not want to say, so the audience is forced to fill in the blanks
> with imagination.[26]

"In general," the letter concludes—as did many—"the film is tiresome, instead of exciting. The next part could be much improved if you take into
account some of what I've written."[27]

Whether letters like these were political in intent or not, their historical
significance for us is politically revealing. If these letters convey anything, it
is the inconclusive impression made by the image of Ivan and confusion
about his historical mission. The film that for so many later (and foreign)
viewers *proved* Eisenstein's entrapment in the Kremlin propaganda machine
was found by many contemporary viewers to lack even the basic ingredients
necessary for propagating state-generated mythology and political imagery.

The reasons for this are, of course, complex, and they involve Eisenstein's
manifold purposes in making the film as well as the processes of censorship
and self-censorship that it went through before reaching the theaters. Here it
should be emphasized that the director and the film industry (and apparently
Stalin himself) all wanted to see this film released, so they each did what they
thought possible and necessary to make it acceptable—and yet it *still* failed
to meet the basic requirements for propaganda. Some of the reasons for this
are fairly well-known. *Ivan the Terrible* was fundamentally difficult and complex because Eisenstein did not want to make Ivan a simplistic hero like Alexander Nevsky, and because his long years of working on the film overlaid
his historical conception with psychological, autobiographical, and political
thinking as well as artistic experiment.

We all know this is a complex movie. But less understood is the fact that
film officials removed elements of the film that would have considerably
clarified Eisenstein's conception of the tsar and would have made his critique
of tyranny far more apparent. The censorship history of this film is filled with
irony. The Artistic Council of the Committee on Cinema Affairs (which made
decisions about releasing films) first met to view Part I on October 28, 1944,
but, having suggested major excisions, was forced to screen it a second time
to make the final decision about its release.[28] The required changes were not
fatal to *Ivan*'s political content, but they did serve to make the film's meanings

more obscure. The film that was released on January 16, 1945 was politically acceptable — just barely — but it offered contradictory indications of the tsar's character and rule. The pre-release discussions of *Ivan* by the Artistic Council are revealing because of what the Council said and did. What they *said* shows that many members thought the film indicted Ivan in ways that made the Stalinist metaphors too dangerous to allow the film's release. What they *did* was remove three scenes that highlighted Ivan's cruelty, treachery and blood-thirstiness.

The first issue of contention was the inscription that opens Part I:

This film is about the man
who in the XVIth century first united our country
About the Grand Prince of Muscovy
who out of separate discordant and autonomous principalities created a
  unified, mighty state
About the Captain who spread the military glory of our motherland to
  east and west
About the ruler who, to achieve these great tasks, first took upon himself
  the crown of Tsar of all Rus.[29]

More confusion has resulted from these titles than from any other aspect of the film. With their clarion-clear statement of the film's subject and their echoes of Soviet propaganda rhetoric, these opening lines tell us exactly what to think as they carefully shape our expectations of what is to come. The titles frame our image of the tsar as bold, victorious, majestic, a Russian national hero; they announce the political mode of the film and they prime us to expect a nationalist epic justifying dictatorship as the path to national unity and international might. More than one prominent reviewer cited them as "the basic ideas, which lie at the base of the film and determine its intrigues."[30] However, the film develops differently. We are immediately and *permanently* distracted from the great cause by the struggle for power within Ivan's entourage and by questions of legitimacy, which soon produce tests of loyalty that almost everyone fails. Betrayals are followed by reprisals which quickly turn deadly. In the midst of military glory, instead of unification we are riveted by terror, murder, conspiracy, treason, accusations, and violent annihilation. Even as early as Part I, the state is not only *not* united, it is ripped apart. Its tragedy is not exclusively due to the opposition of reactionary, selfish boyars, but also to Ivan's own ruthless pursuit of power and his chosen methods for dealing with boyar resistance. *Ivan* Part I is anything *but* "the story of the man who . . . created a unified state . . . spread military glory . . . achieved great tasks." By Part III, it is the story of the man who destroyed every living thing in his country, even the birds, but even Part I gets far enough to show Ivan as a man who decides to trick his people into submission if they do not choose him to rule over them and a man who creates his own army of inhuman sons without mothers or fathers to terrorize his political enemies. And he does so not for some Machiavellian "justifiable end," nor solely because his enemies are obstructionist, but because, as we learn from the prologue, his powerlessness as a child (powerless to protect his mother, his own body, and his country from its ravishing enemies), produces a hunger for revenge.

The essential brutality of these images and of this shadow plot might have been clearer if they had not run counter to the expectations produced by the opening titles. So why did Eisenstein begin *Ivan* in so misleading a way? Because he was forced to do so, at the very last moment, in order to get the film approved. The prescriptive titles that open the film and shape the way generations of viewers have understood (or misunderstood) it were a late addition and a substitution made for purely political reasons. The new titles were drafted by Eisenstein on November 28, 1944, only a week before the second screening was to take place.[31] In the original screenplay the film was to begin with titles that placed Ivan in the company of the other bloody despots of his era: "In the century when Europe saw Charles V, Philip II, Catherine de Medici and the Duke of Alba, Henry VIII and Bloody Mary, the fires of inquisition and Bartholomew's night, to the throne of the Muscovite Grand Princes ascended the one who would become the first tsar and autocrat of all Rus'—Tsar Ivan Vasilevich the Terrible."[32] No lofty aims or political justifications here, only references to Ivan's most bloodthirsty contemporaries. The new titles, with their emphasis on national unity and imperial accomplishment, convey an impression opposite to that of the text they replaced and create an entirely different set of expectations. One might argue that placing Ivan amid the "fires of inquisition" could have been Eisenstein's way of justifying Ivan's actions as typical of his times, or as a revolutionary transcending his times. Even in that case the original titles would still prepare us for the story about violence and power which follows—topics which were far less appropriate subjects for a socialist realist epic than unity and glory. Furthermore, I would argue that we can see Eisenstein's famous capacity for irony here. Introducing the film with a text of high-flown Stalinist rhetoric that frames the narrative with themes continually challenged throughout the film, would have appealed to Eisenstein's sense of humor as well as his sense of self-preservation. The new text was safe, but paradoxical and confusing at the same time.

The other changes imposed on October 28 further obscured the darker sides of Ivan's character and the brutal amorality of the *oprichniki* guards. The Artistic Council called for the removal of two scenes: the "Prologue," which related Ivan's childhood, and the "Oath of the Oprichniki"—two scenes Eisenstein considered critical to understanding Part I.[33]

"Very good," Eisenstein had written to himself in 1942 while transforming the screenplay into a working script, "it forms a closed circle,—from the dark prologue to the dark oath."[34] In his original plan for Part I, the Prologue was to offer an explanation for the ruthless cruelty at the heart of Ivan's later decisions to destroy the boyars. Later inserted early in Part II, the sequence is well-known: it depicts Ivan as a lonely, helpless, and humiliated child whose desire for revenge would compel him to destroy the evil tyrants of his youth but would also lead him to outdo them in tyranny. The Prologue offered both a political and a psychological explanation for Ivan's adult behavior and provided the first clue that the two were intertwined. That Eisenstein was permitted to keep the Prologue in a shorter form and place it at the beginning of Part II gives credence to the Artistic Council's stated objections: that it was too long and postponed the action.[35] The uncut Prologue, however, shows an even greater emphasis on psychological elements in the future tsar's makeup, his childhood fears, and sense of powerlessness that were translated into the adult's hunger for and brutal displays of power—which undoubtedly sat uncomfortably in the anti-psychoanalytical intellectual context of Stalinist times.[36]

The oath scene is a different story altogether. In the released version of Part I, the final sequence at Aleksandrova Sloboda begins with a shot of Ivan in a dark, brooding pose, melodramatically draped over the arm of a chair. These frames appear to represent his anxiety as he waits for the people to arrive to recall him to Moscow and beg him to rule over them. But these shots, in fact, are all that is left of one of the most chilling episodes Eisenstein made for *Ivan*. They show Ivan's reaction to the ceremony in which the new *oprichniki* guard he has just formed swears an oath of allegiance to the "Great Russian State."

Eisenstein found three separate records of the historical *oprichniki*'s oath and he wrote extensively about its demonic moral and political significance in his pre-production notebooks.[37] We hear the *oprichniki* recite the oath again at the end of Part II in connection with Staritsky's murder, but the lines were supposed to be introduced here in Part I, forming a better-paced transition from Ivan's despair at his wife's coffin to the affirmation of his power at Aleksandrova Sloboda. In a somber echo of Ivan's coronation, the new servitors are dressed in black robes and holding tall black candles while they chant:

Before God I swear
A true oath
A grave oath
A dreadful oath

For the sake of the "Great Russian Tsardom," they each pledge:

To destroy the enemies of the state
To renounce my kin and my clan
To forget my father . . . and my own mother
My true friend and my blood brother
FOR THE SAKE OF THE GREAT RUSSIAN STATE.[38]

Eisenstein considered this "dark oath," which placed state interests above friend and kin and the political abstraction above the human, to be the source

74. *Ivan the Terrible:* The Oath of the *Oprichniki.*

75. *Ivan the Terrible:* Fyodor Basmanov taking the Oath.

of all the "sins" of the *oprichniki* and the wellspring of a flood of murderous events culminating in the murder of their leader, Alexei Basmanov, by his own son Fyodor.[39] Eisenstein makes it clear in his notes that *oprichniki* violence was not justified by the glorious founding of the Russian State, but rather deflected progressive political aims onto a path of degeneration and brutality.[40] The oath and its historical context as described in Eisenstein's notes have obvious referents in Soviet history (to the cult of revolutionary asceticism) and in Stalinist ethics (to the legend of Pavlik Morozov, which Eisenstein had depicted in the film that nearly cost him his life, *Bezhin Meadow*). The scene itself has not been recovered, but even in the screenplay it is a desolate image, made all the more so by the gloomy black candles and robes that mirror the pure white of Ivan's coronation and wedding, while foreshadowing the black-clad procession following Staritsky's murder at the end of Part II.

The "dark oath" was slashed precisely because members of the Artistic Council were uncomfortable with its derogatory view of Ivan's policies. As the director of popular tractor romances, Ivan Pyrev stated, "the oath was absolutely unnecessary. The oath lowered the figure of the ruler and his great significance."[41]

Recently, Efim Levin has argued that the members of the Artistic Council failed to perceive a critique of Stalin in *Ivan,* Part I. Levin believed that the Council members were unable to escape their expectation that Eisenstein would follow the state's commission "to exonerate Ivan the Terrible, to show that the blood was not spilt in vain."[42] No one (Levin included) would expect the Artistic Council to refer to the Stalin/Ivan metaphor openly, but comments about the specific historical and political content of the film made at the second screening on December 7 show, in fact, a clear perception of Eisenstein's political challenge. The required revisions and other criticism issued at the Council's discussions show a tacit recognition of Eisenstein's failure to satisfy the state's commission and hint at his flouting of its basic premises. Each of the three scenes the Council removed—the titles, the prologue, and the oath—were explicitly damaging to Ivan in political terms that had modern resonance.

Moreover, if the propaganda value of the film was supposed to lie in its justifying Ivan's cruelty by the greatness of his cause and the perfidy of his enemies, it is striking that almost every member of the Artistic Council was either troubled or confused by characterizations of the cause, the tsar, and the principal characters, even at the second screening. The actor Aleksei Dikii, for example, began by defending Eisenstein against familiar charges of formalism; "there is formalism and formophobia" he said, but at the same time, he found the film historically confusing. He objected that the historical Malyuta had been an "intelligent, significant" figure but here he was "just a pretty stupid fellow [*prosto glupovatym parnem*]." As for Ivan, Dikii stated simply that based on Part I, it was hard to judge Ivan's historical role.[43]

One of the historians present, Mikhail Galaktionov, stated even more clearly that while the film was an artistic masterpiece, transcending debates about formalism and realism, it failed to meet its own goal in depicting the tsar: "Ivan the Terrible should be portrayed as a ruler [*gosudaria*], however, in this film, that is not accomplished." Eisenstein should have explained the tsar's cruelty as a legitimate political response to the enemies who opposed his "great, mighty, rule." But instead, we get melodrama: "the same old poison, the coffin, [and] the enemy [Efrosinia Staritskaya] is just some *Baba-Yaga*, not a representative of a social issue." The *oprichniki* too, were "completely unsuccessful," contributing to his judgment of the film as "unfaithful [*neverno*] not in some trivial sense," but in "diminishing this great figure . . . and his entire cause." He wanted to reconsider releasing the film at all. The young director Igor Savchenko also found the explanation for Ivan's "wicked, cruel, degeneracy," to be unclear and unmotivated in the December 7 cut, and he did not see any redeeming features in the tsar's portrait. "Without the Prologue . . . Ivan is, from the very first episode, immediately evil, he's 'Terrible' and why he's so 'terrible' is incomprehensible."[44] Boris Gorbatov (another historian present) was disappointed that Eisenstein *only* portrayed Ivan as an autocrat, and that the plot revolved around the struggle for power rather than showing how much the historical Ivan accomplished for Russia, "the people he is fighting for, the reforms, the progressive ideas, the *oprichnina,* the 'window on Europe,' the broadening of ties . . . he's a little one-dimensional." Gorbatov also noted that "It is not important to us, who he is struggling against, but what he is struggling for. . . . It is important to show that the *idea* for which Ivan the Terrible was struggling was emotionally close to the people . . . a very difficult task for Ivan the Terrible."[45] Last but not least, Vsevolod Pudovkin defended the film, though not by refuting the political suspicions raised by previous critics; he never said that Eisenstein's Ivan is a great hero or a model for their time. He defended *Ivan*'s artistic complexity, and asked those present to view the film like a great chess match, complicated and with various possible outcomes.[46]

There was a great deal of artistic criticism as well, but it tended to be general in nature. Konstantin Simonov among others heatedly criticized Part I for its cerebral style, its failure to touch the heart.[47] Boris Babochkin (the actor most famous for his role as Chapaev) found the acting atrocious and the film as a whole "very tiresome . . . everything after Ivan's recovery drags, the poisoning of Anastasia drags, the audience will find it hard to watch such slow-moving scenes."[48] But while some of these viewers denounced the film's "formalism," most of them, even those critical of its historical or political presentation, took pains to praise formal aspects of the film's style and, like Dikii, to deflect criticism of its formal elements and defend it against "formophobia." Savchenko went so far to say that *Ivan* would be an immensely influential work and that all his own future films would reflect the impact of Eisenstein's innovation in *Ivan the Terrible*, Part I.[49]

From this discussion it should be clear that Part I failed to match politically shaped expectations that Eisenstein would present a conventional "positive hero," or an accessible, heroic, historical chronicle, with clear lessons about both the past and the present. Instead film industry viewers found its *historical* Ivan a confusing mass of contradictions, anachronisms, and forthright distortions and its *political* Ivan dangerously somber, manipulative, and unheroic. While these first viewers may not have articulated their criticism in explicitly political terms, their criticism of its historical rendering alongside their acceptance of its artistic vision suggests at the very least that they did not see the film as a triumph of Stalinist propaganda. Ironically, the efforts by the Artistic Council to sanitize and clarify Eisenstein's portrait of Ivan only further complicated an intentionally difficult film. While their editing may have prevented the film from exposing an even darker image of tyranny, it was still not enough to make *Ivan* useful propaganda or socialist realist, a fact that was confirmed in the letters from public viewers.

The first stage of the official reception of Eisenstein's *Ivan the Terrible*, Part I shows an artist testing every possible limit and an official cultural institution prepared to negotiate with him. But the debates in the Artistic Council also show that there were limits to official toleration for "variability" in socialist realism and "mutability" of its conventions. The same issues were raised when *Ivan* was nominated for a Stalin Prize. The picture was complicated by Stalin's personal role in the process, first as a shadow over the deliberations, then as final arbiter of the prize in his name.

Leonid Kozlov has argued that Stalin's approval of the screenplay marked a turning point in Eisenstein's conception of himself as a Kremlin toady and eventually forged his determination to challenge Stalin in Part II. But Eisenstein's desire to win the Stalin Prize (and the disappointment he records in his diary when the committee initially voted against it) suggests that his attitude towards Stalin's personal approval was more tortuous.[50]

Few people realize that Eisenstein came very close to *not* receiving the Stalin Prize for *Ivan*. It was rejected at every level of the nomination process and the award ultimately required the personal intervention of Stalin. In the beginning, the Film Section of the Stalin Prize Committee refused to nominate it, preferring to put forward more conventional and popular wartime dramas.[51] Then, when Ivan Bolshakov, chief of the Committee on Cinema Affairs, insisted that its nomination be discussed at the Plenum Meeting of the Prize Committee (despite its having been denied nomination in the section), the Plenum voted 20–12 against recommending it further up "to the highest level."[52]

The Plenum discussion, though carefully coded to avoid all direct political speech, is as interesting for its absences as for its passionate denunciations. At the Plenum meeting on March 29, 1945, the chair Solomon Mikhoels presented the Film Section's nominees, listing the other films in order.[53] Mikhoels then added that there was another candidate, "which had provoked debate on matters of principle in the Section meeting . . . this film is Eisenstein's *Ivan the Terrible.* . . . No one said that the film isn't appealing [*ne tianet*] or that its craftsmanship is on an inferior level . . . but matters of principle and aesthetic positions, its methods, etc. called forth considerable objections."[54] This reluctance to make a decision for a prize bearing Stalin's name, on a film commissioned by Stalin, and clearly about Stalin, is telling. Although almost everyone present agreed that *Ivan the Terrible* was the work of a master craftsman, Film Section members were too uncomfortable with matters both aesthetic and political to agree even to nominate the film.

Bolshakov opened the discussion with a stirring piece of circumlocution justifying his nomination of *Ivan the Terrible.* "A monumental work, in fact a unique work . . . every element of this film represents a new direction in cinema." He conceded that the music and the acting provoked disagreements, and that Eisenstein was "more a rationalistic than an emotional artist," and he insisted that the greatest achievement of the film was that Eisenstein "correctly conveyed the image of Ivan the Terrible." Bolshakov did not elaborate on this ambiguous pronouncement, but his next comment suggests that his criteria for judging the quality of the work were more those of a filmmaker than those of a historian or of a Stalinist political appointee: "Cherkasov's extraordinary acting created the image that we will now associate with Ivan. And therefore we consider that this film undoubtedly represents a major event."[55] After Bolshakov defended the film on official grounds, it was nonetheless vehemently rejected.

Bolshakov was followed by Alexander Korneychuk, the orthodox socialist realist playwright who loathed *Ivan.* "Eisenstein did nothing new in this film . . . individual frames are remarkable, but the film is cold, a rationalist film, which audiences will not understand." Korneychuk then attacks Eisenstein directly: "this is formalism by a master who has made no forward progress but who, from our point of view, has only deepened his errors, . . . he has nothing to teach young artists. He is very far from realism. If he must be allowed to continue to make films . . . we do not need to honor him with a Stalin Prize." The specific causes of Korneychuk's outrage suggest that rationalism alone was not the problem. "Let's look at the funeral. The coffin stands there. But you need a ladder to get close enough to see it . . . There are no people anywhere, there's very little of the epoch, the real Russia—I don't see it . . . And Cherkasov here,—this is a man in a fidget. All I remember is how he turns his head. He is capable of touching no one." Korneychuk concludes by challenging Bolshakov's assertion that Cherkasov's Ivan is historically or politically appropriate, hinting at his discomfort with the film's politics. "It has been said here that [Eisenstein] is the first to show Ivan the Terrible relatively faithfully according to the way he is seen today. But how does philosophical, historical thought see this period? Eisenstein was unable to depict the truly disturbing [*volnuiushchikh*] images and I am opposed to giving him the Stalin Prize."[56]

The great art historian Igor Grabar picks up on the historical objections raised by Korneychuk. Like many historians today, Grabar was angered by factual inaccuracies in films that purport to be historical. He similarly failed to appreciate the differences between his own professional goals and those legitimate narrative and artistic goals of the filmmaker. Then and now critics frequently invoke the filmmaker's failure to represent the past in its proper complexity as a cover for political disagreement.[57]

The historical errors in the film infuriated Grabar particularly because "the author could have avoided [them] if he had only consulted more with historians, but Sergei Mikhailovich Eisenstein was so sure of his own competence that he never did that." In his outrage Grabar recounted an anecdote from the wrong film: "I once said to him in regard to *Alexander Nevsky,* 'How could you have Buslaev say, "Well this is a serious business" [*Nu, eto delo ser'eznoe*], in the thirteenth century, when the word *ser'eznoe* did not appear until the time of Anna Ivanovna,' . . . And Eisenstein had the nerve to reply, 'I did it on purpose.' Only children speak that way." Grabar remonstrated further to the Plenum: "This is trivial of course, no one noticed, except us, poor sinners who know the Russian language and how it developed and so on, but permit me to tell you that . . ." and he went on to list several of the anachronisms Eisenstein allowed to slip into *Ivan:* there were no diplomatic corps in Muscovy at the time of Ivan; Muslims, such as the emissary from Kazan, were never allowed into Orthodox shrines; tsars never gave political speeches in cathedrals; and the unforgettable stream of coronation coins would never be poured in the center of the cathedral but only in the doorway.[58]

Other opponents of the film rose to add their voices to this particular choir. Alexander Goldenveizer, one of the historical experts at the Plenum meeting, complained that no political discussion would have been held in the shadow of Anatasia's coffin; he also objected to the ringing of the tsar's death knells before the tsar was actually dead, and to women singing in church. Vera Mukhina, the prominent sculptor, protested Eisenstein's characterization of Anastasia as an "empty space," when historically she had been a bright, positive influence on the historical Ivan. Mukhina also noted numerous mistakes in costuming and sets.[59] The architect Arkadi Mordvinov spoke in more general terms for all his colleagues in the Union of Architects. Interest in architectural history was high at this time, with the era of Ivan the Terrible holding particular interest, so architects of every persuasion were eagerly looking forward to Eisenstein's film—and, according to Mordvinov, they were all deeply disappointed, finding "neither the style of the epoch nor anything of the Rus of that time." While the Plenum was in session various colleagues incredulously approached him to ask if this film was really going to receive the Stalin Prize.[60]

All historical movies make errors of this kind, so we need to ask if the attention given to them here had any particular significance in the context of Soviet cultural politics, and specifically the Stalin Prize. Was Russian history more sacred than most, or was there a political subtext to these discussions? Anyone familiar with other historical movies of this period will find such a critique of *Ivan*'s historical lapses excessive. Soviet historical films were notorious for their extravagant distortions of known historical figures and events.[61] Perhaps for that reason Eisenstein took great pains to demonstrate his reliance on genuine historical sources. Is it possible that this chorus of trivial historical criticism was a cryptic recognition of Eisenstein's flawed portrait of the tsars of both eras, a convenient veil for rejecting the film's depiction of Russian history?

It is obviously impossible to draw definitive conclusions from such elliptical discourse, but it is just as obviously hard to believe that *Ivan the Terrible* was to be denied the Stalin Prize because of a Muslim in an Orthodox church or a political speech at a funeral. One waits in vain for a discussion of the film's merits or of its value as a representative of the national canon. But those who attacked the film on artistic grounds went no further than to say that the film was, in Grabar's formulation, "cold, cerebral, from the mind and not the emotions of the artist, and everything is done for the sake of effect not for truth."[62] Or as Mukhina added, "in this film everything is from the head and nothing from the heart, an excessively cerebral work," but also there is very little of Russia here, she claimed, "it is almost like a *Ring of the Niebelungs*. Ivan's dress in the final scene is practically Parsifal, this isn't Russian, and there is a great deal that is foreign in these things."[63]

When someone finally did speak out in defense of the film as art, it was none other than Mikhail Chiaureli. Claiming to speak for other Russian filmmakers, Chiaureli proclaimed *Ivan the Terrible,* Part I "such a great film, it should not be passed over." In comparison with other historical films, he said, *Ivan* was great not because it was a monumental work, as others had noted (often by way of lip service), or because it depicted important events, but "because here we see the magnificent [*grandioznyi*] taste of an artist, the gigantic, fascinating contours of an artist. . . . We can't always understand the leading artists of our time, who," he continued, "don't want to follow tradition, but who try to do something new, different and perhaps stronger and more persuasive. He is driven by a desire to liberate us from tradition and make something interesting."[64]

No one on the committee recommended the film as an epic of Stalinist triumphalism. No one sang the praises of its socialist realism or its defense of national unity. No one lingered on its meaningful rendering of Russia's heroic past. Given the film's complexity, perhaps this is not so surprising. But no one *attacked* the film for failure to meet these conventional expectations either. Given that we are examining a roomful of people who wanted to deny the film a prize that carried immense political importance, the silences are significant. It should have been easy to say that *Ivan the Terrible* failed to embody even the basic requirements of socialist realism, or that it tarnished Russia's historical legacy, or even that it portrayed the ruler in any of a number of less than glorious ways. Other works received exactly this sort of treatment, but in regard to *Ivan,* the committee studiously avoided all serious political, artistic, and historical issues.

In the end, Mikhoels offered the thinnest but probably the most honest justification for nominating *Ivan the Terrible:* it was clearly superior to some of the other nominees. He conceded that the historical experts had found errors in the film, but that these were just "pretexts [*poiski*]." By any standard, it made sense at least to nominate *Ivan* and allow the members to vote on it.[65] At the end of the day, everyone agreed, and then twenty of the thirty-two voting members decided against the film.

In all fairness, some people then and now find *Ivan* to be excessively melodramatic and mannered. Pauline Kael is wittiest on this score, but even the humorless hacks on the Stalin Prize Committee are entitled to be immune to *Ivan*'s power and pathos.[66] But except for Korneychuk and Mordvinov, who seemed adverse to all complexity, the other viewers seemed more stunned than confused by the film's ambiguities. At the very least their avoidance of either conventional defense or substantive attack reinforces the impression given by the public's letters to Eisenstein and the Artistic Council's responses to the film—that *Ivan* was from the beginning seen as a complex and ambivalent work, one with no clear message in a period when some degree of clarity was required both as an aesthetic principle and a ticket to political survival.

The avoidance of direct attack cannot be attributed to Eisenstein's stature or international renown. Throughout his career he had been the subject of criticism and controversy; while he enjoyed great prestige in the early forties, with his Stalin Prize for *Nevsky* and his high post at Mosfilm, he had been just outspoken enough to make his position still vulnerable. On the other hand, the priority status Eisenstein received for this project may have engendered or inflamed considerable jealousy. The star director of Soviet cinema, the current favorite of Kremlin patronage, was granted more time, money, and attention for *Ivan the Terrible* than other film projects of the period. Yet what did he produce? A movie that seemed to condemn tyranny while flattering the tyrant, a movie no one could be sure he or she understood, a movie that many considered to be "un-Russian."

This last charge—*Ivan*'s "foreignness"—offers at least a partial clue. The film is obviously cosmopolitan in its borrowings and adaptations, and in the 1940s such a charge would be dangerous by itself. But comments made two years later, after a number of people had seen Part II, make it clear that complaints about cultural "*un*-Russianness" signified suspicions of political "*anti*-Russianness"—and suggest how personal animosity overlapped political criticism. In March 1947, Vishnevsky wrote a long critique of Part II in which he wrote that Eisenstein "is too *western*, . . . He has forgotten about Rus[sian] nature, language, spirit, manner, Rus[sian] passions."[67] A few weeks later, in April 1947, Vishnevsky reported that Alexander Dovzhenko also disliked the film for its "un-Russian" quality: "Eisenstein is a great talent, up to his neck in the debris of the library, in western aesthetics. . . . He will never return. . . . And also, he is always ironical, cynical. . . . Somewhere over the yawning *abyss*."[68] Then—as if to clarify for himself where all this has led—at the end of April, Vishnevsky recorded a single comment about Eisenstein made by Pyotr Pavlenko, who had worked closely with him on *Alexander Nevsky* and on some of his unrealized projects in 1939–1940: "Pavlenko is critic[al] of Eisenstein: 'He sees history through irony. Inside, he is not one of us. . . .'"[69] Or, as Korneychuk put it: "Yes, this is a big work, Eisenstein is an exacting artist, but his manner, his style are too far from everything we maintain about art."[70]

The question remains, however, why attacks on the film had to be indirect and coded. Bolshakov's nomination of *Ivan* offered Stalin Prize committee members an easy choice, which almost no one took. As the official state representative in the film industry and as the individual responsible for arranging Kremlin screenings of new Russian films, his statement supporting *Ivan* should have been taken as the official state-sanctioned position. It was well-known that Stalin had supported the project throughout. He personally approved the screenplay, he approved the release of Part I, and he certainly authorized Vishnevsky's positive review.[71] Had anyone seen the film as conformist or orthodox, committee members could have saved themselves the trouble of an independent opinion by affirming the nomination in the terms Bolshakov set out. Alternatively, and perhaps more dangerously, they could almost as easily have rejected the nomination by claiming that Eisenstein's film failed to live up to Bolshakov's description of it. So why did they resort to coded, ambiguous, and trivial arguments? One can only conclude that viewers either hated the film for its formal experimental style or feared it for its ambiguous politics. If they had seen *Ivan,* Part I as patriotic, heroic, or tragic, they would have said so. But if they did not, that put them—official viewers especially—in a difficult situation: knowing that Stalin had approved the film, but seeing nothing attractive about its content or style, left them without a safe response. And although Stalin had approved the film up through its release, he was known to be terrifyingly capricious and manipulative. If viewers saw the film as (at the very least) contradictory and ambiguous, foreign and cold, it would have been safer to neither approve nor reject the film in clear terms but to bury it in obfuscation.

The final and perhaps most vexing question is not why the committee did not give Eisenstein a Stalin Prize, but why Stalin himself reversed all these decisions and gave him the Prize after all. Did he see the movie as an ode on the order of *Alexander Nevsky?* No one else did. Stalin was, of course, nothing if not unpredictable, so we may never understand this eccentric act. Perhaps Stalin was flattered by what he saw, reading the surface narrative and none of the subtext that other viewers could not ignore. It is possible to imagine that Stalin was untroubled by the demagoguery, manipulation, corruption, and violence accompanying the raw power that Eisenstein attributed to Ivan in Part I. One partial explanation proposes that Stalin offered Eisenstein the prize as a kind of bribe. Stalin had considered Part I to be just barely acceptable in political terms; he knew Eisenstein was finishing Part II and wanted to ensure that it not deviate any further from Soviet aesthetic and political acceptability.[72] But there may have been additional substantive issues at the heart of Stalin's approval of Part I and his enraged rejection of Part II. The campaign to rehabilitate Ivan was always fundamentally focused on state power and its justification in the analogous foundation of a highly centralized state under the control of a single individual.[73] When artists, challenged by the limitations of Ivan's heroism, turned Ivan into a tragic figure, an individual with a multifaceted persona, Stalin, Andrei Zhdanov, and the other managers of the campaign were displeased.[74] While personality and genre issues clearly played a role in Stalin's hostility towards Part II, specific political issues help us understand Stalin's different reactions to the two parts of the film. In his justification of state-building, Stalin made clear his support of state terror as a legitimate weapon against the state's enemies: "one has to wage an unceasing and merciless battle against one's enemies to eliminate them if they are interfering with the development of the state. That is Stalin's position," as related by A. S. Shcherbakov, chief of the ideology section of the Central Committee.[75] In Part I, Ivan unapologetically prepares to do just that and manipulates his various enemies into positions of subordination until the scene at Anastasia's coffin, when he decides to form a fighting force, the *oprichnina,* to destroy them. In Part II, however, he begins to doubt his actions and to question the legitimacy of violence in state formation, an attitude which Stalin found appalling.[76] It is not that Part I presents a more sanitized or heroic Ivan—only that his ruthless pursuit of power was presented in ways that Stalin could still find attractive. Many of the other people who saw *Ivan* in 1945 found this portrait of the tsar far more troubling. Ironically, the fact that Stalin awarded Part I the prize may be evidence of the film's essential *critique* of Stalinist tyranny. Eisenstein seems to have understood that Stalin's blind ambition and his perverted sense of "leadership" would be flattered by a portrait of power based on conspiracy, brute force, and the manipulation of his subjects. He was able to pull off the remarkable feat of depicting unlimited power in a way that both pleased Stalin and laid bare every dictatorial device he used.

In conclusion, while reception tells us little about Eisenstein's own purposes or politics, I want to make two points that are often overlooked when ascribing political meaning to this movie. First, there is no essential *Ivan the Terrible*—there will never be a "Director's Cut." The ordinary difficulties in interpreting this film are compounded by the director's lack of control over its content during the transformation of a screenplay into a film that could be shown in public. Any effort to determine what *Ivan the Terrible* tells us about Eisenstein needs to recognize the fact that the film was intended to be psychologically, historically, and politically complicated, and then was further shaped by compromise and self-protection on the director's part and by political censorship. Second, even if the reception of the film does not tell us what Eisenstein intended to say, it allows us to eliminate readings imposed by viewers following false clues based on historical accidents, events external to the film, or actions independent of the filmmaker, such as the awarding of the Stalin Prize. When even the viewers who were most motivated to praise the film for its totalitarian message were unable to avoid ambivalence and obfuscation, we can see beyond the manichean terms in which Stalinist art is often confined. At the time of its release, *Ivan the Terrible,* Part I was not a propaganda success; it failed to fulfill its commission to present a usable historical pedigree or a socialist realist epic. But we must be careful not to conclude from this that the ambivalent reception in 1945 is proof of the opposite—proof that *Ivan* is a work exclusively critical of Stalinist rule. On the contrary, the discussions of 1945 make it clear that we need to discard the reigning dichotomies of Stalinist cultural studies: dissident/conformist, hero/coward, victim/criminal, lackey/martyr. Viewers in 1945 were bewildered by the film for the same reasons we continue to disagree about its meanings. It is a film in which fascination with absolute power has been read as both approval and condemnation of power.

Ivan the Terrible is a great film precisely because Eisenstein knew its subject from within and without. And he incorporates in *Ivan* the astonishing ability of animated film to transform images into their mirror opposites: to shape-change by sliding seamlessly between characters in ways that reveal the same-nesses among polar opposites and the polarities within.[77] In his political life Eisenstein experienced both complicity with the system and repulsion to-ward it; he understood the allure of power and was horrified at its uses both in himself and in the autocrats he depicted. When we strip away the layers of extraneous rhetoric that Eisenstein and others have imposed on *Ivan the Ter-rible,* we find a work of art that challenges us to consider Russian history in the twentieth century from a perspective that offers no simple solutions. Just as he did not intend *Ivan* to whitewash the medieval tsar, but rather to explore his contradictory legacy and his significance for a contemporary audience, Eisenstein did not seek to exonerate either himself or "the leading figure of his time" but to explore the contradictions and the tragic history that brought them into being. In an era when both politics and culture were often one-dimensional, blandly consoling, and blindly simplistic, Eisenstein's film came as a bombshell. *Ivan the Terrible* is a difficult movie because it was butchered by censorship and self-censorship, but it is a great movie because it makes a mockery of our expectations and challenges us to understand how the best and worst aspects of the human condition can coexist.

Notes

Research for this article was supported in part by the University of Texas at Aus-tin, University Research Institute, and the International Research and Exchanges Board (IREX), with funds provided by the National Endowment for the Humani-ties and the U.S. Department of State, none of which is responsible for its content. For their generous comments and conversation, I am immensely grateful to Naum Kleiman, David Bordwell, Ian Christie, Judy Coffin, Valerie Kivelson, Kristin Thompson, Yuri Tsivian, and Alexander Zholkovsky.

1. Jay Leyda, *Kino: A History of the Russian and Soviet Film* (Princeton: Prince-ton University Press, 1983), 382; *Variety,* March 19, 1947; *New York Times,* March 10, 1947. See also the review in *Time Magazine,* April 14, 1947, 104–105: "bold, fascinating to look at. But . . . as Eisenstein tells it, this vindication of Ivan becomes, by many parallels, a vindication of Stalin and his regime."

2. Richard Taruskin, "Great Artists Serving Stalin Like a Dog," *New York Times,* Sunday, 28 May 1995.

3. Gerald Mast and Bruce Kawin, *A Short History of the Movies* (New York: Mac-millan, 1992), 188; David A. Cook, *A History of Narrative Film* (New York: W. W. Norton, 1996), 361–362.

4. Kristin Thompson, *Eisenstein's* Ivan the Terrible: *A Neoformalist Analysis* (Princeton: Princeton University Press, 1981), 3, 65, 67; and *"Ivan the Terrible* and Stalinist Russia: A Reexamination," *Cinema Journal,* vol. 17: 11 (1977), 30–43.

5. Alexander Zholkovsky, "Eisenstein's Poetics: Dialogical or Totalitarian?" *Laboratory of Dreams: The Russian Avant-Garde and Cultural Experiment,* ed. John E.

Bowlt and Olga Matich (Stanford: Stanford University Press, 1996), 254.

6. Alexander Solzhenitsyn, "Odin den' Ivana Denisovicha (One Day in the Life of Ivan Denisovich)," *Novyi mir* 1962, no. 11, 39.

7. R. Iurenev, *Sergei Eizenshtein: Zamysly, Fil'my, Metod* (Eisenstein: Projects, Films, Method), 2: *1930–1948* (Moscow: Iskusstvo, 1988), 222–223, for example.

8. Sergei Eisenstein, *Izbrannye proizvedeniia v shesti tomakh* (Selected Works in Six Volumes) (Moscow: Iskusstvo, 1964–1971), 6, 548–551.

9. Leonid Kozlov, "The Artist and the Shadow of Ivan," *Stalinism and Soviet Cinema,* eds. Derek Spring and Richard Taylor (London: Routledge, 1993) 116–17, 120–122.

10. Neia Zorkaia, *Portrety,* (Moscow: Iskusstvo, 1966) 131, 138 (cited in Herbert Marshall, *Masters of Soviet Cinema* (London: Routledge, 1983), 227. And here is film critic Maya Turovskaia, in a recent interview, recalling a conversation with her uncle who was working at the time in Eisenstein's crew: "'How can you glorify Ivan,' I asked. . . . Of course we hadn't seen *Ivan Two* . . .'" Quoted in Nancy Ramsey, "Keepers of a Flame that Burned for Russia," *New York Times,* Sunday, July 5, 1998, 14.

11. For a spectrum of late-Soviet and post-Soviet views on Eisenstein's political significance, see roundtable discussions in "Kino totalitarnoi epokhi" (Film of the Totalitarian Era), *Iskusstvo kino,* 1990, nos. 1–3; "Rencontre au cabinet Eisenstein," in the supplement to *Cahiers du Cinéma,* 1990, no. 427, 43–49, on *Cinéma de l'epoque totalitaire,* a retrospective in Paris in 1989; and N. Kleiman, O. Kosolapov, N. Sirivlia, "Eizenshtein segodnia" (Eisenstein Today), *Iskusstvo kino,* 1996, no. 5, 10–21.

12. See in particular Katerina Clark, *The Soviet Novel: History as Ritual* (Chicago: University of Chicago Press, 1981) and her "The Mutability of the Canon: Socialist Realism and Chingiz Aitmatov's *I dol'she veka dlitsia den',*" *Slavic Review,* 43 (1984), 573–587; Thomas Lahusen, "Socialist Realism in Search of its Shores," *Socialist Realism without Shores* (Durham, N.C.: Duke University Press, 1997); Joshua Rubenstein, *Tangled Loyalties: The Life and Times of Ilya Ehrenburg* (New York: Basic Books, 1996).

13. Clark, *The Soviet Novel;* Abram Tertz, *On Socialist Realism* (New York: Pantheon Books, 1960); Peter Kenez, *Cinema and Soviet Society, 1917–1953* (Cambridge: Cambridge University Press, 1992), 157–185; Régine Robin, *Socialist Realism: An Impossible Aesthetic* (Stanford: Stanford University Press, 1992).

14. Sarah Davies, *Popular Opinion in Stalin's Russia: Terror, Propaganda, and Dissent, 1934–1941* (Cambridge: Cambridge University Press, 1997), 4–5; Peter Kenez, *The Birth of the Propaganda State: Soviet Methods of Mass Mobilization, 1917–1929* (Cambridge: Cambridge University Press, 1985); and Kenez, *Cinema and Soviet Society,* 140–156.

15. Ramsey, "Keepers of a Flame," 14.

16. According to Ivan Bolshakov, Stalin once remarked about the dismal state of mind of Soviet filmmakers: "During the War we didn't have the time, but now we'll lick you into shape." Cited in Kozlov, "The Artist," 127; Bolshakov's assistant, G. Mar'iamov, attributes the same remark to Stalin's furious response after watch-

ing *Ivan,* Part II; G. Mar'iamov, *Kremlevskii tsenzor: Stalin smotrit kino* (Moscow: Kinotsentr, 1992), 74.

17. Peter Kenez, *The Birth of the Propaganda State: Soviet Methods of Mass Mobilization, 1917–1929* (Cambridge: Cambridge University Press, 1985).

18. Vsevolod Vishnevskii, "Fil'm 'Ivan Groznyi,'" *Pravda,* January 28, 1945. Further details are available in Vishnevskii's journals, excerpted in "Iz dnevnikov, 1944–1948 gg." (From My Diaries, 1944–1948) *Kinovedcheskie zapiski,* 38 (1998) 65–67; a critical review written by Petr Pavlenko got as far as galley proofs; see Leonid Kozlov, "The Artist and the Shadow of Ivan," 124.

19. B. Romashov, "Fil'm "Ivan Groznyi," *Izvestiia,* February 4, 1945.

20. The letters are preserved in Eisenstein's fond in Russkii gosudarstvennyi arkhiv literatury i iskusstva (RGALI), fond [holding; hereafter f.] 1923, opis' [list; hereafter op.] 1, delo [folder; hereafter d.], 2289. I do not know how they were collected, selected, or preserved. Some are copies of letters sent to *Pravda* in response to Vishnevskii's review, others were sent directly to Eisenstein.

21. Sheila Fitzpatrick, *Stalin's Peasants: Resistance and Survival in the Russian Village After Collectivization* (New York: Oxford University Press, 1994); Sarah Davies, *Popular Opinion in Stalin's Russia: Terror, Propaganda, and Dissent, 1934–1941* (Cambridge: Cambridge University Press, 1997).

22. The one exception, the only purely positive assessment of the film, was a long typed letter from a fan who hoped Eisenstein might jump-start her career in theater: ". . . since childhood, I have dreamed of devoting myself to serve the art of the theater but I have not had the opportunity to complete even a middle-school education . . . ," from Nina Bogdanova, Krasnodar, 11.IV.45, f. 1923, op. 1, d. 2289, list [sheet; hereafter l.] 108.

23. F. 1923, op. 1, d. 2289, l. 109 [n.d.].

24. F. 1923, op. 1, d. 2289, ll. 112–113 [10.IV.45].

25. F. 1923, op. 1, d. 2289, l. 117 [n.d.]; see also ll. 120ff. for more corrections.

26. F. 1923, op. 1, d. 2289, ll. 126–127 [2.I.45].

27. F. 1923, op. 1, d. 2289, ll. 126–127 [2.I.45].

28. The notes of the first discussion have not surfaced in the archive of the Committee on Cinema (Efim Levin, who had greater access to the archive than I, does not mention them in his article about the screenings; I have also been unable to find them), but the actions taken on October 28 can be reconstructed from records of the second screening and other documents in Eisenstein's archive.

29. "Fil'm etot o cheloveke/ kotoryi v XVI stoletii vpervye ob"edinil nashu stranu/ iz otdel'nykh razobshchennykh i svoekorystnykh kniazhestv sozdal edinoe moshchnoe gosudarstvo/ O polkovodtse, kotoryi vozvelichil voennuyu slavu nashei rodiny na vostoke i na zapade/O gosudare/ kotoryi dlia resheniia etikh velikikh zadach vpervye vozlozhil na sebia/ venets tsaria vseia Rusi." On November 28, Eisenstein scribbled more than nine variations before settling on this text; see f. 1923, op. 1, d. 548 [28.XI.44]. The inscription does not appear in the original screenplay (see S. M. Eisenstein, "Ivan Groznyi: Kino-stsenarii," *Novyi mir,* 1943, nos. 10–11, 61–108) but it is printed in the English translation by Ivor Montagu and Herbert Marshall, which was based on the finished film, *Ivan the Terrible*

(London and Boston: Faber and Faber, 1985). This is Kristin Thompson's translation, *Eisenstein's* Ivan the Terrible, 79.

30. Il'ya Smirnov, "Mezhdu dvumia tiranami" (Between Two Tyrants), *Kinovedcheskie zapiski,* 38 (1998), 14. Cf. Iurenev, *Eizenshtein: Zamysly,* 237.

31. F. 1923, op. 1, d. 548, ll. 1–8 [28.XI.44].

32. Eizenshtein, "Ivan Groznyi: Kino-stsenarii," 62.

33. F. 2456, op. 1, d. 957 (Komitet po delam Kinematografii pri SNK SSSR, Zasedaniia Khudozh. Soveta. 7.XII.44), l. 10, 21, 26–27.

34. F. 1923, op. 1, d.565, part 1, l. 27 [4.III.42].

35. F. 2456, op. 1, d. 957, ll. 10 (Pyr'ev), 21 (Pudovkin).

36. Kleiman, *Neizvestnyi "Ivan Groznyi,"* video-CD.

37. Eisenstein and his assistant director, Lev Indenbom, compiled a manuscript of references to historical sources for over two hundred citations from the screenplay—his "Historical Commentary" (although there was little actual comment). Originally Eisenstein hoped it would be published alongside the screenplay; *Novyi mir* refused. The manuscript, *Istoricheskaia kommentariia k tstenariiu "Ivan Groznyi"* [22.IX.43] is in the *Novyi mir* archive f. 1702 op. 1, d. 1061; and has been published in *Kinovedcheskie zapiski,* 38 (1998).

38. Uppercase in the original, *Novyi mir,* "Ivan Groznyi: Kino-stsenarii," 80–81.

39. Originally Eisenstein's plan was: "End Part I with the oath of the oprichniki. The oath is pronounced by Fedor and received by Aleksei (Let the game begin!)." F. 1923, op. 1, d. 155 [4.VII.42], l. 94. See also, diary entry in f. 1923, op. 2, d. 1168 [13.II.42], ll. 5–7, 10–11.

40. F. 1923, op. 2, d.1168 [13.II.42], ll. 6, 8; f. 1923, op. 2, d.125, l. 2; f. 1923, op. 1, d. 561, l. 67.

41. F. 2456, op. 1, d. 957, l. 10.

42. E. Levin, "Istoricheskaia tragediia kak zhanr i kak sud'ba" (Historical Tragedy as Genre and as Fate), *Iskusstvo kino,* 1991, no. 9, 84. Later Levin elaborates in reference to Part II: the Ivan they expected was "a progressive state actor, a wise politician, a visionary and great reformer, who no one disputes was cruel and spilled a great deal of blood, but for a holy cause, sanctioned and justified by history" (87). Levin cites long excerpts from the discussion following the screenings of Parts I and II, but he tends to leave out the comments with specific historical significance.

43. F. 2456, op. 1, d. 957 [7.XII.44], ll. 2–4.

44. F. 2456, op. 1, d. 957 [7.XII.44], ll. 26–27.

45. To this last, Eisenstein himself piped up: "Even harder for me!" f. 2456, op. 1, d. 957 [7.XII.44], l. 34.

46. Pudovkin, f. 2456, op. 1, d. 957 [7.XII.44], l. 18.

47. F. 2456, op. 1, d. 957 [7.XII.44], l. 13.

48. F. 2456, op. 1, d. 957 [7.XII.44], l. 6.

49. F. 2456, op. 1, d. 957 [7.XII.44], l. 31.

50. F. 1923, op. 2, d. 1170 [18.V.45], ll. 12–14.

51. The Stalin Prize committee deliberations are found in RGALI, f. 2073 (*Komitet po Stalinskim premiiam v oblasti iskusstva i literatury*). The nominations are

in f. 2073, op. 1, d. 15 (*Kom. po delam kinematografii pri Sovnarkom*) [28.III.44], l. 72; f. 2073, op. 1, d. 12 (*Protokoly plenarnykh zasedanii komiteta*) [29.III.45], l. 31. The Film Section's nominees were *Kutuzov, Georgii Chaakadze, Zoia, Ona zashchishaet rodinu* (She Defends the Motherland), *Nashestvie* (Invasion), *Raduga,* (Rainbow), *V shest' chasov vechera posle voiny* (At Six p. m. after the War), and *Chelovek No. 217* (Person No. 217).

52. F. 2073, op. 1, d. 14, l. 67.

53. F. 2073, op. 1, d. 11 (*Stenogramm zasedanii plenuma komiteta raboty 1943– 44 gg. Obsuzhdenie doklada Sektsii teatra i kino*) [29.III.45], l. 150–151. The Plenum included the following: Beiseitova, Bolshakov, Gerasimov, Glier, Goldenveizer, Grabar', Kolas, Korneichuk, Mikhoels, Mordvinov, Miaskovskii, Nasyrova, Khmelev, Chiaureli, Samosud, Iura, Mukhina.

54. F. 2073, op. 1, d. 11 [29.III.45], l. 150.

55. F. 2073, op. 1, d. 11 [29.III.45], ll. 151.

56. F. 2073, op. 1, d. 11 [29.III.45], l. 152.

57. The best example is the body of historians' reviews of Oliver Stone's films *JFK* and *Nixon,* in which criticism of the films' historical laspses reflects the political perspective of the author towards the subject of the film.

58. F. 2073, op. 1, d. 11 [29.III.45], l. 153.

59. F. 2073, op. 1, d. 11 [29.III.45], l. 154.

60. F. 2073, op. 1, d. 11 [29.III.45], l. 153–55.

61. "It is true that the overwhelming majority of historical films made anywhere and at any time aims to use the past in order to deal with present problems . . . Nevertheless it is extraordinary how brazenly the directors [of Soviet wartime historical films] distorted past events, distant or recent, in order to make their points." Kenez, *Cinema and Soviet Society,* 203.

62. F. 2073, op. 1, d. 11 [29.III.45], l. 153.

63. F. 2073, op. 1, d. 11 [29.III.45], ll. 154–55.

64. F. 2073, op. 1, d. 11 [29.III.45], l. 156.

65. F. 2073, op. 1, d. 11 [29.III.45], l. 157.

66. Pauline Kael's review is reprinted in *Kiss Kiss Bang Bang* (Boston: Little Brown, 1968), 288–289.

67. Vishnevskii, *Kinovedcheskie zapiski,* 38 (1998), 74 [30.III.47–31.III.47]. To Eisenstein's great relief, the review remained unpublished.

68. Vishnevskii, *Kinovedcheskie zapiski,* 38 (1998), 75 [no date, April 1947].

69. Vishnevskii, *Kinovedcheskie zapiski,* 38 (1998), 75 [27.IV.47].

70. F. 2073, op. 1, d. 11 [29.III.45], l. 152.

71. Stalin's note approving the screenplay on 13.IX.43 is reproduced in Mar'iamov, *Kremlevskii tsenzor,* 70. Mar'iamov, as Bolshakov's assistant, also describes in fascinating, if not entirely credible, detail, Bolshakov's role in screening films for Stalin.

72. Conversation with Naum Kleiman, June 1998.

73. David Brandenberger and Kevin Platt, "Terribly Romantic, Terribly Progressive or Terribly Tragic: Rehabilitating Ivan IV under I. V. Stalin," *Russian Review* 58 (1999), 635–654; David Brandenberger, "'Not So Terrible After All . . .': Stalinist

Historiography's (Re)casting of Ivan IV, 1937–1953" (manuscript). The latter is to be published in a substantially revised version as David Brandenberger and Kevin Platt, "Terribly Pragmatic: Rewriting the History of Ivan IV's Reign, 1937–1956," in the forthcoming *Epic Revisionism: Tsarist History and Literature as Stalinist Propaganda,* ed. by David Brandenberger and Kevin Platt.

74. Brandenberger, "'Not so terrible,'" 15.

75. Brandenberger, "'Not so terrible,'" 9.

76. Stalin's reaction to Part II is well-known and widely described; see "Stalin, Molotov and Zhdanov on *Ivan the Terrible,* Part Two," Sergei Eisenstein, *Selected Works,* 3, *Writings, 1934–1947,* ed. Richard Taylor, trans. William Powell (London: British Film Institute, 1996), 299–304.

77. Anne Nesbet, "Inanimations: Snow White and Ivan the Terrible," *Film Quarterly,* 50: 4 (1997), 20–31.

THE POWER OF GRAMMAR
AND THE GRAMMAR OF POWER
The Childhood Scenes in *Ivan The Terrible*

Alexander Zholkovsky

T he central theme of *Ivan the Terrible*—"Ivan's emergent autocracy"—is richly emblematized in the childhood scene, in which the boy Ivan turns on his powerful and controlling boyar advisers and seizes power.[1] Originally planned as the Prologue to Part I, it was eventually presented as a flashback near the beginning of Part II (shots 133–205), when Ivan recollects his past and uses it as a warning to his erstwhile friend and now opponent, Fyodor Kolychev.[2] Here follows a shot-by-shot transcript of the sequence's dialogue in my quasi-literal English translation:[3]

The sequence begins with the murder of Ivan's mother Elena Glinskaya (shots 133–146; henceforth abbreviated as I-1) and, in the script only, the arrest by Shuysky of her favorite Telepnev, whom the little Ivan is unable to protect (I-2).[4]

> I-1. (136) *Glinskaya:* They have poisoned me! I am dying! (139) My son! (140) They have killed me! Beware of poison! Beware of the boyars! (145) *Voice off:* Elena Glinskaya (146) is dead! . . .
> I-2. [script] *Voice off:* Strangle the Princess' lover! *Telepnev:* Grand Duke of Moscow, defend me! *Shuysky:* Seize him!

Then—after a close-up of the adult Ivan complaining of his lifelong orphanhood (shot 147)—follows scene II-1 in the reception room (shots 148–174), demonstrating that the little Ivan's power is purely nominal. In the name of "the Grand Duke of Muscovy," whose legs are too short to reach the ground (in the script, "to reach the desired support"; shot 174), the matters of state are decided by de-facto boyar rulers, wrangling with one another.

> II-1. (154) *Belsky:* Ivan Vassilyevich, Grand Duke of Moscow (155) has graciously decided to conclude a commercial treaty (156) and to pay duties for the transit of goods via the Baltic (157) to the great (158) Hanseatic league (159) of German merchant towns. (160) *Shuysky:* The Grand Duke of Moscow (161) has reconsidered. He has concluded the

76. *Ivan the Terrible:* Ivan with Belsky and Shuysky.

treaty (162) with the Order of Livonian Knights. (163) *Voice off:* [They] have (164) bribed Shuysky off, all right! *Belsky:* To the Hansa! (165) Hansa! . . . It was also the Boyar Council's decision. (167) *Shuysky:* The Grand Duke can at will annul the Council's decision! *Belsky:* But he has pledged his word to the Council! *Shuysky:* The Grand Duke is the sole arbiter of his word. When he pleases—he gives it, when he pleases [otherwise]—he rescinds it. The Grand Duke's will is law! *Belsky:* But the will of the Grand Duke (168) is to deal with the Hansa! (169) *Shuysky:* The Grand Duke's will is to concede the privileges to the Livonian Order. (170) *Shuysky, voice off:* The Grand Duke's will is law!

Ivan's so-far latent conflict with the two boyars comes to a head in the next scene: as the huge Shuysky and minuscule Belsky continue their squabbling (scene II-2-1; shots 175–178), the boy Ivan suddenly makes his voice heard, challenging the boyars (II-2-2; shot 178).

II-2-1.   (176) *Belsky:* It is necessary to pay the Hansa! *Shuysky:* We will pay the Livonians! (177) *Belsky:* The Hansa is more profitable to the State! *Shuysky:* Not to the State—it's to yourself that it is more profitable! *Belsky:* And you, you have been bribed by the Livonians! It is the Hansa that it is (178) necessary to pay! *Shuysky:* We will pay the Livonians!
II-2-2   *Ivan, voice off:* We'll pay no one! (179) We are not obliged to pay anyone! The coastal towns were built by our ancestors. (180) Therefore, those lands are our inheritance—they must belong to Moscow. *Shuysky:*

No one is such a fool (181) as to give them back?! *Belsky:* What fell off the wagon is lost. (182) *Ivan:* If they won't return them voluntarily, we will take them back by force! (183) *Shuysky:* By force?! (184) *Belsky:* And where would one find such force?

Shuysky then goes on, hubristically, to humiliate Ivan in personal terms by calling his mother a "bitch" and treating Ivan himself as a sort of stray dog. Ivan raises the stakes even higher and avenges all past and present slights by delivering Shuysky to the servants. Having thus availed himself of the "support" of the people, he proclaims his intention to become Tsar (shots 178–205). His punitive and power-grabbing action is cast as a cornered victim's self-defense.[5]

(185) *Ivan:* It's by you that Russia's strength has been frittered away!— lining boyar's pockets! (187) *Shuysky:* You'll have me die laughing! By Gosh! (188) Take your feet off the bed, I say. (192) Take them off the bed of my mother . . . my mother, poisoned by you dogs! *Shuysky:* A dog, am I?! (193) She herself was a bitch! Ran around with that dog Telepnev! (196) No one knows from whom she whelped you! (197) Dogs' offspring!! (198) *Ivan:* Seize him! (200) Seize! (203) *Belsky:* [He] has handed a senior boyar over to kennelmen! (205): *Ivan:* I shall reign alone! Without boyars! I will be Tsar!

The climactic scene II-2-2 in the royal apartment builds on pointed references to the immediately preceding ones. To single out two:

- The close-up of Shuysky's huge foot on the royal bed harks back to the close-up of the enthroned Ivan's pathetically small foot, the figure of the apocalyptic angel bestriding the universe in the background, and the trampling of Telepnev by Shuysky's henchmen (in the script).
- Shuysky's fateful arrest resumes the issue of Ivan's mother's (Glinskaya's) murder. Within scene II-2-2, his seizing is farcically foreshadowed on the verbal plane by the words with which he falls on the royal bed: "Umoril esi" (You'll have me die laughing); plotwise, it is directly provoked by his response to Ivan's mention of the poisoning: Shuysky lunges at Ivan with his staff. In an additional symmetry (so appropriate to the theme of "revenge"), the script also had Ivan replicating verbatim Shuysky's order regarding Telepnev: "Vziat' ego!" (Seize him!).

Especially close ties link II-2 to the preceding public episode II-1 (whose "publicness" will be mirrored by the final entrance of Ivan's servants). It is

77. *Ivan the Terrible:* The child Ivan's small foot does not reach the floor.

78. *Ivan the Terrible:* The dying Glinskaya.

there that Ivan's two contrasting but symmetrical adult opponents make their appearance. At first, both of them, albeit separately, lord it over the minor Ivan, with the "big" Shuysky defeating the "smaller" Belsky—in a zig-zag detour that eventually leads to the triumph of the "smallest of all," Ivan. This typically Eisensteinian reversal—*otkaznyi*—pattern is in this case firmly rooted in the archetypal motif of David and Goliath and its cinematic reincarnations, such as Charlie Chaplin's clownish victories over the "Big Guy" villains and policemen.[6]

The integral theme of the childhood sequence—Ivan's transition from infantile helplessness to autocratic power—is conveyed tellingly through his speech behavior. Throughout the episode in the reception room Ivan keeps silent, as he had in the preceding scene of Glinskaya's murder, where he appeared literally as a speechless creature crawling on all fours. He only starts speaking in the second part of the scene in his chambers (II-2-2). Typologically, his sudden acquisition of speech is akin to the Biblical passage about Balaam's ass (Numbers 22.28) and the corresponding chapter in *The Brothers Karamazov* (III. 6–7) where Smerdyakov, who until then has been silent and considered quasi-human, suddenly joins a theological discussion and is explicitly called Balaam's ass.[7] It ties in as well to the entire *topos* of a cultural hero's miraculously early speechifying—for example, Christ's dialogue with rabbis in the Temple at the age of twelve, just before reaching the age of responsibility (Luke 2.46–47). According to the script, in scene II Ivan is thirteen; remarkably, Eisenstein in his memoirs sees himself as a once and forever twelve-year-old.[8]

Ivan's lengthy silence (the script stresses his growing desire to speak up for himself) is made even more dramatic by an additional contrast. He is not just silent while others are not; the point is that they speak on his behalf, in a solemnly official third person.

Belsky: . . . *The Grand Duke of Moscow, has graciously decided* to conclude a . . . treaty and to pay duties . . . to the great Hanseatic league of German merchant towns . . .
Shuysky: The Grand Duke . . . has reconsidered. He has concluded the treaty with the Order of Livonian Knights . . . *The Grand Duke* is the sole arbiter of his word. When he pleases—he gives it, when he pleases [otherwise]—he rescinds it . . . *The Grand Duke's will is law* (see shots 154–170).

Moreover, the two boyars speak in what could be loosely called performatives: speech acts that despite being couched in third-person, past-tense terms describe, begin to enact, and promptly result in spectacular actions: the handing over of treaty scrolls to respective ambassadors.[9] The *peripeteia* of the argument between the two boyars further dramatizes the irony of Ivan's silence, since his will is invoked in giving diametrically opposite orders.

In the royal apartment (backstage, as it were) the squabbling goes on but gradually shifts from the officially detached third person to more direct forms, as the same arguments are transposed into a lower-style, almost criminal argot. The grammatical perspective starts with such ostensibly normative impersonal forms as *nadobno* (it is necessary) and *poleznee* (it is more useful/ profitable) and the infinitives they govern. But it soon turns out that lurking behind them have been rather personal, if so far inclusive, first-person plurals and even quite brazenly direct and mutually exclusive second-person singulars: "We'll pay the Livonians!—It's to yourself [*tebe*] that it is more useful/ profitable—And [as for] you [*tebia*], the Livonians have bribed you!" This crude personalization of discourse subverts its original solemnity—as have the two boyars' earlier disagreements, which are now laid utterly bare in the *ty*-form. (In fact, even bribery has been similarly first brought up in third-person plural: "They have bribed Shuysky off all right," shots 163–164.)

The impregnability of the boyars' official discourse is graphically breached by the defeat of at least one of its versions: that of Belsky. This offers Ivan the much-needed opening and shows him the way. In fact, emblematically the "arbitrariness of power" has already been formulated quite explicitly and precisely with reference to the power of words, in Shuysky's remark about the Grand Duke as "the sole arbiter [*khoziain*] of his word." (This remark, intended by Shuysky as a mocking repartee, will soon turn out to have been a grotesque foreshadowing of his own demise on Ivan's arbitrary orders.)

To go back to the turning point in the climactic scene (shot 178), Ivan chimes in at a rather high pitch, unexpectedly shrill against the somewhat relaxed background of the boyars' after-the-fact bickering, which this time is constative (stating a fact or situation), not performative (making things happen). Ivan echoes/retraces the grammatical course of their exchange. He starts off by grammatically echoing but semantically negating Shuysky's peremptory line ("We'll pay the Livonians!") in the same inclusive first-person plural:

> "We'll pay no-one [*nikomu*]! We are not obliged to pay anyone [*nikomu*]. The coastal towns were built by our ancestors. Those lands are our inheritance . . . If they won't return them voluntarily, we shall take them back by force [*siloi*] . . . It's by you [*vami*] that Russia's strength [*sila*] has been frittered away!—lining boyars' pockets! . . . Take your [thy] feet off . . ."

Ivan's first words already exhibit a tendency toward exclusion, which is essential for his autocratic drive. It is signaled right away by the multiple negatives (*nikomu, ne budem*) and becomes more and more pronounced as he proceeds from castigating the third-person, absent foreigners to antagonizing the unspecified second-person plural boyars, present and absent, and the present Shuysky himself, unceremoniously identified in second-person singular (*Uberi nogi s posteli* [Take your (thy) feet off the bed]). Ivan's grammatical bluntness is, again, presented as "defensively imitative": indeed, the *ty*-form has already been broached by Shuysky: *Umoril esi!* (literally, Thou hast made me die laughing). The punned-upon word *morit'* (*lit.* to make die) can typically mean "to exterminate by poisoning rats and other vermin," and thus foreshadows the use by Ivan of the word *izvedennoi* (exterminated) regarding his mother's murder. Characteristically, as Ivan quarrels with one boyar, he does not ally himself with the other. In fact, despite their minor previous feuds, the two boyars are shown (in a separate shot, 181) to mock and oppose Ivan together, thus once again pushing him, as it were, to fall back on an exclusive, solitary-autocratic use of force, already prefigured by his insistent references to *sila* (force, strength).

The climax of the minidrama II-2-2 unfolds almost entirely in canine, dog-eat-dog terms: Ivan engages Shuysky in a "bitching match" and effectively "outbitches" him. This Riffaterrean matrix of the scene—in idiomatic Russian terms, *oni sobachatsia*—is likely to have been quite consciously devised by Eisenstein, who insisted on identifying the precise ideological, proverbial, etymological, archetypal, subconscious, and even autobiographical formulae underlying the artistic structures that he analyzed, taught, and created.[10] Several such hypograms—"canine" and other—overdetermine the scene. Among them are:

- The archetypal motif of a manipulative metamorphosis, of the type that underlies the episode in Charles Perrault's "Puss in Boots" where the feline trickster asks the sorcerer-cannibal first to turn into a lion and then into a mouse, at which point he swallows him.[11] Unlike the Puss (and the historical Ivan), Ivan leaves physical action to his helpers, which highlights his superior power—in the spirit of Eisenstein's remark about the superior role of a film director, who need not himself act since he can manipulate the footage.[12] An even closer parallel is furnished by the legend of Actaeon, the hunter whom Artemis punishes by turning into a stag and having his own hounds tear him to pieces. Ivan's deed is couched in hunting/canine terms and casts the avenger in a superior hands-off role.
- Self-fulfilling "performative" proverbs and maxims, of the type *Nazvalsia gruzdem—polezai v kuzov* (If you call yourself a mushroom, go right into the basket), and *Sobake—sobach'ia smert'* (Unto a dog a dog's death), which emphasize the magic power of the word.

- Sergei Eisenstein's and his parents' own canine and "pup-ist" private semantics, where puns like *plodit' eisen-shcheniat* (*lit:* to breed Eisen-pups) were current; moreover, in Eisenstein's memoirs, this "pup" motif is discussed precisely in the context of Sergei's Oedipal relationship with his father, whose method of educating him in the facts of life he compares to the way pups are taught to swim by being simply thrown into the water.[13]

Eisenstein's love of wordplay brings us back to the verbal texture of the childhood sequence—its poetry of grammar, as it were.[14] We have already noted the prominence of quasi-performatives in the official scene, II-1; indeed, the elocutionary force of speech acts offers a perfect linguistic icon for the theme of power. Let us therefore take a closer look at the elocutionary dynamics of the "dog-eat-dog" episode, II-2-2.

The first, as yet rather cautious step is taken by Ivan, who mouths the word "dogs," subliminally prompted by Shuysky's lying with his feet on the bed, like a dog. The script specifies that Ivan mutters this "between his teeth," which connotes a dog-like baring of teeth. Ivan's half-repressed attitude is subtly iconized by the syntactic structure of his very elaborate one-sentence speech spanning shots 188–192. It features a forcefully reiterated imperative *Uberi,* each time accompanied by increasingly peripheral grammatical dependents, *Uberi nogi s posteli! Uberi, govoriu. Uberi s posteli materi. . materi, vami, psami, izvedennoi* (Take your feet off the bed. Take [them] off, I say; take [them] off the bed of my mother, my mother, poisoned by you dogs). The offensive D-word is thus tucked away in the sentence's remotest grammatical corner: indeed, *psami* (dogs) is a noun in apposition to the instrumental-case agent *vami* (by you) of a passive participial phrase (*izvedennoi* [poisoned]) qualifying an oblique-case attribute *materi* (of my mother) of a prepositional object *s posteli* (from the bed). The subordinate grammatical role of the second-person *vami* also reduces that pronoun's predicative and elocutionary potential; the latter is further diluted by the plural number of both words ("you dogs"), which may be plausibly taken to refer to boyars in general rather than specifically to the two who are present.

Shuysky, of course, is not fooled by these grammatical subtleties. Accepting the challenge, he first transposes Ivan's words into a direct, first-person singular nominative-case predicative reference to himself (*Ia—pes?!* [A dog, am I]), which is interrogative in form but a clear threat in speech-act terms (meaning approximately: "Don't you dare call me a dog to my face!"). At the same time, visually he turns into a metaphorical animal. As the script has it: "'A dog, am I?!'—Shuysky bellowed, rearing like a beast from the bed." In the film, this is realized through his beastly look and fur outfit, contrasting with

Ivan's innocent semi-nudity. (To be sure, as Tsar, Eisenstein's Ivan will wear furs himself.)

Shuysky then proceeds to return the insult. He begins in the constative mode (indicative mood, past tense, third person): *Sama ona—sukoiu byla! S Telepnevym-kobelem putalas'!* (She was a bitch herself. Ran around with that dog Telepnev.) But he retains the direct and personal quality of the canine reference—the singular number and predication of his preceding sentence (*Ia—pes?!*). Indeed, he exacerbates the insult by a stinging moral and sexual innuendo. Shuysky's next step is to produce a canine verb that links, somewhat hypothetically so far, the mother's peccadilloes to her son, and to address him in second-person singular: *Neizvestno, ot kogo ona toboiu oshchenilas'!* (No one knows from whom she whelped you), thus impugning Ivan's dynastic legitimacy. He then rounds it all off with a blunt nominative-case noun phrase, *Such'ie plemia* (Bitch's offspring), whose offensiveness is only slightly tempered by its ambiguous status as either a predicative or an appositive phrase. The appositive reading ("Ugh, you [or: you-all], bitch's offspring"), and the noun's collectiveness neatly conclude the circle begun by Ivan's plural appositive phrase "you dogs." Shuysky's accompanying play with his staff, in addition to being a sort of symbolic assassination attempt on the young prince, tends to metaphorically demote Ivan to a dog: a creature to be handled with a stick. (Ivan's earlier crawling on all fours may be subliminally tapped here.)

To Shuysky's upping of all the personal, political, and elocutionary antes, Ivan responds—self-defensively, to be sure—with a similar yet even more drastic violence, based on the power of the word. The repeated imperative *Vziat' (ego)!* (Seize [him]!) crowns the dramatic spiral begun by Ivan's relatively modest initial order to Shuysky to take his feet off the bed and provides closure to the entire childhood plot triggered by the murder of Glinskaya and "seizing" of Telepnev.

The "canine" seme appears to be absent from this last speech act. According to the script, the order, first uttered by Ivan as an "hysterical scream," is addressed to the kennelmen, of whose presence he has now become aware only when he delivers it the second time.[15] In the film, they actually enter only after his first cry, and their professional identity remains indeterminate even as they grab Shuysky. This pause in the development of the canine motif lasts until a shocked Belsky's *ex post facto* clarification: *Stareshego boiarina—psariam vydal!* ([He] has handed a senior boyar over to kennelmen!) (shot 203). This remark is already strictly constative—third-person, indicative mood, past tense—as befits an epilogue-like summary of a dramatic denouement.

The use of the third person here builds on Ivan's preceding words ("Seize him"); Belsky objectivizes this usage and expands it to cover all three actants:

who handed whom over to whom. This results in an overarching plot rhyme to Belsky's opening third-person remark in the earlier scene about what "the Grand Duke graciously decided" to do. The grammatical repetition under-scores the semantic contrast between what was then effectively said and done in Ivan's name and what he has now decisively accomplished himself, prov-ing that he, indeed, is "the sole arbiter of his word" and "his will is the law."

A word's elocutionary force depends on the appropriate sociopolitical status of the participants. In the textbook example, the words "I pronounce you man and wife" are only valid if addressed by a priest (or his civil-service equivalent) to unmarried consenting heterosexual adults. In the scene under discussion (and the film as a whole), political status is precisely what is at stake. Ivan becomes Tsar because he dares and manages to outperform ("out-performative") his opponents. Plotwise, he defeats Shuysky by having him effectively arrested. In terms of speech acts, by having his tall order obeyed he dramatically establishes the desired elocutionary relationship with his in-terlocutors: instead of the boyars speaking and ruling in his name, he now literally has the last word. On the symbolic level, the entrance of professional dog handlers meets one more role presupposition, resulting in a magical metamorphosis: seized by kennelmen, Shuysky in effect ends up a dog, or rather, a wild beast hunted down by kennelmen with the implied help of hounds. In a subtle foreshadowing, the script has actually already described Belsky as "leaping around Shuysky yelping [like a pup]" (this corresponds to the beginning of II-2-1, shot 176).

In the film at large, the "canine" seme echoes the hound leitmotif in the characterization of Malyuta, the boyars' view of Ivan as a "wild beast," and the "beaver" song in the cathedral episode, whereby the killing of Vladimir Staritsky is symbolically transformed into a successful "beaver hunt."[16] In-deed, the seizing of Shuysky by kennelmen foreshadows the death of Starit-sky and, in the script, the scene of *pravezh* (law enforcement by torture), where Malyuta sets the dogs upon a boyar whom he has dressed in a bear-skin.[17] In its turn, Ivan's vow, at the end of the childhood sequence, to become Tsar (shot 205) prefigures the film's closure with Ivan on the throne, sum-ming up both his struggle for and the meaning of autocratic power (shots 723–728).

So far we have focused largely on Eisenstein the scriptwriter, who master-fully interweaves the motifs of official discourse, coming of age, dog-eat-dog hostility, and verbal power, marshalling them in the service of the central theme of autocratic power. It is time to go beyond this structural analysis in order to correlate it with Eisenstein's personality as it comes across in his memoirs. Many parallels have been drawn—by Eisenstein himself and oth-ers—between his works, especially *Ivan the Terrible* and its protagonist, and their real author. I will briefly touch upon some of them.

- The parallel between Eisenstein's own childhood, marked by an Oedipal relationship with his father and other father figures, and the recurrent image of defenseless children in his films, in particular an almost naked child victimized by fully dressed adult antagonists (as in scene II-2). The little Ivan's pathetic undershirt seems to boast autobiographical origins (and parallels in Eisenstein's films and theoretical writings), as do the boyars' innuendos about Glinskaya's whoring, which may go back to the memories of the "undersexed *papen'ka*" leveling similar accusations at the "oversexed *mamen'ka*." The parallel extends to the shot of Glinskaya's being carried away and Eisenstein's mother carried by the father after an attempt to throw herself down the stairwell.[18]

- The connection between the autocratic, sadistic, or otherwise painfully self-assertive motifs in the films and Eisenstein's own confessed inferiority complex and compensatory fixation on overachievement, fame, and power.

- The analogy between the "hunt" motifs in the film and Eisenstein's obsession as reader, director, and scholar with corresponding mythological archetypes and detective plots.[19]

- The close ties between the motif of revenge justified as a defensive payback (in particular, the idea of revenge of a hunted animal/cornered victim/defenseless child turned victoriously punishing hunter) and Eisenstein's consistent theoretical and practical stylistic predilection for symmetrical, mirror-like, rhyming, and immaculately closed structures of the sort exemplified by the childhood sequence.

- The affinity between oppressive physical violence and that enforced by stylistic means, as signalled by Eisenstein's acknowledgement that the overarching invariant of his oeuvre — the theme of "unity" — can only be realized by doing "violence" to the diverse material it has to subjugate.[20] This forms a telling parallel to the price of violent autocracy paid for the unity of Russia in *Ivan the Terrible*. It has been noted that Eisenstein's directorial dominant was achieving an equilibrium of all artistic and technical means at the expense of — by doing violence to — the "live human factor."[21] Eisenstein's confessed "inhuman" fixation on abstract, superhuman formulas and primitive, even prehuman archetypes may explain his reliance, in memoiristic discourse, on stereotypical devices.

- The kinship between the film's words-turned-deeds leitmotif and a similar (auto)biographical pattern. Eisenstein's memoirs abound in subplots where some early culturally encoded or otherwise distinctly structured impressions "come true" in his later life. (These impressions are visual — of photographs, drawings, book covers, postcards, film

sequences; verbal—of episodes from novels and newspapers, of
famous people and places; imaginary—obsessive dreams and desires;
and real-life—of children's games and lonely pastimes.) The memoirist
revels in describing how he eventually got to meet the celebrities, visit
the places, and script, stage, and direct his favorite situations.

The influence of an artist's early memories on his creations is, of
course, a commonplace. Somewhat more specific is the strong self-
fulfilling ("magical") undercurrent: what had been only a memory
becomes enacted in real life/art, vindicating the impressionable,
bookish child-turned-artist. Furthermore, as many of those
impressions had a cruel, sadomasochistic tinge, their enactment puts
Eisenstein in a class with his avant-gardist contemporaries and their
view of art as a vehicle for violence and power (as in Eisenstein's
favorite line from Isaac Babel's short story "Guy de Maupassant"
about the well-timed period at the end of a sentence piercing the
human heart more chillingly than any iron).[22] Finally, and quite
idiosyncratically, such performative vindication of cherished words
and images meant a successful settling of scores with paternal
authority. A graphic instance of such childish revenge is the
spectacular limb-by-limb tearing apart of the statue of Alexander III
in *October,* which Eisenstein himself connected with the long-desired
destruction of the ugly Riga facades built by his Chief Architect father.[23]

Eisenstein's artistic progress, inspired by bookish images of cruelty
and resulting in an obsessive portrayal of violent revenge in films,
drawings, memoirs, and profiles of fellow artists, borders on circularity.[24]
Just as revenge does not break the cycle of vendetta but only turns the
underdog into top dog, so the highbrow recycling of dime-novel
violence by an artist of genius results in what could be called, to
paraphrase Chukovsky on Alexander Blok's *The Twelve,* cowboy movies
played on a gigantic organ.[25]

- The similarity between the dynamics of Ivan's empowerment and that
of Eisenstein's own career. In the childhood sequence, Ivan proceeds
from squirming in the silence imposed by the peremptory,
paternalistic, official, and false discourse of the boyars to acquiring
speech and using it in a bluntly forthright, forceful, and vindictive
way. This parallels Eisenstein's own story as an originally well-behaved
child rebelling against his parents' plans for his career and against
traditional culture in general to become a revolutionary avantgarde
artist. The irony becomes manifest at the "synthesis" stage of the
dialectic triad, with the former rebel entrenched in his own rather rigid
system of discursive power. The stylistic dimension of this dialectic
deserves special attention.

Eisenstein's memoirs are remarkable for the way they are styled. In accordance with his own paradoxical statement, they intend to reveal in order to conceal; yet as usually happens in such cases, they end up being tell-tale.[26] They are written in a brisk, self-assured manner, often in snappy script-like paragraphs cultivated by the Futurists. They pretend to be energetic, free, and open, but already by the time of their writing their manner had become conventional and served to shield the writer's persona from scrutiny. The memoirs make liberal use of stereotypes—as the director frequently resorted to in his films, fully deserving the ridicule heaped on him, for example, for his "fat kulak" in *The Old and the New*.[27] In this respect, especially telling is the passage about the art of finding the proper extras to cast as right and left Social Revolutionaries in *October*.[28] In the memoirs, the massive stereotyping of people (for instance, of Leon Moussinac as a Leftist "d'Artagnan") and events (Eisenstein's struggle to avoid deportation from France as a high-society intrigue on behalf of a persecuted revolutionary) may have something to do with his avowed admiration for Balzac.[29] The hallmark of Balzac's style was the use of conventionalized generalizations—about thirty-year-old women, impoverished aristocrats, foreign-born bankers, provincial students—of the sort spoofed by Chekhov already at the time of Eisenstein's birth and yet praised and emulated by Eisenstein time and again on the brink of his death.[30]

Despite their rhetorical dazzle, erudite intertextuality, and occasional self-revelational insights into the psychology of creativity, Eisenstein's memoirs on the whole read as a coldly detached, superficial account of brief encounters with people portrayed in a cartoon or poster style. This imperviously opaque and condescendingly didactic discourse is naturalized by its being addressed to the average Soviet reader, whom their author rightly assumes to be ill-informed, unsophisticated, and ready to be fed pious propagandistic stereotypes and fall for the game of elitist name-dropping with a Communist flavor. But then, the range of Eisenstein's tastes—from detective novels to Balzac to Sade and Sacher-Masoch, to Disney to cops and robbers and his distaste for Proust—was essentially that of an adolescent who failed to mature.[31] In this, he was ironically part and parcel of his Soviet audience, pointedly kept in the state of permanent adolescence. The best of Soviet literary production was for children or featured essentially boyish characters such as Ostap Bender, while socialist realist literature for adults was such in name only.

The course of Eisenstein's stylistic journey—from a rebellion against infantile acquiescence in paternalistic officialese to the creation/acceptance of new formulaic conventions, which were attractively infantile in form and ominously paternalist in function—is sadly ironic and reminiscent of the story of the young and then grown-up Ivan. To a great extent, this was of course due to the double jeopardy of writing as an intellectual and a homo/bisexual in the time of severest political and cultural censorship. But it remains inescapably true that writing amidst arbitrary arrests and making films that justify them results in an arrested development. To conclude where Eisenstein's memoirs—and Ivan's childhood—begin:

> A boy aged twelve. Obedient, polite, clicking his heels . . . A boy from a good family. That's how I was aged twelve. And that's how I am now that my hair has turned grey [although] at twenty-seven the boy from Riga became a celebrity.[32]

Notes

1. In the formulation of the central theme I follow Kristin Thompson, *Eisenstein's* Ivan the Terrible: *A Neoformalist Analysis* (Princeton: Princeton University Press, 1981), 67–68, and its modification in my essay "Eisenstein's Poetics: Dialogical or Totalitarian?"in *Laboratory of Dreams: The Russian Avant-Garde and Cultural Experiment,* ed. John E. Bowlt and Olga Matich (Stanford: Stanford University Press, 1996).

2. The shots are referenced according to Sergei Eisenstein, *Ivan the Terrible.* (London and Boston: Faber and Faber, 1989), 136–146.

3. The transcript is based on Eisenstein, *Ivan the Terrible,* emended according to the original script and at one point supplemented with unrealized script material. See Eisenstein, *Izbrannye proizvedeniia v shesti tomakh* (Selected Works in Six Volumes) (Moscow: Iskusstvo, 1964–1971), 6, 203–215.

4. Eisenstein, *Izbrannye proizvedeniia,* 6, 205.

5. Thompson, *Eisenstein's* Ivan, 92 and 100–101; Zholkovsky, "Eisenstein's Poetics," 255.

6. David and Goliath are referred to directly in a similar scene in the script of *The Old and the New.* Eisenstein, *Izbrannye proizvedeniia,* 6, 98.

7. For the manifold relevance of Dostoevsky subtexts to *Ivan the Terrible,* see R. Ia. Kleiman, " 'Tol'ko "skvoz' Ivana" u menia interes k nemu . . . ': Eizenshtein i Dostoevskii" ('Only "Through Ivan" Do I have an Interest in Him': Eisenstein and Dostoevsky) *Kinovedcheskie zapiski* 38 (1998), 314–328.

8. S. M. Eisenstein, *Memuary* (Memoirs), 2 vols, (Moscow: Muzei kino, 1997), 1, 31.

9. Performatives in the strict sense of J. L. Austin, *How to Do Things with Words* (Cambridge: Harvard University Press, 1975), in and by themselves constitute the necessary actions, unlike imperatives, which call for a separate realization of the issued commands, as argued by Emile Benveniste, "La philosophie analytique et le language," in his *Problèmes de linguistique générale* (Paris: Gallimard, 1966), 274.

10. In the sense found in Michael Riffaterre, *Semiotics of Poetry* (Bloomington: Indiana University Press, 1978).

11. Incidentally, Eisenstein participated in Meyerhold's staging of Ludwig Tieck's "Puss in Boots"; see I. A. Aksenov, *Sergei Eizenshtein: Portret khudozhnika* (Eisenstein: A Portrait of the Artist) (Moscow: Soiuz Kinematografistov, 1991), 27.

12. Eisenstein, *Memuary,* 1, 276.

13. Eisenstein, *Memuary,* 1, 349–352.

14. On the concept of poetry of grammar, see Roman Jakobson, *Verbal Art, Verbal Sign, Verbal Time.* (Minneapolis: University of Minnesota Press, 1985), 37–107.

15. Eisenstein, *Izbrannye proizvedeniia,* 6, 214.

16. Incidentally, when in the United States, Eisenstein was nicknamed "red dog" and "Mesopotamian mongrel" by conservative journalists and "son of a bitch" by Upton Sinclair's brother-in-law.

17. S. M. Eizenshtein, *"Ivan Grozny:* Neizvestnye stranitsy stsenariia" (Publikat-siia V. V. Zabrodina) (Ivan the Terrible: Unknown Pages of the Screenplay [A publication by V. V. Zabrodin]), *Kinovedcheskie zapiski* 38 (1998), 252–253.

18. See Zholkovsky, "Eisenstein's Poetics," 253; on parallels between the little Ivan's childhood and that of Alyosha Karamazov, see Kleiman, "Eizenshtein i Dostoevskii," 320.

19. See Viacheslav Vs. Ivanov, *Ocherki po istorii semiotiki v SSSR* (Essays on the History of Semiotics in the USSR) (Moscow: Nauka, 1976).

20. Eisenstein, *Memuary,* 2, 297.

21. See especially Aksenov, *Sergei Eizenshtein.*

22. Zholkovsky, "Eisenstein's Poetics," 336.

23. Eisenstein, *Memuary,* 1, 339. Incidentally, Eisenstein *père*'s aesthetic legacy seems uncannily present in the monumental stylistics of the son — judging by the samples reproduced in the recently printed and filmed Eisensteiniana.

24. Perhaps the most telling example is the literary portrait of Kazimir Malevich as a Clint Eastwood-cum-Arnold Schwarzenegger avenger type; see the essay "Nemchinov most" (Nemchinov Bridge) in Eisenstein, *Memuary,* 2, 310–315.

25. Kornei Chukovskii, *Kniga ob Aleksandre Bloke* (A Book about Alexander Blok) (Paris: YMCA Press, 1976 [Reprint of 1922 edition]), 126.

26. Eisenstein's statement is from *Memuary,* 1, 358.

27. See, for instance, Il'f and Petrov's "1001-ia derevnia" (The 1001st Village): Il'ia Il'f and Evgenii Petrov, *Sobranie sochinenii v piati tomakh* (Moscow: Khudozhestvennaia literatura, 1961), 2, 463–466.

28. Eisenstein, *Memuary,* 2, 389.

29. The d'Artagnan comment is from Eisenstein, *Memuary,* 2, 324–333.

30. Roland Barthes described Balzac's style in *S/Z,* trans. Richard Miller (New York: Hill and Wang, 1974). For comments on such absurdly overgeneralized lines in Chekhov as "prosecutors like angling, especially for ruff," and "Students are often blond," see N. Ia. Berkovskii, "Chekhov: ot rasskazov i povestei k dramaturgii" (Chekhov: From Stories and Novellas to Dramaturgy) in his *Literatura i teatr: Stat'i raznykh let* (Literature and Theater: Articles from Various Years) (Moscow: Iskusstvo, 1969), 54. Eisenstein praises these stereotypes in *Memuary,* 2, 424.

31. "I never liked Marcel Proust," he says in Eisenstein, *Memuary,* 1, 19.

32. Eisenstein, *Memuary,* 1, 31.

IVAN THE TERRIBLE
Eisenstein's Rules of Reading

Yuri Tsivian

In nature, the thunderstorm may serve as a prototype of the historical event. Then the movement of the pointer around the face of the clock may be seen as a prototype of the absence of the event.

—Osip Mandelstam

On February 25, 1947, there was the meeting at the Kremlin between Sergei Eisenstein and Nikolai Cherkasov (on the one side), and Joseph Stalin, Vyacheslav Molotov, and Andrei Zhdanov. Zhdanov, then Secretary of the Central Committee, made a remark which was taken down by Cherkasov: "Comrade Zhdanov said that Eisenstein's fascination with shadows distracted the viewer from the action, as did his fascination with Ivan's beard: Ivan lifted his head too often so that his beard could be seen."[1]

Five months earlier (and three weeks after the Party Central Committee's resolution condemning *Ivan the Terrible,* Part II, appeared in *Pravda*) Eisenstein made a diary entry that sounds as if he were anticipating—and, in a sense—forestalling, Zhdanov's remark. Following a detailed analysis of the scene in Ivan's stateroom (Part I) in which the huge shadow cast by Ivan's head forms the background of action (Eisenstein called this a "shadowy commentary" to the scene) we find the following passage whose bulky first word "overburdenedness" (Eisenstein's English equivalent to the Russian term *peregruzhennost'*) not merely communicates but almost depicts the principle of excess central to the aesthetics of Eisenstein's last film: "*Overburdenedness* with shadows—too many images stuffed; [but only] for <u>those</u> who do not '<u>read</u>,' but simply hurry on after the action. That is, for those who came to cinema for telegraphic syntax, rather than for poetic writing with repetitions, illustrations and music—for [those who came for] the anecdote alone."[2] The aim of this article is to outline what may be called, paraphrasing Eisenstein, the "reading rules" of his late poetics—the rules that help to approach *Ivan the Terrible* on Eisenstein's own terms.

THE CREDITS

One such rule—the rule of a good beginning—Eisenstein owes to Arnold Schönberg, whose essay "The Relationship to the Text" (1912) he quotes in a diary entry from the summer of 1940. The composer of songs, says Schön-berg, must not "cling" to the text provided by the poet; on the contrary:

[I]ntoxicated by the sound of the first words of the text, I had finished many a lied of my own without in the least caring for the further development of the poem, without even noticing it in the ecstasy of composing. Only some days later did I think of looking up the poetical content of my lied. To my great amazement I realized that I could not have done more justice to the poet. The direct contact with the sounds of the first words made me sense what necessarily had to follow.[3]

From this Eisenstein concludes: "Without a doubt, the beginning of a text (of a good text) bears the *nux* of emotional imagery which determines the sub-sequent flow not only of the poem itself, but also of the music written for it."[4] Latin for "nut," *nux,* was a stock word that Eisenstein used to describe the node, the germ, the nuclear image of the work—Schönberg's experience re-affirmed that such an image has to be planted from the outset.

I cite this entry to explain why I prefer to start my discussion of *Ivan the Terrible* by analyzing its credits—a textual space that, normally, hardly merits a pause. Not so in *Ivan;* here, the credit sequence nutshells a number of motifs whose true role we increasingly sense as the film proper unfolds. It consists of four elements: a musical theme, a song, changing letterings, and a darkish image of writhing smoke against which the latter appear. The first thing we notice on screen is the title "Ivan Grozny," accompanied by a musical theme that Eisenstein's notes identify as "the theme of Ivan." The theme resounds while the names of the players and *dramatis personae* replace each other, to give way to the song performed by a male choir. The song takes around twenty seconds of credit time, after which the theme of Ivan returns and stays until the credit sequence is finally over.

One motif is the image of smoke seen in the background—later in the film, it appears two more times, both times under different circumstances which thus define the way we read it. This semi-abstract smoky substance is what card players call the "joker"—a card whose suit and value vary from one deal to another. During the Kazan battle (Part I) the smoke is an index of fires. In Part II, smoke marks off a flashback—Ivan's childhood trauma—from the main action, which the flashback is meant to explain. In this context, if we call this "smoke" then we do so only figuratively, as we speak of the "mist" of memory or the "murk" of the subconscious mind.

Since the credits are the first thing we see on the screen, it may appear that it is entirely up to the viewer what to think of the image of smoke—and whether to think of it at all. For want of a story context, broader cultural contexts readily offer their assistance. It has been suggested that the background image might hide a visual reference to the line "His spirit is there—in the smoke of the centuries!"—Alexander Pushkin's poetic tribute to Nikolai Karamzin, a nineteenth-century writer on history (and the one to whom we owe the first "psychological" portrayal of Ivan),[5] a line that posits the historian as the hero rescuing the past from the fires of time. However, once one decides to approach the credits as an audiovisual cluster (or, to use Eisenstein's favorite metaphor, an ideogram) rather than an indifferent combination of sounds and signs, one hardly needs to go that far. We hear the music, listen to the song, and read the words "Ivan Grozny"—the name of the movie and the descriptive name of its hero—overlaying the image of smoke. The context emerges as a real-time trajectory resulting from the interaction of the four.

Western equivalents fail to live up to the ambivalent flavor of Ivan's vernacular sobriquet. While names like "Terrible" or *Schreckliche* mean both fearsome and ugly (an association conveyed in Russian by a different word), the name *grozny* associates fear with admiration for beauty, a mixture perhaps inherited from the word *groza* (thunderstorm) from which it derives. This is not merely an etymological aside. Like many thinkers of his time, Eisenstein shared a faith in primal emotional imagery buried under the surface of words, and held it to be the task of the artist to restore this imagery to its former power. The atmospheric origin of Ivan's name is a case in point. In his research Eisenstein saw it revived in folk songs featuring "Ivan the Thunderous" or in the widespread biographical legend which begins the story of Ivan's life with a description of the thunderstorm that broke out on the day of the Tsar's birth.[6] In one of his preparatory notes for the film, Eisenstein even quotes Pushkin's portrayal of Peter the Great: "The whole of him is like God's thunderstorm," only to annex it in favor of Ivan.[7] Using a phrase that Eisenstein employed as the title for one of his major treatises on art, we may say that even though the action rarely takes place outdoors, "nonindifferent nature" is a major player in this film.

As a *nux* of emotional imagery, the image of the thunderstorm proved particularly helpful because of its acoustic dimension. Outlining the musical theme of Ivan—an outline which Sergei Prokofiev was to translate into music proper—Eisenstein instructs the composer to give it a Wagnerian ring: "[M]usically, the theme of Ivan must take the form of an encroaching thunderstorm, as though one were to compose a piece entitled Thunderstorm (like the beginning of *[Die] Walküre*—storm, thunder, rain.)" and adds: "This theme must underlie the introductory credits."[8] According to this plan, from the outset the rumbling of the musical "thunder" will interact with the words "Ivan Grozny," releasing the etymological energy of this name.[9]

Two other elements that participate in the credits—the smoke and the song—also contribute to the pun. As with Prokofiev's music, Eisenstein's working notes let us track the final text of the song back to the stage of conception. In April 1942, Eisenstein wrote two lines of text intended to serve the poet Vladimir Lugovskoy as a "dummy" to be modified into verse. Imitating the parallelism of folk ballads, Eisenstein links the name to its root:

> *Grozy* (Thunderstorms) were encroaching,
> *Grozny* (The Terrible) Tsar rose against them.[10]

The following quatrain is what we actually hear from the screen:

> A black cloud is rising,
> The face of the dawn is washed with red blood.
> The boyars' treacherous plot
> Is rising for a battle against the authority of the Tsar.[11]

The pun is gone—veiled. Instead, the chorus informs us of a thundercloud, a verbal image that lends its name (writes up a role, assigns a reading) to the visual image of the black smoke writhing in the background. As every element of the credit sequence is thus mobilized to create meaning, we are faced with a composite sign, a multimedia hieroglyph of nonindifferent nature.

MOTIF STRUCTURE

I have lingered upon the credits because they serve to illustrate two principles—from our perspective, two "reading rules"—that Eisenstein adhered to as he was building up the motif structure of *Ivan the Terrible*. First, any motif (e.g., that of a thunderstorm) manifests itself across different classes of sign vehicles—in this case musical, verbal, and visual. At different times Eisenstein referred to this principle under various names: "the monistic ensemble," "audio-visual polyphony," and even "sound-sense spatiality" (*zvukosmyslovaya prostranstvennost'*).[12] We may simply call this "the rule of variety." To demonstrate the second principle (which we may call "the rule of ambivalence") we need to return to Eisenstein's instructions to Prokofiev and Lugovskoy. This principle may be formulated approximately as follows: any motif tends to be distributed across opposing classes of *dramatis personae*. If we compare Eisenstein's plan for the musical theme of Ivan with his instructions for the text of the song, the reader will easily notice that despite the fact that the play on the root *groz-* defines both, the image of the thunderstorm in the music is personified in Ivan, while in the song it betokens his enemies, the boyars. In this, the notion of a cinematic motif differs from that of an iconographic attribute in visual arts. Unlike the conventional lightning that helps the beholder to identify Zeus the Thunderer in mythological paintings,

Eisenstein's thunderstorm is not assigned to Ivan the Terrible as a character, but is a property of *Ivan the Terrible* as a film.

NARRATIVE STRUCTURE

A unique thing about *Ivan the Terrible* is that its story elements tend to develop in a manner similar to the development of motifs. Watching the way in which dramatic situations in *Ivan* parallel, echo, and paraphrase each other, one suspects that most are versions of deeper structures to which Eisenstein ascribes more than merely narrative significance. This suspicion grows into certitude the moment one consults his working records to find most of these listed and named: twin cult, patricide, filicide, bisexuality, birth trauma, or the ritual killing of the king.[13] These *ur*-structures—as well as the very idea that beneath the pall of what film characters say or do lurks a deeper truth that concerns us all—stem from Eisenstein's interest in monistic theories that held sway in turn-of-the-century psychology and anthropology. These theories all proceeded from an assumption that at the bottom of things there is always a key—a kernel myth or a primal something: a scene, a trauma.

According to Eisenstein, one key to the story of *Ivan* is the ritual killing of the old king—a rite which the ancients believed ensured the continuity of power. Like many of his contemporaries writing on the subject, Eisenstein held that vestiges of ritual regicide were found in some harmless (and some not so harmless) medieval customs, specifically in ones having to do with carnival reversals of power. In a diary entry made in January 1945 he taps such a reversal in order to explain the final scene from the yet unreleased (and yet unbanned) Part II: "One finds yet another *antic custom* in *Grozny*: dressing a jester in Tsar's garments and then stabbing him (in lieu of the Tsar). This, in fact, is the pivot [*bolvanka*] of the entire scene in which Vl[adimir] Andreevich is killed ('he killed a jester' and 'the fool likes it on the throne.')"[14]

And pivotal it is. More than once during the sequence Eisenstein replays the primal situation of regicide, shifting characters and their assumed roles in a carousel of fortunes. The events unfold as follows. Sensing a conspiracy, Ivan invites his young cousin Vladimir to a feast. Drunk, Vladimir confirms that an assassin, Pyotr, has been found to kill the Tsar whereupon he, Vladimir, would ascend the throne—more or less against his own will since he feels he is not made to rule. The scene is set: we have three figures: the king, the pretender, and the killer (now standing in the wings). This first ("real") regicide is averted by its mock reversal. Ivan makes Vladimir don regal garments, puts him on the throne and bows before him in made-up reverence. This is the first of two moments marked in the diary entry —"the fool likes it on the throne"—the moment when a new figure is added to the essential triad: the pretender who poses as the king becomes the king's fool. The other moment the diary refers to belongs to the next reversal of fortunes. As Vladimir—still posing as the Tsar but not enjoying the role any more (he feels the game may take a bad turn)—walks, candle in hand, across the cathedral, the killer enters, and stabs him in the back. Captured by two guards, Pyotr discovers his mistake and says he is prepared to die. Ivan slowly approaches; holding his arms from both sides, the guards bend the killer into a bowing position; Ivan gestures to straighten him up and pronounces the line from which the diary quotes: "Why are you holding him? He did not kill the Tsar, he killed a jester." What follows looks like an uncanny encore of the previous scene with Vladimir: we watch the king taking a deep bow in front of the bankrupt killer destined to become his friend in Part III (not destined to be made).

This explains why I find Eisenstein's method of story construction akin to his own way of working with motifs. Here, as there, things only count as long as they recur, but they must recur transformed (the rule of variety) and change hands (the rule of ambivalence). Writing on another subject Eisenstein dubbed such narratives "telescopic"—at various points the story returns to one kernel situation to be replayed in a different mode.[15] Above, I have tried to demonstrate the telescopic quality of one sequence, the final sequence of Part II. If we now change the optical distance and look at Eisenstein's movie as a whole, we see that on the larger scale of the entire film the anatomy of *Ivan* remains essentially the same. Sequences echo, mirror and ape one another; situations turn into their own opposites, lining up telescopic series that span the space of the film from beginning to end.

CORONATION

One such series involves the sequence discussed above. The mock coronation of Vladimir that concludes Part II turns upside down a true one that opened Part I—an unhurried reconstruction of the ceremony marking young Ivan's accession to the throne.

Reconstruction is Eisenstein's word, not mine. He used it in a diary entry made in January 1948 (a month of so before his death), comparing, with his usual flair for unexpected juxtapositions, his first film, *Strike,* to *Ivan,* which he knew would be his last—two movies which, on the face of it, could not differ more. The thing in common, he explains, is that both contain quasi-documentary sequences focusing on the question "how is it done."[16] *Strike* is what Eisenstein calls a "tech-film": a film exploring the technique of underground class struggle. By the same token, the coronation sequence in *Ivan* examines "*how* the anointment is produced." In both cases, he adds, "the method is one of reconstruction: [I reconstruct] typical behavior in typical circumstances."[17] What interested him most during the staging of the coronation sequence was not so much the theater of power but, as it were, the

79. Ivan's gilding ceremony from Alexander Nechvolodov's *Tale of the Russian Land,* 1913.

factory of power: "Ritual is the production process whose output consists of non-material, non-object values."[18]

Hence the care with which he reconstructs two principal rituals of the coronation—robing and gilding—altering them slightly to fit the film's design. As required by the robing ceremony, Ivan receives the orb and the scepter from the archbishop, but when it comes to the ultimate gesture that produces a tsar, the placing of the crown, Ivan does it with his own hands. This, I am told, departs from the accepted practice: although we do witness Ivan take the crown from the priest's hands, Eisenstein's Ivan is a self-made tsar prepared to rule in the teeth of the church.[19]

The gilding ceremony has also been changed. Eisenstein would have known how this ritual looked from an ancient miniature reproduced in Alexander Nechvolodov's *Tales of the Russian Land,* an illustrated history book which Eisenstein frequently used as a source.[20] In this picture, we see the newly crowned Tsar leaving the cathedral in which the robing ceremony has just taken place, while his two brothers are seen showering golden coins in front of him (Fig. 79). Though one of the sketches for the film looks fairly faithful to this source (Fig. 80), in the actual film we find Ivan standing, not walking, in the center (and not on the steps) of the cathedral while the shower of coins keeps pouring endlessly upon his head. Small as it may seem,

80. Eisenstein sketch for *Ivan the Terrible,* Coronation scene.

this adjustment alters the original symbolism of the event: the current of coins no longer refers to the path of gold, but to a golden rain—one of the leitmotifs of Eisenstein's film.

KURBSKY AT THE POLISH COURT

In the opening sequence of Part II—roughly halfway between the straight coronation and its mock reversal—we are shown another theater of power, only this time Eisenstein parodies rather than reconstructs its workings. The props are a sword and a knightly cross; the action, give and take. Kurbsky, the Russian defector, hands his sword to the King of Poland. Lounging in his royal armchair, the King takes the sword and returns it to Kurbsky, who thereby is made the liege of Poland. Next, the King produces a ribbon with a glittering cross, which he puts around Kurbsky's neck—thus making Kurbsky a knight, the King's retainer.

This is more or less what we see happening on the screen. Initially, however, Eisenstein's design had been more complex—or, to use his own term, more "telescopic." As envisaged in the scenario, before we are shown the actual ritual we are supposed to see its mock version—a parody within parody, as it were, given that the knighting of Kurbsky is in and of itself a parody of the coronation ritual shown at the beginning of Part I. This is how the scenario describes the first moments at the Polish court:

> The scene begins almost like the scene of Ivan's coronation
> Something is happening OFF SCREEN.
> And various groups look OFF SCREEN. [. . .]
>
> In the foreground
> A huge white and black ball.
>
> Clustered around it—striped jesters.
> The jesters keep glancing OFF SCREEN.
> And tinkle their bells.
>
> The jesters are mimicking what is happening in the background,
> As yet invisible to the spectator.
>
> Two jesters are balancing on the ball.
> One of them—the chief, browless and moonfaced—brandishes his
>   beribboned jester's wand.
> A third bends his knee before the ball.

The first dangles in front of the kneeler his wand with the ribbon, as
    though to invest the latter's neck with the decoration on its end.
He knocks the second jester off the ball by pushing him from behind.
The second jester falls.
A fourth jester takes a running leap over the ball.
The ball rolls.
The jesters fall in a heap one on top of the other. They freeze motionless.[21]

As shown on a drawing that Eisenstein sketched for this scene (Fig. 81),
the placement and movements of the "chief jester" ordaining his counterpart into the Order of Jesters parallel those of King Sigismund beribboning

81. Eisenstein sketch of jesters at the Polish court.

82. Illustration from Alexander Benois' *ABC*, 1905.

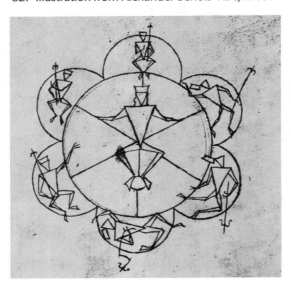

83. Villard de Honnecourt, *The Wheel of Fortune*, c. 1935, pen on vellum.

Kurbsky. Even the props appear to ape each other: the jester's wand with which the mock King decorates the mock Kurbsky's neck is nothing other than a puppet jester whose triple hood recalls the shape of the cross. Virtually everything about this remarkable image is charged with double meaning, including the big ball around which the whole routine pivots—a property whose tongue-in-cheek symbolism becomes apparent as we trace Eisenstein's drawing to its source.

The clue is right before us. Beneath the drawing, we see Eisenstein's note indicating: "A plagiarism from Benois' '*ABC*.' But worked so cleverly into the action, that the sin is justified." The book in question (first published in 1905, around the time Eisenstein was learning to read) is not an ordinary ABC—its designer Alexander Benois thought of it as an artwork as much as a primer. This twofold purpose is also manifest in the picture from which Eisenstein borrowed his jesters and their ball (Fig. 82). Technically, the picture is a rebus: the ball and the jesters stand for the words *shar* and *shuty* illustrating, respectively, the small and the capital variations of the letter ш. But if we take a closer look at Benois' ball, which is not merely a ball but a globe, and at his four jesters—a happy one nearing the top, a frightened one going downward, an angry one under the ball, and a plaintive one standing next to it—and at the king watching their antics with a thoughtful air, we will discover that what they are enacting before the king (and what Benois offers children) is an ironic version of the Wheel of Fortune. This medieval emblem (Fig. 83) features the ruler clinging to a large wheel symbolizing the four stages of reign: *regnabo, regno, regnavi, sum sine regno;* that is, "I will rule, I rule, I have ruled, I am without rule." This mor(t)ality tale and its visual formula is said to descend from the following passage from *The Consolation of Philosophy* by the sixth-century Roman philosopher Boethius:

> Are you trying to stay the force of her turning wheel? Ah! Dull-witted mortal, if Fortune begin to stay still, she is no longer Fortune.
>
> As thus she turns her wheel of chance with haughty hand . . . , fortune now tramples fiercely on a fearsome king, and now deceives no less a conquered man by raising from the ground his humbled face. . . .
>
> "I turn my wheel that spins its circle fairly; I delight to make the lowest turn to the top, the highest to the bottom. Come you to the top if you will, but on this condition, that you think it no unfairness to sink when the rule of my game demands it."[22]

It may appear at first that the philosophical fatalism of the Wheel of Fortune as mimed by Eisenstein's Benois jesters has little to do with the overall story of *Ivan the Terrible*—a film whose visible narrative hinges upon the consolidation rather than the disintegration of power. However, what we see is only part of this story, two-thirds of a work mapped as a trilogy revealing as it unfolds the price Ivan is paying for glory. To appreciate the way Eisenstein planned to make this price known to the viewer, we need to remember "bio-mechanics"—a theory (also an actors' training technique practiced in left-wing theatres in the twenties) according to which stage characters are defined by their manner of movement. A preparatory note (written down around the same time as Eisenstein made his Benois drawing) thus outlines a motor mal-function that overtakes Cherkasov's character as the film moves from its first part to its last:

> In the first episode, Ivan's movements and changes of mood are remarkably *brisk*. . . . In the second one they become *syncopic*. . . . All the mobility and elan [*brosovost'*] of the first episode is reduced here to the movement of the eyes, *hauchement de la tête etc*. During the "Last Judgment" Ivan moves as an unstrung marionette—a parody of his own self of the first episode.[23]

A remarkable thing about this project is that here the biomechanical evolu-tion of the character is defined in the same terms that Eisenstein uses to define the development of the plot—conceived, we recall, as a parade of parodies. First Kurbsky, then the jesters, later the poor fool Vladimir, and now—pressed against the backdrop of the Doomsday fresco—the Tsar is shown putting on a string-puppet parody of himself. Sadly, only a few stills survive from the "Last Judgment," a scene showing Ivan's violent confession shot for the last part of the trilogy. However, a series of sketches made in de-liberately nervous strokes (Figs. 84, 85, 86) also survive and give an idea of the angular uncoordinated motions Eisenstein wanted Cherkasov to perform. Another note (penned in July 1942) specifies Ivan's behavior afterward:

> *After* the "Last Judgment":
> Ivan the *Stony*[24]

and summarizes:

> The 1st episode
> All of him moves
> The 2nd one: only his *eyes* move
> Funeral feast: only his *eyelids* move, his face and his glance are stone-like
>   (use adhesive tape to pull down [Cherkasov's] lower eyelids)
> *Eherne Maske* [an iron mask].[25]

Lastly, Naum Kleiman's theoretical reconstruction of Part III tells us how Ivan would have looked in the finale:

84. Eisenstein sketch for *Ivan the Terrible,* Part III.

"Sallow faced," "drooping"—such were the director's instructions for the make-up and costume artists, and that is how he pictured Cherkasov's acting during the end sequence. We can also read it in the very figure of Ivan as depicted on Eisenstein's drawing entitled "Alone?" It shows the climax of his self-destruction and the deepest point of his loneliness.[26]

Despite the inevitable fluidity of Eisenstein's work-in-progress, we can count up to six transformations (particularly striking since other characters remain ageless) that mark Ivan's itinerary from hope to letdown—a cycle also de-scribed by the wheel of fortune the jesters on the ball perform so well. One

85. Eisenstein sketch for *Ivan the Terrible,* Part III.

may even speculate why Eisenstein thought his little plagiarism to be so clever: the aim behind the act we see Benois' clowns perform before the king—to remind the ruler of the sad trajectory of rule—was, in a sense, identical to his own goal. This theory, of course, can not be proved or disproved, but whether or not Eisenstein perceived his aim this way, Stalin must have: only the first (ascending) part of the story was allowed to come to the screen at the time as the "main spectator" (as they used to whisper in the 1940s) was still alive. Part II was banned, Part III left unfinished.

Let me add that Benois's image is not to be taken as a clue to a direct allegorical reading of the film—not even if it were included in the final version of the movie. Allegory may help to explain the workings of power, but tells nothing about the workings of Eisenstein's film. In effect, the way this film works—and the kind of reading it asks for—is contrary to allegory. Central among the film's mechanisms is a safety device averting direct readings, be they political, historical, or moral. Earlier on in his career Eisenstein used to call this device "conflict" or "collision," and by the time he made *Ivan* he preferred "dialectical struggle of opposites." Alive throughout his work, however, there was a conviction that the true task of an artist was not to shape or educate, but to confuse and jolt viewers out of their comfortably consistent picture of the world.

86. Eisenstein sketch for *Ivan the Terrible,* Part III.

THE MONTAGE-IMAGE

It may sound paradoxical, but in Eisenstein's art theory the smallest indivisible unit always consists of two things, not one. What constitutes the structure of the work is for him not A or B, but the difference, the tension growing between them in their twin cell—until the *nux* outgrows the nutshell (a little organic explosion) only to reproduce the contradiction on a higher level. Speaking of film, Eisenstein dubbed such a unit a "montage-image" (*montazhnyi obraz*). As distinct from images as representations, the montage-image harbors mutually conflicting features.

The montage-image is not only about montage. Actors' movement, lighting, art design—in *Ivan,* any aspect of filmmaking may be found to embody the principle of internal contradiction. Consider a grand mural that covers the walls and the ceiling of the Reception Hall: the space of anger and mercy, used in the film, as in real life, to announce decrees and receive foreign embassies. A miniature from an old chronograph that depicts one such ceremony in amazing detail (Fig. 87; note the throne, the figures seated along the side walls and the entrance wall shown only in part in order not to block the people behind it) tells nothing about any paintings on its walls or ceiling; evidently, the chronicler was more interested in the happening than in the room.[27] Eisenstein, who must have remembered this miniature, remains reasonably faithful to this source as far as architecture and seating arrangement—he even preserves its peculiar sense of perspective down the hall—but adds a big mural of his own. (We happen to know that Eisenstein was very pleased with this choice: an entry made in his diary on March 30, 1942 reads: 'The angel figure in the Reception Chamber is the best graphic image I have so far managed to invent.")[28] The mural shows rolling clouds along the sides (thus recurs the motif of the thundercloud planted in the credits), and, all along the ceiling above the clouds, the Angel of Apocalypse with the balance in his right hand and the sinuous sword in his left.[29] The sun-like face of the angel extends beyond the space of the ceiling and appears hanging upside down from the wall over the entrance (Fig. 88). This, however, is only part of the figure; the whole of it, as seen in the sketch Eisenstein made (Fig. 89), probably to explain this idea to the set decorator Iosif Shpinel, can only be shown in orthogonal projection since the feet of the angel—shown trampling the face of the Universe—fold over the wall behind the throne (Fig. 90).[30] Twice folded, Eisenstein's angel of wrath turns literally into a montage-image—an image impossible to take in at a glance, and also, if one may say so, into a "surround icon"—an icon impossible to escape.

I leave to the viewer the joy of discovering how these two images—the face radiating flames and the face being trodden down—placed, vis-à-vis, on opposite walls yet parts of the same image, are made to participate in the

87. Ivan receiving foreign embassies from Alexander
Nechvolodov's *Tale of the Russian Land,* 1913.

confrontation that takes place between Ivan and Kolychev (Fig. 91), another former friend who, we remember, was side-by-side with Kurbsky in Part I, pouring coins on Ivan's head. Let me mention a visual rhyme I might have passed by were it not for a piece of paper on which Eisenstein sketched two shots storyboarding the prologue—a sequence which, shortly before the release of Part I, Eisenstein was forced to shift to Part II where it now figures as a flashback.

Ivan tells Kolychev why he hates boyars: they killed his mother and

88. Ivan in the Reception Chamber, *Ivan the Terrible.*

89. Eisenstein sketch for *Ivan the Terrible.*

90. Young Ivan on the throne, *Ivan the Terrible.*

humiliated him as a child. Fade-in; black smoking clouds; the last glimpse of the poisoned mother; then, there follows a scene showing two grotesque boyars, thick and thin, misruling in his name while little Ivan is shown sitting on the throne, his foot groping vainly for a foothold. This foot, comments Eisenstein, echoes the foot of the angel seen behind the boy's head in an earlier shot—which explains why we see these two shots juxtaposed in his preparatory drawing (Fig. 92).[31] A system of cross-references is thereby created: foot-foot, foot-face, lack of power, excess of power. This is what Eisenstein has in mind when speaking of the montage-image.

We need Eisenstein to help us read *Ivan the Terrible* because in the film Eisenstein's theory and practice form a vicious circle; unlocking it risks trivializing the film and the theory. Would many of us viewers be able to see a

91. Ivan and Kolychev in the Reception Chamber.

92. Eisenstein sketch for *Ivan the Terrible*.

connection between the foot of a fresco figure visible in shot A and the foot of a film character shown in shot B, or construe, at a viewing, all the avatars of the cloud motif unless prompted by Eisenstein's notes? I doubt it—not because our perceptiveness or visual memory is less than Eisenstein's (perhaps; but isn't this also what makes us admire Joyce or Picasso?), but because, for better or for worse, we simply do not watch movies the way Eisenstein thought—or, at his low moments, wished—we did.

We ought to try to meet him halfway. Not only Eisenstein's vision of things, but also his image of himself, were predicated on the paradox of indivisible duality, a feature which Eisenstein, this intolerable self-observer, thought indispensable for his work to take off from the ground: "My activity: one wing—analytical, the other—imagery." [32] In this sense, Eisenstein *is* a montage-image: the physical body of his film has an invisible twin—the mental movie without which the first is not complete.

Notes

Epigraph quoted from A. Ospovat and O. Ronen, "Tiutchev, Gogol' i Mandel'shtam" (Tiutchev, Gogol and Mandelshtam) in *Tiutchevskii sbornik II* (Tartu: Tartu University Press, 1999), 53.

1. Richard Taylor, ed., *The Eisenstein Reader* (London: British Film Institute, 1998), 162.

2. RGALI (Russian State Archive of Literature and Art), Moscow, f. [holding] 1923, op. [list] 2, d. [folder] 1176, l. [sheet] 53. In future references the last number is omitted whenever the folder consists of a single sheet. Underlinings in quotations from Eisenstein's writings are his own; italics are used to mark English or any other non-Russian words in the original.

3. Wassily Kandinsky and Franz Marc, eds., *The "Blaue Reiter" Almanac*, trans. Henning Falkenstein (New York: The Viking Press, 1974), 95. Eisenstein quotes Schönberg's essay in German.

4. F. 1923, op. 2, d. 1164, l. 18.

5. Viktor Listov, "Near the Altar to the Unknown God," *Kinovedcheskie zapiski*, 38 (1998), 37.

6. K. Valishevskii, *Ivan Grozny* (Moscow: Obshchestvennaia pol'za, 1912), 134.

7. RGALI, f. 1923, op. 1, d. 554, l. 44; on the conceptual importance of this etymology see Leonid Kozlov, "Ten' Groznogo i khudozhnik" (The Shadow of Grozny and the Artist), *Kinovedcheskie zapiski*, 15 (1992), 44.

8. F. 1923, op. 1, d. 568, l. 1.

9. To make sure it worked, Eisenstein even drew a stepped diagram explaining how to synchronize the acoustic "encroaching" on the visuals. Judging by the draft of January 23, 1941, initially the title *Ivan Grozny* was supposed to conclude, rather than open, the credits sequence (as it does in the final version of the film). It was to be preceded by names of the players appearing one by one, in step with the music climbing crescendo (Eisenstein's idea of "encroaching": closer is louder) until the last—the loudest—"peal" of this musical storm would coincide with the

appearance of the words *Ivan Grozny*. As the main title fades out into the dark, the music dies down—and "immediately [there follows] a dolly shot closing in on the face of the child Ivan, [accompanied by] a musical yell" (RGALI, f. 1923, op. 1, d. 568, l. 1). Like the folk legend of Ivan's life, this yell and this dolly would tie in the birth of the hero with the thunder heard in his name.

10. F. 1923, op. 1, d. 568, l. 11.

11. This song originally belonged elsewhere. It had been recorded for a discarded scene in which the *oprichniki* would have been shown taking an oath to protect Ivan from conspiracies.

12. F. 1923, op. 2, d. 1969, l. 46.

13. On patricide and filicide in *Ivan* see *Kinovedcheskie zapiski* 38 (1998), 133–137.

14. F. 1923, op. 2, d. 1172, l. 36. The italicized phrase *antic custom* is Eisenstein's play on the similarity of the words "antic" and "antique."

15. Eisenstein calls Piranesi's structures "telescopic." Eisenstein, *Izbrannye proizvedeniia v shesti tomakh* (Selected Works in Six Volumes) (Moscow: Iskusstvo, 1964–1971), 3, 180; he used this metaphor (as that of "triple arbalest") to refer to the story structures as well (3, 186).

16. F. 1923, op. 2, d. 1180.

17. Ibid.

18. Ibid. Cf. Bourdieu's term "symbolic capital," though of course the capital accrued in *Ivan* is feudal. Pierre Bourdieu, *The Logic of Practice,* trans. Richard Nice (Stanford: Stanford University Press, 1990), 165, 228.

19. I am indebted to Richard Wortman for the historical details on the ritual of Russian coronation. One may also cautiously suggest that Eisenstein borrowed this gesture from Napoleon, who is said to have whisked the crown from the Pope's hands at the time of his coronation.

20. Aleksandr Nechvolodov, *Skazaniia o russkoi zemle* (Tales of the Russian Land) (St. Petersburg: Gosudarstvennaia tipografiia, 1913), vol. 4.

21. *Ivan the Terrible: A Screenplay by Sergei M. Eisenstein,* trans. Ivor Montagu and Herbert Marshall (New York: Simon and Schuster, 1962), 117–118. It is not clear why and at what stage Eisenstein discarded this scene; we know that he thought about casting it—his friend, theater critic Iosif Yuzovsky, was to play the chief jester (*Kinovedcheskie zapiski,* 38 [1998], 63).

22. Boethius, *The Consolation of Philosophy,* trans. W. V. Cooper. (London: J. M. Dent & Sons Ltd., 1902), 28–29.

23. F. 1923, op. 1, d. 570, l. 10. Although, in a technical sense, at this stage of pre-production *Ivan* was still envisaged as a two-episode picture, conceptually it was a trilogy in two parts.

24. F. 1923, op. 1, d. 570, l. 11.

25. Ibid.

26. Naum Kleiman, *"Formula finala"* (The Formula of the Ending), *Kinovedcheskie zapiski,* 38 (1998), 107. The drawing Kleiman is referring to is reproduced in Jay Leyda and Zina Voynow, *Eisenstein at Work* (New York: Pantheon Books, 1982).

27. Reproduced in Nechvolodov, vol. 4.

28. Eisenstein, *Izbrannye,* 6, 496.

29. The source for this fresco, if there is one, is not clear. As Kristin Thompson convincingly shows, Eisenstein's figure has no direct parallels in Orthodox iconography. See Kristin Thompson, *Eisenstein's* Ivan the Terrrible: *A Neoformalist Analysis* (Princeton: Princeton University Press, 1981), 189.

30. The scenario specified that the angel's feet trample the face of the Universe. Eisenstein, *Izbrannye,* 6, 305.

31. F. 1923, op. 1, d. 576, l. 26.

32. F. 1923, op. 2, d. 1721, l. 10.

IVAN THE TERRIBLE AND "THE JUNCTURE OF BEGINNING AND END"

Anne Nesbet

In the last days of his life Eisenstein undertook a protracted analysis of Gogol's terrifying story "Vii" in which a schoolboy, Khoma Brut, is seduced by a witch-girl and, despite his attempt to protect himself from demonic forces by tracing a magic circle around himself, is murdered in an old church by the piercing gaze of the eponymous monster. Everywhere in this story Eisenstein saw reiteration of the most archaic themes of death and sexuality: the name "Khoma" could be seen as a feminized version of "Homo," or "man," thus placing Khoma "in the series of Gogolian b. S. [bisexual] characters."[1] Khoma Brut was also another avatar of Doubting Thomas putting his finger in the wounds of Christ ("towards the reading of 'wound' as 'vulva'," remarks Eisenstein), and Gogol's unfortunate Khoma perishes within a double womb – magic circle / church when those are pierced and betrayed by Khoma's doubts and Vii's gaze. On January 25, 1948, Eisenstein scribbled among his notes, "Despite my sick condition, I am terribly proud of my decoding of 'Khoma Brut.'"[2]

Eisenstein's excursion into Gogol's wombs and tombs was no isolated phenomenon, but rather an integral part of a much larger, and profoundly autobiographical, project. It was during the post-*Ivan* years, during the forced period of convalescence following the heart attack of early February 1946, that Eisenstein wrote his memoirs, and in fact the film *Ivan the Terrible* reflects (among other things) a shift into the autobiographical mode. My focus in this essay will be Eisenstein's turn, in the last months of his life, to a wide-ranging retrospective analysis of *Ivan the Terrible* as a means of meditating not only on his own autobiography but also, more generally, on the ways that life and death intersect.

In Gogol's horror story, Eisenstein found much that could be connected to *Ivan*. The "bi-sex" nature of Khoma and his death within the womb-like circle of the church were reminiscent of the person and fate of that ill-fated royal simpleton, Vladimir. The Tsar Ivan's seduction of his cousin succeeds when he has persuaded Vladimir to don the Tsar's robes for that fateful procession into the cathedral. Vladimir is then "in drag," we might say, as Tsar.[3] (Throughout *Ivan* one finds an unremitting exaggeration of the feminine side of Vladimir's features. His face seems painted as almost a caricature of a woman's face; in a sense he has been in some kind of drag all along.) Vladimir's donning of the costumes of tsardom turns out to be his undoing, of course, as the assassin intending to kill Ivan makes do with the mere caricature of Ivan. Like the frozen mask of the white lady that is the highlight of Fyodor Basmanov's costume during the wild dance of the oprichniki preceding Vladimir's demise (the loyal Fyodor also being dressed for the occasion in "drag"), the Tsar's robes weigh on Vladimir: he walks stiffly as he heads toward what even he senses (as the famous "blue blush" reminds us, a blush that Eisenstein compares to that of the skunk in *Bambi*) are the perilous depths of the cathedral.[4]

The importance of "drag" in these wild and deadly celebrations reveals to us (as Eisenstein explains in some unpublished notes from the late 1940s) the hidden nature of the rituals with which Part II of *Ivan* closes: the dance of the oprichniki is not just an example of the "carnival tradition," and certainly not merely a dance, but at heart nothing less than a *wedding*.[5] The ill-fated "fool" Vladimir, having put on the Tsar's raiment, enters into an ancient exchange whose origins Eisenstein traces to the old marriage custom of bride and groom trading clothes: "The exchange of clothes (and of places) between *king* and *slave* is not only a phenomenon of a piece with the exchange of male and female clothing—but the direct *derivative* of that exchange. A man and a woman exchange clothing, entering into marriage."[6] In the case of Ivan and Vladimir, this "wedding" will find its consummation only in death, as Vladimir is pierced by the knife intended for the Tsar.

The transvestitism of the wedding is itself a kind of substitute for more primitive exchanges: "The exchange of clothing . . . is the exchange of M. and F. essences—*the crudest form* [English in original] of the materialization of these essences is the different sexual organs. Such that the exchange of clothing is the exchange of organs. . . . the exchange of essences."[7] The "wedding" takes its place in a chain of repetitions of the ancient drive towards what Eisenstein refers to as "bi-sex," the combination of female and male "essences" (and their symbolic representations) within one arena.

That "arena" can also be the literal one of the circus or theater. When Eisenstein pondered the multiple layers of meaning in *Ivan,* he returned to the fundamental issue of "bi-sex," he took up a thread he had explored more than a decade earlier, in 1933–1934, a period when he had been particularly intrigued by the archaic imagery at work in the circus: "In a less 'content-oriented' art we should find, more cleanly, a full picture of prelogic and maximum conservatism: the circus! [1] costumed animals; [2] the bisex of costumed clowns . . ."[8] (Eisenstein's theoretical notes on the circus came at a time in 1933 when he was thinking of staging a politically oriented circus

spectacle of his own, "The Hand of Moscow.")[9] His own most circus-like production—the staging of Alexander Ostrovsky's *Enough Simplicity in Every Wise
Man* (1923), that early experiment in bringing the "shocks" of the circus into
the arenas of theater and film—had come to a ribald conclusion around a plot
device of a wedding impeded at every hand. This dramatic moment was
where Eisenstein's first short film intervened to illustrate not only a chase up
and down towers, but also a series of metamorphoses imposed on the luckless
Glumov, the culmination of which was a "wedding" of clowns, in which the
female participant was dressed in men's clothing. The scene ends not with
a kiss, but with rude gestures (a "fig") directed first between characters and
then, in close-up, towards the film audience itself.

Weddings are places where identities get very tangled throughout Eisenstein's life and career. We might want to consider, for instance, the tangled
web of allusions presiding at the wedding of Fomka the bull and his bovine
bride in *The Old and the New* (1929): there the sweet little cow managed to
represent both the underdeveloped Soviet countryside and "Europa," the West
from which Soviet Russia wishes to claim its independence, while Fomka the
bull stood in not only for the "industrial" stimulus so needed in rural Russia
(a stimulus whose bloodlines went back to that Westerner, Henry Ford) but
also for Stalin, progenitor of the future. But Eisenstein's interest in the complex interplay of identities that weddings suggest seems to have significantly
predated his filmmaking career. One of the earliest childhood memories described by Eisenstein in his autobiography is a wedding game he used to play
with his friends:

> Another friend, who was French, and whose name and surname I have
> forgotten, was the son of the owner of the pen factory.[. . .]
>   There was a trio of plays we performed on Sundays, with him, Alyosha
> Bertels, and myself.
>   The happy ending of one of these plays.
>   Alyosha *en travesti.*
>   The French boy was dressed as an English "bobby." And I, for some
> reason, was dressed as a fantastic . . . rabbi (!) who married them.[10]

In this early game, identities, whether sexual, national, or religious, are the
product of costuming; one wonders which irony it is in the young Sergei's
disguise as a "rabbi (!)" that inspires Eisenstein's middle-aged self to append
the exclamation point.

As Eisenstein examined *Ivan the Terrible* in 1947 and 1948, he found in it
not only the repetition of those broad cultural patterns (like the role of "bi-
sex" in marriage rites) that underpin so much of humanity's art and ritual,

but also places where those profound themes were made autobiographical, tied to key moments of Eisenstein's own artistic past.

One figure who resurfaces, perhaps unexpectedly, in Eisenstein's notes of the 1940s is his one-time collaborator and student, the director Grigori ("Grisha") Alexandrov. In late 1947, while pondering the ubiquitous (and co-existing) imagery of "womb" and "phallus," Eisenstein thinks back to his 1923 production of *Enough Simplicity for Every Wise Man.* The actress Vera Yanukova, with whom both he and Alexandrov (who acted in the play) were at that time in love ("and more!" Eisenstein scribbles in a margin), sheds a circular (womblike) skirt and scrambles up a (phallic) pole with a moon-sign at the top.[11] "Reminiscences of *Wise Man* of course lie at the foundation of (Alexandrov's) most successful production, *Circus,*" Eisenstein claims—and considering Lyubov Orlova's sensational "flight to the Moon" in that film, the claim seems thoroughly reasonable.[12] If we take that parallel seriously, then *Circus*'s blond Bolshevik hero becomes a stand-in for Grisha Alexandrov, and Eisenstein must logically be played by . . . the evil German, Von Kneischitz!

In notes from November 1947, Eisenstein reveals another *Wise Man* "reminiscence": none other than *Ivan the Terrible.* "Kurbsky is curious: a double (by design) of Ivan the Terrible—Ivan as a blond!—made similar by typage to the blond aspect of Golutvin (character from *Wise Man*—and to the actor: Gr. Alexandrov!"[13] Then, switching into English, Eisenstein appends a crucial and fascinating comment: "The conflict of Ivan and Kurbsky had to incorporate my conflict with Gr. Alexandroff. Quite consciously. And this conflict helped me to feel the Grozny-Kurbsky drama. The psychology of the f[r]iend Kurbsky and the sufferings of John [Ivan] when he has left him."[14] There is a lovely classical Freudian slip here, because Eisenstein leaves the "r" out of "friend": Kurbsky/Alexandrov, the "friend" and "fiend." So Alexandrov's musical comedy *Circus* and Eisenstein's operatic epic *Ivan the Terrible* can be seen as another set of oddly matched twins, a charming idea that puts yet another "spin" on the carnivalesque atmosphere of the dance of the oprichniki.

In *Ivan,* as in *Wise Man,* Eisenstein muses, a man "liquidates" his rival in a womb-like setting: the cathedral in *Ivan,* the circular arena in the 1923 play.[15] Thus Eisenstein's latest creation reaches back into the director's past and brings back motifs from his creative origins. This thought fascinates Eisenstein—and leads him, on this day less than three months from his own death, to a meta-autobiographical and somewhat melancholy pondering of the relation of beginnings and endings: "This is quite striking—to what degree the juncture of Beginning and End is historically momentous for my work. Is *Ivan* the end of my biography as a director?"[16]

With its repetition of moments from Eisenstein's personal and cultural history and its mysterious conflation of womb and tomb, *Ivan the Terrible* plays through the paradigms provided by another strange work (well known to Ei-senstein) obsessed with the "juncture of Beginning and End": Freud's *Beyond the Pleasure Principle* (1920).[17] This was the essay in which Freud explored those psychic phenomena that seemed somehow to ignore—or predate?—the general rule that "the course taken by mental events is automatically regu-lated by the pleasure principle."[18] At the heart of the mysteries Freud wrestles with in *Beyond the Pleasure Principle* is the "compulsion to repeat."[19] This com-pulsion is also central to *Ivan*—not only in its recycling of themes from Ei-senstein's past, and not only in its formal repetitions of motifs (the shadow, the candle, the eye), but even in its narrative, within which the flashbacks to Ivan's childhood, a kind of psychoanalysis of his motivations, establish patterns that Ivan is destined to relive: all those poisoned women in white, mother and brides.

Freud is led by his discovery of a "repetition compulsion" to acknowledge that there may be some kind of instinct "inherent in organic life to restore an earlier state of things," and that, more dramatically, this drive back towards one's origins is also, since "inanimate things existed before living ones," a way of taking "circuitous paths to death." Viewed most severely, this would permit one to say that "the aim of all life is death."[20] This mysterious bond between "womb" and "tomb" was, as we have already begun to see, very much on Eisenstein's mind in the 1940s. The death of Vladimir in the "womb" of the cathedral—or of Gogol's Khoma Brut in the demon-filled church—were far from the only illustrations of this fundamental and fatal correspondence.[21] Eisenstein found echoes of this profound pattern in many, many places, as his notes of the late 1940s suggest.

One of his more surprising finds was an advertisement in *Life* magazine for Sinclair Opaline Motor Oil.[22] The ad shows Danny Kaye floating through a hoop held by Virginia Mayo ("stars of Samuel Goldwyn's *The Secret Life of Walter Mitty*. In Technicolor"): "Like Magic, Premium Sinclair Oil gives your car more power. Your car's power goes up like the magic of levitation when you use premium Sinclair Motor Oil." On October 16, 1947, Eisenstein gushed happily, "One could write a whole book about this little page of advertising."[23]

> It's difficult to imagine a clearer image . . . in which the theme of unity—
> through substitution (sinking back into the womb and the drive towards
> the womb *ersatz*—"the girl of my dreams") would be presented so
> literally (and at the same time allegorically transposed). The passage
> through the circle—into the interior—*into to girl* [sic; English in original],
> part of whom is that circle <she holds it> and with that the condition of
> "levitation," that is, the *Schwebe-Zustand* [floating condition] within the

Mutterleib [womb] <the psychological condition of levitation and its like attributed to "saints" is a reminiscence of the state freed from the force of gravity—the "gyroscopic" state in the womb>.[24]

With the return to the imagery of the womb comes an interest in the relatively "plasmatic" characteristics of primordial matter (as exhibited in Eisenstein's notes by floating fetuses, amoebas, and Mickey Mouse). This fascination, too, reflects the logical paths set forth in Freud's *Beyond the Pleasure Principle,* in which the "compulsion to repeat" (and the drive to return to prior states that repetition implies) leads to a consideration of life's protoplasmic beginnings: "Let us picture a living organism in its most simplified possible form as an undifferentiated vesicle of a substance that is susceptible to stimulation . . . "[25] The price that this little vesicle must pay for the evolutionary privilege of consciousness is the gradual hardening of its contours, the loss of the carefree "plasmaticness" (as Eisenstein would put it) of its youth:

> Indeed embryology, in its capacity as a recapitulation of developmental history, actually shows us that the central nervous system originates from the ectoderm. . . . [A]s a result of the ceaseless impact of external stimuli on the surface of the vesicle, its substance to a certain depth may have become permanently modified. . . . A crust would thus be formed which would at last have been so thoroughly "baked through" by stimulation that it would present the most favourable possible conditions for the reception of stimuli and become incapable of any further modification.[26]

The embedded story in *Beyond the Pleasure Principle* of the trials and tribulations of protoplasm at the very dawn of the human drives towards death and sex was one that had caught Eisenstein's eye already long before, in 1933, at the very same time he had been pondering the "regressive" and "bisexual" attributes of the circus. On a sheet of notes about the theme of regression in Hegel, Eisenstein added, "Could also refer to Freud: the libido theory . . . is the reproduction of the protoplasmic stage."[27]

In the 1940s, Eisenstein's interest in protoplasm—a fascination that bridged the theme of the return to the womb (and to death) *and* the "omni-appealing" nature of the animated character (as he writes in his notes on Disney)—was especially focused on the mysteries of a contour that has learned to exceed itself. The name he gives this phenomenon is "plasmaticness":

> [H]ere we have a being represented in drawing, a being of a definite form, a being which has attained a definite appearance, and which behaves like

the primal protoplasm, not yet possessing a "stable" form, but capable of assuming any form and which, skipping along the rungs of the evolutionary ladder, attaches itself to any and all forms of animal existence.

Why is the sight of this so attractive? [. . .]

[T]his picture is inescapably attractive through its trait of all possible diversity of forms.[28]

In *Ivan,* however, a film directly influenced by Disney (specifically *Snow White and the Seven Dwarfs*) the contours of the human figure are tortured in order to create a grotesque imitation of a cartoon figure's plasmatic lines.[29] In Disney this plasmaticness of contour leads to comedy, to what Eisenstein calls "formal ecstasy"; in *Ivan* the effect is grotesque, contorted, forever reminding us of the *pain* involved when a figure trapped within a three-dimensional universe where the rules of physics apply—is asked to behave as if he were fundamentally linear. This strain is part of the essential sensibility of *Ivan:* what separates Nikolai Cherkasov from Mickey Mouse is his *crust.* (Later in his life, Nikolai Cherkasov would reflect more than once on the strain of literally embodying Eisenstein's graphic visions, as the endless drawings Eisenstein used as a sort of "first draft" of *Ivan the Terrible* were brought to life—"animated"— by the actors. The director's achievements, complains Cherkasov, came at the price of "not infrequently constraining me within the cruel frames of his graphic and pictorial intent." He adds that "during the numerous rehearsals and shoots devoted to the mental anguish of Ivan, I thus was not once able to free myself from the sensation of physical constraint, which hampered to the highest degree my efforts as an actor.")[30]

The "compulsion to repeat" at work in *Ivan the Terrible* has perplexed and inspired the film's critics. In her analysis of the "excess" at work within (and counter to) the formal structures of *Ivan,* Kristin Thompson shows how even the repeated motifs so central to the film's aesthetic can also work to derail, rather than reinforce, the film's narrative unity. These "floating motifs" can confound the critic who wants to fit them into any kind of tidy formal structure:

[A] single motivation may serve to justify a device that is then *repeated and varied many times.* By this repetition, the device may far outweigh its original motivation and take on an importance greater than its narrative or compositional function would seem to warrant. This kind of excess is extremely common in *Ivan.* The introduction of the bird motif, for example, is realistically motivated: a couple of the objects in the coronation ceremony have historically authentic bird emblems on them

(the scepter, the little rug on the dais). But later the birds become less
integral to the action at hand. [. . .] Indeed, by the time the last bird
appears in the film—the white "Holy Ghost" icon on the ceiling of the
feast hall—I am hard put to assign it any function at all.[31]

The key here would seem to be not the object repeated, but the film's insistence
on repetition, per se. In notes from 1940 Eisenstein had suggested that "repetition" in its "purest form" took shape as "ornament." [32] At that time he recalled
a kind of "repetition machine" that had charmed him in his childhood, by
means of which one could trace an image and have it reproduced precisely,
though perhaps in a different size, by the mechanism's second pencil: "I remember in childhood I had just such an apparatus!" [33] Certainly all those po-
lysemous yet excessive motifs dominating *Ivan the Terrible* serve an *ornamental*
function. The "compulsion to repeat" that the ornament indulges and reflects
is part and parcel of *Ivan*'s ascent/descent into the dark allure of the womb.

As the image, under the spell of repetition, regresses into "ornament," we
face a profound transformation of the dialectical tension between image and
concept that had so long been Eisenstein's central concern. Long before *Ivan,*
as he pondered the significance of the image-driven philosophy of *October*
in 1928, Eisenstein had turned to Hegel as he described the yearning for each
other of "abstract idea" and that idea's "materialization." This longing, it
turned out, was part of yet another story, endlessly repeated over the ages:
"This 'yearning for each other' of two separate or separated elements, dialecti-
cally necessarily monistic, is the most 'lawful' of tendencies. From the Platonic
myth of single creatures separated into two and seeking reunification. . . ." [34]
This very myth, from the *Symposium,* is the story upon which Freud closes
Beyond the Pleasure Principle, as he contemplates the mysteries of the origins
of sexuality: "Shall we follow the hint given us by the poet-philosopher, and
venture upon the hypothesis that living substance at the time of its coming
to life was torn apart into small particles, which have ever since endeavoured
to reunite through the sexual instincts?" [35]

Eisenstein's last years and months were marked by the resurgence of the
autobiographical impulse, the desire to bring together the ideas and discoveries of a lifetime into some kind of greater unity. At the end of 1947, he
proposed to himself a form that had captured his imagination already fifteen
years earlier: the spherical book.

In 1932 1 was preparing to organize my theoretical materials into a book
(fifteen years I have continued to collect these materials)—somewhere I
wrote, "I dream of creating a *book in the shape of a sphere*—for everything
I do touches everything else, and everything crosses into everything else:

the only form capable of satisfying this condition is a sphere: from any meridian transition is possible to any other meridian. <Even now I yearn for this form of a book—and now perhaps more than at any other time.>[36]

Such a book would allow the kind of connection and repetition which other, more linear forms tended to deny; perhaps *Ivan,* too, was a film longing to become more "spherical." The fantasy of the spherical book can also be seen as another incarnation of the "return to the womb" that was such a dominant motif in Eisenstein's last years. Like the "plasmatic" animated character— or the fetus—much of the allure of the spherical book stemmed from the infinite flexibility of its connections: thought itself, within the form of the sphere, would find its contours liberated and newly plasmatic. The sphere is also, however, as Eisenstein remarked, the very shape things take when freed from outside stimuli, as when they are suspended in the liquid environment of the womb.[37] Eisenstein's spherical book would thus be the record not only of his highest intellectual achievement, but also the embodiment of his mind's ultimate regression. A remarkably abstract form, the spherical book could not, in the end, be compatible with the messiness of life: its perfect shape, like that of all originary and final "protoplasms," could only be achieved at the very beginning or very end of all things.

In his last days, Eisenstein took some time away from his other studies to ponder the ultimate mystery of that other state, the ultimate "unity" that is possible only on the far side of the thresholds of birth and death. On February 7, 1948, only two days before his death, he copied out a few paragraphs from a French translation of the oldest of Hindu sacred texts, the *Rig-Veda,* on the state out of which the world long ago emerged and to which we all eventually return. "Here is everything," he mused at the bottom of the page. "The *status quo* of the situation of Unity, which is neither being nor not-being. And the originary indivisibility of things. And the method of attaining that state through immersion."[38] As his own life neared the end of what Freud speculated was merely a kind of detour, an individual's "circuitous path to death," Eisenstein found in the reconciliation of womb and tomb, in the "juncture of Beginning and End," a meaningfulness that neither being nor nonbeing could exhaust.[39]

If that image (or, rather, nonimage) also troubles us, it is because it is— unlike almost any other Eisensteinian image—astoundingly *non*dialectical. It is, rather, a description of the realm in which neither image nor story have any further roles to play. Eisenstein's entire creative life, however, had revolved around bringing things together, often in scandalous combinations, and especially in combinations of abstract ideas and concrete, sometimes bawdy, materializations. Such combinations were most often explosive, hazardous, dialectical: they would not, in fact, lend themselves well to the

93. Saul Steinberg doodle © 2001 The Saul Steinberg Foundation/Artists Rights Society (ARS), New York.

smooth abstract curves of the "spherical book." Eisenstein had always delighted in images, such as this simple Saul Steinberg doodle (Fig. 93), capable of luring the mind onto the curving path of digression and detour. Eisenstein discusses this cartoon, which can be seen as a kind of hieroglyphic encapsulation of the "womb/tomb" paradox, at some length in *Nonindifferent Nature.* "For the uninitiated," says Eisenstein, "this is the point of stopping dead in place."[40] Like any image, this figure arrests its viewer. This cartoon, however, thematizes its own ability to arrest. The naive spectator ("uninitiated") presumably finds himself completely unable to decide which direction "really" leads to the exit, here doubly deferred and displaced. Ambushed by paradox, he can only conclude that in fact there is no exit available to him at all.

Here the imagined naive spectator has made a grave mistake. The exit, of course, is neither off somewhere to the right nor a little bit to the left: it is right here, in the very arrest itself. Like Immanuel Kant's seeming dead-ends that provoke leaps into the sublime, this little drawing supplies the somewhat less naive (the "initiated") spectator with an opportunity, Eisenstein suggested, for ecstasy:

> For the initiated—this is the formula of that double path by which a truly effective work is constructed—equally descending by its roots into the subsoil depths of the accumulation of the past experience of humanity, and by its crown, growing into infinity of heavenly perspectives of the future social and spiritual progress of humanity.[41]

The sign's misleading arrows restrict the spectator to the horizontal axis, but Eisenstein shifts our attention splendidly to the vertical (represented in the drawing by the post holding the sign). He also reveals a great organic image—a figurative tree, with roots in humanity's most distant past and its topmost leaves stretching into the future—lurking behind the artificial and manmade construction of the signboard. Finally, the sign offers another figure of "bi-sex," as the vertical post pierces the closed circuit described by the sign-board's edges, reminding us of the acrobatic exploits of *Enough Simplicity for Every Wise Man* (1923) and also of the unfunny circus arena of *Ivan the Terrible* when the foolish Vladimir enters the church to meet his death. There "womb" and "tomb" come together, as they do again here, in the signpost's paradoxical conflation of "exit" and "no exit."

Sometimes, however, instead of an exit, one finds something else, "neither being nor not-being," as Eisenstein said of the *Rig-Veda,* but rather the state—or status quo—which is always before or after, and where the dialectical language of images, of pictures, must yield to "immersion." Some exits are ecstatic, and from others there is no way out. In his final ruminations Eisen-stein seemed headed for other than merely sublime understandings of the ways things come together: here we move, with him, beyond the reach of autobiography, and light and image, and on into that darker realm where be-ginnings and endings enter their ultimate embrace.

Notes

1. RGALI (Russian State Archive of Literature and Art), Moscow, f. [holding] 1923, op. [list] 2, d. [folder] 416, 1. [sheet] 9. This folder dated "20 January–7 February 1948."

2. Eisenstein's quotes are from f. 1923, op. 2, d. 416, l. 23, and f. 1923, op. 2, d. 416, l. 15.

3. See Marjorie Garber's interesting discussion of transvestitism as a sign of "category crisis" generally in *Vested Interests: Cross-Dressing and Cultural Anxiety* (New York: Routledge, 1992). She defines drag as "the theoretical and deconstruc-tive social practice that analyzes these structures from within, by putting in ques-tion the 'naturalness' of gender roles through the discourse of clothing and body parts" (151).

4. Eisenstein compares this blue blush to Disney's characters' exaggerated blushes; he mentions specifically the skunk in *Bambi,* but for the record we should also recall the blushing faces of several of the seven dwarfs, and in particular the character who is "all blush": Bashful. See S. M. Eisenstein, *Le mouvement de l'art,* trans. B. Epstein, M. Iampolski, N. Noussinova, A. Zouboff (Paris: Les Editions du Cerf, 1986), 230–231.)

5. F. 1923, op. 2, d. 268, l. 3

6. F. 1923, op. 2, d. 268, l. 3, dated "13 September 1947." Emphasis in the original.

7. F. 1923, op. 2, d. 269, l. 24.

8. F. 1923, op. 2, d. 231, l. 4 (Folder dated December 1932–March 1934).

9. See f. 1923, op. 1, d. 848, plans for "Ruka Moskvy." On the second sheet of notes in this folder Eisenstein refers to the "fifteen years" that have passed since the Revolution, giving us an approximate date for the project.

10. Sergei Eisenstein, *Selected Works,* 4: *Beyond the Stars: The Memoirs of Sergei Eisenstein,* ed. Richard Taylor, trans. William Powell (London: British Film Institute, 1995), 117. This reminiscence is dated May 29, 1946.

11. F. 1923, op. 2, d. 268, l. 20. This folder is dated ""13 September 1947–5 February 1948."

12. F. 1923, op. 2, d. 268, l. 20.

13. F. 1923, op. 2, d. 268, l. 30. (Dated November 27, 1947.)

14. F. 1923, op. 2, d. 268, l. 30. The "conflict" with Alexandrov to which Eisenstein refers here would seem to be not merely the adolescent competition over Ianukogo, but rather the betrayal Eisenstein felt when Alexandrov went off to make his own films in the early 1930s.

15. F. 1923, op. 2, d. 268, l. 30.

16. F. 1923, op. 2, d. 268, l. 30. The last sentence is in English in the original.

17. Eisenstein makes explicit reference to this aspect of Freud's oeuvre already in 1933, as we shall see below.

18. Sigmund Freud, *Beyond the Pleasure Principle,* trans. James Strachey (New York: W. W. Norton, 1961), 3.

19. Freud, *Beyond the Pleasure Principle,* 25.

20. Ibid., 43, 46.

21. Eisenstein refers to the cathedral as a womb-like structure in several places. See for instance f. 1923, op. 2, d. 268, 1. 22.

22. This advertisement held in f. 1923, op. 2, d. 268, l. 45.

23. F. 1923, op. 2, d. 268, l. 41.

24. F. 1923, op. 2, d. 268, l. 41. Material in < > brackets appears in English in the original.

25. Freud, *Beyond the Pleasure Principle,* 28.

26. Ibid., 29.

27. F. 1923, op. 2, d. 231, 1. 17, dated "18 November 1933."

28. *Eisenstein on Disney,* ed. Jay Leyda, trans. Alan Upchurch. (Calcutta: Seagull Books, 1986), 21. The Russian edition can be found in A. V. Prokhorov, B. V. Raushenbakh, F. S. Khitruk, editors, *Problemy sinteza v khudozhestvennoi kul'ture* (Problems of Synthesis in Artistic Culture) (Moscow: Nauka, 1985), 205–284. The editor of the Eisenstein material for both editions is Naum Kleiman.

29. On the connections between Walt Disney and Sergei Eisenstein, see my "In-animations: *Snow White* and *Ivan the Terrible,*" *Film Quarterly,* 50: 4 (1997), 20–31, and also Russell Merritt, "Recharging *Alexander Nevsky:* Tracking the Eisenstein-Prokofiev War Horse," *Film Quarterly,* 48: 2 (1994–1995), 34–47.

30. *Nikolai Cherkasov,* ed. by N N. Cherkasova and S. Dreiden (Moscow: Vserossiiskoe teatral'noe obshchestvo, 1976), 101, 158.

31. Kristin Thompson, *Eisenstein's* Ivan the Terrible: *A Neoformalist Analysis*

(Princeton: Princeton University Press, 1981), 295. See, in particular, chapter 4, "The Floating Motif" (158–172) and chapter 9, "Excess" (287–302).

32. F. 1923, op. 2, d. 239, l. 2, dated "23 July 1940."

33. F. 1923, op. 2, d. 239, l. 43.

34. F. 1923, op. 2, d. 228, l. 27.

35. Freud, *Beyond the Pleasure Principle,* 69–70.

36. F. 1923, op. 2, d. 268, l. 37, dated "17 November 1947." Emphasis in the original, and material in < > brackets appears in English. On Eisenstein's "Spherical Book" project, see the article in this volume by Oksana Bulgakowa.

37. F. 1923, op. 2, d. 268, l. 2.

38. F. 1923, op. 2, d. 268, ll. 75–76.

39. Freud, *Beyond the Pleasure Principle,* 46.

40. Sergei Eisenstein, *Nonindifferent Nature: Film and the Structure of Things,* trans. Herbert Marshall (Cambridge: Cambridge University Press, 1987), 188.

41. *Nonindifferent Nature,* 188–189.

ABOUT THE CONTRIBUTORS

An associate professor in the Department of Communcation Studies at the University of Otago, New Zealand, **Andrew Barratt**'s research is centered on twentieth-century literature and culture; he has published books on Mikhail Bulgakov and Maksim Gorky, as well as monographs devoted to major works of Russian literature. In recent years his teaching interests have turned to both film and comparative literature.

Rosamund Bartlett is currently Leverhulme Research Fellow in Russian Cultural History at Birkbeck College, University of London, and Fellow of the European Humanities Centre, Oxford University. Her book *Wagner and Russia* (1995) includes a discussion of Eisenstein's production of *Die Walküre*. She is also coauthor of *Literary Russia: A Guide* (1997) and editor of *Shostakovich in Context* (2000).

The Jacques Ledoux Professor of Film Studies at the University of Wisconsin, **David Bordwell** is the author of a dozen books and some eighty articles on both historical and theoretical topics relating to film. His 1993 book, *The Cinema of Eisenstein,* was winner of that year's Theatre Library Association Award for the outstanding book in film, broadcasting, or recorded performance.

Oksana Bulgakowa is a Moscow-born scholar who spent a number of years in Berlin and is now a member of the Slavic Department at Stanford University. Her writings dealing with Soviet cinema have appeared in numerous German publications. She has written and directed a film about Eisenstein called *Die verschiedenen Gesichter von Sergej Eisenstein* (The Different Faces of Sergei Eisenstein), 1998. Her biography of Eisenstein based on archival materials is scheduled to appear in English in 2001.

Ian Christie worked for the British Film Institute for twenty years, during which time he co-curated a major Eisenstein exhibition that toured the U.K., and presented live orchestral accompaniments of the Eisenstein silents. He has co-edited (with Richard Taylor) a number of books on Russian and Soviet cinema, including *Eisenstein Rediscovered* (1993), and organized two Eisenstein conferences in Oxford (1988 and 1998). He is currently a professor of film and media history at Birkbeck College, University of London.

For many years **Herbert Eagle** has applied his early interest in semiotics and literary theory to the study of both Russian and East European cinema. He is the editor and translator of *Russian Formalist Film Theory* (1981), as well as the author of a score of articles on film in which he has analyzed the work of Eisenstein, Andrzej Wajda, Jiří Menzel, and Dušan Makavejev, has offered broad surveys of East European cinematic traditions, and has provided detailed analyses of individual films. He teaches at the University of Michigan, Ann Arbor.

A professor in the Department of English at the University of California, Los Angeles, **James Goodwin** is the author of *Eisenstein, Cinema, and History* (1993), *Autobiography: The Self-Made Text* (1993), and *Akira Kurosawa and Intertextual Cinema* (1994), and the editor of *Perspectives on Akira Kurosawa* (1994). His current book project concerns interrelationships between photography and literature in American culture.

Professor of Russian at Tufts University, **Vida T. Johnson** has written on both Serbo-Croatian and Russian literature. In recent years she has devoted much of her attention to film and is coauthor, with Graham Petrie, of *The Films of Andrei Tarkovsky: A Visual Fugue.*

A professor of history at the University of California, Santa Cruz, **Peter Kenez** has devoted his career to studying the Soviet Union in the immediate postrevolutionary era. The author of highly regarded studies on the Russian Civil War, he has also carried out extensive research on Russian film, which has resulted in the publication of *Cinema & Soviet Society, 1917–1953* (1992).

A Dostoevsky scholar and a professor of literature and film at York University, Toronto, **Nikita Lary** is the author of *Dostoevsky and Soviet Film: Visions of Demonic Realism* (1986) and is currently working on a study of Viktor Shklovsky's practice and theory of film.

Al LaValley, Professor Emeritus of Film Studies at Dartmouth College, was the first chair of Film Studies at Dartmouth after it became an independent department. He has written widely on American and German film, and with Barry P. Scherr, has taught a course on the relationship between Soviet film and sociopolitical developments in the country.

Holder of a Ph.D. in Slavic languages and literatures from Stockholm University, **Håkan Lövgren**'s dissertation has been published as *Eisenstein's Labyrinth: Aspects of a Cinematic Synthesis of the Arts* (1996). Over the past decade he has published some half-dozen articles on Eisenstein and has delivered papers on him at scholarly conferences throughout Europe and North America.

Anne Nesbet holds a joint appointment in Slavic Languages and Literatures and Film Studies at the University of California, Berkeley. She is the author of articles on Eisenstein, Isaac Babel, Nikolai Gogol, Vladimir Nabokov, and Alfred Döblin. Her forthcoming book on Eisenstein (*Savage Junctures: The Figurative Philosophy of S. M. Eisenstein*) will be published by I. B. Tauris.

Joan Neuberger is a professor of history at the University of Texas, Austin. In addition to her book, *Hooliganism: Crime, Culture and Power in St. Petersburg, 1900–1914* (1993), she has published a series of articles on Russian urban life and is working on a book tentatively titled *Eisenstein, "Ivan the Terrible," and Stalinist Cultural Politics in the 1940s.*

Author of *An Approach to Mandelstam* (1983) and *The Fallacy of the Silver Age in 20th Century Russian Literature* (1997), **Omry Ronen** has published more than fifty articles on twentieth century Russian poets, problems of poetry explication and poetic theory, the history of poetic locutions, and literary history in general. He teaches at the University of Michigan, Ann Arbor.

Barry P. Scherr, Mandel Family Professor of Russian at Dartmouth College, has a particular interest in Russian cultural life of the twentieth century and has published widely on Russian poetry and prose. Recent projects include *Maksim Gorky: Selected Letters* (1997), which he co-edited and co-translated with Andrew Barratt, and *Twentieth-Century Russian Literature* (2000), co-edited with Karen L. Ryan.

While at Gosfilmofond in the former Soviet Union, **Yuri Tsivian** oversaw the restoration of early Russian films, a project which resulted in his co-edited volume, *Silent Witnesses: Russian Films 1908–1919* (1989). Prior to assuming his current position at the University of Chicago, he held visiting posts at the British Film Institute and at the University of Southern California. He is also the author of *Early Russian Cinema and Its Cultural Reception* (1994).

Josephine Woll's research has focused on twentieth-century Russian literature and culture. Her book, *Real Images: Soviet Cinema and the Thaw,* was published in 2000. She is also the author of a book on Yuri Trifonov, and has written on anti-Semitism in Russian life and on dissident literature under the Soviets. She teaches at Howard University.

Born in the former Soviet Union, **Alexander Zholkovsky** was a leading figure in linguistics, structural linguistics, and poetics well before his emigration in 1979. He now teaches at the University of Southern California. He is the author of some fifteen books, among which are *Themes and Texts: Towards a*

Poetics of Expressiveness (1984) and *Text CounterText: Readings in Russian Literary History* (1994), as well as over 190 articles, dealing with literature, culture, and linguistics.

INDEX

(Films, except for those by Eisenstein, are followed by the name of the director; literary and scholarly works will be found as subentries under the name of the author.)